What the Critics Say:

"Not since Max Weber invented political charisma has there been as useful a how-to book on the subject. Doe Lang's book mysteriously draws other books on its shelf closer to it."

—*William Safire*, New York Times

"Doe Lang is a woman with charisma, which she says is 'to imagination as electricity is to the wire that carries it.' Her book is one of the best self-help volumes I've seen." —*Liz Smith*, New York Newsday

"A dazzling piece of work—perceptive, witty, and wise—full of delicious surprises!" —*Celeste Holm*

"Everyone's library should have dictionaries, a thesaurus, the works of Shakespeare, and Doe Lang's wonderful book!" —*Nanette Fabray*

"An exciting book!" —*Rene Dubos, Rockefeller University*

"Supremely knowledgeable exercises. . . . A true gift . . . highly imaginative . . . multifaceted, extraordinary! This book is a treasure."

—*Lisa Curtis*

"This wonderful book will be a bible for many people for years to come."

—*Sir George Solti*

"This book is a prescription for happiness. . . . A wonderfully revealing experience." —*Dr. William H. Frey, Director,*
Psychiatry Research Laboratories,
St. Paul, MN

"An exceptional book. . . . Everybody can find what they need in it—spiritual, emotional, technical, physical. . . . Read it!" —*Janos Starker*

"*The Secrets of Charisma* was . . . an enormous journey. Doe Lang packed virtually everything in the way of liberation, creativity, and personal growth into one book . . . ideas that awaken and energize."

—*Dr. Clark Moustakas*

"A magnificent work, full of psychological truth and humanistic light."

—*E. Andreou, Poet, President of European Art Center, Greece*

The New Secrets of

CHARISMA

How to Discover and Unleash Your Hidden Powers

Doe Lang, Ph.D.

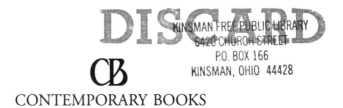

CB

CONTEMPORARY BOOKS

Library of Congress Cataloging-in-Publication Data

Lang, Doe.
    The new secrets of charisma : how to discover and unleash
your hidden powers / Doe Lang. — Rev. ed.
        p.   cm.
    ISBN 0-8092-2826-2
    1. Success—Psychological aspects.   2. Charisma
(Personality trait)   I. Title.
    BF637.S8L347   1999
    158.1—dc21   98-38352
                                            CIP

An earlier version of this book was published by S.P.I. Books in 1994 as *The
Secrets of Charisma: New Ways to Capture the Magic Skills of Leaders and Lovers.*

Excerpt from "Nothing Twice" from *View with a Grain of Sand* by Wislawa Szymborska, English translation by Stanislaw Baranczak and Clare Cavanagh copyright
© 1995 by Harcourt Brace & Company, reprinted by permission of the publisher.

The Social Readjustment Scale (Holmes-Rahe Stress Management Scale) is
reprinted with permission from *Journal of Psychosomatic Research*, 11, Holmes,
T. H., and Rahe, R. H., copyright © 1967, Pergamon Press, Ltd.

Stress Inventory No. 25 is reprinted with permission of H. L. Barksdale, courtesy
of The Barksdale Foundation, Laguna Beach, CA.

Cover design by Scott Rattray
Interior photographs courtesy of Hideoki and Nancy Brown
Interior design by City Desktop Productions, Inc.

Published by Contemporary Books
A division of NTC/Contemporary Publishing Group, Inc.
4255 West Touhy Avenue, Lincolnwood (Chicago), Illinois 60646-1975 U.S.A.
Copyright © 1999 by Doe Lang
Printed in the United States of America
International Standard Book Number: 0-8092-2826-2
99 00 01 02 03 04 QP 15 14 13 12 11 10 9 8 7 6 5 4 3 2 1

Andrea Lang

akal . . . "undying"

TO THE RADIANT, UNDYING SPIRIT
of
ANDREA ILONA LANG

Adored and adoring big sister
of Brian Lang

Incomparable loving heart
* her art*
*   her writing*
*   her healing charisma*
*   Lives and inspires others . . .*
even who never knew her.
Wherever she was, she created beauty
* and humor*

our brilliant darling
* magical grace*
*   dazzling wit,*
*   her luminous beauty,*
*   song,*
*   laughter*

Lost and perished
* in the Painted Cave Fire*
*   Santa Barbara, California, June 27, 1990*

Dearest Andrea
heart's daughter

phoenix soul

CONTENTS

INTRODUCTION

Why do we need charisma in the new millennium? A good question!

Several years ago, when I was first asked to write a book about charisma, I discovered an interesting paradox: although clients of all ages and levels of achievement were anxious to acquire charisma and improve their lives, most academics and media people either knew nothing about it or disdained the whole subject as frivolous!

Though the first edition of this book drew a great deal of favorable response, the initial reaction of many talk-show hosts and columnists ranged from sceptical to hostile. "You either have charisma or you don't—you've got to be born with it!" was a common remark. I had a feeling that these well-known people felt their own sense of "entitlement through talent" was threatened by the idea that "ordinary" people could learn to harness their inner charisma and be more dynamic, exciting, and successful.

Most people remember the word *charisma* in connection with the Kennedys, but it hadn't yet penetrated anywhere else in that era. In the sixties, when the brilliant Joyce Engelson sent her just-published first novel to her alma mater for review, she was attacked for using the word *charisma*! "Where did she get that word!" the professor wrote contemptuously. "She certainly never learned it here . . . at Barnard!" (Actually she had—when she studied Max Weber, who wrote about political charisma in the early 1920s.) As late as 1990, when I completed my doctorate in psychology and communication, the Psych Index (database) still had no entry for *charisma*.

So charisma, for much of our lifetime, has either been beneath notice, highly suspect, secretly fascinating—or any combination of the three. Discredited gurus, dictators, and suicidal cult leaders—who exploited their charisma—deepened public distrust.

But as the communications explosion opened up the world and flooded our consciousness with ever more information, *charisma* became a glamorous buzzword, a star emblem for the mysterious instant appeal of new people, products, and ideas. Today, the hype machinery speeds up celebrity on TV, in print, and even on the Internet, rushing to cloak every new candidate with the instant mantle of "charismatic" (deserved or not). In fact, in the last ten years the use of the word *charisma* has increased over 100 percent in the United States alone, according to a media search in some seventy thousand papers and publications. Self-help books and business studies about leadership now include the nature of charisma and general theories on how to develop it; charisma has become a respectable part of the landscape.

Scholarly academic conferences on nonverbal research used to present innumerable clinical and theoretical studies on communication, without giving people any practical, in-depth help to develop their own skills and overcome their fears. Yet nationwide surveys had long found that most people fear public speaking even more than death! Jerry Seinfeld, in a recent Broadway show, claimed he was baffled to learn that death comes in second to the public's number-one terror: public speaking! "I can't believe it! Does that mean that most people who go to a funeral would rather be in the coffin than give the eulogy?!" A client of mine, a fledgling congressman, said thoughtfully, "Yes! That's *exactly* how I used to feel!"

Since I wrote the first edition of this book, attitudes toward charisma have changed appreciably. My declaration that we all have charismatic inner gifts and can use enjoyable tools to develop the expression of our charisma shocked and startled some people at first. Enhanced by an array of mind-body-lifestyle-spiritual skills, each person's individuality emerges as a power for good in their private and public worlds.

In 1984 an earlier version of this book, *The Secrets of Charisma*, appeared in paperback for the first time. People interviewed then were asked whether they thought they had charisma. They replied confidently, "Yes—when I'm at my best." That was great progress. I was invited to give international seminars on charisma. In Japan a front-page article and photo of Tokyo businesspeople at my seminar was headlined "American actress teaches Japanese to be carefree!" Requests for workshops poured in from England, Canada, and Brazil. The Singapore government brought me there to train the entire civil-service sector of the government in communication.

The Charisma program has since attracted an enthusiastic following in many different cultures. I am not only continually amazed by what clients and students achieve but also touched and impressed by the never-ending flow of grateful, perceptive letters and thought-provoking insights from readers throughout the world.

Foreign-language editions (e.g., Portuguese Brazilian) sometimes use *charisma* in the title, but often the edition's new title reflects national concerns and characteristics. The first Japanese edition, for example, was called *Transforming Weakness into Strength*. There the publishers omitted the chapter on anger altogether, as they considered it a "shameful" subject! I loved the unabashedly metaphysical German title, *The Magnetic Power of Personal Radiance*.

Most provocative was a reader's letter asking plaintively, "How can the Pope and Elvis Presley *both* be charismatic?" When I thought about that I realized this reader was right. Something more was needed to describe different kinds of charisma. That led me to identify thirteen kinds of charisma, which await you in the first chapter.

Let's return to the original question: Why is charisma so vital for the next millennium? Now that charisma has in a sense been democratized, our fascination with it has if anything increased. It seems within reach, and everybody wants it. But do we really *need* it?

In a world of unprecedented technological complexity, with virtually instant access to people and places everywhere and accelerating rates of change, our ability to cope, connect, and communicate well will be critical for both personal and global survival. Most of us probably talk to more people in a week than our grandparents spoke to in a lifetime! This means that everybody needs to become not just computer-literate, but charisma-literate, not as observers but as owners! The "superlanguage" of charismatic power means the skills of speaking and reading people—particularly the skills to *achieve rapport easily and effectively with all kinds of people in all kinds of situations*. The grammar and vocabulary of this superlanguage include your ability to

- be expressive in a positive way, verbally and nonverbally;

- be aware of what's really going on within yourself and other people;

- take responsibility for your own emotions as well as actions;

- focus increasingly fine-tuned social skills on any situation;

- speak eloquently, easily, and well in any setting;

- use your body-mind intuition, compassion, and skills to create positive energy, positive scenarios, and positive outcomes; and

- know how to defuse conflict—even instantly when necessary.

In this thoroughly revised and updated edition, I've provided new resources and additional advanced power tools to accelerate your access to your own unique expression of charisma as a superlanguage.

Intrinsic charisma is a birthright. Some of it is inborn, some must be developed, and some must be rediscovered.

Try everything and then choose the techniques that challenge and intrigue you the most. Those that are hardest might well be the most rewarding; notice which ones delight you (you may be surprised!), because they might be the most valuable of all. Share them with your children, friends, and loved ones. The more you do, the more satisfying and user-friendly your world will be. No matter what your age, location, or status in life, this adventure is open to you. I wish you expansive joy on this fascinating journey and as much surprise as it continues to give me. Nobody has it "all together." As long as we're alive, we are apt to make clumsy mistakes—and I apologize for any I have made here.

Enjoy the trip—and send me a postcard!

The Thirteen Kinds of Charisma

What is charisma? Nobody can tell you *exactly*. In research I conducted with more than two thousand people from all walks of life, I got such answers as these:

> "You either have it or you don't. All I know is that when you have it, everybody wants to do things for you!"

> "It's sex appeal."

> "It's a mysterious charm that draws people to you!"

> "It's a kind of harmony between the person and his or her audience."

> "It's vitality."

> "It's energy."

> "It's never being boring."

> "It's a holistic state—when you're one with the people you're with and everybody feels inspired, excited, enriched, and enlarged."

> "It's a quality of believing your own lies . . . general confidence."

Most people felt charisma is inborn but, paradoxically, could be developed. I asked people when they themselves had felt most charismatic in their lives. The intriguing (and encouraging) response was that nobody, not even the people who regarded themselves as shy and nonassertive, said, "Never!"

So apparently we all enjoy some experience of feeling successful and authoritative—times when we feel effective in expressing our true selves and being understood and appreciated. Both are necessary for a satisfying experience, according to the majority of people I surveyed.

I have always had a secret interest in charisma.

When I was no more than six, I remember trying to figure out just how my older brother had said, "Good-bye, Mom!" in the morning when he left for school. Was there something special in his voice or inflection? My mother always answered, "Good-bye, dear!" to him, and it seemed she never said "dear" to me. What was the secret of his charisma? I had no way of knowing then that the mere fact of his being male had a great deal to do with it!

I suspected that perhaps I was deficient in some way and that was why she didn't say "dear" to me. That was too alarming to talk about or even to acknowledge to myself. I was far too proud to *ask*. . . . Of course I wanted to be liked and loved, but I wasn't sure I had what it took—whatever that was!

Secretly I suspected it had nothing to do with being good, although I was always exhorted to *be* good. Perhaps for girls—although this was never suggested—it had something to do with being pretty? I studied the cool, distant gaze of models in the magazines and the sultry, provocative look of movie stars. I tried to learn how those looks felt from the inside. Somehow, I felt, if I knew *what* to do, I could do it!

In spite of all my efforts, I felt no closer to that mysterious and wonderful confidence some people seemed to have without working on it at all! They could be naughty or outrageous, have a temper tantrum—nobody seemed to mind. On the other hand, I was required to be as perfect as possible. Was it because people thought I wasn't good unless I was perfect? I couldn't be sure, but I put on such a good act that some people thought I had *too much* confidence!

Katharine Hepburn once referred to her arrival in Hollywood by saying, "I was bringing myself as though I were a basket of flowers!" How wonderful to feel that way and to be able to say it! In my home that would have been considered boastful and immodest—not qualities that were admired or encouraged. Yet, if Hepburn hadn't had her confident sense of self she could never have swept through Hollywood as triumphantly as she did. The prevailing ideal of women in her day was cuddly, sexy, pretty (and if possible, blond)—nothing like the independence, aristocratic strength, individuality, and racehorse beauty she projected.

People do walk through the door of your expectations!—especially if the expectations are unquestioning and sure. Katharine Hepburn's sense of self was so powerful that she not only became a star; as everybody knows, she stayed one.

When I was a little girl, I used to pretend I was a princess. It was reassuring to know that I had a strawberry mark on my thigh, because otherwise my real family—all kings and queens, naturally—would never be able to find me. I didn't confide this to anyone, but it was a great consolation to know that I was too fine for my own family and my friends—*and they didn't even know it!*

Meantime, the waiting before the royal talent scouts came to find me wasn't wholly satisfactory because I didn't quite know who I was while waiting to *be* a princess. It was fun to pretend to be other people, and I seemed be very good at becoming different characters and doing all kinds of voices and accents. So I became an actress.

The Tinker Bell Syndrome

The only problem about getting your confidence from performing is that if you depend on it, what happens when you go offstage? Even onstage it's never quite enough. Many performers suffer from what I call the Tinker Bell syndrome. Unless an audience is madly applauding and calling out, "I believe! I believe!" they don't feel worthy or valid as human beings. Brilliant British actor-writer Chris Langham told me that on the night of his triumphant London debut in *Crazy for You*, in the middle of a standing ovation, as he was coming up from a bow, the thought crossed his mind, "Is that all????!!"

Too much is never enough!

There are also negative aspects to being valued for one's talents alone. Other people's jealousy can be very undermining if your personal self-esteem is shaky.

My own experience led to an ambivalence about the business of performing. Growing up, I was admired and praised when I sang, played, or (later) acted. But one little girl, who happened to live next door, was bitterly jealous. Years later I found out her mother had taunted her by saying, "Why can't you sing and play like Doe?" No wonder she hated me! She herself was a pretty, bright little girl, but that apparently was not enough for her competitive and ambitious mother. So we both suffered for it.

And I learned: yes, it's good to have talent, but watch out! You may be hated for it. The same is true for beauty, brains, and other gifts. What I kept searching for was *what made a person* OK—that inalienable confidence in oneself that makes it possible to move through life with unassailable joy and assurance. I used to marvel at people who were neither talented, pretty, nor especially bright, but who had *it*: charisma.

There is a Sufi saying that if you want young people to learn how to deal well with life, tell them to associate with lucky people. People who have positive expectations usually draw positive events to them.

If you think you're lucky, why then you are! Dr. Shelley Taylor, who wrote *Positive Illusions*, found that people who think they are luckier, better-looking, and smarter than they are in actuality are happier and more successful and live longer.

Although I, on the contrary, usually disparaged my own talents, they brought me a series of professional and academic scholarships, and after graduating from Bennington College, I embarked on a career in theater, cabaret, and TV to support my studies as a concert pianist. I knew I was lucky not to have to be a waitress like so many other young hopefuls. I could always earn money acting, singing, or even playing cocktail piano in elegant hotels and clubs. At the same time, I really didn't think I was worthy of notice. In fact, once when the great Duke Ellington himself, who had heard me (when I didn't know he was there) and liked my playing, invited a music critic to come hear me at a club in New York, I cravenly pleaded sudden illness and fled. In view of all this, it seems a minor miracle that I won a Fulbright fellowship to study opera in Italy and professional recognition as an actress, singer, and pianist here and abroad. Of course, in spite of my occasional stage fright, I loved what I was doing—it was wonderful playing Maria in *West Side Story* and the lead in *Mame*, singing *Carmen* and musical comedy on TV with Leonard Bernstein, and playing long-suffering Nurse Karen Adams on *As the World Turns*. How lucky that other people believed in me (especially since I hardly believed in myself). I also knew how lucky I was to have the joy of playing and singing great music with its infinite resources—the language that speaks to us more than all others across cultures and time.

So perhaps it's not surprising that I've always been an optimist after all—even if a sometimes despairing one. I'm the product of a mixed marriage: my father (who sang like an angel) was a pessimist and my mother, bless her, was an optimist.

Anyway, the secret unremitting search went on quietly deep inside me—for what? I knew only that I was searching for something, that it was both terribly important to me and very elusive.

I began to realize that I wasn't the only performer plagued with occasional but troublesome stage fright (or, as it is now known, "performance anxiety"). Other people confessed their own misery about this and fear of the fear they lived with. What a difference it could have made if someone had helped us when we needed it! So I found myself beginning, without conscious awareness of why, to research and put together information and exercises that would help people perform at their best. Remembering that Einstein once said, "I want to be as simple as possible—but no simpler!" I looked for the fastest possible results without being superficial or simplistic.

I wanted so much to help people overcome their fears that I soon had collected and invented a huge arsenal of resources with some near-magic keys to give people. Word got around. Soon I was asked to teach aspiring actors, singers, and instrumentalists at the Columbia University Graduate School of the Arts and the Manhattan School of Music. I discovered that I loved teaching! Serendipitously, when an injury put an end to my performing career, the New School in New York invited me to teach several courses. The first, called "Acting for TV," was a natural since I'd been a regular on *As the World Turns*, *Edge of Night*, and other soaps for several years, but the other course, "Public Speaking for Private People," I agreed to only reluctantly since I had never taught or even taken a course like that.

It soon became clear that communication problems evoke people's deepest fears. Practically everybody is frightened of public speaking. At first I worried—how could I deal with so many people of so many different backgrounds, ages, interests, and educational levels? The assortment was wildly diversified, with ages ranging from sixteen to eighty years. I saw how much people suffered from low self-esteem, their inability to speak up, and panic that they couldn't measure up to their own and others' expectations.

Everything I had been collecting and amassing suddenly became relevant. Realizing I needed "different strokes for different folks," I threw myself into intensive studies of everything from gestalt, transactional analysis, psychodrama, and transpersonal and ego psychology to Ericksonian and clinical hypnosis, neurolinguistics, psychomotor therapy, psychoneuroimmunology, quantum physics, stress management, yoga, Zen, Kum Nye, and several schools of Buddhism and other Eastern disciplines. I discovered that if you go deeply enough into psychology, you hit not China (like the child digging through the sand) but spirituality. I wanted to be able to give people, in all their diversity, whatever keys they needed to become more richly themselves.

People told me their haunting personal stories; I saw how each person developed over the course of a semester, how rapport grew in the group, and the reserves of genius everyone seemed able to draw on. We all realized that deep down we all have much in common and a great deal to give each other. I found it fascinating to help people become what they dreamed of and began to have a deep respect for the inner gifts so-called ordinary people have. I had always been a closet optimist about people. Now I was coming out of the closet.

Then a journalist who had heard about my classes at the New School wrote a detailed and admiring full-page article for *Women's Wear Daily*, called "Doe Lang's Class in Charisma." My first reaction was horror! How presumptuous! Had I claimed to teach charisma? No. The reporter had come and watched, and that's what *she* said I was doing!

I rushed to the dictionary and found to my relief that *charisma* (which comes from Charis, one of the Three Graces in Greek mythology) used to mean the divine gifts or attributes we each have within.

That was exactly what I believed. I saw that my role was to help people trust themselves and, through dealing with their fears about public and private speaking, reach deep places where we share our humanness. I had learned to have great admiration for the creativity, inner gifts, and capacity for charisma every person has, no matter how unlikely that may at first seem. Yes, there are great differences in vitality, education, and expressiveness, but at the deepest level, nobody is boring! What most people present at the surface bears little relation to their real quality and gifts.

Charisma—the Superlanguage

More and more people came to me with urgent communication needs. I began to see that the explosion of technology and the rapid changes we have all been experiencing have made understanding each other more important than ever before. I began to see charisma not as an ego trip, as many brilliant narcissists had used it (often with devastating results), but as a superlanguage that can create rapport and a respectful human relation with others while at the same time helping us realize our own best potential.

This is a powerful message. And every time an article about my work appeared or I was on TV or radio, people from all over the world would write me, asking how to achieve charisma. Most people had been brought up to believe it was either something you had or didn't have, and that there was nothing much you could do to change that. How wasteful and how wrong!

Through my work with thousands of people, I have seen that everybody has great riches within, if only they could accept that. As Liv Ullmann said to me not long ago, "We all have the same deep thoughts and feelings. Opening up to them makes a bridge between people."

I had found some profoundly satisfying bridges to help people experience themselves in a more loving, accepting way and deal with others with the same kind of loving concern they now could give themselves.

Political figures wanted my advice on charisma. Producers from TV shows and publications asked me to analyze body language. Business leaders, actors, professors, computer geniuses, scientists, professionals of all kinds, celebrities, women in transition—people with enormously varying backgrounds—all seemed to need affirmation and techniques to learn increasingly complex and important communication skills. Some wanted a way to restructure their family relationships and create peace and harmony in their lives.

I found that this work is a nonthreatening way for people to reach deep areas of themselves and profoundly affect society as well. Now I've discovered everything I've learned is truly useful. It is my great joy and privilege to be able to help people. That's why I decided to write this book. I wanted to share the work I have done on myself and with others because at last I know what my gifts—what everybody's gifts—are for.

Charisma—intrinsic charisma—is within all of us everywhere. And it's meant to be shared.

As I promised in the introduction, here is a new way of looking at the varied faces of charisma. First, here in a stream of consciousness, is what people in my classes have whispered, shouted, or thrust forward as their associations with charisma: *allure, appeal, attraction, charm, dynamism, presence, magnetism, personality, confidence, vitality, power, persuasive, unforgettable, irresistible, adorable, heart-melting, you forgive them everything, you want to do things for them, you want to be with them, you want to be like them, you want them to like you, you feel more important and charismatic in their presence, empowering, inspiring, uplifting, funny, eloquent, magical, surprising, creative, innovative, larger than life, original, instantly familiar yet mysterious. . . .*

The Thirteen Kinds of Charisma

Add your own candidates—these lists are only a start, and by no means exhaustive. Many of the first twelve categories are based on talent, achievement, or being born in the right time, place, and family.

1. **Performance charisma**: Whether Barbra Streisand, Jerry Seinfeld, Leonardo DiCaprio, or enduring icons like Luciano Pavarotti, Frank Sinatra, Cary Grant, Fred Astaire, John Wayne, Katharine Hepburn, Audrey Hepburn, Charlie Chaplin, the Marx Brothers, Marilyn Monroe, Humphrey Bogart, Jimmy Stewart, Spencer Tracy, Bette Davis, Jeanne Moreau, Monty Python, Bob Dylan, or the Beatles, performance defines the cultural landscape and forms a permanent backdrop for our collective unconscious.

2. **Sports charisma**: Simply think of Michael Jordan, Babe Ruth, Sonja Henie, Tiger Woods, Bobby Jones, Mark Spitz, Tara Lipinski, Martina Navratilova, Michelle Kwan, Sammy Sosa, or Mark McGwire.

3. **Money or business charisma** (may be achievement or family-related): Included are the Rockefellers, Du Ponts, Kennedys, George Soros, Bill Gates, and Warren Buffett, who have more money than some entire countries. Even if they are personally unprepossessing, once it is known that they have enormous wealth, their charisma is immediate.

4. **Spiritual charisma**: With or without temporal power and human or legendary-divine, some people have it—the Pope (any Pope has situational charisma, and some, such as John XXIII, have actual spiritual charisma), the Dalai Lama, Mother Teresa, the Maharishi, Thich Nat Hanh, Buddha, Moses, Christ, the Virgin Mary, St. Francis, St. George, St. Anthony, and all the lesser saints.

5. **Political and leadership charisma**: As Max Weber wrote, political charisma is an up-and-down affair: it may be God-given, but it has to be validated by the crowd. A successful candidate has political charisma when elected, but it probably is temporary! Tony Blair and Bill Clinton certainly have charisma but, by definition, in defeat they lose a good deal of it. Eloquence, sexual magnetism, persuasiveness, personal attractiveness, outrageousness, and a minor flaw are all components of personal charisma. History, however, confers more or less permanent charisma on those whose reputation survives their tenure—Winston Churchill, Franklin D. Roosevelt, Ronald Reagan, and even the evil geniuses of Adolf Hitler, Benito Mussolini, and Joseph Stalin.

    Resurrectional charisma is a specifically American subset of the political and media charisma: for example, Richard Nixon left office in disgrace and still managed to wind up as a respected elder statesman. If the career is big enough, career death is only temporary! Having power does not guarantee charisma, however; for instance, Ken Starr, Newt Gingrich, and Trent Lott at the height of their power still did not have charisma.

6. **Media, fashion, and style charisma**: The household TV gods exemplify this type—Larry King, Mike Wallace, Barbara Walters, Rosie O'Donnell,

Oprah Winfrey (whose plug can make any book a bestseller), Howard Stern, Bill Moyers, Ted Koppel. Creative movie and media moguls such as Steven Spielberg, Woody Allen, and Ted Turner also have immense power, influence, visibility (i.e., celebrity), and wealth. A strong indicator of Woody Allen's charisma is that he can get the biggest stars to appear in his movies without letting them know in advance what they will be doing. Sometimes their parts even wind up not showing them at their best. The Soon-Yi–Mia Farrow scandal had little negative impact on Woody's charisma in the United States and none at all in Europe, where sexual scandal is ho-hum for most people. Fashion moguls Giorgio Armani, Ralph Lauren, Calvin Klein, or Donna Karan and supermodels Cindy Crawford and Christie Brinkley parlayed their charisma into great wealth and influence through cross-over charisma (see #7). Tina Brown, British-born editor of the *New Yorker*, merged magazine, film, and other media in a new charisma "synergy." Buzz is not enough, and media exposure and celebrity are not enough—but they certainly help, for charisma must be sustained to last. Fifteen minutes of fame is only a start.

7. **Cross-over charisma:** Occasionally people, like Ronald Reagan, achieve fame first in one field and then cross over—in his case, from movies to politics. Andy Warhol began as an artist and became famous as an influential cultural icon. Lucille Ball graduated from being a TV comedienne to powerful head of her own studio, as Mary Pickford had done in the early days of Hollywood. In another time and place, Ignacy Paderewski, the great Polish pianist, became president of his country. Václav Havel went from literature to politics, becoming president of Czechoslovakia and then of the Czech Republic.

8. **Cumulative charisma:** Some people have been famous so long that they seem always to have been part of our lives. Elizabeth Taylor and the Kennedys come to mind. A subset is the necrologic cult fame of Elvis Presley, Marilyn Monroe, Judy Garland, and Frank Sinatra.

9. **Situational (including family) charisma:** This type includes royal families. Princess Diana first earned situational (fairy-tale princess) and then media charisma (scorned wife who appealed to the public for sympathy, broke down the royal reserve, and showed sympathy for children and the disabled). Dying young and tragically, she occasioned the most spectacular, technologically awesome, TV-assisted worldwide communal grieving and achieved legendary status. A subset of her situational charisma is the generational legacy: Prince William's charisma is particularly potent because, since his mother's poignant death, his potential as future king and his personal charm have been compounded by journalistic efforts at reparations, so that glimpses of him become more precious because they are rare. Any king or president (and his family) has situational charisma, as do unofficial dynasties in showbiz, like the

Redgraves and Barrymores, and socialite clans like the Rockefellers, Du Ponts, and Kennedys.

10. **Legendary/heroic/mythic charisma:** Historic personages and fictional characters can also have charisma. Think of great explorers Marco Polo or Columbus; kings and queens from King Arthur to Cleopatra and Marie Antoinette; fairy-tale and mythic figures from Cinderella to Paul Bunyan, Ulysses, Johnny Appleseed, and Mickey Mouse, saints (especially St. Francis and St. George), and the Greek gods Dionysus, Apollo, Pan, and Hermes; biblical characters including Solomon, David, the Queen of Sheba, Goliath, and Moses; famous seducers, reprobates, scoundrels, monsters, and dreamers, such as Don Juan, the Marquis de Sade, Dracula, Frankenstein, and Don Quixote.

11. **Literary, artistic, and intellectual charisma:** Writers, composers, philosophers, poets, and artists have great charisma. They include the enduring greats of literature, art, and music like Homer, Shakespeare, Aeschylus, Aristophanes, Plato, Aristotle, Sophocles, Michelangelo, Rembrandt, Dickens, Kant, Freud, Jung, Twain, Wilde, Shaw, Renoir, Picasso, Bach, Mozart, Beethoven, Gershwin, van Gogh, Dickinson, Plath, O'Keefe, Neruda, and many more. Many of these people were superb self-promoters (e.g., Shaw and Wilde). One of the fascinations of Dickinson and van Gogh, on the other hand, is that they became successful only after death.

12. **Scientific and technological charisma:** Galileo, Descartes, Einstein, the Curies, Pasteur, Edison, Darwin, Stephen Hawking, Richard Feynmann, and Robert Oppenheimer have this kind of charisma.

13. **Intrinsic charisma:** The last category does not depend on talent, family, celebrity, or even achievement. We have all known people in our lives who were unforgettable—a grandfather, parent, sister or brother, beloved teacher, or town character.

And each of us has, within, a secret garden of the heart that is rich and charismatic. We are all dreamers. Everybody feels pain, fierce desire, fear, sometimes guilt, anger, or despair; everybody craves joy, peace, respect (or recognition and acknowledgment), and happiness. We resonate with love, magnetism, energy, and vitality because in essence this is our own best speaking to us, reminding us of the riches within, and of our power to connect the dots that are our separate individualities, sensing the ocean in the drops of water.

As Nobel Prize–winning Polish poet Wislawa Szymborska wrote:

With smiles and kisses, we prefer
to seek accord beneath our star,
although we're different (we concur),
just as two drops of water are.

In Nara, Japan, there is a famous meditation garden, Ryoanji, a sunken rectangle of smoothly raked pebbles known for thirteen large, flat stones; people come from all over the world to sit quietly and meditate on the edge of the rectangular space, their feet dangling over the edge. I idly counted the grayish black stones and realized suddenly that there were only twelve! "Wait! How come there are only twelve stones?" I asked the monk who was shepherding us around. He smiled quietly: "Ah, the thirteenth is in your mind."

The thirteenth charisma is intrinsic charisma not only in your mind but also in your heart. Charisma is a basic energy force of nature, like fire or water. It's value-free: it can be either positive or destructive, life-enhancing or imprisoning. Greek poet Evangelos Alexandreou calls it the "jewelry of the human soul."

Claiming your intrinsic charisma connects you not only to the deep best of your private authentic soul but also to other souls in a powerful, mutually fulfilling life dance. That is what this book will help you allow yourself to do.

2

Imagination–Its Care and Feeding

Imagination is more important than knowledge.
—Albert Einstein

*If you learn "tricks," you'll be a caterpillar that flies,
not a butterfly.*
—Baba Ram Dass

Ninety percent of this game is half mental.
—Yogi Berra

People and events do walk through the door of our expectations.

"I'm not sure if it's just my imagination," a client will say to me the first time he or she has tried a new exercise and found it working. People don't always realize that the world is *created* by our imagination.

I remember my first trip away from my New York home. I was sixteen and went to visit my brother in Minneapolis. Very excited at the prospect of traveling so far, I stood on the station platform and thought, with amazement, "I'm getting on the train because I had an *idea*—to visit my brother!" This seemed so simple, almost stupid, that I didn't share it with anyone. Yet it impressed me very deeply.

Years later, my son, Brian, then ten, wrote a poem:

Ideas are a piece of clay that
keeps developing bigger and bigger.
Until it finally shapes itself into
  a sculpture
which is one specific idea.

Life is an idea—an idea never
  to forget—
It keeps on developing forever.

I was astounded. When it won a prize in a poetry contest and was printed in the *New York Times*, people wrote in from all over the country—clearly he had touched universal feelings.

Our expressed and unexpressed ideas control the way we live our lives. Someone once remarked: "There are three kinds of people: those who make things happen, those who have things happen to them, and those who wonder, 'What happened?' "

When we can direct our lives, we feel creative, happy, and, most important, fully alive. As long as we are in an unconscious "victim" position, our suffering is compounded by the bewilderment and helplessness we feel.

The Burning Question

In *Man's Search for Meaning*, Viktor Frankl described the universal human need to see meaning in one's life—and death. This need can even be stronger than the desire to live. A Zen definition of the purpose of life is "to unroll the scroll of meaning." In other words, we have a profound need to discover what we're here for—not why, but what for.

I have found this basic human question to be of burning importance to people on all levels. In my workshops for businesspeople, whether their initial motive for taking the course was to speak effectively, handle interpersonal communication better, get over nervousness in front of groups (and we know that most people are more afraid of public speaking than anything else—even death), or one of a dozen other related pragmatic objectives, when I asked what they perceived as the most meaningful part of their existence, a hush fell over the room. That told me I had "hit a nerve." It was the silence we have all experienced in a group when something important has happened, something that engages our most basic questions about ourselves.

Michael M., a rising young architect, said wonderingly, "I just realized that the most important thing in the world to me is not my work, as I thought, but my relation to my kids. Everything else is really secondary."

He had made a discovery that changed his view of his own life—what gave it the most meaning.

> Close your eyes, breathe slowly and deeply, and ask, *"What gives my life its meaning?"* Allow yourself to feel the answer emerging without your giving it any conscious direction. You may surprise yourself. Take a minute to do that now.

Who's Directing Your Script?

Acknowledging your real feelings is a powerful precondition to becoming the creator and director of your life. A lot of people feel like minor actors in somebody else's production—and a road company at that! They don't like the working conditions, they don't know whether the play is any good, they can't tell if *they* are good enough, and they feel at the mercy of the critics, the producer, and possibly the star; life for them is a misery of anxiety mixed with anticipation:

"When the show opens, *if* it's a success, everything will be OK."

"Suppose the reviews are bad? Suppose my reputation is ruined? Suppose I fail to meet expectations?"

"What if I'm fired?"

Meantime, the stress buildup is tremendous. Everybody's nerves are frayed. Tempers are short. The uncertainty robs good moments of joy.

"How can I play with my children when I'm worried about business?" moans Donald T.

"I can't get to sleep because I keep thinking about all my office problems and what I have to do tomorrow. I can't relax," says Madelaine, a top government official.

"I can't seem to stop worrying," says a mother of three.

"We wouldn't be as successful and productive if we lowered our stress level," avowed a group of top women radio and TV executives. They were not willing to pay that price.

We tend to equate any kind of "letting go"—even relaxing—with loss of control. In other, more traditional societies, certain days are designed for a mass letting go to relieve people's consciousness of the burdens of the tight, structured lives they live the rest of the year. Mardi Gras in Catholic countries, the Indonesian Monkey Dance (*ketjak*), festivals in Italy, whirling dervish Sufi dances—all these are responses to the deep human need for relaxation of tension and freedom from our own and others' expectations of "appropriate behavior." From masked balls to drugs to nightclubbing, societies have always provided outlets for the need to let go. The curious paradox is this: if we are not to lose control entirely, we must occasionally let go.

It's no longer enough to take a vacation a couple of times a year. We need to *de-stress daily* to protect our health. Then we can increase our creativity and enhance our joy in life.

We are, after all, creatures of rhythmicity: in-out goes our breath. Systole-diastole, up-down, tense-relax, and ebb-flow are in our blood. Our functioning is related to the tides of the moon, the pull of the sea, the movement of the planets. In the last few years science has confirmed what earlier societies knew all along: we are creatures of perpetual change. We are all works in progress.

It has been estimated that at any moment the mind can store a *quadrillion* bits of information. Most of this we are scarcely aware of at all; our cells and life functions take over and run us on automatic pilot. What a power plant of possibilities!

Though internally we are immensely responsive to our environment, most of us don't even notice the reaction of our bodies to the stresses of our lives. But the organism is devilishly clever. We can lie to the mind:

"I feel fine! There's nothing wrong with me."

"That shouldn't bother me. It's a detail. Trivial!"

"Why should I care about that?"

Meanwhile, that magnificently faithful seismograph—the body—is quietly registering (and responding to) the flow of feelings and perceptions we are experiencing, *whether we realize it or not*. The knees get weak, heart pounds, stomach tightens. We try to pretend none of that is happening. Ignore it long enough and the body will produce some gross imbalance: illness or accident—even hypertension, heart disease, or cancer. That is its way of saying, "Hey, listen to me, you're not paying attention to my feelings!"

Sometimes people who have been overworking will suddenly break down. ("But he was never sick a day in his life!") Type A people (angry, compulsive workaholics) don't allow themselves to stop until they suffer a heart attack. They are the personality type most likely to be struck down by sudden cardiac collapse.

"Death," as some wag remarked, "is Nature's way of telling you to slow down."

In our Puritan-based culture, we have not been trained to nurture ourselves. Many, many people drive themselves mercilessly on the unspoken assumption that only after they have worked hard do they really have a right to enjoy themselves. Many of us feel deep down that if we do enjoy ourselves, we will be punished for it. Having postponed for so long the human need to enjoy and savor the texture of our lives, we are often unaccustomed to (and uncomfortable with) feeling good. Only being stressed feels familiar. The familiar, even though unpleasant, will seem reassuringly like home.

The Importance of the Unimportant

Marcus L., a brilliantly successful industrialist, had struggled for twenty years to achieve power, wealth, and fame. On the way up he had risen to every challenge; he had beaten down every setback and competitor. He came to me because he had now achieved everything he had always wanted but couldn't enjoy it. He felt a curious emptiness and hopelessness.

"Isn't there anything else? What's it all for?" he blurted out. He couldn't understand why life should suddenly seem so pointless to him. He had used his body like a well-made machine that he had to respect and care for, but he had forgotten to enjoy it. And the inner demon (we are all deeply moralistic in our inmost hearts) nagged at him unrelentingly. He had earned his pleasures, but they suddenly seemed worthless. He made love to a succession of desirable women, drove fast cars, dined in the great restaurants of the world, and was a patron of the arts. He was powerful and respected—but the underlying grimness of his drive to succeed had robbed him of the habit of joy.

Joy had, without his even noticing it, been sent packing years ago. We are a product-oriented, result-oriented, end-oriented society. Marcus had fulfilled his own and society's expectations. What was wrong? *Where was the payoff?*

A sense of emptiness—really despair—overpowered him. He felt cheated.

His vision of the meaning of his life was not large enough. When he learned to understand the importance of the unimportant, to get in touch with his unacknowledged inner self and contact all those deeply human centers that had nothing to do with power, success, fame, or wealth and that were in fact shared with every other living being, his whole feeling about his life changed. Learning to meditate expanded his experience of his own world and opened him to a new sense of value, lightness, and fellowship with other human beings. During his first meditation, he laughed—it was the first time he had, he said, in eight months.

Maurice Maeterlinck's famous parable about the bluebird of happiness illustrates a profound insight about the quest for happiness and meaning. The point is not that the foolish hero went around the world looking for the secret when he might have stayed in his own backyard because that is where it was all the time. The point is that he had to make the journey in order to experience his own happiness.

We see only what we believe, what we're prepared to see. Yet the clues to a new state of development are probably there all the time if we could only see them. All of us can remember opportunities missed, people neglected, chances ignored because we were not ready for them.

Our "ideas" were in the way.

Every era produces its own meaningful myths in whatever form is most popular. For ours it may be film. A powerful Japanese movie, *Rashomon*, tells the story of a forest murder (based on a 1915 short story by Akutagawa Ryūnosuke) from the separate viewpoints of the main people involved. At the end of the film, we don't know if anybody was lying. Everybody was telling his own truth, although their stories conflicted with one another's. Very puzzling! What remained was a basic human mystery.

The old certainties are gone. We must be able, in this new age of shifting realities, to tolerate much greater ambiguity than ever before. How are we to steer, then, without the lodestar of the old certainties, the old values?

The answer may be that *we can only judge the truth by the reality it creates*. Let me hasten to add here that this refers to nonverifiable parts of experience—larger issues than "Who forgot to put the cap on the toothpaste?"

What we imagine becomes true because we act as if it is, creating a reality by the very assumption.

For instance, if you walk around assuming that people are no good, somehow your experience will confirm it. You expect to be cheated—and you will be. If you assume people are not to be trusted, every negative experience you have will reverberate in the light of your inner conviction.

Your Hidden Assumptions—Are They Good for You?

"People are no damned good."

"I can't win."

"Nobody cares."

"I love people."

"Why does it happen to me?"

"Every guy wants only one thing."

"I'm lovely."

"Somebody up there loves me."

Each of these basic, hidden assumptions creates experiences of life that match a perception of meaning. Whatever happens then provides its own justification.

"I'll believe it when I see it" is like saying, "I'll go in the water when I can swim." We have been taught, because of the old faith in objective evidence, to see things backward. Yet it is only by an act of imagination (a kind of faith)—before reality provides evidence—that realities begin to happen.

Strangely enough, the old saying "Results count," which used to be the battle cry of result-oriented, materialistic people, is now the touchstone for a new, more organic groping toward human meaning. The question is "What *effect* does my view or attitude produce?"

We are learning that through imagining, we can tap enormous potential. By imagining we are, as Anne Frank said, "really good at heart," and by imagining that we feel love—or at least by extending our hopes and wishes until they are realized—we can begin to direct energy toward those expanded states of being.

Attention is energy: what we imagine begins to happen.

The Great "As If" Principle

Uta Hagen often tells her acting students to "act as if." And in life, no less than in acting, this is how reality is created. In the next chapters we will explore how to open ourselves to these new enlarged ways of functioning and feeling—tapping our deepest creative potential to express our own gifts and communicate productively with others.

> Visualize a person as perfect, whole, at his or her best, and project that certainty, if possible when that person is asleep. It's not necessary to be in the same place.

One of my students created a very imaginative adaptation of this mental gift giving. She was trying to help a friend who was experiencing a writing block. She thought to herself, "What can I do?" Nothing, she felt, directly. Then she thought, "What if I do three things that I hate to do and mentally dedicate to my friend the energy released by my doing those tasks?" So she cleaned up her closet, her desk, and her refrigerator. Then she told her friend. Indeed, her friend experienced a certain inexplicable flow of ease and ability to work, perhaps triggered by the generosity of her friend's act.

This was an empathic act—to do something difficult yourself to help someone else. There is, of course, no way of knowing precisely what does help. The alchemy of freeing energy is capricious.

Research tells us it is the right hemisphere of the brain that perceives sudden shifts in feeling. We have all experienced that when a depression lifts, a sudden insight gives a new feeling of lightness, or fear gives way to relief and the world is suddenly bright again.

The left hemisphere, concerned with linear thinking, logic, analysis, and sequential thought, is the plodder, the analyst, the critic, and the relentless logician. The right hemisphere is intuitive, deals in imagery and spatial or musical matters, and operates swiftly to change gestalt or feeling states—often mysteriously. It is the artist, singer, child, romantic.

We need both hemispheres to function well. Language, although mainly located in the left hemisphere, also involves music, so when we speak we are using both hemispheres. Western education and thought tend to develop mainly left-brain-oriented processes, and the latest findings have shown that we need to involve learners in more right-brain activities to enhance and facilitate ease and depth of learning.

When you're in a rut mentally, you tend to pace up and down. Dance, sing, paint, jog, or recite poetry—and you free the right brain and trick the left into accepting some help.

Interrupting or changing the psychophysical processes that correspond to the mental blocks are ways of getting out of our mental traps. The intuitive right brain would be responsive to someone's gift of mental energy or positive vision of functioning beautifully, and it could immediately integrate that into an entirely different feeling state than the problem level—which is full of reasons, history, explanations, grievances, and complaints (rational and "stuck").

Studies have shown that plants that are prayed over grow bigger and produce larger and more exceptional fruit. At Findhorn, a spiritual community in Scotland, the size of the fruits and vegetables has astounded botanists.

I once witnessed a dramatic episode involving the power of group thought. One day a young singer, one of my best students, was absent from my class at the Manhattan School of Music.

"Where's Kathy?" I inquired.

"Oh, didn't you know? She has a brain tumor, and she's been in a coma for three days," answered one of the other young women in the class. I was horrified. Although I had never done anything like this before, I gathered everybody into a circle and for the next hour and a half, standing with hands joined and eyes closed, the ten of us visualized Kathy as completely healed and sent her our collective healing energy. Although I had no experience doing anything like this, and no idea if it would work, I just felt we had to try to do *something*. Many other people in the school, we heard later, were also sending Kathy healing energy. That afternoon Kathy came out of her coma.

William Tiller of Stanford University suggests, on the basis of his research, that the intensity of the coherent group-energy field (which means a group of people on the same wavelength with the same intentions at the same time) is not the sum of the number of group members, but the *square* of the number of people in the group. In other words, the power of a group of 200 people whose energies were coherent would have the numerical value not of 200 but 40,000! As Dr. Larry Dossey and others have shown, studies confirm that patients who are prayed for—even if they don't know it— have shorter hospital stays and get well faster.

W. Brugh Joy, M.D., writes in *Joy's Way: A Map of the Transformational Journey*, a book about healing with body energies:

> The induction potential of a group field can be very powerful. Furthermore, one or two individuals with strong energy fields centered at the heart level are capable of igniting the rest of the group into that same level of consciousness.

Of course, this accounts for mass hysteria as well. Anybody who has ever been in an audience mesmerized by a powerful speaker or a great performance has known that sense of exhilaration and oneness that unites the whole crowd. I remember hearing the great pianist Vladimir Horowitz play at Carnegie Hall, and I remember being one of eleven thousand people at a women's conference in Albany, swept away with the sense of exhilarating unity. And who has not been at great football or soccer games, or experienced the powerful charisma in action of pop singers from Sinatra to the Beatles to Madonna? On the demonic side, we have seen newsreels of Hitler addressing stadium crowds whipped into frenzy.

Tapping into Your Charisma

Dr. Robert Ornstein, author of *The Psychology of Consciousness*, says, "Mental control of physical states can show individuals that they have absorbed from their culture a radical underestimation of their possibilities."

Thousands of people have tapped into expanded learning capacities through Suggestology, a poorly named but remarkably effective teaching system developed by the distinguished Bulgarian scientist Dr. Georgi Lozanov.

As Sheila Ostrander and Lynn Schroeder report in their book *Superlearning*, in the mid-1960s Dr. Lozanov pioneered a new system to effortlessly learn and remember information. He was able to prove what he had suspected—that the human ability to learn is virtually limitless. In the first experiment with fifteen professional people, aged twenty-two to sixty, the group, at first disbelieving and skeptical, learned a thousand French words in one day—almost half the working vocabulary of a language! Using relaxation exercises, stately slow music, and differing intonations for reading aloud the material to be learned, this pilot group not only scored an incredible 97 percent on the test but also enjoyed the whole experience. (The number of new pieces of information usually acquired in conventional learning sessions is fifty to 150.)

In subsequent courses people who tried the system noticed that their lives improved—small health problems dropped away, neuroses cleared up, and self-confidence increased along with their ability and pleasure in learning. "They begin to grow into a larger notion of what they are and what they can do." This worked with people of all ages and levels. Every human being seems to have the capacity to perform at something like a genius level!

Lozanov's research convinced him that when people use both body and mind harmoniously, they can expand their mental capacities and awaken and enhance their creativity and intuitive abilities. No special equipment is necessary, and it's effective with young, old, mentally challenged, and brilliant alike. In Iowa, after a year's teaching in the public school system, Suggestology produced significant leaps in student achievement. What a profound difference it would make if this method were adopted by our schools.

Originally a doctor and psychiatrist, Lozanov didn't set out to be an educator—he was studying the nature of the human being in all its potential. As Ostrander and Schroeder point out, "Lozanov devised ways to open the reserves of the mind, to heal mental and physical disease. But in investigating what the whole human being can do, he couldn't help being drawn into creative and intuitive areas."

This remarkable method paralleled and reinforced my discoveries in teaching people how to communicate comfortably and effectively, and, in effect, *tap their own charisma*. We work with the whole person—body, mind, lifestyle. By ironing out blocks in the energy flow—which may be the result of fear, negative self-judgments, momentary tension, early childhood conditioning, poor self-image, or a lack of confidence in one's abilities—people begin to be able to express their best selves, feel confident and capable, deal calmly and effectively with hitherto frightening communication situations, and best of all—*know that they can always do it*. No more hit-or-miss hoping or purely verbal or purely experiential approaches—with this holistic approach to communicating, you master the tools and resources that put you in a state of calm, relaxed, pleasurable functioning. This intuitive, creative state can produce what some Russians call "bio-rapport."

Bio-rapport is the vehicle for experiencing your own charisma. When the vibes are good, you feel accepted and liked, you are in resonance with your audience, and others have a positive experience of you.

In *Superlearning* Ostrander and Schroeder write:

> Bio-rapport—messages pulsing in widening circles out of the whole person—probably lies at the heart of charisma. This is the between-the-lines communication of powerful artists and leaders, and of great teachers. It makes the message take, it reaches and moves us, even to the barricades. . . . Underneath the separate surface of things, there is a connection, a dynamic network, flashing countless messages everywhere, anywhere, perhaps faster than the speed of light. Time and space do not seem to affect these life signals. We are just beginning to realize how we influence and are influenced by thoughts and feelings pulsing along the network. . . . Like the old telephone system, this is a party line, and we're all on the line. . . .
>
> As Donald Hatch Andrews remarked, "In shifting the basis of our ideas about the universe from mechanics to music, we move into an entirely new philosophy of science and a fresh way of looking at things for the rest of us. . . . We form the resonance, we are the music and the message."

Everybody has had the experience of walking into a room feeling great—perhaps you just fell in love! People all sense a certain glow about you. When you smile, they respond. When you look or act gloomy or have a chip on your shoulder, the chances are that people respond to that negative message. Interestingly, negative messages are usually misunderstood. People generally interpret negative feelings as being directed toward *them*, and may perceive you as angry, sullen, arrogant, snobbish, cold, or mean when you are actually feeling worried, apprehensive, shy, or sad. You are putting out signals on the telepathic network we are all involved in.

Later I will show you how to program yourself for a positive outcome before an important meeting, presentation, or encounter in your life. *People will walk through the door of your expectations*—if these expectations are real enough for you.

Unfortunately, it doesn't do any good to say with only the top layer of your mind, "I will do it! I will get that job! I will make a good impression!" If your body is caught up in unconscious tension, your electromagnetic field will not reflect that positive image because it wasn't put in at a deep enough level.

The late Itzhak Bentov, the brilliant charismatic author of *Stalking the Wild Pendulum*, asked what happens to your consciousness if you're knocked out in a dark alley. Your body can't worry that your wallet is being stolen. Your waking consciousness is certainly no longer aware of what is happening, but your rudimentary consciousness is keeping the machine going. Your heart is still beating, blood is pumping, and you are breathing.

Ben, a wonderfully sunny, funny, spiritual genius (who could hold audiences spellbound for eight hours), used to say that a rudimentary consciousness is like the "janitor who minds the boiler room." Now if you give the "janitor" instructions to clean out all the rooms in the house (translating that into whatever you want to do well, from playing tennis to addressing a board meeting) and your body remains tense with anxiety, it's as though you asked him to do a wonderful job cleaning up the house— but left all the doors locked! "Damn," complains the janitor. "How do you expect me to do that? You're lucky I'm taking care of the furnace."

Many people try to bully themselves into relaxing by saying to themselves, "That shouldn't bother me!" or "Shape up! Stop behaving like a fool. Pull yourself together!" None of this impresses the janitor. He just shrugs. And you feel angry at yourself for not being able to control your nerves, tension, or scared feelings. Your voice shakes, your legs quiver, you can't remember what you wanted to say, your stomach knots up, and your hands perspire. And the more you berate yourself, the worse it gets.

In the next chapters we will explore ways for you to change how you react to stress by learning breathing, psychophysical, and visualization skills that will give you the techniques and confidence to be at your best even when you don't feel like it. Through role-playing and courage exercises and some fun-to-do assignments, you will discover for yourself the secrets of exploring and projecting your true voice, your own insights and perceptions, your warmth and feelings. You'll learn how to read people and situations accurately so that you are really "tuned in." The ancient knowledge that mind, emotions, and body are all one can be implemented with new techniques to help you achieve your potential beyond your wildest dreams.

The Dance of Communication

Have you ever watched fireflies blinking in a bush, off and on, off and on? Pretty soon they're doing it in unison. Nature likes to do things economically. The Dutch scientist Christian Huygens noticed the phenomenon of two-pendulum entrainment in 1665. Scientists sometimes call this "mutual phase-locking of two oscillators."

This entrainment is observable in human relationships as well. For instance, Dr. William S. Condon made amazing discoveries about the "subtle, largely unseen conversational dance": listeners were observed moving in precise though unconscious synchrony with a speaker's words. This process appears to be a universal characteristic of human communication. During conversations, people engage in intricate and shared movements across many subtle dimensions, yet are strangely unaware that they are doing so. Even total strangers will display this synchronization.

When people synchronize breathing in a shouting match or singing, chanting, or marching, they feel good about each other. We now know that the brain waves of the participants synchronize, and a feeling of harmony results. "The closer you move in rhythm with someone," Condon asserted, "the closer you become with that person." Sensitivity to different rhythms can mean the difference between hostility, incomprehension, or boredom and a feeling of intuited understanding.

When unpopular children are taught to be aware of other children's body language as well as of their own, they become more popular. This is part of what Daniel Goleman calls "emotional intelligence"—and it can be learned. While doing my internship at Creedmoor State Hospital on Long Island, I helped schizophrenics learn to be aware of their own and others' body language. This gave them new social skills and a sense of community with others, which greatly diminished their paranoia.

The One-Minute Verbal Free-for-All

Here's an exercise I have found enormously energizing and freeing. I use it with my classes, asking people to divide into pairs, face each other, and shout at each other nonstop for one minute. The only requirement is that they yell as loudly as possible, not stop for a second, and continue until the minute is up. People who find it difficult to "hold the floor" or grab attention are amazed how hard it is for them to keep it up. They often feel foolish or embarrassed at first. But once they get into the knock-down, drag-out spirit of it, they find it a tremendous amount of fun, and everybody feels alive, warm, and energized. In fact, it is one of the fastest ways to bring up the energy of a group of people. The mock battle leaves everybody breathless and laughing, and has the effect of breaking down barriers of shyness and inhibition.

If you consider yourself shy, or if you'd like to improve your verbal fluency and spontaneity, try it! Stand facing your partner (or a wall), set your stopwatch, and begin to talk vehemently, as loudly as possible without straining, for one minute. No less! If you shout continuously, you take in more oxygen, which stimulates more brain activity, and there is a greater flow of energy and ideas. The loosening of your blocks has the effect of unleashing a veritable flood of rich material. Over and over I have marveled at the funny and imaginative tirades that people come up with out of the reservoir of their own experiences during this exercise—without effort! If you can once break through the barrier of initial shyness, the flow is apt to be torrential!

Sometimes people protest, "But I'm not angry now. How can I yell when I'm not angry?" This is usually a form of embarrassment at revealing how they might behave when they do let go. Anger is terrifying to many people. They're afraid of simulating it or, in some cases, expressing it at all. In later chapters, I will show you how using anger productively can enormously enhance your powers of expression—without losing your friends.

The power to switch emotions—to quickly call on and enact emotions you may not be feeling at the moment—gives you access to emotional flexibility. For many people it lessens the fearful power of taboos about expressing negative feelings (or, in surprisingly many cases, *any* strong feelings).

The Keys to Your Charisma

Each of us in our own lives is a vehicle for change. When you make changes in the way you *imagine* your life and its meaning, your ability to affect others' lives grows powerfully and dramatically. Throughout these chapters, I will give you practical tools for understanding *how* we communicate to other people *what* we are feeling and *why* our sense of meaning (what is true for us) is communicated clearly to those around us even when we don't express it openly. Even when we ourselves are not aware of our true feelings, they can change the outcome of our interactions with people.

Imagination has been so undervalued as a practical tool of life that we need to find ways to relegitimize it—not just for artists, poets, and similar visionaries, but for everybody. You have begun to understand how the right hemisphere, which controls our states of feeling, can trick the left hemisphere—the rational, logical part—into dropping its resistance to change, to leaps of imagination, to risks, to confidence. We have to learn to mother and father our unborn selves; we are constantly changing, evolving, growing, shedding old mind-sets and personalities that are too limited and limiting for our lives today.

Some of what I describe may seem irrelevant at first—but nothing is unimportant. We will commute from the micro to the macro level, and I will show you techniques of reconceptualizing your communication with yourself and people around you so that you can be, at once, most fully yourself and most productive with other people.

We will dart acrobatically from inside to outside, from front to back, from body to breathing, mind, and lifestyle—because everything counts. *Only you—once you have a range of resources wide enough to choose from—can pick a key to unlock the secrets of your own charisma.*

Novelist Elizabeth Bowen once remarked, "A novelist is a person who invents the truth." I have since come to see that we are all artists of our lives. *A person is a truth who invents reality.* Each of us has an inner truth, and we can contact it in ways that I will specifically explore in coming chapters. *We each have all the gifts we need to live vitally creative lives.*

Many people have remarked, "All children are geniuses!" Marshall McLuhan observed, "Education is a process of shutting off our talents." It need not be. It *must* not be. With the shrinking of the world into a global village, the rewards and knowledge have grown as great as the risks. We now can know how to contact those unused parts of our selves. With practice, we can become more skillful at tapping into these inner sources of power.

We need to be curious and interested in the questions, rather than the final answers. Values must be reevaluated in the shifting light of change.

Dreams—Our Inner Messages

Every human dreams. A Malaysian tribe, the Senoi, have a crime-free, mental illness–free society because they have learned to work with their dreams—to accept feelings and transform them. In psychodrama workshops I have been deeply moved time after time by the beauty of imagery, the depth of perception, and the sheer eloquence of people speaking out of their deep feelings, unburdened by clichés from their ordinary levels of existence.

Becoming aware is a prelude to conscious integration at a higher level. Accepting the dignity of your inner gifts makes them real . . . ized.

Bali is the only society on Earth where it is taken for granted that everybody is an artist. As part of religious observances everybody paints, sings, dances, sculpts, weaves—nearly every possible form of human expression gets free rein. The result is a healthy society and an astonishingly high level of artistic achievement.

Our Western conception of the artist as a suffering genius who has little or no relation to ordinary mortals is part of the old dichotomizing split between mind-body, god-devil, good-evil, pleasure-pain. When we are reunited with all our amputated possibilities, we no longer need to make the artist a devil or hero. The Russians, for whom poets have always been the suffering surrogates of the entire popular consciousness, recognize the power of poets and writers to polarize the feelings of the nation. Writers have been thrown into prison, insane asylums, or shipped to Siberia. Russian people know that the fate of their poets somehow affects the population deeply, because to speak truly is to give voice to essential human feelings. Such people are valuable—and dangerous! Yet people speaking directly from their deep consciousness are as simple, clear, poetic, and moving as the greatest writers.

Most of us have a great deal invested in our automatic ways of behaving, our carefully learned *un*consciousness. The process of expanding behavior styles or opening to new experiences, of expressing feelings openly, may be frightening to many people.

"I feel silly," said Malcolm N., trying to permit himself to do The I-Don't-Care Swing (page 223). Yet we can't grow properly without laughing. Exercises and activities that may at first seem "silly" await you in the next chapters. Nothing is irrelevant. The most surprising little memories, actions, and dreams can trigger growth, change, and illumination. Irreverence, whimsy, and humor are natural relaxation and survival mechanisms, personal "tuning forks." Humans, like metals, break under too much stress. For all recorded history, one way of diminishing stress has been to *laugh*.

The shared experience of celebrating pain lightly provides a feeling of unity that counteracts the most devastating load of private misery.

My adopted Hungarian grandmother, Mimi, who survived endless changes of country, government, mind-set, and lifestyle, once told me, "Laughter is a soul bath." In Nazi-occupied countries of Europe during World War II, jokes were a defiant code that gave people courage and relief. Author Norman Cousins described in *Anatomy of an Illness* how he cured himself of an incurable disease with heavy doses of comedy films and laughter.

Our infinite human capacity to transform and transmute our lives is quickened by the capacity to laugh. Jokes often depend on the juxtaposition of the unexpected with the familiar. A person who can make others laugh is generally much valued. The trick is to use humor without straining. Have you ever winced at jokes carefully, painfully planted in a speech by a speaker who clearly finds nothing a laughing matter?

I will show you how to be funny in your own way, by relaxing and sharing in the common experiences of your audience and yourself. *No tricks!* Instead, when you know how to begin the process for yourself, the results will be like all good performances—surprising but right and inevitable—the best creative interaction between your own intuition, experience, and feelings and those of your audience.

I'm not going to *give* you a fish; I'll show you how to catch all the big ones yourself out of the rich and surprising aquarium of your own inner resources!

Technology of Trusting Yourself

Whatever you learn from this book will need to be filled in with insights, feelings, and experiences that are yours alone. Call it the "technology of trusting yourself." By merely imagining (and then practicing), you can move into a new, expanded charismatic self. *The discovery of your charisma begins with the cultivation of your own trust in yourself.* Much of that depends on garbage removal, clearing away the psychophysical blocks that stand in your path.

When students begin work with me, I tell them, "People are going to ask you pretty soon what you've done to yourself. Did you have a vacation? A new hairdo? Are you in love?" (This last is really significant, since more than 45 percent of the people replying to my charisma questionnaire said that they had felt most charismatic when they were in love.) Most outsiders won't know exactly what's changed about you. They will just sense *something* has. A new confidence, a sense of yourself as more valid as a person and more connected to others at the same time—all this will change the way people perceive you.

They *will* walk through the door of your expanded expectations. It seems like magic. But magic is only a name for what we don't yet understand.

To Grow You Have to Forgive Yourself (and Others!)

We will be exploring many ways you can seduce your left brain into letting go of the small self's fears and old ways of doing things, and allowing the creative, intuitive, holistic part of your brain—the right hemisphere—to make a quantum leap forward.

It is important to recognize—without self-blame—the fear you may have of changing, the fear of losing the self you are familiar with.

"But that's not me!" protests Janet L.

"That's the way I am," says Bruce B. firmly.

These are the last stands of the early resistances of the "small" self. Once, long ago, they helped you become an individual in ways that were safe in the milieu in which you grew up, which protected you from being overrun, violated, or even destroyed. But that was when you were small. They may no longer be useful. To change, you have to acknowledge their value to you in the past and respectfully ask permission of that resistant part of you to accomplish its goals of survival and growth. This means *not* being angry at yourself for failing to change as rapidly as you would like to.

The only way to grow and move ahead is to throw out self-blame, perfectionism, and anger at yourself for not achieving your ends as fast as you would like, and to acknowledge exactly what you feel without feeling that it defines you. We are infinitely malleable and, in the process of self-transformation, we must nurture ourselves in order to move ahead as quickly as possible to the next-higher stage of evolution.

St. Francis said, "Be gentle with yourself. Forgive yourself each day." And this is *what works*. The next chapter describes the Anti-Judgmental Notebook—as the initial step in this process.

If you can't immediately imagine being confident, charismatic, and irresistible, have patience. *Feelings change*. Endlessly. Always. They pass like clouds across the horizon, waves across the sea. Patience with yourself gives you the necessary detachment to face your worst failings, take responsibility, and gently encourage yourself to grow—without judgment.

Remember the story of the two caterpillars inching their way along the ground? Suddenly a bright golden butterfly flashed by them.

"Hmph!" said one of the caterpillars, pausing for a moment. "You'll never get *me* up in one of those things!"

3

How to Stop Putting Yourself Down

(Or Whose Side Are You on, Anyway?)

Life is a fairy tale in reverse.
—Isak Dinesen

The basic question for every human being is—
is the Universe friendly?
—Albert Einstein

In answering the charisma questionnaire, one out of four interviewees reported feeling most charismatic "now" or "when I was three [to five] years old." One out of three said, "When I am in love."

Most of us can remember some time when we felt loved, accepted, in tune with the world. When we feel like that, it's as though we can do no wrong. Our bodies feel light and free (if we're aware of them at all), we feel happy and at ease, life seems full of beautiful possibilities. The world seems friendly. It's hard to imagine we'll ever feel differently. The sun shines for us, and we are in tune with everything.

Remember, no one who answered the questionnaire wrote that he or she had never felt charismatic. It appears to be part of our natural heritage. Why, then, is it so difficult to hang on to that marvelous sense of being totally at home in the world? More important, *how do we get back to it?*

To discover, nurture, and enhance your own natural charisma, you have to play detective with your mind and body and feelings. By discovering what roadblocks you put up—which first take the form of negative thoughts and then are translated into physiological symptoms that interfere with full natural breathing and functioning—you will have the tools to clear the way to the kind of natural, easy functioning we've all experienced at good moments in our lives. You will be able to make them happen at will.

Imagine for a moment a garden hose spraying water full force. The force of the spray is very powerful; the water shoots across your garden in a splendidly concentrated arc. Now imagine that you bend the hose and make a kink, a small stoppage, at one point in the line. This is comparable to what happens when you have a negative thought and your body tenses. *Your electromagnetic field literally weakens.* Your breathing grows shallower; less oxygen reaches your brain, which uses three-quarters of your oxygen supply, and so you can't think as well.

When I was a young actress going for auditions, I was so nervous I'd forget the names of the people I met. "What's the matter with me?" I wondered. "It's as though there's a hole in my head. When I'm nervous, I forget everything! I feel so stupid." I didn't realize then that I had practically stopped breathing. Holding your breath when you're nervous (which most people do without realizing it) lowers your IQ instantly, at least temporarily.

Muscle-Testing Your Emotions

To demonstrate to yourself how your negative thoughts and feelings literally weaken you, try the following experiment: Stand facing a friend and put your left hand on his or her right shoulder. Now ask him to extend his left hand, palm down—elbow straight, wrist slightly higher than the shoulder (you can reverse it—it's not important which side is used). Tell him to think of something very pleasant. When he's ready, tell him you're going to try to push down his extended hand and he should resist your pressure. (The idea is to test his strength, not to suddenly overwhelm him and knock the arm down.)

Put three fingers on his arm just past the wrist (between the elbow and the wrist) and press down. Notice how strong the resistance is. Now ask your friend to close his eyes and think of something very negative. Give him enough time and ask when he is ready. Then put your right hand on his arm again the way you did before and press down again. You'll be surprised—and so will he—when his arm goes straight down, as though there were no strength in it at all! Then let him test you. The same thing will happen. People are always amazed by this test.

When you want to restore your strength, simply tap your tongue behind your front teeth (with your mouth closed) on the upper gum (the alveolar ridge) a few minutes. When your friend tests you again, your strength will be completely restored! (See chapter 5, page 80, for a more complete description.)

This kinesiological testing can also be used to test foods and drugs, to see if your body finds them positive or negative. Test with foods, drugs, or vitamins by holding the substance at the center of your chest with one hand, and have a friend test as usual with the other. It doesn't matter whether or not you know what you're holding. For instance, if you wrap up a cigarette for a smoker, the reaction will be weak even if the person is an unregenerate smoker and likes cigarettes! The test isn't affected by your likes and dislikes but by what really strengthens or weakens your system. Again, the body doesn't lie!

This is particularly important to protect yourself against prescription drugs that may be harmful to you. According to a 1997 study at the University of Toronto, 100,000 people died from prescribed drugs. Seventy percent of the doctors did not inform patients of the possible side effects of the drugs they had prescribed! So before you take any drug, be sure to read labels (many doctors don't!), discuss possible side effects and drug interactions with your doctor, and have someone muscle-test it on you. Herbal remedies are also a possible option. If your doctor is not open to these ideas, find one who is!

It's impossible to be relaxed and anxious at the same time, and that's not as obvious as it sounds! Using this clue, I am going to show you how to free your energy flow and unlock your charisma.

Freeing Your Energy Flow

Since we know that everybody has had the experience of feeling charismatic—that is, comfortable, at ease, effective, alive, and in joyful communication with the world (bio-rapport)—we're going to learn how to produce that psychophysical state quite deliberately. This is a five-stage process:

1. Identifying the interferences (the kink in the hose interfering with the water—your energy flow) when they are

    a. thoughts and feelings (including negative self-judgments)

    b. physical tensions and irregular breathing

2. Learning relaxation techniques to deal with the specific body tensions that *you* experience

3. Reframing negative thoughts—aloud

4. Practicing new breathing processes that will change the chemistry of your consciousness and help you maintain a calm, powerful energy flow—even under stress—so you can be at your best when you don't feel like it

5. Learning and rehearsing "power amplifiers" so you can be on a natural high *at will* to give you a heightened energy flow

A good detective needs a greedy eye for detail. Your clues will be the trivial moments that trigger negative feelings. Sherlock Holmes, Hercule Poirot, and all good detectives unravel the most complex mysteries by keen attention to significant details. Most of us are more like Watson in our unawareness and disbelief; when we start paying attention, we say, "Elementary, of course." The "crime" is the fatal leakage of energy and confidence caused by negative thoughts, experiences, and tensions.

"Who was the most negatively critical person in your childhood?" I asked a group, as I always do at the beginning of the course. People shifted in their seats, smiled, looked surprised or uneasy. What did that have to do with communicating well? Public speaking? Charisma? A great deal, as you'll see.

"And what," I asked, "were some of the verbal and nonverbal messages that you got as a child and never forgot about what you were or should be or do?" Now the answers poured out.

"My mother: she always told me I was clumsy."

"Both my parents: nothing I did was ever right."

"My older sister kept telling me I was stupid and I'd be found out."

"My father said people were no damn good. He also gave me the feeling that whatever I felt or did, he just wasn't interested. I wasn't important."

"My grandmother: 'Stop, you're a bad boy. You must never get angry. Don't be disobedient.' "

"My older brother: 'You're a dumb klutz—you're clumsy, you're awkward. You're ugly.' "

"My aunt: she said I should be a little lady; 'You're too shy.' "

Many women had heard these repeated messages:

"Be a lady!"

"Keep your elbows in; keep your legs together."

"Do what's expected of you."

"Be nice."

"Don't raise your voice."

Often people reported contradictory instructions. One woman, a writer, said she was told, "Be aggressive, don't be shy," and at the same time, "Be obedient and do what you're told!" An amazing number of people, including some high up on the corporate ladder, had been told they were stupid. One executive, who kept deploring that he exploded regularly at his subordinates, said he just couldn't stop. He stuck out his jaw like a rebellious little boy: "That's the way I am; I can't help it!" he declared. His early message from his father had been that he was stupid. He began to see that every time he ordered himself to do something ("Every morning I yell at myself, 'John, today don't be such a jerk, don't yell at everybody,' and then I go right out and do it!"), his inner self would rebel against that bossy voice that talked to him exactly like his father, who had called him "stupid."

Often, people are unconsciously obeying old cultural messages. When I was invited to Singapore to train government employees in communication, no one in the group would speak up! Ninety percent were Chinese, and their childhood message was "Be quiet! The nail that sticks up gets hammered down." On the other hand, as adults they were supposed to be *kiasu*—enterprising; this created a great conflict for them.

Knowing what are your hidden self-put-downs can save you from sabotaging your own performance. I have found it crucial to help people unearth their personal and cultural negative self-images—only then do they realize they're not true or useful.

Most of us suffer from at least an occasional nagging doubt. It's important to recognize these little devils when you're making a speech, meeting new people, or facing new challenges. Perhaps you say to yourself:

"I'm not clever enough."

"I'm not attractive enough."

"I'm not young/old enough."

"I have no right to be happy/successful/famous."

"My vocabulary's not good enough."

"They'll think I'm a hick."

"They'll think I'm boring."

"Who am I to sound like an expert?"

"I'll probably louse this up."

"*They* will resent it if I act sure of myself."

"*They* won't like me—why should they?"

"*They* won't be interested in me."

"I'm not as good as I was/he or she is/I should be."

Etc., etc., etc.

You may not even be aware that you have some doubts and negative beliefs about yourself. But when you're in a new or challenging situation, they may show up and shoot you down *if you are not aware of them.* Recognizing them as temporary roadblocks will prevent them from taking over.

On the surface, you may be capable, attractive, and apparently sure of yourself. But if a small inner voice tells you you're really going to mess up, and this little imp constantly nags you when you're not paying attention, watch out. It's practically impossible to fake an air of authority and ease. (When there is a conflict between verbal and nonverbal signals, studies show it is the nonverbal ones that are believed.) You may find you shrink, bluster, stumble, fall silent, laugh apologetically, talk too much or too little, and betray by a hundred little signs that you're not feeling very comfortable. Afterward you beat yourself about the head (mentally) and think of ten splendid things you could have said but didn't. You can't understand why you didn't think of those things in time, but it is, alas, too late to retrieve the situation. This is known to the perceptive French as *l'esprit de l'escalier*—"the wit of the staircase"—what you think of as you're leaving, or going down the stairs.

Each time you don't speak up when you have something to say makes it harder to assert yourself the next time.

Your Verbal Polaroid

You'll use your trivia triggers to clue you into the secret of your own mystery. Since we need to find the negatives that interfere with the flow of creativity and power, I have found it most productive with thousands of people to start with the negatives—the Anti-Judgmental Notebook.

Nothing is irrelevant or arbitrary here. Every question has a direct bearing on how we unconsciously sabotage our own power. You may find it surprising, possibly painful. But please bear with the process—there is a positive payoff within only a short time, and I'll explain that immediately after discussing the Anti-Judgmental Notebook.

Get yourself a small (three-by-five-inch) spiral notebook. *Take this everywhere*—in your purse or pocket, keep it with you. Whenever something triggers a negative judgment (it may take some noticing at first to realize exactly what is or isn't a judgment), write it down, along with the date, the time, and (if you know) a brief note on what set it off. *The only essential is what you said to yourself.* Do add what you felt in your body when the painful thought occurred to you.

Write down these details:

1. What happened, externally or internally;

2. What you said to yourself (e.g., "You're stupid!" "You messed up again!");

3. What you felt in your body; and

4. What happened to your breathing.

Important: don't be misled if your trigger moments seem trivial. What's really important is never what seems to be going on. That's one of the cagey disguises of our inner messages. We often feel ashamed to acknowledge that something so *trivial* as a chance remark or tiny incident or an unfavorable comparison with someone that we ourselves make can upset us.

"Don't be ridiculous—that shouldn't bother me! It's so petty!" This lightning inner response can make the original perception slink back into the underbrush, cowed, discouraged. You have no *right*, you're telling yourself, to feel this way. Not so! At this point stand up and say *aloud*:

"I HAVE THE RIGHT TO FEEL WHAT I FEEL!"

Say that three times. Go ahead. How does it sound? Angry? Defensive? Apologetic? Practice saying it *as loudly as you can*—at least three times a day—until it stops feeling foolish and silly or frightening. *What you say inside your head is not the same as saying it aloud.* One of the most important prerequisites for beginning to feel you have the right to speak up in any situation and share your information, experiences, and perceptions with others is **giving yourself permission to feel whatever you are really feeling.**

Many people are afraid of feelings they don't approve of. They think acknowledging them means they're giving in to those feelings. "If I have jealous feelings, I must be a jealous, rotten person. I don't want to be that." Or "If I'm so angry, I must be a bad person. Anger is bad." Many people, having been brought up by parents who themselves did not know how to handle anger, are convinced that natural, normal feelings of anger—which everybody has sometimes—are evil, that *they* are bad or undeserving if they experience such feelings. Sometimes the parents expressed anger themselves but didn't allow their children to.

Scraps of psychotherapeutic jargon often become weapons in the war against the self. "You're neurotic!" is the latter-day version of the old message to a child, "You're bad, you have a devil in you!"

Many people put themselves down for feeling something they don't approve of by telling themselves, "That's sick!" or "I'm being compulsive again." The discouragement of succumbing to a negative pattern is compounded by self-blame—or used as a justification. "Hopeless, helpless, or defiant—that's the way I am."

When I was teaching at Columbia University, a student flounced into a department meeting where she had been asked to explain why she hadn't done any work in her courses. She stared defiantly at the assembled professors and announced, "Well, I can't help it. I'm an anal compulsive personality." With that triumphant announcement, she swept out of the room.

Whether you take refuge in a label or judgment or are crushed by it, it prevents you from moving ahead to another stage. Part of this is a misunderstanding about the nature of emotions. We all are capable of innumerable feelings, from ecstasy to blind rage—this doesn't make us bad or evil. Emotions are, as many Eastern writings have taught us, like clouds passing across the sky or waves across the ocean. Our mind is a screen across which changing emotions and scenes pass. If we identify with any of them, act them out, or hang our self-image on them, we'll be unable to let go of the negative emotions or go on to experience others. Emotions are *not* behavior. But if we refuse to acknowledge strong negative feelings, they may erupt as "unskillful action" (the Buddhist term) or what psychologists call "acting out."

As Buddhist philosopher Chogyam Trungpa Rinpoche remarked:

Negative emotions are like manure. If you recycle them and work with them, they become like a compost heap; they nurture growth. If you don't deal with them, but just push them aside, or ignore them, they are nothing but a pile of shit!

We've all seen little children playing together. Suddenly a great fight erupts. There is a lot of yelling and wrangling, maybe even hitting. Then, as though nothing had happened, they'll be playing together peacefully again. This is a perfect demonstration of what happens to feelings when they're fully expressed. There is an almost magical transformation; having been expressed fully, the anger disappears. Often it is not convenient or appropriate to express feelings openly in a social, personal, or business setting. Then what can we, as adults, do?

The key to letting go of negative emotions is full acknowledgment without judgment. (You may have to talk to yourself quickly!)

Imagine a little girl or boy who comes crying to you because he or she skinned a knee or had an argument. You can say, "Stop crying. Don't be a baby!" Or you can say, "You really feel bad, don't you? That really hurt when you fell down!" Which response is going to feel better to the child? Try it. You'll see: the first will make your child cry harder and feel worse. The second will be comforting.

We tend to think we have to solve problems for people. We offer advice, suggestions, or pep talks. We do the same to ourselves. And the child part that is feeling anger, hurt, or fear gets enraged at this message that seems to say, "You have no right to feel what you feel," or "If you feel like that you're no good," or "Get on with it! You're being an idiot, ridiculous, babyish." Result? You feel discouraged, blocked, and depressed.

We're all complex combinations of many different states; sometimes we feel grown-up, sometimes childish, sometimes detached, sometimes emotional; our needs change. Feelings are just emotional equipment. If we lay judgments on them, it becomes impossible to follow the Ariadne thread to the minotaur in the cave and find out what the real monster looks like. *The monster is not us.* The deeper you go, the better the news is. Messages of doubt, put-down, and self-hate prevent us from using our true gifts—our real charisma.

The monster is ignorance of our true feelings. *Critical voices* are not the voice of truth; they are simply "taped recordings," old messages that aren't true, ones you do not have to identify with. Not anymore!

Notice your judgments (sometimes they're elusive). That's the first step. Sally R., a beautiful woman in her thirties, said, "My sister, who was seven years older and very jealous, always used to tell me I was stupid in math, that I couldn't hide how dumb I was; I'd be found out. So I want to deal with my math anxiety and fear of public speaking—then at least *that* won't be stopping me." She didn't realize as she spoke that her negative "tape" was giving a leapfrog judgment: "Well, kid, you can get rid of one or two fears, but *you'll fail anyway* because those old messages were really true—you *are* stupid and you *will* be found out." When I pointed this out to her, she gasped, "Oh, my goodness, I guess I really feel deep down that I am all those things—I didn't even notice I was being judgmental then." That awareness was the beginning of change. Most of us never stop castigating ourselves and have completely forgotten that originally those put-down messages came from other people and are *not* the voice of truth.

Lawrence M., a dignified, highly respectable investment banker who rarely smiled, admitted he was angry about the Anti-Judgmental Notebook. "Frankly, I was horrified—I realized this week that I'm judgmental about everything in my life, all the time. With my friends, my wife and children, my colleagues, my business associates—I'm always involved in a running dialogue of put-down and self-criticism. And I'd never been aware of it before. No wonder I find it hard to speak up in a group or be spontaneous! This inner critic is telling me all the time I'm going to botch it up. By the time I've subjected what I wanted to say to my inner critic, it's no longer appropriate to say anything."

Wrong Doors I

When you have become aware of all your hidden judgments, you can identify "wrong doors" and cut off the old tapes. Once you realize that these critical voices are tapes from your past, not real evaluations, it's possible to shake free of their heavy judgments and begin to appreciate and acknowledge yourself. That is the beginning of true growth.

"But my mother didn't *mean* to be so negative," protests one woman, distressed. "She meant to be a good mother."

Let's detach right now from blaming your parents for the negative messages they gave you. They probably were programmed that way by *their* parents. You are responsible, however, for having responded to the message in the way you did. The point of the Anti-Judgmental Notebook is not to lay blame at the door of others or your own, but just to recognize that these are mere messages, not the "truth."

Inside, most people are instant moralizers. Even people who don't admit their doubts to themselves or anybody will blame others or act them out and then wonder about why they behaved the way they did.

Ronnie R. had no trouble talking, but, laughing, said other people complained that *he* didn't listen. He was a good speaker. He did not show up for the breathing exercises because he thought he really didn't need them. People wondered why he had taken the class (I wondered too!). Then I invited him and four other students to appear on a TV program. The others had never been on TV before. The host of the program, Bill, was a young, attractive man, recently promoted to network TV from the "sticks." Before the show I asked him, "Bill, would you mind my asking what fears or uncertainties you had when you started?"

"No, that's fine," he answered. But evidently he really did mind, because when I asked him that question on the show, he snapped back angrily, "Fears? I have no fears! If I did, I wouldn't be in this business!"

"Oh," I retorted innocently, "congratulations! You're the only person in the world with no fears!" Bill was so furious that he turned to Ronnie and blasted him: "Well, what about you? Are you blocked?" Poor Ronnie was so stunned he froze. I knew he was trying to figure out what to do. Should he make a joke? Hit the host? Be pleasant? He was totally immobilized. Finally, Bill turned to the next student, who, fully prepared by long, slow breathing, answered him coolly and with poise. (Ronnie was so dismayed by his own inability to function that he took the course over again. This time he learned the breathing exercises. "Now, my wife says I listen," he said proudly. "It's changed my life!" He had become aware of his own feelings *and* other people's.)

Jennifer L. was unable to understand why she had forgotten a very important party. She had noted it in her appointment book but still had forgotten all about it.

"I must be losing my mind! How could I forget a thing like that?" she complained.

"Did you have any ambivalence about going?" I asked her.

"Well," she admitted, "I really wasn't crazy about the people giving the party, but I told myself I should get out and socialize more and I shouldn't feel that way about them."

I pointed out to Jennifer that she had given herself information about her feelings and had then told herself that she had no right to feel them! So, like mischievous gremlins, they crept underground and undermined her conscious decision to go to the party. It's as though the unacknowledged, unrespected feelings said, "Aha! You won't listen to us, we'll fix you! We'll put you in a trance, and you'll do what *we* want, not what *you* want, and you won't even know what hit you!" In Romans, chapter 7, verse 19, St. Paul puts it this way: "For I do not do the good I want, but the evil I do not want is what I do."

Why do we try to hide our feelings from ourselves? For these three reasons, mainly:

1. We're afraid we will take on unpleasant qualities of negative emotions we feel. ("Your face'll freeze!" Grandma used to tell me when I cried.)

2. We're afraid that if we recognize it, the emotion will be fed and will increase.

3. We think we're being self-indulgent and self-pitying.

But, far from fanning the negative thoughts, full acknowledgment leads to the release of those painful feelings. Allowing yourself to experience the pain of whatever feeling you're experiencing (without judgment, blame, or shame), noticing its exact location in the body ("When I see my husband out with another woman, I feel jealous. My throat tightens and my chest hurts, and my heart beats so hard I feel it'll burst my chest."), is the first step toward feeling better and changing patterns of behavior, even though for the moment it feels worse.

Allowing yourself to notice all the feelings you are feeling, not just the ones you approve of, gives you more information on which to base your action; it gives you *choice*. For instance, Jennifer might sit down and write out her thoughts:

Positive

"I'd like to meet more people."

"They've invited me, and I know I could meet some people at their party."

"It's sometimes fun to be with new people."

Negative

"I don't like Tim and Jerry."

"I can't stand their smoking."

"Their taste in music isn't mine."

"I don't like their friends."

"I don't feel good around them."

Then, with this full range of information, she could decide whether to:

a. Go for a short time

b. Set up another appointment so she would have a reason to leave early

c. Not go at all, but take a rain check

d. Seek out other friends and social situations that would respect her needs but not conflict with her preferences

In short, she would be able to make a *real choice*, one that satisfied her.

Next time you find yourself making one of these judgments, *stop!* Take out your notebook. Write it down. Try whenever possible to record your feelings *immediately*. Should you find yourself in a social situation where this might be difficult, make a mental note and write it down later, but always on the same day. Don't let more than a day pass; if things pile up, they'll never be written down at all.

You'll recognize the importance of recording (and doing it immediately) over time. You'll be able to determine a pattern of judgmental behavior. You'll probably notice, as most do, that your times of discomfort and alienation from yourself are confined to a few situations and are not global. You might observe that you're confident at cocktail parties but not at the office; that you're generally at ease over dinner with friends but not at family gatherings. Being able to monitor your unique patterns will yield insight and attention to those facets of yourself that require more work than others and those that require no work at all. As a log of your growing self, the Anti-Judgmental Notebook will become your best tutor: a set of guidelines by, for, and of yourself.

Being gentle and understanding with yourself will make you more tolerant of other people's failings.

You Choose

Making an active choice is always more satisfying than being led around by unconscious drives. Acting out unacknowledged feelings makes one feel helpless, out of control. Just recognizing and voicing your desires, doubts, and feelings is, strangely enough, more important than getting what you want!

If you can't communicate well with yourself, you'll find it harder to communicate with others. Speaking up has to start at home. The first line of communication has to be a check with your inner feelings. Otherwise you'll soon find you don't know what they are.

When I was a little girl, I remember my brother asking my grandfather, "Grandpa, what's so terrible about lying?"

"Oh, nothing much," he answered innocently. "Just one little problem. After a while, if you keep lying, *you won't know what the truth is!*"

Not being honest with ourselves has the same result.

How can the Anti-Judgmental Notebook help you get in touch with your real feelings, liberate your courage, and open the door to a new expressiveness and charisma? Just observing your feelings dispassionately gives you a sense of detachment and greater control. It's suddenly very clear that *you are not your feelings*—you *have* feelings and they change. You no longer confuse character with behavior, behavior with identity. By getting in touch with the repetitive tapes you may be running in your head, you can separate those messages from your automatic pilot and unmask them as thieves of your charisma.

There is a big difference between saying, "I never do anything right" (and the accompanying "sinking" feeling) and "I never do anything right . . . Oh! that's judgmental—throw it out!" At least you're not identifying with your own persecutor anymore!

Wrong Doors II

Whose side are you on, anyway? If there's no answer to a question, it's probably the wrong question. Yet some of the most painful questions we put to ourselves seem unanswerable. Have you ever tortured yourself with these:

"Why *me*?"

"Why can't I ever get things right?"

"Why does everybody let me down?"

"Why can't I find love?"

"Why do other people have so much more luck than I do?"

"Why am I such a loser?"

The sense of helplessness, frustration, and low self-esteem such questions produce can be almost unbearable. When you were an adolescent you probably wondered, "Will any girl/boy really like me?" "Will I ever stop feeling clumsy, awkward, and uncomfortable?" As time went on, your problems probably lessened or disappeared. You didn't notice, however, the exact moment when you got an *answer* to the question. Or, indeed, whether you got an answer at all. At a certain point, the question simply seemed irrelevant. I remember saying to my mother in a panic, "How can I go to high school? I've never been!"

Is there a question that you ask yourself over and over again that has tortured you for years and seems to be unanswerable? I call that a wrong door. Once you recognize such a question as a dead-end attack that leads nowhere, the next time it comes up, you can say to yourself, "Uh-oh! That's a wrong door! *Don't go through it.*" A wrong door leads only to anguish, nothing else.

There is an odd paradox here. Emotions are usually based on old thought patterns or early assumptions:

"Mommy doesn't love me because I'm unlovable."

"I always goof up because I'm stupid."

"People laugh at me because I say the wrong things and have the wrong feelings."

"It's bad to feel mean."

"Nobody believes me when I tell them how I feel."

"Men don't like me because I'm small-breasted."

When one extricates the wrong doors and early messages from the negative feelings, it is then possible to isolate a lot of mechanical, automatic, pain-producing mechanisms and just turn off their power!

You're still aware of thinking those things, but now they're almost "in quotes"; *you know they're not real*. Remember the old joke about the psychiatrist who told his patient, "Madam, you don't have an inferiority complex—you *are* inferior!" Most people are afraid that in some way this is really true of them. But when you're in harmony with yourself, you feel you have value, human worth, and capacity for love; then all fear and pain from negative self-images drains away.

We can look at the same group of facts and, according to what they're named, wind up with entirely different results. It's the old "Is-the-glass-half-full-or-half-empty?" story.

"Bah! Humbug!" said Scrooge. We have a habit, in our puritanical Judeo-Christian culture, of imagining that being tough on ourselves is realistic. Actually, having confidence in ourselves works much better and, happily, this is a skill that can be learned. Most people, I find, need to increase their self-affirmation. If you were fortunate enough to have grown up in a family that gave you a feeling of "OK-ness" about yourself and your feelings, you'll have had a head start. But as a friend of mine observed, most people have led "wounded" lives, so that most of us need very much to increase our self-affirmation. This means changing habits of thought.

Most people are confident in some respects but not in others. We all can expand our powers and skills in communication. I've never met anyone who was perfect or perfectly at home in every communication situation. Maybe it isn't even possible!

Some people are very comfortable talking to a few people but uncomfortable with large groups. Others are at home with multitudes but uncomfortable with a few. (Leonard Bernstein once announced to a huge audience that he planned to give up smoking—something he had not confided to a soul before then.)

It's often a surprise—and a source of encouragement—to my class members when someone they had perceived as highly competent and effective admits he or she is, in fact, feeling insecure and nervous. Realizing that other people put themselves through the same painful "hoops" can amplify your compassion for others and increase your ability to listen "between the lines." Understanding your own processes gives you the tools to see people as they are, rather than as extensions or projections of your own fears. And you will begin to see that you have more margin than you think—you don't have to be perfect to be charismatic! "Ninety percent of success is just showing up," Woody Allen once remarked.

New Strategy

When someone is unpleasant or hostile, the wrong door question is: "Why doesn't he like me?" and the sinking feeling that follows leads to the old trap, "Nobody likes me!"

The right question (one that will yield an answer) is: "What's he feeling?" You may not always be able to find out, but just asking this question will shift the focus of your attention, probably more realistically. You may think (and feel free to give your imagination full play):

"He had a fight with his wife and is feeling grumpy."

"Big parties make her feel shy and uncomfortable."

"When his ideas are challenged, he feels his right to exist has been threatened."

None of your guesses may be right, but at least you won't shoot yourself down in the line of fire between another person and her or his private problem.

When my daughter, Andrea, was about seven years old, she asked me one morning, "Mommy, are you mad at me because of something I did or because you got up on the wrong side of the bed?" I was amazed that she was able to make that distinction. Certainly, at her age, I couldn't have. Many adults I know see everything that happens to them as a reflection of themselves. Everything negative is their "hard luck"; "It could only happen" to them. Transactional analysis calls these negative expectations *scripts*; that is, people have made unequivocal decisions early in life, usually below the level of awareness, and they operate on them for the rest of their lives unless they ferret out these unrewarding patterns and decide to change them. If you're convinced that all men are beasts and that it's dangerous to love a man because he'll leave you, you'll probably choose partners who fulfill your unconscious expectations. If you think all women are bitches, you'll be drawn to the ones who will treat you badly. If, because your older brother laughed at you and constantly interrupted when you tried to speak up at the dinner table, you find your voice is mousey and timid, you may actually feel it is *dangerous* to talk louder, even though you're perfectly able to.

Lucy G. came from a family of "interrupters." Now middle-aged, she had a husband and children who never listened to her. In my class, she was so timid that she asked if she could remain seated while she spoke. Why was she taking my class? I asked.

"Well," she said with a nervous, apologetic laugh, "I want to learn how not to be so boring. I can't hold people's attention. At a dinner party, I can't even finish my sentences. People start talking and I never get to say what I want to, so most of the time I don't even try." Lucy held her shoulders hunched around her ears. Her eyes darted timidly back and forth. She spoke so softly and hesitantly it was difficult to hear her words. Her expectation was that nobody would listen to her because of her assumption (judgment) that she was boring. To her, it was actually frightening to stand up and say what she felt.

By the time she had completed the course, she was standing up straight and speaking in a firm voice. Two years later, Lucy was directing a volunteer program for reading aides in her local schools, training new volunteers for (and speaking on behalf of) the whole program to community groups. The change began when she kept her Anti-Judgmental Notebook, noting whenever she told herself she was "boring." She learned to tell herself, "Judgment—wrong door!" and to drop her old, negative expectations.

People are always amazed to find that they can *choose* to change characteristics they think they're stuck with. Being "boring" is not like having blue eyes; it may be learned, but it is not genetically determined or immutable. Have you ever noticed how people pick up the speech and behavior patterns of those they associate with? Even dogs seem to acquire personalities that are like their owners'!

It's fascinating to see how differently people react to similar situations. In the class with Lucy was a young engineer, Bob R., who said, "I come from a family of interrupters, too, but I talk louder than they do! You can't stop me!" Bob's self-judgment was "I can't let anybody get behind my facade because they won't like me if they do. I'm really *not likable* unless I'm being witty or giving information." Secretly, he, too, felt he was boring. But how differently he projected his judgment. Some of his family messages had been "You can't trust people," "Don't let anybody know you well," and "People are no good!"

The upshot was that Bob never looked anybody in the eye and hardly ever stopped talking. Through our listening exercises he found that he didn't have to *talk* to communicate with another person. Gradually he began to change his self-image as he allowed himself to trust other people a little more. It was a hard struggle for him to let go of his wariness and his need to chatter. For Bob, the meditation exercises (see chapter 12) and the discovery that people *really wanted* to be helpful and supportive gradually calmed him, so that by the end of the term he was able to look people in the eye, listen, and really hear what they were saying. He reported with pride and pleasure that people at work had remarked on how much he had changed for the better. "I actually like some of them now!"

Some people can give themselves a kind of pep talk that helps them get moving. "C'mon, now, let's go! Get your act together and stop horsing around!" one woman told herself when she got upset. She was judgmental of herself and of other people, but she was able to notice that she was being "melodramatic" and cut short the "garbage" *without feeling put down.*

Working with the Anti-Judgmental Notebook

It's not so much what you say but how you feel about it that counts. If your inner dialogue has a painful quality and leaves you feeling low in self-esteem and depressed, that's perfect material for your Anti-Judgmental Notebook. Whip it out and jot down as briefly as possible whenever you hear yourself saying something, aloud or to yourself, that is a judgment, or a wrong door. Note the date, the time, and what you feel physically (e.g., my stomach is all knotted up, my heart is beating very fast, I have a throbbing headache, I have a dull feeling all over . . .). Notice also what happens to your breathing. "I'm tense—I almost stopped breathing and blacked out," a lawyer told me, "when I felt I couldn't make a good impression in court. Until we started to do the breathing exercises [see chapter 12], I never realized that I practically stopped breathing when I got nervous. That's why I was always afraid I'd black out and faint in court."

For a week or two, keep your little notebook with you. If you're not able to write it down immediately, go to the bathroom to make your notes or update your book before you go to bed at night. *Don't let the day pass without writing in it.* This is your instant verbal Polaroid for checking what you're actually feeling.

Someone asked, "How do I know I'm being judgmental? For instance, how can I improve if I can't correct myself when I've done something wrong?"

"That's easy!" I answered. "When you have a purely pragmatic 'should' ('I must get to the bank by three o'clock so I can get some cash before it closes.'), this is straightforward and nontoxic. But watch out for a little hook of anguish, a little catch at the heart, when you say something negative to yourself ('Why am I *always* late?'). *That's* how you know you're being judgmental; those are the tapes left over from early messages, now counterproductive and useless."

Sometimes you'll get the feeling without words. It could be the look someone gave you or something somebody did or some piece of news that triggers a feeling of anger, jealousy, hurt, self-mistrust, or loss of self-esteem. (Gore Vidal once said, "Every time a writer sees another writer have a success, something in him dies a little.")

To escape noticing painful emotions we often distract ourselves by talking, smoking, drinking, eating, or burying ourselves in some activity—playing cards, watching television. Bad idea! If you're feeling judgmental and disgusted with yourself, it's because you haven't gone deep enough. You can be sure that *if you go deep enough,* the news is good! It's important to learn to observe one's feelings *without blame*—only then can you make any real changes.

"But," objected another student, "if I don't criticize myself, how can I improve?"

"Tell me," I asked him, "when you put yourself down, how do you feel? Does it make you want to go rushing out and do a dozen good things? Or do you feel dispirited, discouraged, maybe even *immobilized*?"

"Yes, that's true," he admitted. "When I put myself down, I don't want to do anything." Heads nodded around the room. Someone asked, puzzled, "But why should that be?"

In *Inner Tennis*, Timothy Gallwey described what he called "Self 1 and Self 2." Self 1 is the critic, the "teller" who keeps up a running tirade of directions, judgments, and (often) abuse. "What a ninny! Why did I do that? What a stupid thing to do! Won't I ever learn!"

Self 2 is the "doer," unconscious, automatic. It includes the memory and the nervous system, never forgets anything, and is anything but stupid.

We have all noticed that there seem to be several voices inside us—and not always friendly ones, either. One way to look at those voices is to remember the right and left hemispheres of the brain. The left brain (logical, sequential, deals with formulating language and rational thinking) corresponds roughly to the critical Self 1. Self 2 has a lot in common with the right hemisphere (intuition, music, spatial thinking, feeling states or emotions). It's more like the child in us, plunging eagerly into new activities, learning without quite knowing how or why; certainly it's not stopped by inhibitions, fears, and worries about whether we'll make fools of ourselves or annoy the neighbors.

In other terms, you might think of Self 1 as the critical parent (as in Eric Berne's transactional analysis) and Self 2 as the free child, spontaneous, impulsive, and uninhibited. First off, the part of us that's impulsive and free will do something joyously, spontaneously—only to have Self 1, the critical side, jeer and criticize. Then, poor Self 2, exactly like a child that has been bawled out, will balk. Will she jump to improve and change? No! She will figuratively fold her arms and sulk. "Oh!" that self seems to retort silently. "If you're going to be so nasty, I'm not going to do a damn thing! Try and make me!" Scold, urge, cajole, try as we will, we don't budge. We have effectively locked ourselves into a double bind. Result? Inaction. Frustration. Discouragement. And, like an angry executive yelling at his employees, we are bewildered and helpless at our own "stuckness."

When we are very small, our minds are like the untouched wax of a phonograph record before pressing. Each experience makes grooves in our neurological system, which become embedded in our mind-body armor. Each time the message is repeated, the groove is deepened. This is why, as adults, we lock in messages we have forgotten, sometimes physically. One middle-aged man was sensitive along his arms and chest. He couldn't bear to be touched there. He didn't remember that he had a bully for a father whom he was not allowed to hit back. The stifled impulse to return his father's blows had recorded itself on his muscles, *even though he had no conscious awareness that he had internalized his angry response to his father's brutality.*

The messages we absorbed from the important authority figures in our childhood become so familiar that we forget who originated them; now we say them to ourselves and think they're true. This is rather like the story of the monkey who belonged to a British colonel in India. Whenever the monkey misbehaved, the colonel would slap his pink bottom and throw him out of the window to teach him a lesson. Soon, the monkey was so well trained that when he misbehaved, he would slap his own bottom and jump out of the window!

By the time we reach adolescence, we make full-scale, harsh judgments of ourselves, thereby causing ourselves a lot of misery. "I'm ugly!" "I'm stupid!" "I'm clumsy." And on and on.

It helps to recognize that whatever it is that we find difficult to do, we have some good interior reason for feeling as we do about it. When we're able to accomplish something that is hard for us, our own acknowledgment solidifies our "ownership" of it. The importance of this cannot be overemphasized.

A cynical father I know once berated his wife, "Why are you so encouraging to the children? Are we supposed to applaud because they don't 'go' in the middle of the floor?" Well, what about that?

Many, many people come from families who expect them to do well but give neither praise nor encouragement for success. Achievements are taken for granted and elicit no appreciation. If there is *no* positive feedback, it's not easy even to *know* what we're doing right, or to want to do it again!

If You Don't Know What You Know, You Might as Well Not Know It!

Evelyn M., a troubled young woman who had a disastrous family history, spoke very little during our first few sessions. Her alcoholic father had deserted the family. Her mother had committed suicide. Evelyn had had several breakdowns and was seriously overweight. It was clear that she had a very poor self-image. Yet she was bright, articulate when she did speak, and eager to learn. Her first talk, candid and interesting, elicited a warm response from the class. The following week, Evelyn came in and told us, "I did something yesterday that I've never done before! I read a short story I wrote aloud to a group of writers, but I'm very upset."

"Why?" the class wanted to know. "Didn't you get a good reaction?"

"Oh, yes," she answered, "everybody said very nice things, and they all seemed to think highly of my story. But afterward the teacher spoke to me and I couldn't get away. I really had to leave because I had an appointment, but I just couldn't tell her. I just stood and waited until she finished." Evelyn's distress was evident. Her lower lip trembled and her face flushed.

"But don't you see what a remarkable thing you did?" I asked her. "You've always considered yourself so shy, and now you've read your own short story aloud to a group of strangers! That was really courageous!" Heads nodded around the room.

Shaking her head sadly, Evelyn said, "But I couldn't get away from that teacher. I just didn't know how to tell her I wanted to leave. I'm so ashamed of myself!" We could not console her. She was so used to thinking of herself negatively that she had to seize on one tiny part of a remarkable achievement to reassure herself that she was still a failure in her own eyes. The act of acknowledgment was so foreign to her that she could not allow herself to enjoy her own progress. And so it was lost to her. "Awareness of transformation," as George Leonard observed, "IS transformation."

The Three As: Acknowledge–Appreciate–Absorb

Do you deny yourself the pleasure of your own good moments?

"Nothing succeeds like success," we say. It's true, so why not learn from it? Take time at the end of your day to appreciate the good moments in it.

If you did something well, allow yourself to feel pleased about it—even though it might have been a small thing that would not have meant much to anybody else, but one that was not easy for you. Perhaps you cleared your desk or made a difficult phone call. Close your eyes, breathe deeply, and spread the pleasure of that small achievement throughout your whole body. Feel it in your fingertips, your arms, your toes, your solar plexus. You're nourishing yourself in the most practical way, feeding your positive expectation. Next time will be easier! After a while, the good moments may become the major part of your day.

Do the Acknowledge-Appreciate-Absorb exercise at least three times every day.

Many of us walk through our lives with a pall hanging over us. Nothing is really terrible, yet the whole world seems gray. Lawrence, the dour investment banker, who was angry at me for making him do the Anti-Judgmental Notebook, was horrified to find that he constantly made judgments about himself.

"It never occurred to me to take *pleasure* in anything I did," he said in an astonished voice. "I was so busy being dissatisfied with myself that I felt gloomy all the time and didn't even realize it!"

At the end of the course, people were telling him he looked, sounded, and acted ten years younger. He smiled, laughed, and displayed his considerable wit to the delight of the entire class. He even did a very credible Cary Grant imitation.

Our judgments are not *us*. Our joy is. All the techniques in this book lead to new ways of being and doing. They need to be learned, practiced, and reinforced. They are not quickie gimmicks that will instantly transform your image and self-image; they are skills that once acquired will serve you in every aspect of your life.

"I'm OK, but That Other Guy's a Bastard!"

The next step is to let go of judgments of other people. When I asked people in the class to describe somebody they disliked or hated, here's how they replied:

"She's a pill!"

"He's a bastard!"

"He's a rotten son of a bitch!"

"She's obnoxious!"

Everybody had a lot of fun with that, grinning as they unleashed their verbal brickbats until I asked, "How much information does that give you?"

People looked surprised, a little crestfallen. "Not much," admitted one young woman, "but it sure feels good!"

"How do you feel about the person you hear making nasty remarks about somebody else? Does it make you trust that person?"

"No. As a matter of fact," remarked one man, "it gives me a kind of funny, uneasy feeling. I think, 'Well, if he talks like this about so-and-so, what does he say behind *my* back?!'"

"Does it give you information about the person he's talking about? Does he make you feel the same way about the person?"

"No," offered another student, a woman. "All we know is that the speaker feels strongly. We don't know why—and there's no reason for *me* to feel strongly."

"Then, in terms of communication and persuasion, judgments haven't been very effective, have they? Now, think again of that person you dislike so much, and describe the behavior that bothers you."

Now the responses were informative, detailed, interesting—and persuasive:

"He never listens to anybody and has no regard for other people's feelings."

"She's constantly criticizing people."

"He treats people with contempt."

"He flies into tantrums when he doesn't get his way. You never know if he's going to be nice or unpleasant when you see him next."

"All right," I said. "What's the difference between describing behavior and judging character?"

"Well," answered an eager young social worker, "for one thing, I feel sympathetic when I hear about the behavior because I'd probably react the same way the speaker did. At the same time, I don't feel he's being vindictive, so I trust him more. And I know a lot more about the situation than I did when I just heard the judgment. That gives me a good feeling that the speaker has trusted me with his observations and experiences."

"Good! What else?"

"I get the feeling that the person the speaker is describing *could* possibly change," offered a retired police captain. "So I think it helps me to feel that people can change their behavior. They're not locked into certain patterns forever."

"Yes," added his wife, "don't we tend to see people according to our expectations of them?" She looked mischievously at her husband. "For instance, for years you were sure I was going to mess up my checkbook, and I expected you to be clumsy in the kitchen, and we went right ahead fulfilling each other's expectations!"

"Right!" he laughed, a trifle wryly. "But now that I've taken Chinese cooking lessons, and you've somehow gotten much better with your checkbook, I'm sorry I made you feel stupid all those years. Actually, you're one pretty smart lady!"

They beamed at each other, having overcome their own early judgmentalism.

Sticks and Stones Can Break My Bones, but Names CAN Hurt Me!

When we were children, we were taught that "names can never hurt me." But that's far from true.

In a massive study of shy people conducted at Stanford University, Philip Zinbardo found that 90 percent of the sample felt they had been shy at some time in their lives. The "shy" group would complete the statement "I feel uncomfortable at a cocktail party where I don't know anybody . . ." by adding "*because I'm shy.*" Those who didn't think of themselves as shy simply added a period, so that the statement read: "I feel uncomfortable at a cocktail party where I don't know anybody."

So people who damn themselves with the judgmental word *shy* blame themselves for their feelings. Worse, they set up the expectation that the same thing will always happen. Ergo, when they go to a cocktail party they expect to be uncomfortable because, according to their judgment, that's their nature, being shy! They've "programmed" themselves into a little box. That makes it difficult to have a different experience the next time.

To confuse behavior with character is dangerous whether you do it toward yourself or other people. Nobody, child or grown-up, does well when the worst is expected of them.

Watch Your Language!

Try this exercise: For one whole day see if you can *avoid* making judgments of *other* people! (If you've been keeping your Anti-Judgmental Notebook, I hope by this time you aren't judging yourself.) If you catch yourself in a negative remark about someone, immediately reword your statement to avoid any "judgment" words (*arrogant, lazy*, etc.) to describe the person.

One of my students, a seventy-five-year-old patent lawyer who made a successful second career acting in commercials, told me that this one exercise had changed his "whole way of being in the world."

"I come from Boston," he told me, "and up there, there was a lot of judgmentalism. Mine was an old WASP family, you know, and I really didn't even *see* a lot of people who were automatically considered 'out' by my early family and social standards. I was terribly narrow. Now I go into the subway and catch someone's eye. It doesn't matter who or what he is. We have a moment of eye contact, and I feel close to that person because he's human, just as I am, even if his background and experience are totally different from mine. You have no idea," he added, "how that has changed life for me! I really feel at home anywhere, and I just don't meet anybody I don't like. I know that sounds Pollyannaish, but it's true."

One time, he told me, his son had come to visit him, and they went to a coffee shop run by a "really crabby woman" who never had a good word for anybody. " 'Wait,' I told Don. 'By the time we leave, she'll smile at me and be my friend.' And, by God, she did!" There's always some good reason why people behave badly. They're having family troubles or something else is wrong, but if you're pleasant, eventually they just have to respond.

This reminded me of a story I heard about two men who walked to work every day past a newsstand owned by a disagreeable man. Every day, the first man would greet the grouch pleasantly, despite the fact that he received no response other than an occasional surly grunt. Finally his friend said, "Why do you bother? That guy is so nasty!" "I'm just not going to let him ruin my day!" the first man replied. Sooner or later, the newsman would respond. It was inevitable.

If you find yourself going around with a chip on your shoulder, take the responsibility for your angry feelings and make a small step toward transforming them.

There was a period in my life when I yelled at strangers a lot. Why were they always doing things to aggravate me? Finally I realized it was my own anger that was bouncing off everybody because I didn't dare express my feelings to the people who were close to me—only to strangers.

In the chapter on anger, you'll learn how to use the power of anger—its energy and information—in ways that are productive for your charisma. Properly used, anger is a great natural resource. Best of all, practicing detachment from other people's anger helps lessen your own. If you cut down on your judgments, you'll feel less anger toward other people, kinder to yourself—and less afraid other people are judging *you*!

Pleasure Points

Begin to collect Pleasure Points. Find three moments during each day when you're aware of experiencing pleasure. Spreading your Pleasure Points gives you a natural protection against low-level judgmental anger. Once you have found what pleasures you (the play of sunshine on your roof, an unexpected smile from a stranger while you're both awaiting the elevator, or a little child's pudgy fist waving in the air), notice how your body *feels*.

What is the difference in local body sensations between the shock of recognition when you unexpectedly see a friend and the joy of contemplating a beautiful painting? *Memorize each sensation.*

Next, take three opportunities during the day to produce Pleasure Points *without any occasion*, without any external stimulation whatever. I mean pure, free-floating pleasure!

Now, are you ready for a real challenge? When you've acknowledged your judgment, transform it into pleasure. Let go. Relax your shoulders, your stomach; slow your breathing; straighten and relax your back. *For no reason . . . enjoy!* You're entering new territory—the unfamiliar, yet deeply remembered, world within the heart that is always yours. In the following chapters, you'll learn how to retake it at will, how it can shelter and revitalize your charisma, first for you and then for everybody else.

4

Your Tension Inventories and What to Do About Them

"What I was going to say," said the Dodo in an offended tone, "was that the best thing to get us dry would be a Caucus-race."

"What is a Caucus-race?" said Alice.

"Why," said the Dodo, "the best way to explain it is to do it."
—Lewis Carroll, *Alice's Adventures in Wonderland*

Our bodies know a lot that we're unaware of. Some people deal with their bodies as though they were enemies. Others ignore them until they break down. Many people are becoming aware that treating the body intelligently (and making it move the way it was meant to) yields extraordinary dividends of mental and emotional health, clarity, pleasure, and fulfillment.

In a Charismedia workshop, Barbara R., a capable, attractive fashion executive, did the One-Minute Verbal Free-for-All with great facility and enthusiasm. When it was over, a look of shocked surprise came over her face. "My goodness, my heart is beating so hard and so fast—I feel as though I'd just done something very dangerous! I had no idea I felt like that. I thought it was easy for me to yell—I've done so much of it!" The fact that her body could tell her things she *didn't know intellectually* impressed her so deeply that it was the beginning of a real breakthrough in letting go of some very old problems. She had found an extraordinary new ally—the information and feedback her own physical tensions could give her.

Getting in touch with your body and finding out where your tension points are is a crucial part of unearthing and enjoying your charisma. Your body and mind are the wire through which your electricity flows. If you blow a fuse because the wire is frayed, there won't be any light at all. Reduction of energy or burnouts result either from underutilizing or overloading the circuits.

Luckily, the body is a responsive instrument—if you're prepared to tune in to it. We get messages from the interior and exterior all the time. Yet many of us try to ignore them as long as possible. We pay no attention until they become so insistent that we are forced to deal with what has turned into a big problem—an ulcer, a bad back, a stroke, arthritis, even cancer. We don't want (most of us) to be hypochondriacs. On the other hand, most people have a secret feeling that the body is beyond their control anyway and, with a shudder of almost superstitious fear, hope that not noticing aches and pains will somehow make them go away.

Faith in technology has fostered a habit of turning over mechanical problems to specialists. Go to the doctor and he'll give you a pill or potion to fix the difficulty. Many people have little sense of the interconnectedness between problems of the body and the mind. "Oh, it's all psychosomatic" means to many people you are either faking or that your ailment is not serious—certainly not quite respectable. We're so quick to de-legitimize our suffering!

As early as the fourth century B.C. the Greek philosopher Plato avowed that "all diseases of the body proceed from the mind or soul." People have always reacted physically to their emotions—cried with joy or grief, paled with fear, reddened in embarrassment or anger, thrown up in fright or disgust, trembled in anguish. Only poets or philosophers paid attention. Language, being more intuitive than we are, is full of expressive reflections of the true connection between our minds and feelings and our physical bodies:

"My heart is heavy."

"I feel light as a feather when I'm happy."

"There's a stone in my chest."

"She's all tied up in knots."

What are *you* experiencing physically and emotionally? Where do *you* feel tension in your body when you experience apprehension, anger, or nervousness? (Where do you feel joy, satisfaction, or pleasure? You've already begun—with the Pleasure Points—to actually *produce the desirable feelings at will*. First, though, it's important to deal with the negatives—the obstacles that *stop* us from enjoying our power and charisma and block the flow of bio-rapport with others.)

Here are some physical feelings that people in my workshops and private counseling most commonly report when they're uptight or nervous or unhappy, in public or in private:

Stomach knots up, hurts

Shoulders and back of neck tense

Hands clench

Knees lock

Butterflies in stomach

Trembling

Palms perspire

Throat gets tight

Lower back aches

Legs shake

Heart beats fast, thuds

Mouth becomes dry, or else has too much saliva

Voice gets high, squeaky, shakes, or gets weak

Feel faint

Nausea

Dizziness

Pounding of the temples

Flushing or blushing

Suddenly have to go to the bathroom

Hands, toes, nose feel cold

Can't hear well

Don't see well

Break out in a cold sweat

Armpits perspire

Head hurts

It's hard to breathe

Chest feels tight

Obviously, a lot goes on!

While the autonomic nerves tense and tighten muscles, the heartbeat speeds up and blood vessels constrict, raising blood pressure and almost completely closing the vessels just under the skin. Your face muscles may contort, but the stomach and intestines temporarily halt digestion. The muscles controlling the bowels and bladder loosen. Many people have experienced embarrassment ("I was so scared I wet my pants!"). Soldiers terrified of battle have lost control of their bowels.

While all this is happening, autonomic nerves directly stimulate the adrenal glands to release some thirty hormones—the surest signs (in lab experiments) of stress. Your cholesterol level shoots up without your having eaten a thing! Epinephrine, thought to be associated with fear, produces the heady exuberance (mixed with anxiety) that we call "the adrenaline flowing." This is by no means all bad. It helps in moments of danger or trouble, so that you can leap higher, lift greater weights, run faster, or achieve faster reaction time. Many performers, musicians, and sports figures feel that heightened sense in their best moments.

The tricky part is that our bodies go into an elaborate and complicated stress reaction even when *there is no physical danger*, no actual threat or need—when we can't return the system to normal by either fighting or running away.

Your boss may have said, "This report is late. I don't like the way you're handling this project!" Suddenly your mouth goes dry and your heart races; you are experiencing a fight-or-flight syndrome. Or your friend or lover says, "Why do you treat me this way?" Or somebody gives you a nasty look. Or the most important person in the room walks out during a presentation you're giving. Or you're terrified of making a speech—a thousand triggers, large or small, can set off these reactions. *Your feelings are causing real physiological changes.* Imagine what a stress-filled business lunch does to your system—think, eat, be on your toes—no wonder many executives get ulcers.

Here, your Anti-Judgmental Notebook and attention to trivia combined with your sense of what is happening in your body will pay off. An amazing number of people never think about their bodies except when something breaks down. They are astonished to discover that their bodies never lie. By respecting physical signals, as we learned to do the emotional ones, we can clear the path to being centered and using our charisma.

Reactions are highly individual, so what upsets you might leave someone else quite cool and undisturbed, and vice versa. And what bothered you a year ago might have little effect today. What you find stimulating at one time might be a stress at another. Don't judge yourself or be angry if this happens. Judging only prevents you from being aware of, acknowledging, and then releasing the stress. Body sensing with detached interest is of immense value and a skill that has to be learned.

The "Three Eyes"

We have many different ways of "seeing" things.

The great St. Bonaventure, a favorite philosopher of Western mystics (the great Doctor Seraphicus of the Church), wrote that humans have "three eyes," three ways of gaining knowledge.

The "eye of flesh" sees the external world of space, time, objects, and living things. Animals also have the eye of flesh—if you throw a stick down, a dog will respond; a rock won't. The "eye of reason" deals with philosophy, logic, the mind itself. You can't smell or taste mathematics, and no one has ever seen a square root or a quark. But no one would deny that these mental realities have drastically changed our physical world. The third eye, the "eye of contemplation," transcends the mental realm. It gives us a sense of oneness with the cosmos—that inexpressible and wordless experience we all have at some time in our lives and lack words to describe. Psychologist Abraham Maslow called these moments "peak experiences." Carl Jung talked about the "oceanic consciousness."

Lawrence LeShan, in *The Medium, the Mystic, and the Physicist*, described what all three have in common at their best: one is not aware of oneself as separate from the rest of the world; there is a sense of unity—past, present, and future are all rolled up in one. For some people, this may be a religious experience; for others the sense of oneness comes while making love, performing or listening to music, communing with nature, running, or dancing. Some people have experienced it under the influence of drugs. Terminal cancer patients who were given LSD experienced a sense of peace, calm, and oceanic oneness with the cosmos, even if they had no religious background or belief.

(At this moment, close your eyes, breathe deeply, and go back within to a place where you were completely happy and relaxed. Be there for a few moments, totally . . .)

This experience of ultimate reality that comes through the "eye of contemplation" we also know as the sense of "flow," a term coined by Mihaly Csikszentmihalyi. When you are experiencing a feeling of your own charisma, you are in that state of "flow."

Selye's General Adaptation Syndrome

Dr. Hans Selye, the famous Canadian stress researcher, worked out a detailed sequence of stress reactions, which he called the General Adaptation Syndrome.

The first part, or "alarm reaction," roughly corresponds to a "fight-or-flight" response. Each additional stress makes everything harder to bear. There is a sort of "cost-overrun" of the original stress. Perhaps you had a fight with your wife at breakfast and then took a pleasant walk to the office; although you thought you were completely calm again, when the elevator in your building shows no sign of appearing, you suddenly feel angry enough to yell at somebody—and whether you do or not, you feel it. In the second part, the "resistance stage," the stressed animal's functions normalize and its resistance to further stimuli rises. If severe stress continues (the third and last stage), total exhaustion may set in. This time, when the alarm symptoms appear they are irreversible; a laboratory animal dies.

Instead of having more oxygen, you feel you're getting less under stress, that your senses aren't taking in as much information as usual. In general, you're actually suffering from impaired functioning. Our systems get the signals mixed. When we can't fight or run away, the buildup of symptoms is no longer functional. The effort not to show what you're feeling adds to the stress you're already under. Denial increases the physiological and emotional toll of the original stress. Now we can understand why (according to the U.S. Senate Committee on Nutrition and Human Needs, chaired by George McGovern) most of the deaths in this country can be traced to stress-related diseases. One out of three men will die of heart disease or stroke before the age of sixty, as will one out of five women. (Undoubtedly, as women move into more high-level positions, that figure will rise.)

Two psychiatrists, Thomas Holmes and Richard Rahe, of the University of Washington's School of Medicine, have created a Stress Measurement Scale so people can score themselves on how much life stress they experienced within a two-year period before taking the test. If your point total for each year is 150 or less you have a 30 percent chance (1 out of 3) of getting sick in the next two years. A score of 151 to 299 gives you a 50-50 chance. Watch out if it's 300 or above—you have an 80 percent chance of falling sick. The chance of getting a serious illness such as cancer, heart disease, or psychosis is greater for those with scores above 300.

What's the Point of Scaring Yourself to Death?

Awareness and acknowledgment—remember these keys. If you recognize what a stressful time you've been having (your marriage broke up, you changed jobs three times, you became a vegetarian and remarried), that recognition alone reduces the stress! Positive events like buying a home, getting an award, or getting married also carry a stress quotient. As Will Rogers noted, "We know lots of things we used to didn't know, but we don't know any way to prevent 'em happening."

Factory tests showed that workers who were about to get married made more mistakes than usual during the week or two before the ceremony!

Holmes and Rahe asked four hundred men and women of varying ages, religions, and marital status to compare marriage with forty-two other events (all known from clinical tests to be stressful) and to give each event a numerical value higher or lower than fifty. Marriage was used as a comparison point, since the most severe stress apparently comes from family relationships.

Look on the following page and count up the number of points that apply to you and add up your total.

Critics have pointed out that the Holmes-Rahe scale seems to overemphasize male problems. Such crucial events in a woman's life as menopause or a mastectomy are not mentioned.

Sally M., in two years, saw her last child go off to college and her husband leave her. She also had a hysterectomy and went back to work as a bookkeeper. Through all the crises she had undergone she had held up

Holmes-Rahe Stress Measurement Scale

Life Event	Number of Points
Death of Spouse	100
Divorce	73
Marital Separation	65
Jail Term	63
Death of Close Family Member	63
Personal Injury or Illness	53
Marriage	50
Fired from Work	47
Marital Reconciliation	45
Retirement	45
Change in Family Member's Health	44
Pregnancy	40
Sex Difficulties	39
Addition to Family	39
Business Readjustment	39
Change in Financial Status	38
Death of Close Friend	37
Change to Different Line of Work	36
Change in Number of Marital Arguments	35
Mortgage or Loan over $10,000*	31
Foreclosure of Mortgage or Loan	30
Change in Work Responsibilities	29
Son or Daughter Leaving Home	29
Trouble with In-Laws	29
Outstanding Personal Achievement	28
Spouse Begins or Starts Working	26
Starting or Finishing School	26
Change in Living Conditions	25
Revision of Personal Habits	24
Trouble with Boss	23
Change in Work Hours, Conditions	20
Change in Residence	20
Change in Schools	20
Change in Recreational Habits	19
Change in Church Activities	19
Change in Social Activities	18
Mortgage or Loan under $10,000*	17
Change in Sleeping Habits	16
Change in Number of Family Gatherings	15
Change in Eating Habits	15
Vacation	13
Christmas Season	12
Minor Violation of the Law	11

*In today's economy, the original figure of $10,000 would be equivalent to $100,000.

remarkably well, but when she began to meditate as part of the charisma workshop, she complained that it made her tired; she was sleepy all the time. Meditation had made her aware of really feeling the accumulated stresses of her life. The tremendous strains she had undergone demanded rest and repair. If she had not started to meditate, she probably would have suffered a physical breakdown because she was driving herself without rest or recognition of what she was really feeling. After a month or so, she found she no longer needed excessive amounts of sleep; and the meditations brought her renewed energy, as they usually do.

People often handle extraordinary crises remarkably well, as though the body knows it can't afford to fall apart; sometimes sheer survival depends on the ability not to. During World War II, a friend survived hair-raising adventures: escape from a Nazi labor camp; near death by shooting, bombing, and minefields; and loss of his parents and most of his relatives and friends. He lived mostly on dry bread and bacon, which he could carry in his pocket. *He didn't even get a cold.* Such stories are not uncommon—this superhuman strength seems to be a common protective mechanism. After the danger is over, we can afford to collapse.

During a time of great national or international crisis and upheaval, people's best qualities often emerge. The heightened danger provides heightened opportunity to be of service, to act and feel like a worthwhile human being. (The Chinese pictograph for crisis is a combination of the symbols for danger and for opportunity.) During the London blitz, the English experienced their "finest hour."

We've all heard stories of superhuman feats ordinary people performed at extraordinary moments—a woman who cannot swim jumps overboard to save her child from drowning or a man finds the strength to lift a car to save a friend trapped under the wreckage. At such times, we seem to be able to tap into near-miraculous reserves of power. The satisfaction of meeting such challenges seems to offset a great deal of the negative stress of crisis. But if you live your whole life as a long, unrecognized battle (or have suffered grievous emotional losses), you don't realize what havoc this is wreaking on your body. Prolonged stress *without perceived meaning* can be devastating—even fatal.

Happy events can cause stress, too. If you're irritable or jumpy after something exciting or pleasant has happened in your life—winning a prize, having a baby, getting a promotion—it's the change that is affecting you. Of course, we'd all much rather have that kind of stress than the other! "Oh, I can deal with that," said one man with a broad grin when he was asked how he would feel if he won the lottery.

Anything can contribute to stress. It's important to know what you're experiencing, since acknowledgment is a dandy detoxifier even if nothing else changes. Thinking aloud with someone who is sympathetic amplifies the de-stressing effect. You can set up your own tension inventory if you're not feeling at your best. *Self-communication is the first line of defense against stress.* Some sources of tension need to be checked every day, others only occasionally; it's like maintaining your car. The habit of noticing stress will enable you to be more and more in touch so you can intuit changes and handle unexpected situations—be centered and moving at the same time.

Everything in the world is moving. The only security is not to stand still and resist, but to maintain your center so you can flow with events in a way that feels right to you. We always know it when that's happening. Here's another paradox. People who cling to old ideas or ways of doing things find themselves increasingly bewildered by the world they live in. They know when they're not with it.

Are Old Ideas Doing You In?

"I don't know . . . Young people today are no good. . . ."

"Children should be seen and not heard."

"A woman needs a man to protect her."

"What's the use—you can't beat the system."

Pessimism is a perception of the dark side of life, never the whole. If your general attitude is pessimistic, it probably means loss of personal control. But personal tragedy surmounted can be inspiring and charismatic.

Former Superman, Christopher Reeve, who became a paraplegic after a devastating riding accident, is now a film director and a passionate advocate for the rights of the disabled. (Of course it helped that he was already rich and famous, but that would not have made him a heroic, charismatic figure.)

When you locate your inner charisma and trust your intuition, if you then can't move in one direction, you'll find a good way to move in another. You'll dance with the world, even without legs.

Knowing that the world comes to meet you at least halfway, you can act "as if." Try acting "as if" you are in love for a single day. What is the feeling? Self-acceptance and joy and the lovely sense that wonderful things are happening and that more are still about to happen will change the way you feel about every moment of your day. Other people will remark on how well you look: "Have you had a vacation? Are you in love?"

Energy, life force, appetite, enthusiasm—we need several hundred ways to evoke these qualities in ourselves, because they are the true substance of personal charisma.

Now, how do you check out your tension inventory? The main categories are body, breath, mental, emotional, and social sphere. (For much of this formulation I am indebted to Sidney Lecker, M.D., *Natural Way to Stress Control*.)

There are two kinds of tension you will want to notice. One is the *emergency tension* you feel when you're on the spot. I'll give you emergency first aid for some of the most common problems. The other is more long range—

the negative judgments that come from early negative messages and how they may be affecting your mind, body, and social self. All symptoms are important and potentially useful as sources of information.

When you realize that everything is relevant, you can direct your energy flow toward enhancing your charisma by eliminating roadblocks and potholes. You'll become increasingly ingenious about making small changes that produce a different feeling, a feeling of control and mastery. "What's really important is never what seems to be going on," according to Buckminster Fuller. Whether you decide to run downstairs in your building instead of taking the elevator, cut out sugar and cut down on salt, take up Sumi painting, tai chi, chamber music, or crystallography, or simply walk to work by a different route, you have, by choosing change, cut down stress and opened up the channels to your charisma—magnetism and joy in life.

When people who took my workshops filled out questionnaires, the largest percentage (approximately 70 percent) said they felt tension in their throat, neck, head, shoulders, or chest. When you remember that *this is where speech emanates*, these answers seem very understandable. Another 30 percent felt tightening or pain in the stomach (an assorted miscellany experienced other symptoms). So here's emergency first aid for releasing tension.

Emergency Tension Release

Whenever you face a tough situation, *stop*, recognize the feelings you're experiencing (mental sensations and physical symptoms), and begin very slow breathing. Verbalize your feelings, aloud if possible or mentally if that's not practical. You'll feel better within minutes.

On the following page you will find another stress evaluation scale. Score as follows (each score shows how true *or* the amount of time you believe that statement is true for *you*):

0 = not at all true for me
1 = somewhat true or true only part of the time
2 = fairly true or true about half the time
3 = mainly true or true most of the time
4 = true all the time

A Personal Stress Factor (PSF) of 5 indicates an essentially stress-free life. A PSF of 15 is a definite handicap to your emotional well-being. A PSF of 25 indicates a severe handicap, and one of 50 or more indicates serious emotional problems and a definite threat to your health. Achieving sound self-esteem is definitely the most effective remedy for eliminating stress.

How to Change the Chemistry of Your Consciousness

This is easy to do but takes awareness and practice. So practice *before* you experience an acute difficulty.

STRESS STATEMENTS*

_____ 1. I feel inferior and inadequate compared with others.
_____ 2. I feel unworthy and guilty when criticized and condemned.
_____ 3. I am easily frustrated.
_____ 4. I have a compulsive need to prove my worth and importance.
_____ 5. I am anxious about my future.
_____ 6. I have trouble making decisions and sticking to them.
_____ 7. I am afraid of death.
_____ 8. I am easily angered.
_____ 9. I resent people who don't do what they should.
_____ 10. I am badly upset by disappointed expectations.
_____ 11. I have a strong need to dominate and control others.
_____ 12. I blame myself for my mistakes and defeats.
_____ 13. I have a strong need for confirmation and agreement.
_____ 14. I habitually put off doing what I should do.
_____ 15. I have an intense need for approval and acceptance.
_____ 16. I am fearful of undertaking new endeavors.
_____ 17. I am sensitive to social pressures.
_____ 18. I have an intense fear of failure.
_____ 19. I have trouble admitting I am wrong.
_____ 20. I worry about my loved ones.
_____ 21. I am pressured by responsibility.
_____ 22. I am afraid to let others see the real me.
_____ 23. I have a compulsive need to meet others' expectations.
_____ 24. I have a compulsive need to win.
_____ 25. I am impatient and worry about getting things done in time.

_____ PERSONAL STRESS FACTOR (PSF) (sum of all scores)

*Stress Inventory No. 25. Copyright H. L. Barksdale. Courtesy of Barksdale Foundation, Laguna Beach, CA 92651.

1. Sit down and time your breaths (counting each breath as one inhalation and an exhalation) for one minute. Most people breathe somewhere between twelve to eighteen breaths per minute. If your rate is higher, you are operating under too much stress. If you breathe seven breaths a minute or less, you will be seen as more composed, more authoritative, more "together"—and indeed, you actually _will_ be.

2. Now, consciously slow your breathing.

The Breath Balloon

Exhale fully with a big, audible sigh (particularly if you're already stressed) and stay empty for a few seconds. Let go of any tightness you feel in your face, neck, jaw, shoulders, head, back, chest, and belly. As the air is coming through your nostrils, imagine you are breathing it as though you're filling a balloon from the bottom. (The balloon is your lower belly.)

Imagine the balloon as very beautiful; make it your favorite color (whatever comes to mind first). Never mind the actual physiological process; this visualization gives you access to an instantaneous, complex de-stressing that will remove the buildup of lactic acid from your taut muscles and calm, oxygenate, and revitalize your whole system *within seconds.*

Hold—check to see if your shoulders are relaxed.

Exhale steadily to a very slow count of seven. See the balloon deflating slowly as you exhale.

Hold for a count of one. Begin again.

Keep this up for five minutes or as long as you like.

In chapter 6, I will explain why this exercise is a magic weapon to be used anytime, anywhere. *It's important to practice this when you don't need it* so it becomes so easy and natural you can do it whenever you want, without giving it your full attention. Concentrating on what is usually a completely automatic process is unusual for most people, so it's absolutely essential that you practice it when nothing else is going on. That way you can explore how it feels. Otherwise you will never, in the hurly-burly of panic, excitement, tension, and crisis, remember to breathe slowly. Your conscious mind would probably say, "Oh, shut up and leave me alone—I have important things to deal with—don't bother me with *breathing*, for God's sake. I've got enough on my mind as it is!"

There is almost a feeling buried somewhere in our psyche that by breathing harder we're *helping* ourselves handle the problem; that's how we recognize "this is serious." We identify so closely with the problem and the emergency that we actually *push* it with our breath—out of some feeling that this will help. Can you remember the last James Bond movie you saw when the whole audience was holding its breath and saying "uh-oh"—as though that could help the hero?

If you were pushing a great load with twenty other people, your hard breathing *would* actually help mobilize you to perform some feat beyond your normal strength. But most of the time holding your breath or breathing irregularly or shallowly—as most people unconsciously do under stress—makes it much harder to deal with the emergency. Your brain is deprived of the increased oxygen it needs, and the tension this causes interferes more and more with the superfunctioning that the original stress reaction was designed to provide.

The mental equivalent of that strained sympathetic breathing is worry. Most people worry because they unconsciously feel it's going to help; it reassures them (that tough inner censor) that they're good, they care, they're concerned and responsible. ("If I worry about doing a good job, I'm worth what they're paying me at work." "If I worry about my children, I'm a good parent.")

Arthur L. said, "I *need* anxiety to get me worked up so I can accomplish things." He was in the habit of taking Valium to cut the level of anxiety to manageable proportions. After he began the breathing, he found he didn't "need" the anxiety anymore; he was productive and relaxed at the same time.

Unfortunately, worry is no more productive than shallow breathing. By identifying with fear and limitation, we cut our supply lines to intuition, resourcefulness, and inner strength. So do practice the breathing when you have nothing else to think about. You may be surprised to find, as many people do, that it's rather scary, at first, to breathe slowly; it brings you smack up against an awareness of your own mortality.

Billy R., a young, athletic lawyer in my workshop, said, "Gee, it's so much *work* to breathe slowly—I felt exhausted when I finished. My stomach was tense with anxiety. I couldn't wait to get the next breath—I had to gulp in air." I asked him if he knew whether his birth had been a difficult one. "No," he said slowly, "but when I was an infant, I almost died of a serious intestinal problem and they cut out part of my intestines before I was a year old." His body and nervous system had retained the physical memory of that early trauma, and his breathing reflected a fear of dying that was an early infant experience.

I invented a gentle self-massage exercise for him, which in twenty minutes totally changed the way he had been breathing all his twenty-eight years. After that, he was able to do the slow breathing and sense with his whole body the deep ease and relaxation it brings.

Malcolm N., a political candidate who was a successful industrialist, came to me because his speaking style was choppy and he didn't always project with authority. He, too, had an uneven breathing pattern. He, too, was surprised to find it felt very alarming to breathe very slowly.

"I don't know why that's hard," he said slowly, "but I find myself gasping for air after the long exhalation, desperate to get in another breath as fast as possible. I can't seem to take it in slowly."

Since I have noticed that breathing difficulties sometimes go back to traumatic births, I asked him if he knew anything unusual about his own birth.

"Well, as a matter of fact," he said with a look of surprise, "I almost strangled at birth—the cord was wrapped around my neck!" Buried inside this fifty-five-year-old man was a terrified infant struggling to get enough breath to survive—*with each breath*. After he had flashed on that memory, he was able to breathe more easily. For the first time in his life he was able to breathe slowly and consistently. Interestingly, this simple breathing change gave him more concentration and improved eye contact. He had remarked that people complained he didn't really listen to them, and his wife, a sharp observer, criticized him for constantly looking around while people were talking to him. Breathing slowly and consistently, once it became a habit, changed the quality of his awareness. He found he had more patience, was able to center himself in the now instead of always thinking about what had just happened or what was going to happen, and really listened to people when they talked to him.

This gave him more opportunity to observe the totality of what people were communicating. He found them much more interesting than just their words, which he had tended to jump ahead and impatiently complete for them. He now found he was getting subtler and more complete information and also better feedback from people. They in turn knew that he really was interested in them. They felt flattered by his steady attention and gaze. It was a remarkable series of changes—all triggered by the change to slow, even breathing. His charisma in the next political campaign was much more powerful. In fact, he won!

Another client, a brilliant Freudian psychiatrist in his forties, also noted with astonishment that he went through a real panic reaction the first few times he did the slow Basic Breath Tranquilizer (see chapter 12). He reported with great satisfaction the following week:

> I determined to stick it out even if I died in the attempt—and it felt as dangerous as though I was faced with the prospect of drowning. Knowing I could choose to go through with it gave me the strength to do it over and over. Finally, it was no longer frightening. I know now I can control any panic I suffer before giving one of my lectures, because it'll never be as bad as that again! This sense of potential control gives me enormous satisfaction. I'm very pleased with myself that I was able to overcome my terror and stick with it.

His face, habitually rather gloomy, broke out in a triumphant grin. Gradually, through that first crucial victory, he was able to liberate his sense of humor and enjoyment of speaking, and he has become a popular and successful lecturer.

The Rush Act

Now you're ready to learn of a very effective secret weapon against the stress of rushing. All of us have moments when there are nineteen things to be done and far too little time to do them. Here is an extraordinarily effective way to be efficient, calm, and collected while rushing. The secret is this: *the more rushed you are, the more slowly you should breathe,* even if you find internal resistance or an obligation to worry ("What are you doing? I *have* to breathe fast to move fast, stupid!").

The best way to practice (before you're under stress) is by walking first slowly and then increasingly fast. Experience the complex sensation of *slowing your breathing as you increase your pace.* Make sure your shoulders are relaxed; we shouldn't be able to see any evidence that you're breathing deeply. A certain mischievous pleasure comes with this contrapuntal breathing. You'll feel a delicious satisfaction in the fact that you *seem* to be rushing, and nobody but you knows that actually you're moving very slowly (since your breath carries the movement) and have all the time in the world. What's happening? Your actual perception of time expands, unfolding like a paper flower in water.

Here's the usual jerky, spasmodic, uncoordinated behavior that characterizes rushing—"Oh, my God, where are my keys? What did I do with my briefcase? Did I turn off the stove? Lock the door? Remember to call the plumber [carpenter, wife, boss, children]?" You know the kind of last-minute details that fall out of our heads like dropped papers when we're rushing around. "Chicken without a head" is a perfect expression for that feeling of being "headless" that rushing often produces. Instead of all that almost spastic, lack-of-flow movement, now you're moving in a continuum of slow, gentle breathing that utilizes all the adrenaline shooting through your system, sending energy and information to the brain. This creates such a detailed, complex perception of every micromoment that in the expanded sensorium there is *time* for everything you need to accomplish and a feeling of sailing easily through crisis.

The Throat Clutch

One of the most common difficulties people report is that their throats close up or tighten. Voices rise embarrassingly or get practically inaudible, which can ruin anybody's confident and authoritative image.

Joanne L. told her group, "I was so humiliated! I'd just started to give a presentation for twenty men and felt my voice shaking and actually cracking. It was all I could do to get through it. What can I do? I don't ever want that to happen again!"

Here are some exercises to keep your throat open and your voice grounded in the body so you can use your full range, even when you're nervous. All these must be first practiced when you *don't* need them.

Basic Yawns

First, YAWN! That's right, a nice rude yawn. If the yawn doesn't take over and do *itself* after you've started, you're not really yawning. Yawning is one of the great natural relaxers, like laughing. If you have trouble starting the yawn, lift your lips up, away from the teeth, as though you're snarling, inhale, crinkle up your eyes, and then open your mouth as wide as you can, in all directions, so that the muscles in your neck stand out and you hear a roaring in your ears—now YAWN! No halfway measures, please! Only by exaggerating can you really get into the feeling that will take over and thoroughly relax your whole face, neck, and throat. You're learning to imitate your own natural processes so you can use them when you need them. Try that a couple of times, until it's easy for you to do at will. If you feel silly doing these exercises, try them in the privacy of your bedroom or bathroom, but full out! Otherwise, they won't hook into your natural relaxing mechanisms and won't be any use to you.

You may find that once you get started it's hard to stop! Good! Keep going until you are all "yawned out."

Once you've got that so you can induce a yawn anytime you want to, *do it with your mouth closed*. We all can remember doing this when we're bored and don't want to show it—at a dull meeting or party or with someone who bores us. Now, however, be very aware of your muscular reactions. The tongue is as low as possible at the back of the throat and lying on the bottom of the mouth, the tip flat (not drawn back), and the sides in contact with all the gums; press the middle of the tongue down as hard as possible. This enlarges the space inside the mouth.

The Helium Ball Yawn

Imagine there is a huge ball of helium in your mouth, pressing the roof up, the back out against the back of your neck, and the sides and bottom down. If you put your fingertips against the sides of the neck in back, you should feel the muscles expanding outward and downward when you yawn, either with mouth open or closed. Your ears go back, too. The back of the tongue goes down. If you want to help get the feeling, put a spoon on the back of your tongue the way the doctor used to use a tongue depressor when you were a child to see the back of your throat. If you expand the throat downward in back of the tongue, you won't gag when you do this. Gagging means you've closed the throat up at the back.

Once you can do this helium ball expansion at will, begin to hum, with a *phmmmmmm*. Notice if you start the sound of the hum with a little click in your throat; that's called the *"glottal catch."* When I was acting in TV daytime dramas, we referred to certain emotional scenes as "glottal stop scenes." They all started with a very effective catch in the throat: "Oh, John, please . . . I can't . . . I . . . I . . . I (gasp) . . . I, oh . . . I don't know what to do . . . Aren't you? . . . Are you? . . . I know but . . . I . . . I can't!"

The glottis is that little fleshy protuberance atop the vocal cords in the back of the throat. A glottal catch means you start a word that begins with A, E, I, O, or U by momentarily closing the throat to start the sound. It's an effective way to emphasize the word. But many people begin *all* words there, and the sounds get trapped in the throat, deprived of the rich vibrations that your breath can give coming through the trunk and mixing with the sounds your vocal cords produce and send up through the head cavities. When the throat closes, you cut off three-quarters of your resonating space.

It's important for your charisma that you free and use your whole, true voice. (See chapter 8.)

Magic Jaw Looseners

A great deal of tension settles in the jaw. Here are a couple of jaw looseners.

To free the throat: Open your mouth as wide as you can, scrunch up your eyes, and stick out your tongue as far as you can. Now, press your chin in with your index finger and hold the chin steady—don't let it move! (It will try to get in the act!)

Now circle your tongue all around your mouth, keeping it extended as far as possible. At first it may be very unwilling to move smoothly, but keep trying until it makes a complete circle as smoothly and continuously as though it were being pulled around by an outside hand. Try to aim for touching your nose on top, your cheeks on the sides, and your chin on the lower part.

When you've circled your tongue slowly clockwise, stretching as far as you can three times, reverse and do it three times in the other direction. (This brings blood to the throat area as the circulation increases—great for a sore throat!)

You will find that your throat feels more open and lighter when you are finished.

Now take your chin between your thumb and index finger and, letting your mouth fall open, wobble your head back and forth between your fingers by moving the jaw. Don't move the jaw itself; let the fingers do the moving. If your jaw is very tight, you may find that the hinge doesn't want to move at all at first. Keep trying until the whole hinge moves and shakes your head when you push it back and forth with your fingers.

How to Free Your Face

Have you ever watched a horse as it stands in the sun, swatting away flies and blowing gently? That's what you're going to do to loosen up your face.

The Horse Laugh

Start with your lips tightly together as though you were going to say *P*. Blow outward to let your lips ripple continuously like a little motor. Hardly a child alive has not tried this at some time or another. It's impossible to be dignified and do this, so be prepared again to feel foolish. So what? But don't laugh until you run out of breath! Do this over and over until it's easy. Now sing a little, running up and down the scales as you do it.

"My goodness, I can't do it at all," mourned one tense young woman, Jane S. "My lips just won't move!" That shows Jane needed the exercise badly; tension will prevent you from being able to do it. As with so much else, you do this by *not* trying. Just let go of your lips and make them as limp as you can.

If you're having trouble with this, try Idiot Fingers. Making a small continuous sound, move your index finger up and down rapidly across your absolutely lax limp lips—as kids used to do when they were playing Idiot! It's guaranteed to make you feel pretty idiotic! The virtue of this "dumb" exercise is that you'll get the feeling of loose lips, and that's vital for relaxing the face and jaw tension.

Now you've got the feeling of loose lips. If you need an image of what that looks like, remember Charles Laughton, whose lower lip always seemed to be hanging open. (I didn't say it was necessarily attractive!) If that picture doesn't appeal to you, you can tune in a mental image of Marilyn Monroe's luscious, half-open lips. Feel what it would be like to have your mouth be exactly like that. Uta S., a German actress with a thin, tight mouth, came to me to free herself of tensions. When I mentioned Marilyn Monroe's ripely relaxed lips, she gasped, "My mother says she looks like a slut!" No wonder poor Uta's mouth was tight!

The Wibble Wobble

Now, keeping your lips limp, make a small continuous sound and shake your head rapidly from side to side as though you're saying "No-o-o-o-o." Important: let your cheeks and lips wobble, as though they were hanging off your bones. (The late S. D. Szakall and Charles Coburn of the movies had the wonderful wibbly-wobbly jowls that this exercise suggests.)

If your head gets stuck or the movement is jerky, you have a lot of neck tension. Keep at it till the movement is fast, continuous, and smooth.

The Pleasure Purr

Now, yawn again with your mouth closed and hum *phmm*. This time think of something you love doing—eating chocolate mousse, making love, stroking fur, smelling burning leaves—whatever sensual memory turns you on. Spread the feeling of glow all around your head, throat, and neck, keeping your throat open and relaxed with your tongue lying low and flat. See if you can distribute humming vibrations evenly throughout your head and neck, as though you were massaging the inside of your skull with sound. You *are* actually doing that! Make the hum as quiet as the purr of a kitten or a very fine Rolls-Royce motor. Make sure you start each sound with the breath snorting through the nostrils (lips relaxed, though), a *phmm* so that it does *not* start from the glottal catch. Make it as even, easy, and continuous as you can. Breathe deeply, close your eyes, and turn on the motor.

After five minutes you will feel thoroughly relaxed and pampered. (By the way, this low "white sound," turned down as far as you can without catching, is a wonderful way to put yourself to sleep. Breathing slowly, you purr away and you'll automatically fall asleep.) Anytime during the day when you feel stressed, just begin to use this helium ball hum (the bottom of your chin should visibly expand to look like a duck-billed platypus, as the tongue presses down the glands under your chin). And keep purring.

The Payoff

If you've faithfully practiced these exercises so that you can do them easily anytime (even if woken up in the middle of the night from a deep sleep), then, as you get up on a platform to speak, all you have to do is open your mouth slightly, allow your lips to be as limp as possible, and, gently, silently blow your breath past your lower lip. This will remind your whole face of the entire sequence of exercises that you practiced so faithfully and will achieve exactly the same results as if you had *done the whole series*!

Warning—This will *only* work if you *have* practiced the whole series beforehand, so your face will pick up the cues it remembers from that final moment.

The aim of all of these exercises of course is to change your physical sense so that you instantly put yourself in a relaxed state with any part of the body, face, or breath. When you practice the exercises, your body is learning a new way to experience itself. This should return you to a sense of freedom and ease you haven't felt since childhood. It's no accident that many of these exercises are things children do idly all the time while growing up. *If it makes you feel silly, it's probably good for you!*

It's instructive to notice what makes you feel foolish. If you can allow yourself in the privacy of your home to do things that make you feel "silly," you've broken down some of the shyness barrier that prevents you from expressing your charisma. Remember, it takes relaxation, freedom from tension, *and* practice in new behaviors to give you the full freedom you need to be truly expressive and eloquent.

Your Inhibition Inventory

Score yourself as follows. Privately (or with one person) or in public, each statement is

    0 = not at all true for me
    1 = somewhat true (part of the time)
    2 = fairly true (about half the time)
    3 = mainly true (most of the time)
    4 = true all the time

	In Private	In Public
I would feel silly (or embarrassed) to		
1. cry	_____	_____
2. yawn	_____	_____
3. dance	_____	_____
4. run	_____	_____
5. shake or move my body rapidly	_____	_____
6. do any kind of physical movement	_____	_____
7. move my pelvis back and forth	_____	_____
8. shake my shoulders	_____	_____
9. shake my feet or legs	_____	_____

(continued)

10. tell a joke	_____	_____
11. open my eyes very wide	_____	_____
12. open my mouth very wide	_____	_____
13. yell	_____	_____
14. scream	_____	_____
15. admit I'm wrong	_____	_____
16. apologize	_____	_____
17. accept compliments	_____	_____
18. make a mistake	_____	_____
19. act in front of people	_____	_____
20. sing for people	_____	_____
21. be asked to read aloud	_____	_____
22. have to play charades	_____	_____
23. wear a costume	_____	_____
24. express emotions	_____	_____
25. express opinions	_____	_____
TOTAL	_____	_____

Add the scores for both columns. 0–15 = You don't always use discretion or listen to others enough. 16–50 = You go with your gut feelings, are expressive, enjoy life, have a good sense of humor and a balanced attitude. 51–90 = You envy people who are more relaxed, you are more timid than you'd like and less spontaneous, you fear rejection. 91–130 = You feel that everything you do is not good enough, you're afraid of social disapproval, you seldom depart from routine, you don't like to make a fool of yourself. 131–170 = You are held back by many fears, you're easily shocked, you don't like to take chances, you have rigid expectations. 171–200 = You feel life is dull, boring, meaningless, your inhibitions overwhelm you, your self-esteem is very shaky, and you're unable to express your potential. Your health is affected.

I hear you saying, "But why do I have to feel silly? I'm a grown-up. I want to have *more* control, not *less*, in my life. You're asking me to behave like a child, and I don't see the point—I certainly wouldn't want to behave like that in public. In fact, it's a secret nightmare of mine that I *will* do something silly in public—you're asking me to deliberately practice silly behavior. I don't get it."

Ok, ok, don't go away mad!

Let me explain. Relaxation from stress is essential to break up the buildup of tension. Between birth and age six, children learn more than at any time during their lives. There is now evidence that children have more brain synapses than adults. Children are more physically active and use their senses more fully. The constant stimulation of the cerebral motor cortex and the challenge to all the senses in turn stimulate greater development of the complex brain centers and fantastic leaps in growth.

By returning to some of a child's repertoire of vocal and motor exercises, we stimulate our own regeneration and give ourselves a welcome antidote to gravity: levity! Everything can seem so grim when we're adults that we can't relax and play. The best work is always accomplished in the spirit of eager play. The natural curiosity of a child and instinctive use of all the senses are things we have to painstakingly find our way back to as grown-ups—so here is a Child-Adult's Garden of Absurdities.

Give yourself permission to behave like a fool. To change your behavior style from A to D you have to go way out to X. That's the Bluebird Principle: it isn't the destination but the journey that makes the difference! When you have allowed yourself to be silly, use some of your expanded sensorium and let go of your dignity. At this point, *results don't count!* But having done some absurd and extravagant exercises will loosen you up in your daily life, with little special effort required.

Six Somersaults a Day

(Please be careful—I don't want any injuries!) Roll over as limp and roundbacked and relaxed as you can—and be sure to have something soft under you!

The Silly Super Shakeout

First shake out one hand, then the other, then shake your head like a rag doll (let your mouth hang loose). Then shake out each leg. Then hop, shaking the other foot. Then jump and wiggle your pelvis and throw your arms and elbows and hands all around, every which way, and make some noises while you're at it! Keep this up for three to five minutes.

The Sexy Dancer Bit

Turn on some jazzy music, turn the lights off, take your shoes and socks off, and dance for fifteen minutes or until you fall exhausted—whichever happens first. Try to move parts of your body that you don't usually move. Move everything. Flail your arms about; move your legs. Shake, rattle, and roll. The harder, the better. Really throw yourself into this. You may find you're inhibited even when nobody is there. Good! Now you know what you have to overcome. Nobody's watching, so knock yourself out. Then reward yourself by lying on your back for fifteen minutes and letting go completely. Be aware of exactly what your body is feeling. Feel your heart beating, your muscles vibrating with the unexpected exertion. Enjoy the luxury of letting go completely. Feel supported and caressed by the floor.

The Cat Stretch

When you wake up in the morning, and at any other time that it's convenient, stretch as slowly and luxuriously as a cat. Feel the energy going down to your toes and beyond, and out through your fingers and beyond. Don't let it short-circuit halfway. Visualize yourself as your favorite dancer, sexy and lithe. Really get into it; whatever shape your body's in doesn't matter. Feel the beautiful, supportive structure underneath, and *stretch*. Breathe . . . Stand up. Feel your rib cage pulling up out of your waist, your waist up out of your hips, your hips pulling away from your thighs, your thighs pulling downward toward your toes, your knees and calves reaching downward; feel the energy pulling down to your feet and up through your hands to the ends of your fingers.

Rainbow Power

Now breathe deeply and bend your hands backward at the wrists, so the palms are facing upward, fingers extended as straight as you can, as though you're supporting the world on your flattened palms, arms straight. Now raise your arms straight above your head. Keeping the palms facing upward, the heels of the palms forward, the backs of the hands pressing down, slowly move your hands outward as though your body were being pulled apart, in a rainbow arc of power. Keep the energy flowing all the way out through your fingertips *and beyond*, as taut and stretched out as you can. When you have brought the hands down to shoulder level, feel your upper back muscles stretching and the inner arms stretched as though you were outlined in fire.

When your hands and arms are level with your shoulders, hold for ten very slow full breaths. Keep mouth closed, shoulders down, neck long. Your fingers will probably tingle! Keep resisting the air with your palms, as though you were pushing away two walls at the ends of your hands.

Now move your whole torso as far to the left as you can—as slowly as possible—turning your head to lean into it. Breathe in and stretch as far as possible, then return to center, exhaling. (Bend the left knee as you stretch.)

Now push to the right side, again following the movement with your head and eyes, bending your right knee. Your feet are solidly planted about two feet apart. Feel the stretch along the opposite side when you lean in each direction. Make sure your body remains straight, not tipped over, so your head, shoulders, and arms keep the same relation to each other. Do this stretch five times in each direction.

The Swinger

Clasp your hands behind your back (if you can't, put your hands on your shoulders, keeping the shoulders down). Swing your whole torso and head to the left, breathing in. Then swing to the right as you exhale. Do this twenty times. Imagine there is a point in the middle of your chest and you're suspended from the ceiling by a string attached there. Feel the two "wings" of your back touching—your chest should be very open.

You will feel completely energized and any shoulder tension will be greatly relieved.

Here is another great shoulder and midback de-tenser for when you've been bending over a desk or hot stove all day: Stand with your back to a desk and place your hands on the desk behind you at your sides. Bend your knees a little, curve your whole body forward as though you were deeply ashamed, and bow your head. Now press down on your hands, inhale (mouth closed, of course), and stretch backward until your body is arched like a bow, head as far back as it will go. Rise on your toes, press them against the floor, and hold for a count of four. Then exhale and slowly curve over again. Do this two to three times. (The height of the desk should be a little lower than you can put your hands on easily—so that you have to bend your knees a little.) This is the best and fastest back de-kinker going.

When I did a TV series on how to de-stress at your desk, these were the most popular exercises because they're quick and effective. They don't take much time. They do need to be done with your full attention.

Next, try the all-time champ of neck relaxers, the Pointillist Necklace.

The Pointillist Necklace (also known as the Drunken Head Roll)

Drop your head from the first few vertebra until your chin practically rests on your chest. Now imagine that there is a necklace around your clavicle and that someone will press gently at each point on it, and this action will move your head. It's going to start moving of its own weight without your help. At each point, moving as slowly as possible without actually stopping, ask yourself, "Is my head as heavy as possible? As heavy as a cannonball? Is my neck as long as possible? Are my shoulders relaxed?" Imagine that there is a ball bearing inside your temples that is moving your head around because its weight shifts—don't lead with your face, but with that imaginary weight inside your head at eye level. It makes your head roll slowly, slowly around. As slowly as possible, circle clockwise. When you hear cracks and clicks, gently go back and "iron" them out. Do this three times around and then three times in the other direction.

This head roll is wonderful when you're tense or as a general relaxer; it is the best exercise for neck and shoulder tension. Do it anytime. It's excellent before going to sleep. Most important—*do it as slowly as possible.* Imagine your head rolling from your shoulder, to your back, to your other shoulder, to your chest, as smoothly, lazily, and continuously as you can. Keep breathing steadily. If it hurts at some point, and it may because you're unkinking a lot of accumulated knots, just breathe more deeply (you can open your mouth a little, but breathe mainly through the nose) and *relax* the rest of the torso.

Tips—always remember to keep the shoulders relaxed; don't hunch them around your ears! Don't let your body tip over—stay upright. Keep your stomach relaxed.

After the Exercises

After each exercise, scan your body from the inside: notice how you're breathing. Lie down and enjoy the expanded sense of ease, space, and power; memorize it so you can get back into that state with less and less exertion as your body begins to learn how to produce that natural unstressed state with ever less effort. Consciously let go more and more. You may find you're feeling lighter and more relaxed than you have in years. Many people report that their breathing eases; they feel suddenly more cheerful, hopeful, and energized. Lie down and enjoy your well-earned rest.

Ready to get up? First rotate your limp hands at the wrists, as though you were oiling the joints by rolling them around. Make the movement as smooth and sinuous as you can. Now try rolling them in the other direction. If you hear a snap, crackle, or pop, make the movements even gentler and subtler and more snaky. Then draw your knees up like a baby, and begin to rotate your feet at the ankles. You'll probably hear a lot of snap-crackle-pop there; our poor feet, mostly encased in shoes, don't usually get enough expressive movement to free the energy locked in them. They're lumpishly dropped at the bottom of the elevator shaft that is our bodies.

You're waking up your system by activating the sensitive micromuscles in your feet and ankles. Like your hands, they can be expressive energy terminals. In foot reflexology, you dissolve body tensions by massaging the feet, because every part of the foot has a corresponding energy center in other parts of the body.

Roll the feet around as smoothly as you can, keeping the hands going, too. (If this is hard for you to coordinate at first, do the feet alone, then add the hands.) If you are really up for a challenge, try rotating the hands and feet in opposite directions. Not easy, but new brain pathways are made when you practice coordinations that had been difficult or impossible. You actually make yourself smarter when your physical functioning gets more adroit and sophisticated.

Take it at your own pace, and don't be discouraged if it seems impossible at first. Stop a moment, knees up, and do it *mentally* for a few minutes. Then do it again physically. This kinesthetic practice greatly enhances functioning.

In experiments with sounds, clinical researchers found that when people *thought* a certain sound, there were tiny movements in the middle ear; athletes who mentally practiced their skills could also cut practice time very substantially. Golfer Jack Nicklaus always rehearses his plays by seeing them in his mind's eye and mentally feeling himself going through the moves. You can greatly improve your own coordination with little or no muscular effort by this kind of mental rehearsal.

After you have done the circling about ten times with both feet and hands, rub your hands together vigorously until you feel they're very warm; then rub your feet together hard, grab your knees, and rock back and forth gently on your spine. Then when you feel it is the right moment, sit up. You will be immensely *alive, awake, refreshed.*

NOW LAUGH FOR THREE MINUTES! You think this is easy? Try it! I guarantee you'll feel revved up, stimulated, totally energized. At first it may wear you out; laughing continuously takes a lot of energy, but it also produces a lot by relaxing a great many involuntary muscles and stepping up oxygen consumption and circulation. Try it with your friends and family.

One entertaining variant that I often do with business groups is to have everybody lie down, each person with his or her head on someone's stomach; then the first person begins to laugh and soon everybody's roaring. It's an amazing feeling to feel that tide of laughter sweeping through everybody's gut and vibrating the floor underneath you.

Heart Relaxer

Every half hour or so, if you're having a hectic day, drop your jaw suddenly. As you do that, breathe, shrug your shoulders, and rotate them fully—back, down, front, up—in generous smooth circles as high, wide, and handsome as you can make them. When you bring them around to normal position, make sure the back muscles of your shoulders have really relaxed. And when you shrug, keep the jaw dropped and relaxed. It's a little like patting your stomach with one hand and rubbing your head with the other!

Holding on produces a tight jaw and sore shoulders. People who carry a lot of burdens generally have tight shoulder and neck muscles. You're beginning to tighten up for the fight-or-flight syndrome. "Crouched for action" can whip the heart into a spasm. If you do this exercise for ten seconds every half hour, it will counteract the buildup of the heart's tendency to spasm. The brain wave, which slows down in older people and those with heart disease, will switch to a normally functioning one.

After a while, you can begin to get the exact "feel" of this relaxed-heart brain wave. Even Type A, uptight personalities can help prevent heart attacks by practicing this normalizing exercise—and feel the new calmer functioning that it engenders in their brains and hearts.

The Caveman Whump

If you feel a lot of anxiety in your chest, lock yourself in the john and lightly beat your chest, shoulders, and back with your fists for two or three minutes. (A low, steady *ughghgh* helps!)

This will break up the tight feeling and stimulate circulation. For more daily and emergency tension-reducers, see chapter 12 for lots of other great Charisma-cises. You'll discover which ones feel best and most effective for you. Try them in the suggested sequences. Then, by noticing what feelings they produce, you can have a short or extended routine that will always keep you in condition to handle the tensions that result from challenges, whether speaking in public, dealing with difficult interpersonal situations, or just facing a time pressure.

Now you know *what*, *why*, and the beginnings of *how*. From here on, the Dodo—who was no dodo—said it best: **"The best way to explain it is to do it."**

You may find that the breathing alone will make the difference between handling a situation well and feeling out of control. Breathing may even make it possible for you to stop smoking, if you are a smoker (more about this in chapter 6).

You're becoming aware of your internal thought, emotional, and body processes, and have some new tools to deal with the most common tension problems most people experience. The exercises in this chapter and later will help you to undo the accumulated knots that have tied up your inner gifts.

You're beginning to stretch and experience the full magic of your own body-mind. Now you'll find out how you can get in touch with your "heartfelt" inner self and share it (safely!) with the world around you—how to create your own inner radiance and resonate with the warmth, love, and acceptance that is waiting for you in others.

5

What's on Your Body's Mind?

*"The body is a pair of pincers set over a bellows and a
stewpot, and the whole fixed upon stilts!"*
—Samuel Butler

"The body is a temple."
—The Bible

If you're paying attention, your body can give you a lot of information
about what's really going on in your life. Most people are unaware of their
body's distress or pleasure signals until they get too urgent to ignore.

Jerry S., a venture capitalist with high blood pressure, remarked, "I
really don't feel any tension—I hardly notice my body at all." His voice rose,
"But people are a headache! My wife, my kids, my colleagues—they all
drive me crazy!"

"Would you like to reduce the stress you suffer in relation to other
people?" I asked him.

"Well, of course!" He shrugged somewhat skeptically. I suggested that
whenever somebody annoyed him, he pay close attention to what was
really going on with his body as well as with his thoughts. I taught him
the Two-Minute Body-Mind De-Stressor, and after practicing it a few
weeks, he began to sense for the first time what was happening in his long-
ignored body. One day he reported with amazement, "This is very interesting. I'm noticing a consistent pattern. Whenever I get annoyed with
people, I feel intense pain right here." He pointed to his temples. Surprise!
Never before had he realized that he was giving himself headaches from
annoyance. Everything had always been other people's fault.

His wife, Linda, on the other hand, was painfully aware of all her
tensions. Terrified of making a mistake and not living up to Jerry's
expectations, she nervously interrupted her family, talked fast, and was
subject to panic attacks. Self-doubt and the fear that she couldn't stand on her
own feet gnawed at her.

As Jerry gradually became more aware of what he was really feeling
beneath the numbness he had imposed on himself since childhood, he grew

fascinated with the messages he was getting from his body. Without any special effort, he became more patient and empathetic with Linda, his children, and his associates; his blood pressure dropped and he stopped getting headaches from sheer annoyance. His friends told him, "Hey, you're much less abrasive than you used to be!" Jerry grinned sheepishly. "I'm certainly feeling different. And for some weird reason people don't irritate me as much anymore."

As for Linda, she now recognized that her daydreaming, lack of concentration, nervous anxiety, and inability to be on time all stemmed from her early need to protect herself against her mother's attacks on her self-esteem. To learn how to pay more loving attention to her body, she too began regularly practicing the Two-Minute Body-Mind De-Stressor.

This is how it's done:

The Two-Minute Body-Mind De-Stressor

Part 1: When something *unpleasant* happens, notice

1. where you feel it in your body,

2. what happens to your breathing, and

3. what thoughts just went through your mind.

NOW,

4. take a deep breath, drop your jaw and shoulders, and relax the whole body;

5. *smile*—say aloud slowly, **"I am relaxed, energized, and calm!"** and

6. (continue the secret smile) breathe six very slow, even, deep breaths through the nose, keeping the lower jaw relaxed, lips slightly parted, and tongue tip resting on the alveolar (gum) ridge just behind the upper front teeth. (With each slow, smooth exhalation, relax the body further.)

Part 2: Do the same sequence for *pleasant* experiences. After you begin to smile (#5), say aloud slowly, "I'm really enjoying this!" Stretch it out, and extend it through your whole body.

The Magic Tongue-Tap

Here is another powerful way to restore your confidence and equilibrium any time you feel under attack. Simply keep tapping the tip of your tongue on the alveolar ridge (the ridge behind your top front teeth) with the mouth closed (without moving your jaw, so nobody sees you're doing anything!). This usually works within sixty seconds. (You can prove to yourself and anyone else that this works by muscle testing, first neutrally, then with a negative thought—your arm will go straight down. Then do the Magic Tongue-Tap; in one to three minutes, when you test again, your strength will be completely restored, and in fact, you will be stronger than before! This is a mini-miracle resource.)

The reason this works is that when you tap the alveolar ridge, you are actually stimulating the thymus to secrete thymosine—one of the prime ingredients of our immune system. The Chinese consider the tongue tip the meeting place of the yin and yang meridians in the body, another explanation for the powerful effect of this simple, invisible exercise.

Almost immediately, Linda began to notice good things happening. Not only did she feel calmer and more centered, but learning deep, slow breathing and muscle relaxation also reduced her anxiety level dramatically and made her feel more in charge of her life. Her voice grew stronger. "I never thought I'd be able to control my mind and actions. It makes me feel so . . ." she paused and laughed a little shyly, "well—grown-up! Here I am, the mother of two. It's about time, isn't it?" She laughed, her eyes shining. "Oh, and Jerry now lets me give him a massage. He's really more interested in his body than he used to admit!" She added shyly, "That and his new . . . uh . . . tenderness to me has certainly improved our sex life!" (Although men can often detach sex from everything else, nonmasochistic women in a long-term relationship usually resent having sex with a partner who seems uncaring in other areas.)

Everybody needs to experience authentic expression, even if, like Jerry, they're very out of touch with their bodies. Sexual pleasure had always been an available instinctual outlet for Jerry, but it became more subtle and satisfying when he grew more aware of Linda's needs and feelings. She found his new patience and caring sexy, and he discovered he was now capable of a certain dreamy, relaxed, non-orgasm-oriented attention and playfulness that made their lovemaking fun and exciting.

Other ways of using the body expressively—dance, drumming, playing musical instruments, and (to a lesser extent) jogging or sports—also create a deeply satisfying aliveness that powerfully amplifies not only your vitality and health *but also your charisma.*

The combined impact of *feeling and intention* is so profound that even the severely disabled can express their emotions through the body, changing the quality of their lives. Manfred Clynes describes in *Sentic Cycles* how he helped people express a range of seven basic emotions using a little machine he invented called a "sentograph." When subjects were asked to press down a lever with their third finger and concentrate on recalling anger, hate, grief, love, sex, joy, and reverence in turn for five minutes each, they reported experiencing an amazingly satisfying emotional catharsis. Similarly, I have found in working with thousands of clients that as they practiced my Charisma-cises (see chapter 12), they discovered that expressing a full range of emotions with intentionality is both emotionally freeing and deeply satisfying. For many people it is also the beginning of profound positive changes in their lives.

Clynes once gave his sentograph to a quadriplegic confined to an iron lung. Her only means of expressing her grief and frustration was to press down the lever with her chin, the one part of her body she could move. Amazingly, after this experience she was able to sleep better, enjoy music, and suffer less pain. In fact, Clynes reported, her spirits improved so much that "it became a real pleasure to be in Mrs. C. N.'s company; a radiance issued from her that affected others who came in contact with her."

At the other end of the physical spectrum, champion ice-skater Michelle Kwan once said, "If you believe and imagine yourself performing, it's already done in your head before you step on the ice." Whether your body is very limited or very developed, the power of your mind and imagination to amplify your experience is virtually limitless.

In the West we tend to split the body and mind in two, as though they were unconnected. The psyche, located somewhere in the skull between the eyes, and the soma, or body, living and moving underneath, coexist uneasily. All our institutions and medical and cultural processes reflect this split and fragmentation. A doctor who tells his patient, "It's all in your head," is an unwitting heir to this Cartesian tradition. Somebody in Colorado left a will offering a million dollars to anybody who could find the exact location of the soul: so far there have been no takers.

Eastern cultures, on the other hand, always considered the body and mind inseparable, and so did the Greeks. We are at last beginning to realize the underlying truth of this approach, and every year sees more and more research on the subtle, complex interactions among mind, body, and spirit. The young field of psychoneuroimmunology is exploring how our cells and thoughts are connected. It is encouraging to know that to a large extent we do create ourselves in our own image. Five factors shape us: (1) heredity, (2) physical activity and exposure, (3) nutrition, (4) environment, and (5) our emotional and psychological experiences, past and present.

Looking at our own splits and imbalances helps us understand more about these fascinating curious connections. Let's look at what the body tells us.

Right and Left Halves

The right side of the brain controls the left side of the body, which is usually considered to represent the feminine aspect: emotionality, passivity, creativity, holistic expression, visualization, yin or receptive forces, and music. The left hemisphere (with its predominantly logical, analytic, verbal, and mathematical functions) controls the right side of the body, the "masculine" side. Right-side personality traits are assertiveness, aggressiveness, and the yang forces in Chinese cosmology.

Reaching out with the left hand is passive and receptive, whereas gesturing with the right is active and aggressive. This doesn't seem to be affected much by whether you're right- or left-handed.

Actor John Barrymore was able to cry out of either eye, *or both*, at will! Once, while making a movie, he asked director Elia Kazan, "Now, how do you want these tears—all at once or a little at a time? And from which eye—or would you like them simultaneously from both?" (He claimed that he had practiced his crying techniques from the time he was a tiny child.) When I tell people in my workshops during a deep relaxation and imagery session that "one side will feel lighter than the other and will continue to tingle even after you have completed this," those who need to assert themselves will feel the tingle in the right side, and those who need to validate their inner selves will report the left side is light!

Chinese facial diagnosis explores the left-right relation in great detail. For instance, the right cheek represents one's mother's influence; the left, the father's. One cheek is usually a little wider than the other. Interestingly enough, the yang cheek (the more contracted one) represents the dominant parent in the person's life. Try it. It's surprisingly accurate.

Meet Your Bottom (and Your Top) Half

The lower half of the body, the part that contacts the earth, is concerned with stability, moving, balancing, rooting, supporting, and feeling grounded. The top half deals with seeing, hearing, introspection, emotional stability, homeyness, dependency, and the alternation between motion and stasis. Outward expression and interpersonal communication, socializing, self-assertion, personal aspirations, manipulation, and action are concerns of the top half.

Have another look at your own body: How is the weight distributed? Where is your center of gravity? Are you bottom-heavy or top-heavy? Forget about disapproval, and let's examine the implications of these divisions.

When the lower half is larger than the upper, the person usually feels more at home dealing with the grounded, private aspects of his or her life. Usually this person cultivates a lifestyle that reinforces these relationships. The top half, remember, is concerned with self-expression, self-assertion, and communication. Which parts of your personality have been given the most attention and support throughout your life? Think how your children, friends, and strangers respond to you and you'll find out.

Most women find one breast is slightly larger than the other. Usually the larger one corresponds to the side of her personality that she has been using more. If the left side is larger, the more feminine, passive side of her nature has been dominant in her life; if the right side, it's the more aggressive, active parts of her personality. This is uncannily accurate, based on observation and informal questioning.

If you've overdeveloped the private (lower) aspects rather than the expressive upper ones, you may feel more comfortable expressing inwardly than outwardly. Emotions express themselves naturally and are released through hands, chest, heart, mouth, jaws, and eyes (the windows of the soul).

"Feeling" or "being" is more characteristic of the lower-dominant person. She or he may find it hard to express feelings to other people. Here is an apparent paradox: many women who have lived homebound, family-oriented lives are "feeling"- or "being"-oriented: they come to my workshops to learn how to express their feelings openly, how to speak up and hold their own. Many come from families that did not express feelings. Sally R. complained mournfully, "There's no connection between my gut, my brain, and my mouth!" Yet women are generally more aware of their feelings than men are, even if they haven't had the opportunity to express them. Many upper-oriented men, who have no trouble expressing themselves, are extremely uncomfortable in voicing feelings. They've been brought up to think that emotions are "messy," not "manly."

The "action" or "doing" person may have a large chest, skinny legs, and contracted buttocks. The assertive, outgoing, upper-dominated person may well be an "oral" type, interested in eating and drinking (the stereotype of the old-fashioned Hollywood producer!). The weak legs and thin hips may reflect a lack of groundedness, stability, and emotional self-support.

Not surprisingly, the best-coordinated parts also escape injuries more than the others. Imbalances may turn up in the opposite ends of the body. The bottom-oriented person might be subject to tension headaches, asthma, arthritis of the wrists, or a nervous stomach. Underdevelopment of the lower half may show up in sprained ankles, varicose veins, sexual dysfunction, or flat feet. But just as with right- and left-hemisphere activity, there is often a crossover of functioning. It's possible to have tension headaches and flat feet!

The two halves of the body, however, can actually learn from each other. The "stuck" lower part, through jogging and stimulating action, feels more active, and the immobilized upper becomes calmer and freer. (If you have trouble doing the One-Minute Free-for-All, do it while jogging: nobody is boring while jogging! Somehow it stimulates the flow of energy and words as well.) When you're stuck in one area, it may be a good time to get going in another. Then the momentum of that success can be transferred to the stuck area. ("A rising tide," John F. Kennedy once said, "lifts all ships.") Suddenly what was difficult becomes easy and natural, even without working on it.

Now take another look at the relative grace or awkwardness of your body's various parts. What are you secretly vain about? Disgusted by? Deposits of fat are considered by many body therapists to be stagnant energy. If you're more talented with the upper body and awkward in the legs and hips, you're probably more involved in upper-body aspects of your life. The opposite (healthy, active legs, a troublesome spine, clumsy arms) might suggest an overemphasis on lower-body aspects.

To some extent most of us are mixtures. A woman who finds it hard to be assertive might have tension in her right arm. This may produce weakness in the joints, tight muscles, or a tendency toward injury in that area. If the same woman has trouble asking for love, or accepting it, the tension might show up in the left arm.

Someone who has a hard time "taking a stand" (our bodies are very literal-minded) might have problems in the right leg (the assertive side, moving forward in the world). Pain in the legs often indicates a fear of taking action; foot pain can be a fear of being oneself.

"That's ridiculous!" Laurie S. protested. "Can I help it if I was born with flat feet?"

"No, of course not," I told her, "but I want to suggest that there's an emotional component to every physical characteristic." Our bodies offer us intriguing clues about our personalities, weaknesses, and values.

Front-Back Split

This is the third important psychosomatic separation. Your front side represents the social (conscious) self: what we present; the side we see most often, look at most affectionately (or angrily) in the mirror; the clearest image of ourselves.

There is some evidence that men are more prone to back trouble than women, possibly because they have been conditioned not to acknowledge their feelings. Lower-back pain has been interpreted as a repressed desire to shit on the world, to get back at it. At one time, most of the top executives of a major New York newspaper were suffering from lower-back pain! Back trouble often shows up in people who're not used to exploring their own emotions or facing some of their darker feelings. The private, unconscious elements are reflected by the back side: all that I don't want people to see or probe—emotions and feelings.

Women also have these problems. Claudia T., a superb horsewoman, golfer, and ice-skater, has horrendous attacks of lower-back pain. She is preoccupied with her symptoms but pays little attention to her feelings. She and her mother have spent their lives manipulating men to get money and power. Denial of feelings was one of the ways they practiced Christian Science (a misapplication of the Christian Science principle of healing yourself through faith).

The Inner Mirror Views the Outer Mirror: Centering

See if you can feel where you are centered. Is it the head? Stomach? Legs? Solar plexus? Be aware of whether you feel balanced. Imagine a plumb line running from the sky through the crown of your head, your forehead, throat, heart's center, solar plexus, navel, and genitals, and plunging to the ground; then transfer all your weight to the right foot, lifting your left a little. (Don't lean onto your hip.) Keep breathing easily (we tend to hold our breaths when we make an effort). Keep imagining that plumb line and breathe easily. Hold your balance for six slow breaths. (Later you can expand that to ten, twelve, and then twenty.) Feel the earth supporting you (it is!).

When you feel comfortable, extend your arms, slightly rounded, to your sides. Balance yourself easily and lightly, again for six breaths. Then return to center and gently transfer your weight to the left leg (don't sink onto the hip—imagine the weight still is centered between your legs). As before, hold your balance for six full breaths, each consisting of an inhalation and an exhalation. Anytime you feel off center, do this centering exercise, called the Plumb Line, and you'll immediately feel lighter, calmer, and at the same time more solidly balanced, strong, and secure.

Now stand centered and at ease. With your inner mirror tuned to your balances, look in the outer mirror and begin to observe, with detachment and nonjudgmental interest, any outer imbalances. The major ones to look for are a great difference or inconsistency between front-back, top-bottom, right-left, head-body, or torso-limbs. These observations are going to be useful to you in "reading" other people as well.

Remember to be interested and curious, but not angry or disappointed, with yourself. Look at your body as a beloved cousin—lovable, familiar, and a little strange all at once!

Mirror-Matching

Notice how the person you're talking to is sitting or standing. Is he leaning back, legs crossed or uncrossed, hands clasped or unclasped? Then match his posture (reversed of course, if you're sitting opposite). If it seems too obvious to copy the other person's gestures right away, do it a moment later. At first you may feel absurd and think the other person will suspect you're mimicking him. Oddly enough, if you're unobtrusive about it, most people do *not* notice.

When people are getting along very well, they are often mirror-matching unconsciously. It happens automatically! When you breathe or move like another person, you are, as the saying goes, on his or her wavelength. The result is, literally, bio-rapport.

Here's an astonishingly effective device for making yourself comfortable socially when you're not feeling that way. Let's say you're at a cocktail party: if you're talking to someone, try mirroring his or her posture, angle of head, and hand and feet positions. Also mirror the level of energy he or she sends (unless it's very low, in which case you might both fall asleep!). We've all seen this at work when one person leans forward and the other then leans forward with great interest. It seems very natural. It is.

In films of successful negotiations, the matching of gestures and body language is strikingly evident. People who communicate well do the mirror-matching instinctively. (Children who are popular do this too, an instinctive social skill that makes others like them and want to be with them.) So by utilizing natural techniques that happen automatically when everything is going well, you can actually create a flow of rapport with *anybody—because you know how.* And if you succeed in overcoming your initial discomfort with this strategy, it quickly elicits a warm response, which in turn makes you feel more comfortable. Soon special effort isn't necessary.

Vocal mirror-matching is also a powerful way to turn a potentially negative, hostile encounter into an experience of solidarity, as we'll discuss more in a later chapter.

Self-Sabotaging Shoulds and Other Little Devils

Now that you've started to practice letting go (hopefully) of your body-disapproval baggage, it's time to look at the mind again.

"I should have . . ." "If only I had . . ." "I'm so . . ." *(undisciplined, compulsive, driven, aimless, overcontrolled, uncontrolled, passive, aggressive,* etc.) Fill in your own self-accusations. Who hasn't sometimes laid on these hopeless wrong door self-reproaches? One of the most difficult tasks for people who blame themselves rather than other people is to move beyond self-judgments and instead to neutrally (as in the Two-Minute Body-Mind De-Stressor) observe the constantly changing cloudscape of the body-mind's shifting feeling-sensations. When you let go of judgments, you can also let go of anxiety, fear, and regret. In that surrender, a whole new world can emerge within moments. (When was the last time you "lost" yourself listening to music, lovemaking, skiing, or lying on the beach?) The more you can relax body and mind and be present in the moment, the more flexible, strong, and stress-proof you'll be and the more you will enjoy life!

One of the great values of Zen and other meditation training is learning to relax the body and the mind *at will,* staying in the "now" no matter how demanding or difficult life may be. This gives us tremendous resilience. Most of the time, in the grip of our restless "monkey mind" we are so busy obsessing over the past or the future that we almost miss the present entirely. Curiously, the discipline of relaxing the body and training the mind to stay "empty" temporarily releases us from the twin prisons of time and self—what Buddhists call "the continuum of self-grasping." What a paradox that letting go is the beginning of real control!

Human beings have always deeply craved a change of consciousness as relief from their sufferings. We depend on music, contact with nature, sex, food, drink, social life, or drugs and alcohol—on sensual, artistic, intellectual, physical, spiritual, and emotional pleasures of all kinds. We long to produce altered states at will, not simply wait for their random appearance in our lives. Since the beginning of recorded history, people have been looking for effective ways of creating "highs," with liquor, coffee, mushrooms, cocaine, and all kinds of natural and unnatural substances.

At the end of a century of overwhelming scientific and technological achievement, two world wars, and the unprecedented horror of the Holocaust, our needs have skyrocketed. With our violence-saturated TV and culture, the breakdown of traditional family and social-support systems, and the widespread availability of drugs of all kinds, people are increasingly desperate to escape into altered states. On the other hand, the information explosion has brought us scientific discoveries of brain-mind-body-spirit connections (e.g., how to produce your own pleasure endorphins without drugs) and stimulated a worldwide explosion of interest in ancient esoteric traditions. ("When the iron bird flies," runs an ancient Tibetan prophecy, "the dharma will travel to the west.") Meditation and yoga are even fashionable. Celebrities such as Madonna and Diane von Furstenberg, magazine publishers, rap-record magnates, real estate company presidents, and finance zillionaires now have meditation and yoga rooms. They are not afraid to publicly declare the importance of serenity in their lives. The rich and famous style leaders are not usually the first, but they do lead the way for the mainstream. In a recent *House & Garden* magazine poll, over 80 percent of the respondents agreed that having a quiet place in the home for meditation is a necessity. Still, while nearly everybody has the menu, not everybody's going to order.

The burning question now is whether we will resort to more and more destructive ways of trying to escape suffering or instead learn the skillful means to achieve personal and world peace. Now it's abundantly clear how interconnected we all are, how much we affect each other and the ecosystem we inhabit. The fall of a sparrow, the rise and fall of governments and the stock market, the rain forests in Brazil, human cloning, global warming, antibiotics and organ transplants, the spreading AIDS scourge, nuclear explosions—everything good and bad affects us all, and more immediately than ever before!

The personal is indeed political. The big news is that the *respect, love, and compassion we can give our own hearts deeply affects society.* No more either-or thinking—we're living in the era of "both-and"! From Confucius to Calvin, the predominant values of denial of self and denial of joy have led to hatred and war.

Our Birthright Is Joy

When you can take a fierce joy in even small things, sadness and disappointment fade, and your radiance becomes irresistibly charismatic. (Who can forget the glowing tear-stained face of Giulietta Masina at the end of Fellini's classic film *Nights of Cabiria*? Cabiria, a prostitute, has just been robbed and betrayed by a man who had promised to marry her, and her hopes of a new life are destroyed. Wandering dazed and grief-stricken down a village street, she is suddenly swept into a local parade, full of clowns and musicians. She begins to smile and irresistibly gives way to delight, even though her heart has just been broken. Audiences find this scene inexpressibly moving and somehow healing. It's like watching a child who's just been sobbing inconsolably burst suddenly into irrepressible laughter: all but the most damaged children have access to instant joy. Perhaps we recognize dimly that we, too, could recapture that capacity that most of us have all but lost?

The Inner Mirror

Secret negative self-judgments can poison our feelings about our bodies. No matter what shape they're in, most people are dissatisfied—too thin, too fat, too tall, too short, too weak, too flabby! A negative body image can seriously interfere with the ability to project charisma.

Hallie S., a ballet dancer with exquisite long legs and arms, said, "I hate myself when I gain a few pounds!" The rest of the workshop thought she was kidding. But she meant it. At one time, in fact, she had been seriously anorexic.

Celeste J., a pretty and slightly plump arts administrator, mourned, "When I meet people, I'm sure they're thinking 'Oh look at that blimp!' and if *they're* fat, I can't stand being with them. I guess I should be more tolerant, but I *hate* fat people!"

Mary R., a lawyer, confessed, "I've always resented being short! Unless I wear terribly high heels, people treat me like a child, and when I have to look up at them—especially men—all my authority goes out the window."

"I'm so mad at my damn leg," said John R., whose left leg was slightly crippled from childhood polio. When he practiced feeling tender and affectionate toward this vulnerable part of his body (which at first was very difficult for him), he was then able to visualize it as functioning well. Eventually, he was able to walk more easily and to carry himself with a new assurance and dignity. Workshop members began to notice the full power of his eyes and strong torso, and to comment on his strength and dignity. Now, his slight limp seems distinguished rather than apologetic. His injured leg will never be as strong as the other, but he feels centered and balanced as he never did before.

People dislike their bodies for many reasons. An injury, an illness, or a weight gain or loss can trigger intense self-disgust. When you hate your body, it's hard to feel loved or lovable—and almost impossible to feel charismatic.

Your Body-Image Test

To get a clear idea of how you actually feel about your body, try this experiment.

1. On a large sheet of paper draw an outline of your body.

2. Color the parts you like best, using your favorite colors.

3. Now fill in the parts you dislike.

4. At the side of the page, write down the "messages" you got from (a) parents, (b) siblings, (c) peers, (d) your loved one(s) past and present, and (e) the media about the parts of your body you *don't* like.

5. Draw in all the locations where you've suffered pain, accidents, illness, or injuries.

6. Color (with other favorite colors) those body parts that give you the greatest pleasure or joy. Some of these may overlap the parts you like best (see #2). Which parts do you consider most vital and healthy?

7. After you've finished, look at yourself in the mirror and try to sense which parts of your body project charisma (i.e., vitality, magnetism) to others. Do your eyes shine? Do you have great hair? A sensual mouth? Are your hips expressive? Your hands? Do you like your pecs? Oh, go on, admit it!

8. Color in the auras projecting outward from your most vital parts on your drawing.

9. Make one drawing for the front and one for the back.

The Cultural Mirror

You may be surprised to find many of your negative feelings about parts of your body are related to media messages and cultural stereotypes about what's (currently) sexually desirable.

Alix R. confessed, "I've always been ashamed of having small breasts, even though a lot of models do. Most of the men in my life prefer Playboy Bunny types." Alix is not alone. Although the women's movement encourages greater self-acceptance for a woman's natural endowments, many women still risk their lives and health getting breast implants. In the hit musical *Chorus Line*, a dancer sang a song called "Tits" about how she became successful only after she acquired larger breasts. Yet small breasts are more sensitive and responsive to lovemaking and certainly don't sag as much when a woman grows older. In other societies, small breasts have been considered charming and desirable. The French ideal was that each should fit into a champagne glass!

Men don't escape physical stereotypes either. They've been programmed to believe you need a large penis to be a successful lover, and if theirs is small or average they may suffer agonies of shame and sexual insecurity. Popular ads trumpet "Who says size doesn't matter?" (supposedly about all kinds of other things). Everybody knows what that's *really* about! When

James Cameron triumphantly accepted his Oscar for *Titanic*, the most expensive movie ever made, he brandished the statuette aloft and shouted, "I'm king of the world! Who says size doesn't matter?" The growing market for penile implants proves it does to many men. So does the edifice complex of real-estate developers like Donald Trump, intent on "getting it up in public" and erecting the tallest building in the world—despite the congestion, increased pollution, and overcrowding this would cause.

Yes, when it comes to big grosses, success is sexy, and nothing succeeds like excess! But when it comes to the vulnerable human body, emphasis on mere size is both dehumanizing and demoralizing.

With a Forgiving Affection—Practicing the Three As

Fitness is fine, but beyond taking intelligent care of ourselves, it's important to cultivate a forgiving affection for our own flawed bodies with all their limitations. This is our vehicle, this time around at least, and it will serve us better if we can appreciate day by day what a gift it is, through all the changes that living, bad habits, and disasters bring.

In the privacy of your own room, take a good look in the mirror at your nude body—this time *without* hating your weak ankles, cellulite, extra poundage, or other aspects you've been deploring. See if you can find something to take real pleasure in, no matter how subtle: the curve of a palm or back, nice ears, or whatever! Practice the three As—**acknowledge, appreciate, and absorb.** This may feel embarrassingly self-indulgent, but it is actually essential nourishment for your emotional immune system. *The ability to feel and express pleasure is an essential component of charisma.*

You may begin to realize that physical characteristics subtly correlate with personality traits or individual history. Is one side stronger, one shoulder higher? Arthur G., whose father had criticized him unmercifully, suddenly realized that all his adult life he had habitually hunched his shoulders as though expecting to be attacked. Until the workshop, he had never understood why some people thought he looked fearful and wary. Acquiring a straight, proud posture (which took time and effort), Arthur found he felt more assertive and confident, people seemed friendlier, and he smiled more often—life didn't seem so deadly serious as it used to.

Emotional experiences are registered in the body throughout our lives and become just as much a part of it as purely physical ones do. How we learn to express or not express our emotions affects all our relationships, which further complicates how stress is felt by each individual. How well we feel we can cope in turn profoundly affects our lives, and our psychosomatic reactions then contribute to our vulnerability.

However, the body has its own wisdom and protective mechanisms, and we often have the virtues of our vices. "The soles of my feet," remarked artist Sally N., "are terribly thin-skinned—like me! As a child I was annoyed when mother told me, 'Dear, you're too sensitive!' She was right, of course.

But now that I accept that, I've learned to protect my nervous system and see the big picture; I don't take things so personally—most of the time! And now I value the insight and awareness that go with the sensitivity."

Jenny S., a well-known actress who had gained thirty pounds when her husband left her for a seventeen-year-old, couldn't get rid of her big stomach even after she had successfully resumed her career and rebuilt her life. When I asked if the weight might be her body's protection against unbearable emotional pain, she gasped, "I used to wonder where the pain went—I knew it was there, but I couldn't feel it." The first time we massaged her stomach, she burst into deep racking sobs, releasing old, stored grief. She had to "thank" her stomach for protecting her from pain with the extra flesh before her stomach would begin to soften. Then, at last, she began to lose weight and the unwanted bulge. *But as long as she only hated it, it wouldn't budge!*

Letting go of body disapproval gives us access to extraordinary emotional, intuitive, and physical healing resources. Our inner and outer body language never lies! When we pay respectful attention, it tells us what's really going on in the depths. Recognizing and expressing embedded anger, grief, and fear is so freeing that alone it deeply affects unconscious processes and initiates positive change. Once we have acknowledged and expressed our true feelings, the body no longer needs to somatize (i.e., express physically). Then it can initiate its own self-healing and a sometimes astonishingly rapid return to health (unless the pathology has gone so far that it's irreversible).

Few of us could duplicate the feat of a yogi I once saw create a cyst on his hand *within minutes* and then make it disappear! But the yogic training in relaxation, concentration, and visualization that produced such a feat now makes it possible—with such modern shortcuts as biofeedback, acupressure, and hypnosis—to mobilize our own healing powers and achieve more control over our own lives.

An attitude of compassionate detachment toward the body is very helpful. At the dentist remind yourself, "I am not my body!" Jack Schwarz, the remarkable Dutch spiritual teacher, could put a sailmaker's needle through his arm without bleeding or experiencing pain. He explained that when he did this, he thought of his arm as "*an* arm" (not as "*my* arm"). Through imaging, mental control, and self-hypnosis, many people learn to stop bleeding, shrink tumors, and cure many ills.

Whatever the state of your health, feeling kindly toward and at home in your body is a path to feeling at home in the world.

The body's mind is intimately connected to our deepest hopes, fears, and dreams at a level where all of us are connected with one another. (Thich Nhat Hanh, the great Vietnamese spiritual teacher, calls that "interbeing.") We're all works in progress, and no matter what our inner-body images express, we can learn to live fully and connect with that interbeing which is our true charisma.

6

Breathing—the Bridge to Comfort and Connection

Pneuma:

1. A breath, breathing.

2. Soul, spirit, according to some ancient philosophers, the universal spirit or primordial substance.

3. The life-giving principle, and the Spirit superior to both soul and body.
—Webster's New International Dictionary,
Second Edition, Unabridged

. . . an intermediate nature, which, though distinct from the mortal Soul or Pneuma, is the source of vital activity.
—Hippocrates

. . . a dream, a breath, a froth of fleeting joy.
—Shakespeare (*The Rape of Lucrece*, 212)

You can live without food and drink for some time—but not without breathing. Because we take the process so much for granted, most people don't realize how the very quality of their lives can change radically when they learn to regulate their breathing.

The vitality of your personality, the alertness of your brain, the steadiness of your nerves all depend to a large extent on your breathing. With so many different interwoven systems contributing to the complicated interactions between your mind, body, and spirit, and the society and time you live in, breathing is about the only one you can totally control. Luckily, that can have a powerful, positive impact on everything else.

Breathing: The Mind-Body Link

Breath, in fact, is the link between body and mind. In the sea of emotion in which we live, breath is the intermediary that changes the chemistry of consciousness. For centuries yogis have known detailed ways of controlling the body and the mind and have used elaborate breathing practices to produce whatever states of consciousness they wished. With our Western taste for mechanized technology, the simplicity of *breathing* still seems to many people more primitive than using medicines, drugs, jogging, machines, or weights to harmonize, heal, and make ourselves whole.

For most male Americans, breathing instructions came from a quasi-military tradition. "Suck in your gut!" barked countless coaches and Marine sergeants. "Shoulders back, stomach flat, and BREATHE!"

The harsh strain of effortful breathing, divorced from the tender belly and gut feelings, is an integral part of our jock sports, loud, assaultive advertising, driven business life, and generally high-stress existence. Perhaps in some way it's also a legacy from our Puritan heritage. The delicate filaments of breath that have been known for centuries to mystical traditions as the doorway to expanded consciousness, health, longevity, altered states, and remarkable feats were, for a long time in our macho society, invisible, even unthinkable.

For women, too, instruction would come as a tag-end reminder: "Mary, stand up straight and *breathe*!" or "Don't get angry—just take a deep breath and count to ten!" At the same time, everybody was told, "Hold in your tummy!" So now we have a society of uptight men and women cut off from their gut feelings.

Uptight is beautifully descriptive of what happens physically when people are tense. The center of gravity (which ought to be about two inches below the navel—what the Japanese call the *hara* and the Chinese the *dan tien*) shifts upward because the stomach is held taut. Deprived of support and oxygen and with their upper body tight and strained, most people resort to rapid, irregular chest breathing.

The effects on personality are profound. Inside you're likely to feel nervous, anxious, worried, or irritable (if you're even aware of your feelings). It's difficult to act spontaneously. When the pressure gets too intense, you may blow up or withdraw from the situation. You look for distraction so you won't notice that you're pretty uncomfortable a lot of the time.

How Many Breaths Do You Breathe per Minute?

Most people breathe between twelve and eighteen breaths a minute. If you are breathing more than that, you are under very heavy stress!

Now count the number of breaths you take in one minute (each inhale and exhale counts as one breath)—without making any effort to slow down or otherwise alter your normal breathing pattern. You may notice that your breath is uneven, choppy, or shallow; there may be a pause between inhale and exhale. Your breath may be noisy, or your nose stuffed a good deal of the time. But that's just a minor inconvenience, not worth bothering about—right? Wrong! Scientists are paying increasing attention to the little-noticed subtle interconnections between brain function and breath. We now know that not only are all emotional states connected to particular breathing patterns, but also that just by slowing and deepening your breathing you can achieve all these things:

- Overcome anger and fear

- Put yourself to sleep

- Expand your magnetism

- Cure insomnia

- Lower high blood pressure

- Give yourself courage

- Alleviate pain

- Calm your own nerves

- Calm other people around you

- Increase your personal charisma

- Stop smoking

- Strengthen your will

- Clear your mind

- Improve your digestion

- Regulate your heartbeat

- Increase your vitality and pleasure

- Improve mental functioning and concentration

Since we are creatures of rhythmicity, ebb and flow, systole and diastole, we need an alternation between effortless, relaxed, steady deep breathing and at least ten minutes a day of intense, continuous activity (if we're physically able)—preferably around some greenery.

When we increase the depth and energy of our breathing, we immediately feel more connected with the energy and rhythms of the universe. The worldwide passion for jogging and aerobics is evidence of the need to reassert our natural sense of psychophysical aliveness in the face of increasingly denatured living conditions. Deadened commercial foods (stripped of nutrients and loaded with chemicals to guarantee a long shelf life), the increasing incidence of stress-related diseases (which account for 80 percent of our national mortality rate), the staggering costs of hospital care, drugs, and iatrogenic (doctor-induced) illness all have alerted growing numbers of people, at last, to the need for taking responsibility for their health and the quality of their lives.

What's Your Score?

If you breathed more than eighteen breaths a minute, you are under very heavy stress. As you know, chronic heavy stress can lead to serious health problems, even death. When your pace is eleven breaths or slower, your pituitary gland begins to function more efficiently. When you breathe seven breaths or less, your pineal gland is activated. *The simple, astonishing fact is that when you breathe seven breaths a minute or less, your entire metabolism changes!* Not only do people perceive your personality differently, they also experience you as more composed, authoritative, and vivid—because *you actually are.*

The breath, which is an incredibly subtle register of all the shifts in your thoughts and feelings, is the single most potent tool for releasing your charisma. Recent studies confirm what everybody has always known intuitively: when we're happy we breathe deeply and fully. Nervous or angry people breathe shallowly, unevenly, and mostly from the upper chest. Depressed people tend to have uneven, labored breathing. Not only are these emotional states characterized by specific breathing patterns, but the breathing itself can actually induce the emotions! Chest breathing, all by itself, can produce unsteadiness of mind and nervousness. (Any well-trained actor can produce hysterical sobs at will within moments by breathing chaotically.)

The average adult inhales about half a quart to four or five quarts of air on each breath. This is shallow chest breathing. Abdominal breathing can more than double this. During strenuous exercise, a person can take in more than 100 quarts of air. With the Magic Breath (see next section) you can increase your vital energy and take in thirty or forty quarts of air, probably ten times what you're now getting. This produces a tremendous change in the way you feel and what you project to others. Increased oxygen means better heart and lung condition, better skin, more complete digestion, and improved morale. When the lungs fill with air from the very bottom upward, they compress, giving a gentle massage to your heart. The diaphragm, too, by contracting and relaxing, massages the heart, liver, and pancreas, and it improves the functioning of the spleen, small intestine, stomach, and abdomen.

The Magic Breath—in Three Stages

You can integrate the new, deepened abdominal breathing so important to giving you control over the quality of your life by a three-stage process. Rather like the evolution of the computer, each stage is necessary for the next, and each succeeding form takes less time and effort but would have been impossible without its predecessors.

Stage I of the Magic Breath—lying on the floor—can be compared to the original room-size computer because it not only takes up the most space and the most time but is also the basis for the others. Since the floor is supporting your spine, no exertion is necessary: this is the easiest and best way to learn to experience a deep level of relaxation every time. When people first lie down, I always ask them to take a "mental Polaroid" of how their bodies feel before they begin. At the end of the sequence, they invariably report feeling "different."

"My body feels lighter," or "It feels heavier"—in either case they notice feeling closer to the ground (with more points of contact) and profoundly relaxed. Some people experience tingling in the arms and/or legs. Breathing in a slow, even, calm way, everyone feels deep peacefulness. "I can't remember when I last felt so relaxed!"

Some people almost fall asleep. But their bodies are learning how to remember this state. "Memorize this feeling," I suggest. "That will make it easier to get back to it quickly." If you don't know what you know, you might as well not know it!

Previously, the class members had registered the number of breaths they took in one minute. After finishing the breathing floor exercise, while they were still lying down, I asked them to check the number of breaths they were now taking per minute. The number usually drops dramatically, often by as much as half!

If you practice this for a week, morning and evening, it will do three things for you. In the morning it will energize you, and at night it will relax you for a peaceful night's sleep. Third and best of all, your body will be relearning the abdominal breathing we all did as children and have since forgotten. (If there are any small children in your family, watch them when they're sleeping; you'll discover that their stomachs *naturally* move out and in as they breathe.)

Stage II, the Magic Breath—sitting erect in a straight chair—is comparable to the desktop computer; it's more compact than the floor model. Practice this stage twice a day (or more often if you can) for a week before going on to Stage III. The main difference here is that *you*, not the floor, have to keep your spine straight.

Stage III of the Magic Breath (which is also called "the Seven-One Magic Breath") is as miniaturized as the microchip. It's invisible, can be done anywhere, and nobody knows you're doing it! It can keep you calm, alert, relaxed, intuitive, and quasi-telepathic in all situations. Even more important, this truly magic formula will make it possible for you to improvise without any preparation: the right words will spring to your lips and surprise you!

If you want this technique to be available when you need it, you have to *practice it when you don't need it.* Think about this practice constantly, and do it not only when you're alone but also when you're with people (whenever you're not actually speaking), and it will reward you by becoming semiautomatic. The Seven-One Magic Breath is also a noninvasive way of calming hostile vibrations. And nobody knows you're doing anything! One man reported that by using the Seven-One Magic Breath he believed he had actually stopped a fight between a couple of teenagers in the subway—*without saying a word.*

Note that it's important to do the three stages of the Magic Breath sequence in order. Go to Stage II only after you've completely mastered Stage I, even if it takes more than a week (it probably won't if you practice it faithfully twice every day). When you're up to the chair breathing of Stage II, you can still do the floor breathing of Stage I whenever you need the deepest relaxation.

You can practice Stage II anywhere—office, restaurant, home, car, bus, even on the subway. Since an erect spine is a crucial component of the Magic Breath at Stage II, both your posture and your charisma will automatically benefit. Nobody can sound or look charismatic with a crumpled spine—it telegraphs shame, discouragement, and defeat.

At first you may have to remind yourself to straighten up and breathe from the gut, but soon it will become almost effortless. When your body and its new habits have been fully prepared by Stages I and II, you're ready for Stage III: the Seven-One. It will come easily at that point and actually be fun to practice. It's rather like having a secret toy that nobody else knows about!

Not only is the whole sequence essential for making the forgotten abdominal "child's" breathing once again an organic part of your everyday life, but later it will also provide the base for your true, best voice. Best of all, you gain tremendous confidence because you know you can always count on yourself, no matter what else is happening.

How Imagery Can Help

Even old patterns are usually backed by a subconscious picture. When I ask people in my Charismedia groups how they visualize breathing, most people smile and wave airily up and down the length of their bodies. A few suggest hesitantly that the movement of air is spherical, but they usually only know this intellectually and can't put it into practice. When you ask a group to take a deep breath, you see shoulders go up, stomachs pulled in, and chests thrust out with convulsive gasps. Then looks of apology appear, because people clearly can't go on doing that—it's too exhausting!

When people change their images, the body-mind instantly internalizes all the information necessary and integrates it into a new process. If you tried to describe it in words, it would take pages and pages and still be hard to follow. The great advantage of learning from an image (right hemisphere) instead of a linear, verbal description (left hemisphere) is speed. Information is compressed into an immediate image, which then breaks up into components that can be recalled and reassembled where and when they're needed.

Think how difficult it would be to give a linear description of even such simple actions as walking or lifting a finger. I once spent two hours watching a swan on the lake in Central Park to see if I could predict the exact curve of its neck as it slowly, again and again lifted it out of the water. That non-linear movement was so varied and subtle, slow-motion photography would probably show it was never exactly the same twice.

Breath Balloon

A slight detour is in order here. The best way to discover how we're really meant to breathe is to lie on the floor on your back (on either a rug, carpet, or padding), with your hands at your sides. If there is a hollow between the middle of your back and the floor, raise your knees until your back is flat on the floor along its whole length. Put a small cushion under your head if you're more comfortable that way. Now you're almost ready to start the Breath Balloon.

Imagine that your entire torso, from the shoulders to the groin, is a beautiful balloon in your favorite color. You are going to *breathe from the tiny opening—the mouth of the balloon—*located in the genitals! Be prepared to feel your abdomen and sides swell evenly all around, exactly like a balloon. Now put one hand low down on your abdomen (just above the groin) so you can feel and see it slowly expand as you inhale, starting from

the small, secret source, the mouth of the balloon, and moving slowly and evenly upward and all around. Since the mind can process millions of images in a microsecond, this single image of your favorite-colored balloon will be the perfect wordless teacher for your new breathing process.

Visualize your Breath Balloon as exactly and vividly as possible, noticing how it gets lighter as it expands slowly upward—and darker as you exhale, your ribs contracting like the staves of a rubber barrel. If you visualize it as exactly and vividly as you can, you'll be able to get a uniform swelling of the whole area from the groin to the lower ribs—front, sides, and back—in the most unforced and organic way. Then allow the top part of the balloon to expand your ribs and upper back as well, feeling the breath push against the floor. (Important—do *not* start the breath up there. If you do, you will have bypassed the abdominal breathing and wound up with the same old, ineffectual, shallow chest breathing that only uses one-third of your lung capacity. And that kind of breath is all over before it can do you any good.)

But first—**before starting your new breathing, empty the balloon!**

Most people never fully exhale. So many toxins are left stored in the body that there isn't enough room for new breathing energy to come in, not to mention the residual tension that remains in the muscles if they're not "vacuumed" by breath. So now take **three giant, garbage-out breaths!**

Inhale as powerfully as you can all the way up to your shoulders; hold the inhalation a few moments, tensing everything as much as you can. Then release all the breath and tension with a nice, loud *groan of relief.* Don't be polite! The more noise you make with this, the better.

Do this three times. Imagine you are releasing not just today's tension, but yesterday's, last month's, and last year's, your whole life's! Make each one a fuller and more total release than the one before.

Stay empty a few moments. Then begin filling the balloon *from the bottom*—the beginning of the inhale should be almost imperceptible.

The most common mistake people make is rushing convulsively, as though they won't have room or time to get enough air. Make the beginning of the breath the smallest, quietest, and smoothest you possibly can. Keep seeing your beautiful balloon—watch it expand luxuriously and then slowly deflate.

Buddha Belly

I have a little jade statue of a laughing Buddha with a round belly. I ask my students to run their hands over it, because it helps them get the feeling of the swelling breath and makes it easier for them to internalize it in their own bodies. You needn't be afraid you'll have a fat belly though—just the opposite!

Now you're ready, at last, for the Magic Breath. Keeping the image of your favorite-color Breath Balloon, we begin. You're lying down . . .

The Magic Breath—Stage I

1. Lying on the floor, exhale completely—all the way down to the groin. Stay empty a few seconds.

2. With your mouth closed, begin a very slow, even, and continuous inhalation, counting to eight in about eight seconds. Inflate evenly and smoothly from the base of your groin, air coming in from the genitals. (This will relax them—a good deal of tension is often held there.) When the balloon is fully expanded,

3. Hold the breath for a count of four. (If your shoulders have risen, relax them now. If you have high blood pressure, skip the holding part for the entire exercise.)

4. Exhale with a slight hiss (as small and steady as a whistling teakettle) for sixteen slow, even counts. If you run out of breath before the end, you've probably let out too much at the beginning. Finish completely by sixteen.

5. Repeat the whole pattern once more:

   • Inhale—eight counts (mouth closed)

   • Hold breath—four counts

   • Exhale (on hiss)—sixteen counts

   Next, increase the count:

   • Inhale—ten counts

   • Hold—five counts

   • Exhale—twenty counts

   Do each pattern twice.

Continue in this pattern, as shown in the chart below. After a repeat, the inhalation is increased by two, held for half the count, and then doubled for the exhalation.

Breathe In	Hold	Exhale	Do
	Counts		
8	4	16	Twice
10	5	20	Twice
12	6	24	Twice
14	7	28	Twice
16	8	32	Twice
18	9	36	Twice
20	10	40	Twice

Your vital capacity will increase each time you do the exercise.

Like honey, which can either tranquilize or energize, the Magic Breath will supply whatever your body needs most—relaxation (before sleep) or quickened energy (in the morning).

(My *Magic of Breathing* tapes will help you practice this exercise on your own, or you can make a tape yourself.)

The Magic Breath—Stage II

Sit tall in a straight-backed chair, with your back pressed against the chair. It's helpful to check this out in a mirror to make sure you maintain the posture, with tranquil shoulders and chest held high at all times.

Pump the stomach in and out a few times. Exhale, stay empty a moment, and begin to inhale slowly, starting with eight counts (as in the Stage I sequence).

Keep your shoulders relaxed and the chest as stable and high at all times as they are at the end of the inhalation. This teaches the body how to isolate the shoulders—which tend to rise and try to get into the act—from the lower abdomen and diaphragm. The beauty of this control is that it's invisible! You can practice in a crowded room or business meeting or at a party, and nobody will know you're doing anything special.

Each time you inhale, imagine vital energy (what the Chinese call *chi*) entering your body and circulating through every cell and the entire system. Like the Indian *prana*, *chi* isn't chemical but spiritual, the elemental life force of the universe. You can store up this energy with each breath you take, and it will give you increased vitality, radiance, and composure—all vital elements of your charisma.

Just as we are sensitive to people's voices, we are also unconsciously responsive to their breathing patterns. We say things like "Oh, he's so tense" or "She's so easy to be with." The emotional response to life that we are sensing is expressed through people's breathing patterns, though we seldom realize it.

You may discover that it's difficult to take a really full, complete breath. Some people who have a rigid self-image find it difficult to exhale fully. They're afraid to let go and express their real feelings. (For learning to let go, the anger exercises, the Karate Chop, the Ape, the Great Wow!, and the Butterflies Chaser help release feelings safely—and "juice up" the whole organism!)

One psychiatrist felt panic the first time he practiced the first stage of the Magic Breath. "It really made me aware of my mortality," he observed. But after doing Stage I for a week, he felt a depth of calm and confidence he had never experienced before.

When you start practicing these rhythmic patterns, you'll find they have a profound effect on your confidence and well-being. In the sixth century B.C., Lao-tzu wrote, "The land that is nowhere, that is the true home," beautifully describing the calm that this anxiety-reducing breathing produces.

Since anxiety is behind all addiction, it's not surprising that many people give up smoking spontaneously after practicing the Magic Breath. The need to smoke is partly a need for more breath (which relieves the underlying anxiety). Because you get smoke each time you puff, instead of breath, you must come back for more. Addiction is a raging desire that can never be satisfied. You can never get enough of what you don't really need.

When you begin to breathe in this new profound way, you may find that for the first time, you're getting what you need and crave and can at last become a nonsmoker.

If you fly off the handle or burst into tears more than you like, you'll notice after practicing Stages I and II of the Magic Breath that you're able to control your temper and emotions more easily. People who lack confidence become more self-assertive and sure of themselves. People who don't listen, or who can't concentrate, begin to be able to pay attention.

The Magic Breath—Stage III (Also Called the Seven-One Magic Breath)

This is the remarkable payoff for all your efforts with Stages I and II. Start by sitting in a straight-backed chair (as in Stage II).

1. Inhale from the lower abdomen, of course, to a slow count of seven.

2. Hold for one count, making sure the shoulders are relaxed and the chest is high, as you did before.

3. Exhale to a slow, even count of seven. At first, do this with the same small, steady hiss as you did in Stages I and II, with your lips slightly parted. After the first ten sequences, you will be able to "miniaturize" further: while counting, with your mouth closed, make small unvoiced "hm" or "furnace" sounds inside your throat that only you can hear.

4. Keep repeating this pattern.

This remarkable exercise will keep you alert, relaxed, and quick-witted. The seven-one ratio is a profound one—it echoes cosmic ratios, such as the height of an ocean wave to the breadth of the wave, the relation of the head to the body, and the rotation of the earth's ionospheric cavity at approximately 7.1 or 7.2 hertz per minute.

When you breathe seven breaths a minute you are in synch with the rotation of the Earth and, therefore, in "tune." This enables you to react instinctively and accurately in any situation; you "pick up" information without knowing quite how, which can be quasi-telepathic.

In a large corporate workshop, after we'd been doing the Seven-One Magic Breath, one man suddenly asked, "Is somebody here thinking about cashing a check?" On the other side of the room, a woman gasped, "Yes, I was! How did you know?"

It guarantees you'll be able to ad-lib just the right remark when someone throws you a curve. At a press conference, when the head of a large auction house was asked whether he was disappointed at the failure of its first sale of computers, he paused, breathed, smiled, and retorted, "Not at all. It takes a lot of runway to get the plane into the air!"

When heiress-socialite and etiquette authority Charlotte Ford was introduced to a distinguished literary audience as the "*son* of Henry Ford," she strode to the microphone and without a moment's hesitation quipped, "Thank God I wore my pantsuit today!" The audience roared and applauded. Later she told me, "Thank God I was doing the Seven-One while waiting to be introduced—otherwise I would have frozen!"

Controlling your breathing gives you access to expanded aspects of your own personality. Your "witness" consciousness begins to operate. You become more objective, and once that happens you never feel as helpless and out of control again, even when you experience negative emotions. When I first discovered this, I was very excited—I thought I had invented it! Then I found out it's some five thousand years old, an ancient Buddhist meditation called *Vipassana*.

Lauren M. said in a Charismedia workshop, "I have to tell you what an amazing change the breathing has brought about for me. I've been married about two years, and I've always been terribly jealous. I kept imagining what would happen if I found my husband with somebody else. I thought I'd kill him and then I'd probably die too. Well, last week, the worst happened. He didn't come home, and I found out he'd been with another woman. Then a funny thing occurred. I'd been practicing the breathing, and I did the Emotion Cooler (see page 110) and the Magic Breath when I spoke to him on the phone. Ordinarily I'd have ranted and raved, but I found myself talking to him very calmly. I asked him when he was going to be home so we could talk. I think he was surprised I was so collected. Well, he came home, and I was still doing the breathing so I stayed calm. I never screamed or even cried or yelled. I'd thought I couldn't survive his infidelity. Now I found myself thinking, 'Gee, I wonder what he's like with this other woman? He must be a different person with her.' I was surprised to find I was interested and curious.

"Suddenly he seemed like an interesting stranger whom I didn't know very well. At the same time, I knew deep inside that I wasn't going to die of this, no matter what happened. I would be all right, even if he left me. Never, never could I have imagined thinking that way before! Well, he was so surprised at the calm way I acted that he began to talk to me; we talked all night. I think it's the best talk we ever had. I don't know what's going to happen, but I do know that whatever it is, it'll be all right.

"I feel something very important has happened to me—it's like I found myself as a person. I could even see things from his point of view and understand his feelings, without feeling mixed up and hurt and furious and wildly jealous the way I usually do. I feel very good about myself. It's like there's some new strong person inside me I didn't know was there, and I'm proud of the way I behaved. I see him looking at me differently, too. That's nice, but strangely enough, that's not the most important thing to me anymore."

The Nose Knows

If you're feeling angry, upset, tearful, anxious, irritable, or nervous, the Emotion Cooler (described later in this chapter), when you breathe only through the left nostril, will change and balance your emotions within less than five minutes. How can that be?

It's a little hard to believe that such a humble organ as the nose is intimately connected with profound complexities of human functioning. There is something faintly comic and ridiculous about the nose. Nonetheless, you may be surprised to learn that the nose performs close to thirty functions. It doesn't enjoy the dignity or respect of the eyes ("the windows of the soul") or the mouth. It can be a source of embarrassment because it's so subject to dripping, running, and reddening. People often are dissatisfied with the shape of their noses (which enriches plastic surgeons). An exposed and slightly shameful air hovers about the nose, implying that it's grateful to be admitted to polite company but may at any moment compromise its owner in some unexpected, indelicate, and socially or sexually unsuitable way. Moderate sneezing is acceptable, but blowing, picking, scratching, and fingering are distinctly out, sources of sudden disgrace. (In a hilarious episode of *Seinfeld*, Jerry delivers an impassioned parody of Shylock's speech from *The Merchant of Venice* because his model girlfriend wouldn't answer his phone calls after she'd caught him off guard in a supposed nose pick.) And then there are the indignities of smells (another favorite subject of *Seinfeld*).

What has this slightly ridiculous, ingeniously designed body part to do with your charisma?

The nose, humble though it is, is a powerful asset in your arsenal of resources for putting you at ease, keeping you well, and making the most of your powers, including your ability to achieve bio-rapport with others. *How* we breathe is important, since we breathe some eighteen thousand to twenty thousand times a day. The nose happens to be the narrowest place in the respiratory tract, yet it filters, moisturizes, directs airflow, conveys smells, warms incoming air, brings in oxygen, creates mucus, acts as a drainage passageway for the sinuses, and—most important—affects the nervous system. The constantly changing phenomenon of airflow is both a cause and a result of emotional, mental, and physiological states and functions.

We have both an internal and an external nose. There we're unique! The ape, for instance, has no external nose. The shape of our noses has a lot to do with what climate our forebears came from. People from cold climates or very dry ones, like the Middle East, are apt to have long noses. In the tropics the inhabitants have wide-open nostrils, since the air needs less processing. (For some inexplicable reason, however, a lot of Scandinavians have short noses.) The outside, or external, nose gathers the air and accelerates its flow into the cavity of the internal nose.

Inside, the nose is a complex, interesting place. Its "floor" is also the roof of the mouth—the palate. If you move your tongue backward, you find a place where suddenly the roof becomes softer. At the back of that spot is a little teardrop-shaped fleshy organ called the uvula. The roof of the nose is also the floor of the brain and the eyeball cavities, just the way the floor of the nose is the roof of the mouth. It's a kind of three-story house with the brain, eyes, and optic nerves on the top floor, the mouth on the bottom, and the nasal cavity in between.

The Nose, the Brain, and Your Nervous System

Few people realize how closely related the internal nose is to the brain, the nervous system, and the pituitary gland (on the floor of the brain). The cranial olfactory nerve has nerve endings in the upper part of the compartment. Inside the nose is a bumpy, lumpy terrain cleverly designed to move the air in certain directions. If you tilt your head and look in the mirror, you can see the turbinates, three shell-like bulges that stir and circulate the air and protect the sensitive tissues of the lungs, adding moisture and humidity. The turbinates baffle the air, stir it up, and indirectly cause our winter-drippy noses (as you exhale, the moisture in the warm air condenses on the outside). The mucous membrane also helps the inside of the nose cleanse itself—because it picks up dust and microbes and, since there's constant movement, carries the undesirable debris out. The "mucous blanket" (as it is called), with its millions of cilia (minute, hairlike structures), is a clever device to keep all the microbes moving, so they don't settle down and cause infection.

It's a brilliant system, but it doesn't always work. If the mucus is too thick, it dries out and forms a crust; if it's too runny, you get a watery nasal drip.

How What You Eat Affects the Nose

Your diet has a great deal to do with the texture and amount of mucus your nose produces. Milk products and citrus fruits like oranges, as well as sugary, starchy foods, produce a thicker mucus. The mucus is not only a secretion to protect our lungs but also an excretion, when the other excretory organs (lungs, skin, bowels, liver, kidneys, and uterus) can't rid the body of accumulated waste. Everything is connected! Processed foods clog the digestive system, antiperspirants prevent the skin from taking its share of excretory functions, and lack of fiber causes constipation. The systems back up. The body responds to overeating, a poor diet, or constipation by discharging greater quantities of mucus. Behold! A cold!

What to Do

Eating only greens for a day or two, cutting out meat and dairy products, taking a laxative, drinking a teaspoon of apple cider vinegar in water several times a day—these are quick ways to restore the body's alkaline balance and avoid the decline into colds and respiratory infections. (Tincture of echinacea helps boost your immune system, too.)

Most organs echo others in the body. The curve of the pelvis is repeated in the palm, the ear, and the hollow in the throat below the Adam's apple. The hands and feet are related, too: through reflexology, pressure on sensitive points on both can relieve organs all over the body.

Sex and the Nose

The nose, interestingly, is related to the sex organs. Underneath the mucous membrane is a spongy layer of erectile tissue, also found in the genitals and breasts. Freud wrote about the interaction between the sex organs and the nose. Originally, he developed his basic theory through correspondence with the ear, nose, and throat specialist Wilhelm Fliess. Both men were interested in the reflexes that link the nasal lining and reproductive organs. They thought they could "cure" menstrual cramps by anesthetizing certain parts of the lining of a woman's nose.

Speaking of synchrony, an interesting phenomenon called "honeymoon nose" is familiar to ear, nose, and throat specialists. Continual sexual stimulation during the honeymoon causes the erectile tissue of the nose to become chronically engorged—like aroused genitals!

Nostril Dominance and the Brain

The links with the brain are also profound. Usually air flows through first the right, then the left nostril, alternating every ninety minutes to two hours. This is a natural biological rhythm, named "infradian rhythm" by Western scientists who "discovered" what the ancient yogis knew thousands of years ago. Certain activities are more appropriate for right-nostril flow, others for left.

Research has shown that nostril dominance cross-correlates with whichever brain hemisphere is more active. In other words, if you're breathing predominantly through the left nostril, the right hemisphere—involving emotions, images, and musical memory—is more active, and if you're breathing through the right nostril, it's your left hemisphere—the rational, logical, linguistic, and verbal part—that's most involved.

Physiological and psychological states are reflected in nostril dominance. By controlling which nostril is functioning, it's possible to "tune" to the activity you're involved in. For instance, before eating, the right nostril should be open; before drinking water, the left. Breathing through the left nostril generally connects with the right (or "emotional") side of the brain and produces a quiet, more inner-directed state.

Cosmic Cycles and the Breath

The cycle of breath alternation follows the cycle of the moon. At dawn there is a natural polarity of breath, depending on whether solar or lunar energy is dominant. The new moon initiates a left-nostril cycle, the full moon a right-nostril one. Solar energy is more constant; it's never altogether absent during the day, and its cycle lasts a year. The moon, of course, waxes and wanes regularly, and its 29½-day cycle governs the ocean's tides.

The moon also affects people profoundly, since about 70 percent of human body weight is water. The night of the full moon traditionally causes a kind of madness: dogs bay, people go haywire; these are times of high tides. In the darkest night, when the tides are at their lowest ebb, human emotional power is also at its weakest.

Swar (breath) yoga details the best activities for whichever nostril is dominant. There's no need to worry if the wrong nostril is clear. You can tell what side is dominant by closing off one side with one finger and seeing if the air flow is cooler there than on the other side or the other way around. After some practice, you can check this out even without closing off one nostril as you become more aware of the subtleties of breath flow.

How to Change Nostril Dominance

There are several ways to change the airflow from one side to the other, if you want to. If you lie on your left side, the right nostril will open. The pressure on the arm and side of your chest sets up a reflex that automatically dilates the open nostril and closes off the other one. This can take from three to ten minutes. (Putting your fist in your armpit will give the same result!)

After meals, lie on the left to stimulate the digestive process with the open right nostril. When you go to bed, if you lie on the left side for five or ten minutes, the opened right nostril will create increased body heat. When you're warm and comfortable, turn to the right; that lets the left nostril open. Then you're relaxed, calmed, and ready for sleep.

Sometimes air will flow equally through both nostrils, but if one side is closed for as much as six to eight hours, some illness is on the way. The breath is related to the flow of energy (*prana* or *chi*); imbalance always precedes the appearance of disease symptoms.

The *Swar* yoga calendar precisely correlates nostril dominance with many activities and aspects of human existence. Great importance is given to living in harmony with natural cycles. That means getting up at least twenty minutes before sunrise every morning to prepare for the day, to be cleansed and sit quietly. At yoga ashrams, or spiritual communities, everybody gets up at 3:30 A.M. for a two-hour stint of chanting, exercise, and meditation. Many people in the West practice these disciplines before going off to their work as lawyers, teachers, or whatever.

If, when you wake up, the wrong nostril is dominant, change it right away; otherwise, the day may be negative and present obstacles. All this develops a much greater sensitivity to subtle cues of body, mind, and feeling, plus a host of practical strategies to cope with imbalances that arise.

Swar Calendar

Right-Nostril Breathing	Left-Nostril Breathing
Left hemisphere dominant	Right hemisphere dominant
Sun	Moon
Electrical	Magnetic
Acidic	Alkaline
Hot	Cold
Operates after sunset	Operates after sunrise
Operates for one hour after sunrise following full moons	Operates for one hour after sunrise following the darkest night or new moon
Descending moon cycle	Ascending moon cycle
Fire	Water
Air	Earth
Sunday—east	Wednesday—west
Saturday—north	Thursday—south
Tuesday	Friday, Monday
Unstable short-term jobs for immediate profit	Peaceful, long-term activities not for immediate gain
Eating, sleeping, defecating	Drinking, urinating
Bathing, studying	Playing music
Hatha Yoga	Getting married
Mantra chanting	Healing pain or depression

Both Nostrils Operating at Once
Hemispheres in equilibrium
Operates exactly at sunrise and sunset
Operates briefly during the hourly transition from one nostril to the other
Ether
Concentration
Meditation
Worship

Good Morning!

One of the most pleasant pieces of advice emerging from this ancient tradition is this: when you wake up in the morning, notice which nostril is open, then kiss the corresponding palm and stre-e-e-tch. Then give thanks for the day and step out of bed on, of course, the corresponding foot. (A gentle saltwater nostril wash clears any mucus from the nose and leaves you feeling clearheaded and wide awake.)

The constantly changing patterns of airflow are "apparently like a central clearinghouse, or switchboard, where all the body's functions are having an effect, and in turn being affected," write Rudolph Ballentine, M.D., and Swami Rama in *Science of Breath*. "The flow of air touching the surface of various areas of the turbinates triggers neuronal responses that set up reflexes throughout the body. In other words, a specific current of air sends out ripples into both the lungs and the nervous system that affect the whole person."

The Emotion Cooler (or Left-Nostril Breathing)

Now that you understand how open or closed nostrils can impact the brain and emotions, here is the amazing, indispensable Emotion Cooler. When you breathe solely through the left nostril, as in this exercise, you are clearing the right brain, where emotions and images are located.

1. Put your right thumb on your right nostril, lightly closing it off. You are going to breathe only through the left nostril.

2. Exhale a long, slow, even breath visualizing it as a black cloud full of all the anger, tension, and other negative emotions you are feeling.

3. Inhale a long, slow breath through your left nostril, visualizing it as golden light and going up your nasal passage and across the corpus callosum to the right hemisphere of your brain, filling it with pure, radiant energy.

4. Continue to inhale and exhale for twenty-six complete breaths.

   • Make them as long, smooth, and even as possible.

   • If there is any obstruction in your nasal passage, imagine a tiny stream of air bypassing the blockage and making its way smoothly up into the right hemisphere.

   • With each exhalation, release all the tension, anger, annoyance, hurt, or other negative emotions you are feeling; visualize them all draining out of your body, emptying from every pore. Each time you exhale, let go of more—not just what happened today, but last week, last year, and all of your life, until you are completely released and clear.

   • Stay empty for a second or two at the end of each exhalation before you begin the next inhalation. Enjoy the increasing relaxation of your whole body and mind.

   • The black stream of your exhalations may gradually grow lighter until, at the end of the twenty-six breaths, both the inhale and the exhale are pure white light.

Allen S., a sales executive, reported, "I often have difficult phone calls to make. One client, particularly, has a tendency to get abusive over the phone. Now when he screams and yells, I do the Emotion Cooler, and I find he doesn't 'get to me.' I just let him rave on—without saying a word—and instead concentrated on exhaling what I was hearing, so it wouldn't affect me. After a few minutes he must have sensed something, because he stopped, suddenly calmed down, and began to talk in a normal, reasonable voice."

Elizabeth R., a high school teacher, told us, "One day I had an unpleasant argument with one of the students who got very rude and insolent. To my horror, I realized I was on the verge of tears. To cry at that moment would have been disastrous. I excused myself and went to the ladies' room to do the Emotion Cooler. In a few minutes, I was not only perfectly calm, but I knew exactly what to do and how to discipline that student effectively. If I hadn't done the Emotion Cooler, I'd have lost my authority entirely, and I couldn't have pulled myself together as I did."

A student, Beryl S., who had never got along well with her father, reported that now when she speaks to him on the phone, she keeps her thumb on her right nostril the whole time, breathing only through the left. "The first time I tried it, I had the first conversation with Dad since I moved away from home when I didn't either fight with him or cry. Suddenly I realized that he was unhappy, too, and I could just listen without getting defensive."

Here's a tip for quick energy: reverse the nostrils, that is, close off the left one with your left thumb. This brings you energy through the right nostril (affecting the *left* hemisphere of the brain). Exhale and inhale twenty-six times.

Just as some people find it harder to take attention than to give it, some express through their shallow breathing the difficulties they have in asserting themselves. They lack the basic confidence to take a deep breath and dare to live fully. It doesn't seem to matter whether you start from the inside or out. In fact, it's easier for many people to start with the breathing—the subsequent opening up that begins to happen is effortless and remarkable. The quality of life changes.

There is a Chinese saying, "He who masters breathing can walk on the sand without leaving footprints."

Suddenly a woman decides to go into business for herself, something she's always wanted to do but didn't have the courage to attempt. A young man who worked in a bank and hated it leaves to become a journalist. A pianist who had always been shy dares to form his own orchestra; he is even asked to head the jazz department of the university where he'd been teaching. He also began to give TV lectures. People change careers and directions, take off forty pounds, begin to find themselves in new, expanded lives—basically because the breathing put them in touch with their own gifts, their own charisma. Then they were able, often for the first time, to go out and express it in their own lives.

Meditation Is a Natural Resource

Having deeply relieved the body and mind of stress (de-stressed it) through breathing, it's only a short step to meditation. People begin to fall into meditation naturally, in fact, when they do the Magic Breath. The two are closely related.

"Say, this feels familiar somehow," an individual will say. "I used to be in this state pretty often when I was a kid."

It's a good feeling. Everybody has had moments of "flow"—complete absorption in something beautiful—music, a landscape, sailing, lovemaking. This selfless involvement is almost dreamlike; we soon realize that our most creative impulses come from that mysterious place just beyond waking consciousness.

Who Needs It?

Given the inroads of stress, we probably all do!

Since we are so result-oriented, we all need a mode of trusting our subconscious to come up with magical solutions, new perceptions, and an unprogrammed processing of the problems in our lives.

The remarkable thing about the nervous system is its natural tendency to evolve. Given half a chance, the nervous system takes precisely what it most needs from meditation. People who need stimulation become more lively. Those who are too "hyper" become calmer. This effect all happens without your doing anything at all except allowing yourself to be "empty" (which I grant you is very difficult).

Mantras and How to Use Them

There are many different mantras ("mind control"). Transcendental meditation (TM), one of the most effective forms for reducing stress, assigns mantras by age and sex. Masters like Yogananda usually prefer one or two. I will use *Ram* as an example, pronounced with a rolled *r* and the *ah* as in *far*. (This is particularly good for confidence.) The Sanskrit letters contain special qualities that produce specific effects on the body. Your mantra should be exclusively associated with your private meditation, so it's best not to talk about your mantra with anyone. Then the deep rest you experience can be transferred to your day. It's like a still pool of clear water that you dip into whenever you need to, that gives you calm and peace in the midst of turmoil. If you prefer, you might use *so ham* (so hum) or *sat nam* (sät näm)—truth, essence. *Once you choose your mantra, stick with it.*

Meditate twice a day, before breakfast and late in the afternoon (when you generally feel a drop in energy). Some people meditate before going to sleep, but you may find it keeps you awake—usually meditating will give you energy, and a regular meditator not only needs less sleep but also is, on average, twelve years younger physiologically than nonmeditators of the same age.

Prepare by breathing ten breaths as slowly as possible. Or do alternate-nostril breathing. Clear your nose by taking a deep breath and holding it as long as you can (usually, two or three of these will clear your nose completely). If you're feeling particularly distracted or jumpy, either jog or do the active stage-fright exercises (see chapter 10) for five or ten minutes—when your body's tired, your mind will relax and let go more easily.

Turn off the phone and make sure you won't be disturbed for the next twenty minutes. Close the door. Loosen any tight clothing. Try this process.

1. Sit motionless, with a straight back and the feet on the floor or cross-legged. Keep a watch or clock where you can see it.

2. Place the hands on your knees, palms upward, the thumb and second finger touching lightly. (Don't worry if they fall open later.)

3. Close your eyes and roll upward to the "third eye" (between your eyebrows) or crown center.

4. Begin to say "*Rr-ahhhh-mmm, Rr-ahhhmmm, Rr-ahhhh-mmmm.*" Feel the vibration throughout your body. Say the mantra at least ten times.

5. Whisper the mantra ten to twenty times.

6. Go to silence, repeating it mentally.

7. When a thought crosses your mind, just notice it, without being annoyed at yourself and getting "off the track." Go back to repeating the mantra. Each time you find your mind wandering, observe it and gently return to *Rahmm*.

8. Sit for twenty minutes. Open your eyes to check the time; if it isn't time, close them again and return to the mantra. If you feel impatient, that's when you need the meditation most!

9. You may feel lightness or as though your body has disappeared. You may be aware of a sudden pain here or there or an itch. Remain as still as you can. Meditation puts you in touch with what your body is really experiencing. Each time will be different. Don't look for any special results. The most important thing is to do it faithfully every day.

10. When the time is up, sit a moment and enjoy the peace you feel. Never rush right out of a meditation; that shocks the nervous system. You have been in a deep state of awareness, even though you may feel you were on the verge of sleep and sometimes had no thoughts (that's the deepest rest of all). If at the end of the meditation you feel tired, that shows that your body and mind were really exhausted. Lie down for five or ten minutes, and you'll be completely refreshed. Usually the meditation will give you fresh energy. If you have a performance or a crisis or can't sleep, do an extra meditation.

11. Begin to whisper the mantra, then say it aloud as you did at the beginning.

12. Rub your hands together gently and stroke your face upward. Sit a few moments to allow your system to get used to waking consciousness

again. Observe how the room looks to you now. Brighter? Sharper? More detail? You've just cleansed your perceptual motor system!

Find a time when you can meditate every day; make it part of your routine. It takes forty days for a lasting change of consciousness to take place.

Playwright John L. was en route to Florida when he saw a bad review of his new play, which had just opened. He laughed ruefully when he told us, "I began to meditate on the plane. By the time I got there, I had distanced it enough so the terrible notice didn't bother me. It was very different from trying to tell myself that I didn't care. I really *didn't* care!" Studies show that meditators are able to recover from shocks faster and more easily than nonmeditators.

Louise R., a retired fashion executive, asked if she could tell the class her experience with meditation. "I used to be married to a very difficult man," she began. "Last time I went to see him in New York, I was so nervous that I fell out of the cab and broke my wrist. This time I prepared for days by doing the breathing and meditation. Well, I can't believe how calm I was. He never got my goat once! In fact he didn't want me to leave. We had a very pleasant dinner. At one point I thought, 'Oh, my goodness, I have no lipstick left,' and then I thought, 'That's all right. You're fine just as you are.' And I really felt that. Normally it would have bothered me a lot not to look my best. But the whole quality of the evening changed. In fact, even when we were married, we never had such a pleasant time."

The idea is to gradually become so calm and compassionate that there is no difference between meditation and nonmeditation. You will find your intuition and creativity greatly enhanced. "I get some of my best ideas when I'm meditating," Paul, a TV executive, remarked.

When the mind is unstressed, the larger possibilities that were hidden from you earlier suddenly emerge—without effort.

Sometimes other people notice the effect on you before you do yourself. Generally, however, there are small but dramatic changes in perception and the quality of your life. It may happen immediately; sometimes it takes a while. Everyone reacts differently. There is no question that you will find relaxation, peace of mind, and interesting experiences at the "still point of the turning world."

Think Pink

The Rosicrucians, whose metaphysical knowledge is one of the oldest traditions in the West, have given us their knowledge of using "color breathing" for healing. The power of thought to change matter, to heal and rejuvenate, is very real.

If someone you know is having emotional problems that are causing illness, visualize a pink or rosy pink color surrounding him or her. It's good to do this when you think the person is asleep, although they don't have to be in the same place or even the same country to feel your healing thought. First meditate to clear your own consciousness, then visualize the person you want to help, sending a feeling of love to surround him, using the most appropriate color.

When the illness is not emotional but physically debilitating, visualize a bright orange color. Many people use color breathing every day for health and healing. Carrie S. wraps herself mentally from head to foot with a spiral rainbow before she leaves her house in the morning. Everywhere she goes, people are extremely friendly. The rainbow, she says, attracts people!

Others use color breathing to protect themselves from the energy drainage of city crowds. See yourself surrounded by white light—I have done this walking down a dark street late at night. Even those who can't see auras somehow sense this field and respect it.

Heal Yourself Before You Can Heal Other People

Meditation and the Anger Transformer exercise (see chapter 11, page 242) will help ease afflictive emotion. If you find it hard to forgive someone, *ask to be released from your resentment.* Breathe in your unhappiness fully, then exhale all the joy you can remember.

This is an ancient and profound Buddhist practice called *TongLen*—which in Tibetan means "giving and receiving." It sounds paradoxical, but it really works. It's training in opening the heart—the most powerful, healing thing we can do for ourselves and others. In this practice, instead of exhaling the negative, and taking in positive feelings, you do the opposite.

Facing your unpleasant feelings with honesty ("I really hate that person!" or "That sick old drunk disgusts me!") and without self-hatred ("I'm an awful person if I feel this way!") helps develop compassion—first for onself and then for every other suffering human being. This is how it works. (The first two steps prepare you.)

1. First, when you become aware you're feeling anger, pain, hatred, aversion, or any negative emotion, see yourself on a mountaintop, breathing in pure mountain air in long, slow, even breaths, with a vast, peaceful panorama all around.

2. Let go of the blaming or hurtful words, thoughts, and judgments ("I hate him!" or "Why did she do that to me?" etc.), and concentrate on the sheer energy of the feelings in your body.

3. Now bre-e-e-athe in slowly—inhale all your unhappiness, pain, or misery on one long, slow deep breath, and *at the same time, think of all the other people in the world who are also suffering from these feelings right now.* Wish that you could help them and yourself. Realize that we're all human, nobody's exempt, and we all suffer from painful emotions.

4. Then exhale, bre-e-e-athe out, in just as long, slow, and continuous an out breath, sending out relief, spaciousness, and happiness, and showering all the pleasant and joyful experiences you can remember on yourself and everybody else in the world who is suffering just as you are.

5. Keep this up for at least ten breaths or as long as you need to. Within five breaths, you should feel a surprising relief.

If it's too intense or difficult, find something less challenging—where the heart is open—like thinking of a dog you love. As the wise American Buddhist nun Pema Chodron tells us, "The circle of your compassion will widen, and four months from today, you'll be able to deal with something that is too painful now. Compassion begins to develop through *maitri*—respect for and honesty with oneself."

The more compassion grows, first for ourselves and then for all the other suffering people in the world, the more we are able to deal with challenging situations without, as Pema Chodron says, "throwing up, breaking down, having a heart attack, or flying into a rage!"

Imagine doing *TongLen* in a traffic jam! Your compassion will grow for every other poor soul who is feeling exactly as edgy, furious, angry, and stressed as you are. If everybody practiced *TongLen*, the traffic accident rate would drop dramatically!

The long, slow breathing alone helps calm us, and the powerful added intention of having the courage to face the pain of our feelings, recognizing that millions of people share these, then wanting to shower joy, peace, pleasure, and spaciousness on ourselves and every other person is the most healing thing we can do for ourselves and others. If at first you can't let go of your angry feelings, just forgive yourself and say, "As I breathe in I wish that I and others could be free of pain, and as I breathe out, I'd like to send out relief." Pretty soon, you'll actually be able to. When you're free of your own anger and pain, you can surround yourself and the person you were angry at with a generous gift of warm, golden light, see him or her as happy, smiling, and content. The next time you meet, you may find the rift between you has been healed.

Not only does letting go of our anger and negative emotions make us happier and more generous human beings, but it can actually help us reverse the aging process. People used to say, "When you're twenty you have the face God gave you, when you're forty you have the face life gave you, and when you're sixty you have the face you deserve!" Of course plastic surgery has given all of us new options to look good as we get older, but if you habitually scowl or knit your brows in worry or have a sour expression, the lines of anger and negativity etch themselves deep in your face. "It's not sex that's the little death," remarked Brian Lang, "but anger." He's right!

The chronically angry are also more susceptible to atherosclerosis (as content-filtered voice tests have demonstrated). Meditators, who in a deep state of relaxation often find themselves gently smiling, are physiologically twelve years younger than nonmeditating contemporaries.

Kirlian photography has actually photographed auras in color, and Yvonne Gary of Indiana has developed a system of *color breathing* to restore youthfulness with some success. Try it and see how it works for you.

1. Start by breathing very deeply and clearing your mind.

2. Choose an area to work on, perhaps the bags under the eyes. Spread them smooth, seeing yourself without them.

3. Breathe in pink air (or a color you really like).

4. Hold your breath and visualize the skin smooth and unwrinkled.

5. Exhale slowly. Repeat the breath and visualization twice more.

6. Now take another area and do three breaths there.

7. Do it in the morning, when you wake, and just before going to sleep at night.

It took Yvonne eight months to accomplish her objective, but it was worth it. Her wrinkles and bags disappeared; her vitality and general health improved steadily.

The desire to heal, to send love, is powerful. If your intention is powerful, it will transcend space and time. Expanding your charisma with breathing and loving emanations will draw a responsive resonance from the world around you.

It cannot be faked. When your charisma and loving intention are there, people feel that and respond intuitively. You have the light within. See it pouring down on you, limitless and golden. *Become the light:*

> *When the heart is light, the breathing*
> *is light, for every movement of the breath*
> *affects the heart. . . . In order to steady the*
> *heart, one begins by cultivating the breathing*
> *power. The heart cannot be influenced directly.*
> *Therefore breathing power is used as a*
> *handle, and this is what is called protecting*
> *the collected breathing power.*
> —Lao-tzu

7

Anger—Fire in Your Boiler Room

Anger is a vehement heat of the minde, which brings palenesse to the countenance, burning to the eyes, and trembling to the parts of the body.
—J. Smith, *Mystical Rhetoric*, 1657

Anger is a brief madness.
—Horace

Anger is one of the sinews of the soul; he that wants it hath a maimed mind.
—Thomas Fuller (1608–1661)

Anger makes dull men witty, but it keeps them poor.
—attributed by Sir Francis Bacon
to Queen Elizabeth I

What about your anger? Is there any value in it? How do you use it productively? How do you keep from hurting yourself and other people with it?

Everybody gets angry now and then, except perhaps some very advanced souls who have outgrown it. Often people were brought up with conflicting messages about anger. Mostly it's "If you get angry, you're bad." The unspoken part is "Only we parents can get angry—you children must not!" Other messages include "Anger means hatred," and "Anger means you don't love me."

My students tell me, "It's more manly to get angry than to cry and show I'm hurt," "When I get very angry, I burst into tears," "Anger is frightening. I'll do anything to avoid it," "When I get angry, watch out. I let it out on anybody and everybody around me. I have a short fuse, but that way I'll never get an ulcer."

Anger's two powerful components are information and energy. When people deny their anger because they don't approve of getting angry at all, they lose contact with the information as well as the energy. Depression often is anger turned inward. Depression is immobilizing, unproductive, and painful. Often people don't know why they're depressed because they have successfully hidden the messages in their anger, even from themselves.

Some people think "positive" thoughts on the conscious level, although underneath they are experiencing fear, anger, and conflict. Nobody is fooled except the person him- or herself.

Anna A. came into class one day after having been beaten by her husband. In a high, thin voice she said, "He can't help himself—but I'm not angry at him; I just want to help him." Her hands twisted a handkerchief, and her knuckles were white (as though she were wringing his neck), but she was unaware of her real feelings because she was determined to have only "positive" thoughts. Her anger was clear to everybody in the room, but her voice was flat, colorless, *unconvincing*.

Denying your true feelings robs you of your charisma. Your feelings, perceptions, and experience are the gifts that constitute the inner landscape of your soul. Real feelings, no matter how negative, are better than sham ones. If you think of emotions as clouds passing across the sky or waves across the sea, you can allow yourself to flow with the negative feelings so they can become new feelings that may be quite different.

If you're keeping your Anti-Judgmental Notebook, you'll be able to spot your anger and begin to observe it with detachment. ("Oh, I feel so angry! Isn't that interesting?") But if you're not going to deny it, what *do* you do with it? It's like a hand grenade that people toss gingerly from hand to hand until it explodes. Obviously that's not a satisfactory way of dealing with hand grenades or anger. Innocent people get blown away.

"Damn him, why does he treat me like this? I'm a person; can't he realize that?" "My wife is always cutting me down in public. I could kill her." "Man, you touch my things, and you won't know what hit you!"

Anger and hurt usually *want* something. Dissonance—as in music—yearns for resolution. Angry people often think they want revenge, but their real need is deeper—to protect or affirm their sense of dignity, self, or value as a person (or, with a social reformer, that of others). An angry person *can* be charismatic, if the level of intensity and emotional power meshes with others' needs.

Demagogues such as Hitler, Stalin, Napoleon, and Joseph McCarthy voiced the rage and fear of the masses they addressed. The "angry young man" of John Osborne's plays or the brooding intensity of James Dean and Marlon Brando touched some responsive chord in audiences for whom they personified larger-than-life feelings. Even now they exert an enduring fascination.

Anger can be a constructive spur to social and political reform and personal growth—if the energy is not short-circuited by fear. But if you don't examine your feelings, you may be completely in the dark as to what they really are.

Are You Running Your Anger or Is It Running You?

If you must get angry, make it a *conscious* decision on your part. Then, as the eminent yogi Shyam Bhatnagar says, "You will be *angry*, not *anger*." Words are potent weapons, so when you fight, avoid vicious, bitter remarks that may boomerang or scar people for life.

You can probably remember idle or deliberately cruel words that were once hurled at you and penetrated so deeply that you never forgot them. There is no way to take back or un-say, "You'll never amount to anything!" "You're stupid!" "You're ugly!" "I never loved you!" "I never wanted you—I wish you'd never been born!" or "Your sister doesn't do half as much for me as you do, but I love her more." Author-actor Malachy McCourt says, "Resentment is like taking poison and waiting for the other person to die!"

The desire to harm someone you're angry at eats you up inside. When you take responsibility for dealing with (and processing) your own anger, the desire for revenge will fade.

How to Lengthen a Short Fuse

Continual anger is an explosive turnoff. If you are always simmering or "on a short fuse," people may be afraid of you or avoid you.

"I haven't had any tantrums this week," reported Matt, very pleased with himself. "I did the long, deep breathing and did not explode once. That was a good feeling. Even though my life was not so great, I handled it very well. I felt power and control because I used my anger in a more productive way than usual. My nineteen-year-old son called long-distance to tell me he was thrown into the brig in the Marines. Instead of yelling at him, I was able to talk calmly to him. To my surprise he admitted he was at fault—something he's never done before. I could tell he respected me more because I didn't yell."

Some people constantly "blow up." Their rages are an attempt to prove to themselves that they're not weak and fearful. Underneath, they may really be terrified of losing love and respect or feel compelled to hang on to their anger, for fear of being left like a turtle without its shell, intolerably vulnerable. The yelling is a "Don't step on me" message that says, "I exist. I *have* to yell to prove it to myself and you."

"I don't get ulcers—I give them," declared one corporate giant proudly. Another successful but inwardly frightened businessman was extravagantly generous with his employees. He bought them all health-club memberships and raised their salaries far beyond the norm for the jobs, but periodically he raged irrationally at his colleagues and his children. People never knew what to expect from him. He could be charming, perceptive, and gentle one moment, a furious tyrant the next. Fiercely competitive, he needed to earn more and more to assure himself of his own worth. But no matter how much money he earned, he didn't feel safe.

Disproportionate anger in his case was actually (as it often is) a sign of inward panic, weakness, and fear, which he managed to disguise most of the time in frenzied activity. Some people, you'll have noticed, yell deliberately, as a strategy. It's one thing to decide to get angry, but quite another to find yourself out of control.

Are You on Anger Overload?

Signs:
1. Do you *have* to be right?
2. Do you find it difficult or impossible to apologize?
3. In an argument do you assume the worst of your opponent?
4. Do you blame others for your anger? ("Why does he [or she] always have to make me mad?")
5. Are you unwilling to accept others' explanations or apologies and get over your anger?
6. Do you find at least three to ten things a day make you angry?
7. Are you a grievance collector?

If there is a raging authority figure in your life, it may help to remember the next time he or she screams and yells that those may well be cries of pain and insecurity. ("If I don't yell, nobody will listen to me.") Real authority doesn't need to rant and rave to make itself felt.

John C., who came into the group to learn to communicate better, admitted that periodically he would get drunk, yell at his children, and furiously break everything in sight. "I don't know whether I drink because I'm angry or whether I get angry because I drink," he said sheepishly.

I asked him to keep an Anti-Judgmental Notebook and for a week to put down all his feelings whenever he became aware of them. At the end of the week, he realized with amazement that what he was feeling most of the time was not anger but fear. Once he had discovered this, he no longer had to drink and break things. He could begin to confront his real problems.

Lee M., a paddle tennis champion, came to class one day very discouraged. "I got so angry this week, I really behaved like a bitch," she said sadly. "First I grabbed the phone from my eighteen-year-old son and yelled at the travel agent, who had screwed up reservations for the fifth time. I was afraid Timmy wouldn't get back to school on time. But I shouldn't have grabbed the phone. I apologized to Timmy later. Then the next morning, in the airport, the clerk was having trouble charging my reservation with the computer. So I said, thinking it would help her out, 'Oh, I'll pay cash for it.' Then she snapped at me, 'Well, you might have told me before!' I yelled back at her, 'You're supposed to be a service person; you don't have to be rude! Now you just void that ticket!'" Lee looked mournful. "I'm ashamed of myself. I don't know what got into me. But I just couldn't help myself; I felt so furious!"

Jason R., an architect, reported, "I yelled at an associate in my office yesterday. He does everything possible to be uncooperative. I completely lost my temper. Now, of course, everything is much worse."

The Power of Admitting You Might Be Wrong

A great many people go through their whole lives without ever apologizing. Countless family members suffer when a father or mother blows up, abuses them, or says hurtful things without ever saying, "I'm sorry!" Unfortunately, many people think an apology is an admission of weakness. Actually it's a sign of strength to be able to apologize without feeling crushed or resentful. If you can say to the other person, "I realize I did something wrong or hurtful, and I am sorry," the other person will feel that you respect and care about his or her feelings. We all make mistakes! If a parent can say to a child, "Gee, I'm sorry I yelled at you, Jimmy. I shouldn't have done that," the child not only can and will forgive (unless it's just lip service and the offense is chronic) but also will see a good model of generosity: life is "safer" because a strong person has acknowledged a mistake. This is just as true in grown-up relationships, whether business, family, or social. A secure person can acknowledge an error, lapse, or misjudgment without feeling humiliated. In fact, it can be endearing and reassuring to others; nobody's perfect! In business settings, tolerance for mistakes can spur creativity—if you never tried anything new, there would be no innovation! NASA calls failed experiments not mistakes but "negative findings," and it rewards creative attempts, even when they are not successful.

How to Handle Your Anger

Whatever triggered your anger, if you want to deal with it productively, it's important to separate the information from the energy. First, take responsibility for feeling angry. Recognize that whatever someone else does, it's *your* anger. There will always be negative and annoying people around. *You* must decide what to do with it. An explosion may cause irreparable damage to others, and repression may hurt *you*. Illnesses such as arthritis, heart disease, and ulcers are often correlated with anger. As we saw earlier, what your mind won't recognize, your body will internalize and may express in the form of illness, injury, or disease.

Often people find that a series of little irritations and unnoticed anxieties build up until a tiny incident (as with Lee) suddenly produces an unexpected explosion. Many of us have a backlog of unexpressed angers simmering just below the surface. Your cholesterol level goes up, your heart races, all the stress hormones are pouring into your bloodstream, and lactic acid builds up in your muscles. *What are you going to do with all that?*

Separate the information from the feelings before responding to annoying situations. It's not easy! But since neither an explosion at the person who triggered your fury nor repression is a good idea, you need other ways of releasing the anger so you can discharge the stress buildup and begin to think coolly. As long as there's "blood in your eye," it's like trying suddenly to reverse a car going ninety miles an hour without first going into neutral. You'll strip the gears and maybe wreck the car. Speaking of cars, "road rage" has been blamed for more than half the yearly fatal car accidents in the United States.

Anger CAN Be Valuable!

Many studies have shown that breast cancer patients who were angry, uncooperative, and antagonistic to medical personnel at the time of diagnosis had higher rates of survival than those who were resigned, passive, or appeasing.

The danger is not in having negative emotions but in denying them. Dr. Lydia Temoshok and her associates (1985) found that patients who denied strong feelings of anger, sadness, or fear (which showed in their facial expressions and psychophysiological responses) had greater tumor density. Roger Dafter of the UCLA School of Medicine wrote (*Advances,* Spring 1996), "Emotions . . . are a source of connection between mind and body, as well as a stimulus to action. Chronic denial, dissociation, and repression of emotions destroy important access to part of this connection. The key to the 'negativity' of an emotion is not its content, but whether it is acknowledged and expressed."

All emotions are valid—they're part of our natural resources. When anger and sadness are expressed and processed, they then can lead to other emotions. In studies of the long-range survival of cancer patients, Dr. Sandra Levy (University of Pittsburgh) discovered that *those who survived longest were the ones most able to feel and express joy.*

We've all seen children get angry, blow up, yell, and five minutes later go back to happily playing together. Somewhere on the way to adulthood, we're taught to de-synchronize the free expression of anger. What was once a total release through voice, body, and speech becomes a strained, painful double bind. Part of you says, "Let's go!" The other part commands, "Hold back!"

I devised the anger exercises to reintegrate our original happy coordination of body, thoughts, voice, and feelings and to safely discharge all that massive buildup of anger not *at* anyone else, but privately, where no one can be hurt by it.

Strangely, to obtain relief from angry feelings it's neither desirable nor necessary to vent them on the people who triggered them. We get the same satisfaction from physically and vocally discharging rage *with nobody present* (though at first this may feel foolish). The first impulse of an angry person is to get revenge, but that's seldom the action we take on cool reflection. The anger exercises give you a safe, swift release for the powerful anger buildup, so you can shift to neutral and decide exactly *how* you want to handle the problem in a way that will be most effective and satisfying. It's impossible to make the best decision until you've acknowledged and released your feelings offstage, away from the conflict.

What to Do

Close the door to your room and warn your family you're going to make some weird noises and not to worry. If you're concerned about what the neighbors will say, put some loud music on or turn up the TV to drown out your yelling!

1. The Pillow Pounder

Put a couple of heavy sofa pillows on the floor or stand next to a firm bed. Inhale, raise your arms as high as possible so you feel the stretch all the way down to your stomach. Then bring your clenched fists down as powerfully as possible while you bend your knees and yell "*EEEEEYuhhhhh!*" Keep your throat open and relaxed. Do this five to fifteen times, or more if you like, as powerfully as possible. Consciously direct your fury downward through your fists with your full force.

2. The Tennis Racket Rumble

Take a tennis racket and beat the bed as powerfully as you can, again and again, making a loud noise (it should come from your gut) each time you deliver a blow. Use all your anger as energy and hit the bed as hard as you can.

3. Vah! Shah! Aggression Release

Stand with the knees slightly bent, feet apart, and shout or whisper, "*Vah! Shah! Vah! Shah! Vah! Shah! Vah! Shah!*" Bounce, jabbing fiercely down with your fists on each word, as short, sharp, and intensely as you can. Do this twenty-six times, then inhale slowly—deeply. Release. Relax.

4. Beat Out Anger Release

If you don't have a tennis racket, roll up newspapers very tightly or use a cardboard mailing tube and *go*—beat the bed, a pillow, anything you can safely release your anger on. Shout "NO!" or "I won't!" from the gut with an open throat. Do this at least ten times, and follow with slow, deep, even breathing.

5. Tantrum

Lie on the bed or floor and pound with your legs, fists, and feet continuously, yelling exactly like a small, angry child.

6. *Pressure Breaker*

Lean forward onto a desk, arms extended, head down. Inhale; hold breath. Jog in place twenty times as hard as possible, as though racing. Exhale all the way with a sigh. Then inhale, hold, and jog thirty times. The harder you jog and the harder you hold, the more tension you will release. Follow with slow, deep breathing. (Don't do this if you have high blood pressure.)

7. *"You Bastard!"*

If you hate to use the word *bastard*, you can substitute *dastard*. Draw it out as long as possible with the throat open:
YOU - U - U - U - U B[D]A - A - S - TARD!
Stand with the feet firmly planted, about as wide as your shoulders, knees a trifle bent (to give your feet a good grip on the floor). Relax your hands at your sides, and begin to swing your arms up together in an arc, like a golf swing, from left to right. Practice a few times (bending your knees as you swing), swinging as high and freely as you can. Breathe *in* on the first swing to the left (mouth closed). Exhale on the second swing to the right, inhale (with mouth open) on the third swing to the left. Then (after this three-swing preparation) on the fourth swing (right) shout as loudly and as long as possible:
YOU - U - U - U - U B[D] - AAA - A - A - A - S - TARD!
Add a fifth swing left on a long exhale.

Begin the whole sequence again with the three-swing preparation (inhale-exhale-inhale). Then shout again:
YOU - U - U - U - U B[D] - AAA - A - A - A - S - TARD!
Swing right for the shout and then swing left.

Repeat the sequence at least ten times.

Important! Make sure the sound of your voice is completely coordinated with your body as you swing from one side to the other. Stamp your foot for emphasis exactly at the top of the swing when you say the word. Be sure to get everything working together. You might notice that you're holding back by tightening your stomach or squeezing your throat. Or the words tumble out before or after you stamp or have swung your arms. Make the sound come from as deep inside as possible. Keep your throat totally open and unconstricted, and hurl it at the next street or at the horizon. It's surprisingly tricky to coordinate. Any uncoordination between the sound, breath, body, and words will weaken the anger release. To get the full benefit of this powerful discharge, it all has to work together. Because so many mixed messages about expressing anger were dinned into us as children, we dilute the expression of our feelings by not letting everything go at the same time (something we all knew how to do as children). Pay attention— are you stopping your breath between the words *you* and *bastard*? It should run smoothly, one into the other. Try stamping your foot before you say the word. Once you get into the swing of it, you'll find it a lot of fun and extremely satisfying. Make sure everything is happening *together*. (It can be startling for outsiders. Once at a large workshop, sixty people were all shouting "You bastard!" together when the door opened. It was too late to stop a delegation of Japanese teachers politely waiting to observe the class. They looked a trifle stunned as they received the full brunt of sixty enthusiastic people hurling "Youuuuu baaaaaastard!" in their direction.)

Concentrating on the physical coordination focuses directly on the release mechanism and bypasses the frustration of "stuckness" that primal screaming or uncontrolled angry yelling produces. Giving in to sheer fury can make us shake with bottomless, seemingly endless spasms that often swell and intensify until we're drained and *still not* satisfied. The advantage of the consciously controlled release is that you feel the satisfaction of *directing* your most powerful negative feelings in a purposeful way toward maximum psychophysical release. Perhaps one reason why uncontrolled screaming anger is so upsetting is that it utilizes the same tight, only *partially* realized patterns of release that kept residual anger trapped in your body so long. In addition, focusing on the resentment content of rage feeds it further. The anger exercises instead acknowledge the feelings and then concentrate your energy on achieving a complete body-voice-feeling release. The emphasis is not on outside factors (people or situations that "made you" angry) but on taking responsibility for discharging the anger and freeing the mind and body for other emotions. That's why the anger exercises should be followed by the Anger Transformer (see p. 269) and the Great Wow!

The Great Wow!

Crouch down near the floor. Begin very small and gradually increase the size and volume of your "wow." Think of it as excitement, anticipation, and pleasure. Take the adrenaline that you have released through the anger exercises, and use it for joyous, uninhibited expression. (This completes the cycle of emotional transformation—from anger to celebration.) *This transformation is crucial* so that you won't get trapped in an ascending spiral of escalating negative feelings.

The first "wow" is quiet, almost a whisper, with your hands opened out, palms away from you as you say the word. The second one is bigger, though still not voiced. The energy is increasing—all the "wows" are lyrically extended as though you were exclaiming at some great natural marvel: a mountaintop, a waterfall, a volcanic explosion. Do eight "wows," progressively louder and larger both with voice and body. The last shout is accompanied by a triumphant leap into the air, as high as you can. Shout as loud as you can make it, arms flung overhead, face upturned to the sky.

Some people frighten themselves the first time they hear their full voices and feel their bodies, breaths, and voices released all at once. Then an enormous exhilaration sets in; there's always a lot of laughter. People often feel silly at first. But then, invariably, they find it's tremendously cathartic as well as a lot of fun. Lee said, "Oh boy, for the first time all week I really feel I got my anger out. I feel tremendously energized. I was so tired when I came in." Jason grabbed a cardboard tube at the office after everybody had gone home the next time a problem came up with his associate. After he had whacked it so hard that it fell apart, he felt freed of his anger. Then, calm again, he came up with a plan to give the other man more responsibility and at the same time remove him from a heavy traffic area where he grated on other people's nerves. Because Jason now felt "clear," he could present this arrangement neutrally, without anger, and the other man was satisfied, too.

May L. said she was able to assert herself quietly but firmly with her boss for the first time. "He listened to me," she said proudly. "I was neither overbearing nor tearful and apologetic; I got my points across."

Louis M., an advertising executive, did some of the anger releasing exercises in the men's room after running into a problem with a printer who hadn't completed a job the way he was supposed to. Since there were people around, he used the Vah! Shah! Aggression Release, and the Karate Chop, and the Steam Engine (see page 223) to discharge anger, so no one heard him. Having released his anger in the men's room, Louis was able to communicate more information about the urgency of the job and the distress he felt that it wasn't up to standards. In an unprecedented move, the printer offered to do the whole thing over again for nothing. "That *never* would have happened before," Louis reported in amazement.

Callie O., who had a demanding, manipulative mother, was able after doing the "You Bastard!" exercise to smile and stand her ground when her mother began her usual entreaties and manipulations. She felt calm, amused, and in control instead of dissolving into tears or giving in as she usually did and getting a migraine headache.

At the end of the Charismedia course, many people remark that *these exercises did more for them than any other*. One man, whom I had despaired of helping because he seemed very withdrawn and not particularly bright or articulate, told us in his final group speech what the anger exercises had done for him. "I can dance for the first time in my life! I was always too self-conscious before. Now I go disco dancing with my wife and she is delighted." This breakthrough had other effects. When we shared a group panel show, he unexpectedly turned out to be the wittiest member of the panel. I could hardly believe he was the same person.

To get the maximum mileage from the "You Bastard!" exercise, make sure your arms are relaxed when they swing way up to the side. One woman objected that doing it in slow motion felt too "dancelike" to release her anger. I had suggested slow motion to help people release the tension in their arms. I added, "Then please intensify the momentum each time, so it *won't* feel lyrical. What would give you the right feeling?" I asked her. She thought a moment and said, "Getting ready for a pillow fight!" And she swung her arms in exactly the right free and easy full swing to the sides.

The power of an image is always the best way to get the information into your body. I realized then that any completely expressed movement, if done very slowly but in continuous slow motion, will look dancelike and smooth! A discontinuous, jerky, or spastic motion won't. Take a great batter's swing or Michael Jordan's leap for a basket or Tiger Woods's golf swing, show them in slow motion, and you'll see a dance, unmistakably liquid and molten.

How to Avoid Getting Defensive

One of the hardest accomplishments in a tense situation is to avoid getting defensive. The minute you do, you've lost ground—and charisma—and it's not easy to recover.

Ann M., a mother of three young children, reported that her oldest child's French teacher had complained that her child wasn't paying attention in class. "She leaned forward as though she were attacking me. Her voice grew very loud.

"I would have reacted very badly to that before," admitted Ann. "I felt as though my 'honor' as a mother was at stake. This time, I looked at Miss Cook, leaned forward, too, and said, 'Isn't it awful? I really need your help on this. What can I do that would be helpful? I'm furious with him!' She immediately softened, and said, 'Well, maybe something is bothering him. He's really a very bright, nice little boy, and I know he *wants* to do well. Don't be angry with him. I'll try to get him interested in a special project. Maybe he needs a little extra attention.' And do you know, it worked!"

Important—if you're going to "blend" (join) with your antagonist, it's crucial to keep your own strong center. Keep your consciousness at the *hara* center (as the Japanese call it) or *kath* center, two inches below the navel. Otherwise you'll feel as though you are collapsing in or toadying to the other person, which is totally unsatisfactory.

"But how can I be sure that I'll react this way, even if I know the right thing to do?" many students ask. This is where the Visceral Rehearsal comes in.

The Visceral Rehearsal

In your nightly rerun of today's "film," stop at any episode you didn't like. Was there something else you could have done? Could you have behaved differently? Would it have made a difference either in what happened or your feelings afterward? If so, run it again, and this time program the new behavior; see yourself responding as you would like to. For example, if you didn't speak up when the cabdriver overcharged you, prepare what you want to say and then rehearse the scene. If you snapped defensively at someone who criticized you, try the new nondefensive way of responding. *Practice relaxing when you are attacked, instead of automatically tensing.* Remember that your self-worth is *not* at stake, no matter what the accusation, and rehearse your new response. By rehearsing the new responses, the next time a similar situation comes up, your visceral response will be the newly learned behavior. Please notice that whatever unpleasant situation happens, something similar will happen again—until you learn how to deal with it. "The universe," said researcher Itzhak Bentov, "is a learning machine." You can do one of two things: respond externally in a different way or change your internal reaction if no outward change is possible.

In chapter 6 you saw how using the new slowed breathing at times of sudden stress helps you change your old unsatisfactory responses so that you can tap into better ways of dealing with people and situations. When you're mentally rerunning your daily "tape," remember to *breathe very slowly and evenly*. If you feel a flash of anger, fear, or other negative emotion, deliberately relax your body and slow your breathing before you go on with the visualization.

Jason R., a burly management consultant, said, "Well, my image for myself is a smooth basketball—light but substantial and able to really fly. I used to have a tendency to get into confrontations with some of my clients. I guess I'm a rough diamond!" He grinned wryly. "But when I was doing the Visceral Rehearsal one night, the image of a basketball popped into my mind. It keeps me agile and on my toes, and I can really move. I don't knock people down now. I just challenge them and we *play* together. It sounds crazy, but my work is more fun now. We 'make baskets' together. Both they and I feel good about that. With that image in mind, I rehearse things coming up and I think of ways to handle things that never would have occurred to me before!"

From Black and White to Full Color—Reclaiming Your Whole Voice

When you use anger exercises to release both your current and stored-up anger, all the energy locked in your tight muscles and tense body will be newly available to you. In addressing a large or small group, if you want to use your anger productively your voice will be strong, vibrant, and sure. Your mind will be clear. The right words will be yours without effort. You will *choose* the way you express your anger (if you decide to) for maximum effect, instead of being shaken by it the way a bone is shaken by a dog. An interesting side effect is that your voice will become more varied, expressive, and energetic.

People with monotonous voices have invariably been conditioned to repress anger. Not only is the negative side of their feelings unexpressed, but the positive feelings are, too. It's as if when some strong feeling is disapproved of, then we unconsciously protect ourselves from criticism by hiding *all* strong feelings, including the positive ones. We lose the natural responsiveness of our voice to our feelings. To recover childhood's full spectrum of pleasurable expression, it's important to hear and experience yourself voicing those negative emotions. When we give ourselves permission to express the least-accepted feeling (without constriction or strain), we gain access to the whole rich spectrum of varied emotional expression.

Then and only then does the sound of your feelings have all the richness, variety, and color of your full emotional range—that's charisma!

8

How to Find Your True Best Voice

1. The Magic of Sound

O what is it that makes me tremble so at voices?
Surely, whoever speaks to me in the right voice, him or
her I shall follow.
—Walt Whitman, "Vocalism," *Leaves of Grass*

Voices—I think they must go deeper into us than other
things. I have often fancied heaven might be made of voices.
—George Eliot

She has a voice full of money.
—F. Scott Fitzgerald

Sound has the power to change worlds. And the sounds of our own voices change with our own changes. They deeply affect how we perceive ourselves and how other people react to us. A whopping 90 percent of respondents to the charisma questionnaire agreed that voice was one of the most important elements of charisma.

Often in my workshops or lectures I ask people if they would like to see me undergo a complete personality change in one minute. Everybody is immediately curious and skeptical. The room gets very quiet. I stand still and concentrate hard for a second or two (at one point in my life, I used to sound the way I'm now about to talk; these days it takes a deliberate effort). Then, speaking from the face, feeling no connection with my body at all, I say in a dull, innocuous voice, "This is the way I sound when I talk with no vibration at all. That's the only change I'm making. But I'd like you to notice any difference you see in my personality!"

Usually I hear gasps . . .

"You sound so boring!"

"You don't even look like the same person . . ."

"You look inhibited . . ."

"Your voice sounds thin, unsure . . ."

"Right, uninteresting, not friendly . . ."

"You seemed to shrink . . ."

"Yes," I add, "and I also *feel* different—timid, unassertive, dull, rather fearful. I'm aware of a tightness in my shoulders, neck, and head. My head feels very far away from my feet. I'd really get a headache if I kept that up!"

Amazingly, I told the group, the only change I made was that I used *no vibration*, either in the head or the body. I spoke from the throat and face as though my face were a mask and there was nothing behind it or below it.

I remember so well the feeling that voice gave me when I was very young and unsure of myself. I didn't know then, of course, that it was possible to change one's feeling about oneself by simply using the full vibration of the body with the voice. Like most people, I was barely aware of the psychophysical and physical force of my discomfort. I just felt when I was uncomfortable that it *took effort to be audible*. When I felt happy and at ease, my voice felt rich and full. It never occurred to me that I could put myself in that state at will. That was to come much later.

Ever since the first century A.D., when Quintilian, the Roman rhetorician, described vocal quality and quantity, poets, phoneticians, philosophers, and physicians have been fascinated and baffled by the elusive characteristics of the human voice. The ancient world knew that there was a profound connection between voice and personality. The word *personality* itself comes from the Latin *per sona*, literally meaning "through sound." The *persona* was the mask actors wore through which their sound (their characters) emerged. In classical Greece, with its stable authority system (people even rebelled according to set rules!), conflict arose from individual opposition to the system, but there was no concept for the self as we know it today. Homer's poetry doesn't even have a word for "person" or "oneself." Gradually *persona* came to mean not the mask but the actor himself, then the "person" in drama.

> Persona—a type of personality conceived as the full realization of oneself; a character in a play or novel.

Eventually the word meant *any* person and lost its original association with the human voice. But the dim awareness that there was a profound connection between the voice and personality remained.

The first systematic attempt to analyze the voice in terms of human emotions was made by Giovanni de la Porta, a medieval Florentine physician and playwright (considered one of the six great men of science in his day). Nothing more seems to have happened until Freud, along with Karl Abraham and Sándor Ferenczi, investigated conscious and unconscious speech expression and their links to neurosis. Almost sixty years ago Wilhelm Reich, and later his disciple Alexander Lowen (founder of bioenergetics), showed how people's voices and speech patterns reveal character structure.

Today, the "masks" of modern communication—tapes, CDs, telephone, movies, radio, TV—flood our consciousness, and the cult of personality is a dominant part of our culture. For the first time in history, humanity can *hear* itself mirrored. Before photography was invented, there were painted portraits but never any acoustic equivalent. Most people are surprised and less than pleased when they first hear themselves recorded ("Gee, do I sound like that?"). The sound we hear inside our heads is, of course, apt to be *very* different from the sound other people hear. Students tell me:

"God, I sound so boring!"

"My voice is so nasal I can't stand it!"

"What a flat sound I have—I can't believe it!"

"I sound like a hick!"

Taping your voice can be extremely helpful. Now you can hear yourself and learn to sound as interesting and expressive as you were meant to be. Everybody instinctively responds to the power of a fascinating voice. (According to Dr. Albert Mehrabian's studies, 37 percent of vocal communication is affected by voice quality itself.)

Since behavior changes consciousness and you become what you act, if you use your voice fully to express your true feelings and develop its timbre and range, *your* "persona" will involve your full self, not a facade. This kind of authentic and organismic voice can give you a sense of integrity (wholeness). People with interesting voices unquestionably have a decided advantage: they seem more fascinating, more attractive. And how disappointing it is when a beautiful person opens her or his mouth and out comes a high, unpleasant, or thin, weak sound. Your charisma emerges with an interesting voice, and people begin to respond to it.

Voiceprints are as individual as fingerprints. Now computer devices are used in business and police investigations to spot lies, confusion, or mixed motives. Changes in attitude and feelings show up as alterations in pitch—not always audible to the naked ear. That's why speakers are often surprised that the audience doesn't realize their nervousness, even though they can feel the changes in their own voices. Of the three complex variables in the human voice—pitch, loudness, and complexity—pitch is the easiest to measure. When you feel a stressful emotion, the hypothalamus gets the message and sends it instantly to your larynx, or "voice box." The larynx gets tighter or looser, depending on what you were feeling, and that changes the pitch. Computers can be programmed to measure these changes and determine the depth of emotion behind the spoken words. Pitch changes, beyond certain well-defined limits, usually indicate confusion, lying, or fear.

As usual, involuntary physiological response is more reliable than conventional testing results. Commercial market research has found this tendency to be particularly valuable. Consumers are not always able or willing to verbalize their real feelings (for instance, when children are asked about soft drinks or teenagers about sex). Voiceprints can also be used to find out if psychiatric patients with anxiety or depression are getting better or worse. Studies have shown that personality disorders (which used to be called neuroses)* and schizophrenia can be spotted through voice and speech patterns alone.

Everybody who has suffered from nervousness before a speech or a performance or the prospect of meeting someone important has experienced vocal unsteadiness, dry throat, and pitch changes. We all recognize the sound of irritation or annoyance accurately, whether or not the words match the message. It's only when these aberrations are constant, when the voice quality is consistently out of sync with what the person is saying, that a personality disorder is indicated. In the last years of her life, Judy Garland's voice held a throbbing vibrato of near hysteria no matter what she was saying or singing. The disturbed patterns of her life, the constant turbulent emotionalism, had become part of every sound she uttered.

When your voice says one thing and your words another, it's the real message that gets through—your underlying feelings—even when you think you're hiding them. Martin M., a trial lawyer, came to me to improve his communication with his clients. "They find me abrasive," he said. He got annoyed with people easily, and often found them irritatingly "stupid." When I asked him to do the "You Bastard!" anger exercise (see chapter 7) he said, "I don't want to do that. I never swear!"

He smiled proudly when he said this. "One of my clients called up my partner today and started screaming that I swore at him. My partner, who knows I never swear, said, 'Exactly what did Martin say? He never swears. Ask anyone who knows him.' The client sputtered a minute and then said, 'He called me an—ashtray!'" Martin grinned broadly.

"And did you?" I asked him.

"Yes," he said. "That's right, I did."

"Well, he got your meaning, didn't he? He knew you were actually calling him an asshole."

"Yes, but I didn't say that!"

---

*Interestingly, in the third edition of the American Psychiatric Association's *Diagnostic and Statistical Manual of Mental Disorders* (DSM-III), "neurosis" was out and "panic disorder" in. This is a healthy shift from a flat judgment to a process-oriented description. It's easier to prescribe treatment if you describe the problem more exactly. This is an index to our changing view of people from the medical model to the growth model. All states are changing all the time. Here is another clear reflection of the new concepts in physics and the influence of Eastern thought. With so many psychologists and psychiatrists studying meditation, transpersonal psychology, Zen Buddhism, Mahayana Buddhism, and other Eastern disciplines, there is bound to be a profound effect on the way we see ourselves. A paradigm shift, as Karl Pribram remarked, is a new way of looking at old problems.

"He understood you very well. So you really abused him even though you didn't swear. Your voice told the story as clearly as if you had."

I would rather be kicked with a foot than be overcome by a loud voice speaking cruel words.
—Elizabeth Barrett Browning

Martin smiled sheepishly.

"Would you do the anger exercise with 'You dastard!' instead of 'You bastard'?" I asked him. "If you allowed yourself to ventilate your anger privately, you wouldn't have to release it directly at clients. You saw by the satisfaction you got that you *needed* to release it. You weren't fooling your client."

Martin's relations with his clients improved dramatically after he acknowledged the power of his feelings and vocalized them in private.

Her voice had jutting corners he could bark his shins on.
—T. Gertler, *Elbowing the Seducer*

Never Yell at a Chrysanthemum

Not only people are sensitive to anger. Plants are, too. Dr. John A. Pierrakos, reporting experiments with his colleague Dr. Wesley Thomas, tells us that when a person shouted at a chrysanthemum from five feet away, it lost its blue azure color and its pulsation diminished to one-third. The poor plants that were kept near the heads of screaming patients (three feet away) for more than two hours a day withered within three days and died!

The more we know about the "invisible," the more we see that everything is a form of vibration and all vibrations are related and sometimes translatable into another form.

I remember singing the *St. Matthew Passion* with the Collegiate Chorale. Conductor Robert Shaw began the first rehearsal by drawing on a blackboard the musical lines as they rose and fell in the opening bars. To our astonishment, they formed the magnificent soaring spires of a Gothic cathedral. That was my first insight into the mysterious synchrony of sound and form.

Sounds and colors are related, too. When a mother yells at her small child in an angry voice, the child's energy fields lose color and slow down. If you shout angrily and bang on the table, your field becomes red, streaked as though with porcupine quills, and the pulsatory rate doubles. The auric field of a person sobbing convulsively becomes deep purple, particularly over the chest, and the pulsation increases.

The voice expresses or blocks vibration from the very ground of our being. Since we are not "solid" (as we thought before the theory of relativity and quantum mechanics turned our ideas about reality upside down) but patterns of waves, our thoughts, emotions, actions, and relationships with others create constantly changing designs of colors, lights, sounds—a dazzling kaleidoscope of shifting energies. Human consciousness is capable of astonishing feats when we begin to respect and work with these subtle emanations.

Since vibrations are life force, sound has a mysterious potency. "In the beginning was the Word," begins the story of Creation. *Logos* (the Word) is sometimes translated as law or, more deeply, archetypal pattern. The Greek philosopher Philo wrote, "His image is *the word*, a form more brilliant than fire—the Logos is the vehicle by which God acts on the universe, and it may be compared to the speech of man." The "word" must have been sound. Pythagoras, too, wrote that sound is a creative force.

The ancients knew that music is therapeutic for the body, mind, and spirit. According to the Mystery Schools, rhythm is related to the body, melody to the emotions, and harmony lifts our consciousness to spiritual awareness (perhaps because it blends the individual with the group, the solitary wave with the throbbing force field of its environmental sea).

The history of civilization could be written in terms of vocal expression. Nobody knows exactly how many languages and dialects there are at the moment; the guess is that there are at least 6,500. We know from the evidence of ancient fossils that languages originated more than a million years ago. Through all recorded history, humans have raised their voices (the primary musical instrument) to control nature and each other, as well as to express their joy, sadness, anger, fear, or yearning through sheer sound.

Our very first breath becomes a sound, a life-giving cry of protest. To speak up is our birthright! The baby quickly learns to associate pleasure, comfort, and food with his mother's voice and touch—the first harmony in his life. His breathing and vocalizing reinforce each other. Later, when we're frightened or upset, the coordination between voice and breathing is disturbed. That throws off the normal rhythms of vocalization and likely plays havoc with the heartbeat's steadiness as well. Since everything is connected, we then feel and sound thoroughly off balance and uncomfortable.

It's fascinating that all over the world children begin to articulate sounds in the same sequence—regardless of what language their parents speak. The sequence starts from the lips (p, b, m) to the tip of the tongue (t, d, l, n) to the back of the tongue (k, g).

Babies often sing before they speak, and long before understanding words the child has already learned much of the vocal language of emotions. The acoustic impressions with which a baby picks up other people's moods and the kinetic urge to re-create sounds begin in the womb. The early impression of sounds is very acute, which explains some of our adult reactions to voices. For instance, once it is associated with fear, a particular sound will always have that meaning—even though as an adult we have no idea why. "My father used to scream at me when I was little," remembered Rosa N., "and then he'd beat me. Whenever I hear a man yelling, even now, I get very frightened."

Oo-La-La (or the Fun Starts)

Babies have perfect voice production! Their breathing (at least in happy babies) functions perfectly, and the vocal cords operate in complete harmony with the breath. *Babies never get hoarse!* If mothers sing to their babies, the child's development moves easily to the next stage. If children aren't allowed to vocalize freely, there may be serious disturbances in breathing and speaking later.

To get in touch with the mischievous and playful freedom a small baby has, try this:

1. Breathe deeply (all exercises start with that "clearing the decks") and empty your mind of words.

2. Pretend you're a tiny baby, and play with sound combinations just to feel the pleasure of making sounds through your voice, lips, and tongue. Forget about the usual way you pronounce words. It'll probably feel very silly and aimless; if it does, you're doing it right! For instance, try: *ma-ma-ma-ma-ma; da-da-da-da-da; la-la-la-la-la; oooooooooookoooo-oooooookooooooooookoooooooo; dee dee dee dee dee dii dii dii dii da-doo da-doo da-doo.*

3. Keep your lips very, very relaxed and say *bhu-bhu-bhu-bhuh* and other sounds that are not in the English language but that a baby discovers for itself. (Sanskrit has fifty letters, the only language in the world that includes all the sounds that infants make as they are learning to speak. This is one of the reasons the yogis were able to come up with mantras that have profound effects on the human organism—because they include all the possible sounds.)

4. Notice how it feels to you physically and how the vibrations affect you—*muh-muh-muh*—as though you had nothing in the world to think about except the feeling of these sounds. Try bubbling (not very adult, for sure!) and keeping the little sound going for a while as though it were a delicate thread of sound you are spinning out of your mouth like a snail's trail. See how many places in your mouth, tongue, and throat you can combine—and which you don't ordinarily use in speech.

5. Vary the pitch and the length. For instance, after *puh, puh, puh, puh* (with the cheeks puffing lightly), do it in a sustained way: *puuuuuuuh, puuuuuuuuh, puuuuuuuuh.*

6. As "research," observe a real baby and notice all the sounds it is making.

7. The last step is to internalize the pleasure of using your tongue, lips, and throat for nothing but sound. Add breath before, during, or after and see how a sigh or a quick breath or a slow intake changes the sound.

8. Do this entire exercise with small subtle sounds, like the very beginning of speech—which it is.

9. At the end you'll feel very relaxed and somehow tuned up. It'll be a pleasure to put together words after having gone back to the dawn of speech!

Around the first year, the child begins to learn words. Its echolalia (rhythmic repetition of sounds and syllables) gives way to one-word, then full sentences. A small child knows exactly how much air she or he needs to speak and figures out how to breathe quietly through the nose with small amounts of air and deeper inhalation through the mouth, using more air just before speaking. As always, body wisdom is instinctive and accurate. (Mentally retarded children manage this less well.)

Blah Blah Blissout

To further relax your lips and tongue and get in touch with that delightful stage of totally relaxed and playful experimentation, try the following (use as big a vocal range as you can):

Bluh, blah, bluh, blah, etc. (start slow, get faster until you're going at top speed)

Bidda, bidda, bidda, etc. (again slow and then faster)

Puddah, puddah, puddah, etc.

Matta, matta, matta, etc.

Kicka, kicka, kicka, etc.

Go back to the beginning and start again (*bluh, blah*, etc.). This time, take away the *b*, until your tongue is flipping back and forth in a continuous *l*. Try your own combinations, all loose-lipped and loose-tongued. Make sure it's only your tongue, and *not* your jaw, that moves.

In nursery school a child meets other children and a teacher. At this point if children are told, "You can't sing!" or "You talk too loud!" inhibition will set in that permanently affects their voices, self-confidence, and sense of well-being.

Paul S., a tall, very thin money manager, came to me to get over his shyness in giving presentations. He hadn't had overly critical parents, but remembering his adolescence, he flashed on the painful experience of being called on to stand up and read in class.

"I was the tallest, skinniest kid in the grade, and everybody made fun of me. When I had to get up to read, my voice cracked, and I felt horribly embarrassed. I guess I always associate getting up and speaking with that adolescent torture. Deep down I'm sure people are going to make fun of me, the way they did then!" He looked surprised. In his mid-thirties he had become very successful in his career, and it was only now that he realized that he couldn't go any further until he could get over that early painful association. He was still narrow-chested and breathed shallowly. The Elbow Propeller (page 256) and the Magic Breath (pages 96–104) developed and expanded his chest. They helped him feel like the authoritative adult he really was when he got up to address his business associates. His whole personality noticeably expanded when he overcame that early association. The fear of being humiliated had locked him into a dull, timid sound and body posture.

Author Elizabeth M. also had a painful childhood memory that affected her voice. Whenever she spoke in front of more than two people, she lost her voice. Now she had to go out on a book tour, and she was panicked that her voice would disappear as it always had. When I asked about her earliest painful association with speaking, her face grew white and her eyes suddenly filled with tears.

"My father died of pneumonia when I was ten. I remember one day the teacher asked every child to stand up and tell what her father did. When my turn came, I was absolutely unable to tell the class that my father was dead. I felt like fainting—I just stood there, unable to say a word until the teacher took pity on me and told me to sit down. During the time he was sick, I had to go around on tiptoe and never speak louder than a whisper." The realization of the source of her difficulty, combined with breathing and courage exercises, gave her the confidence to begin to speak up—within a few weeks she was enjoying her new sense of maturity (it still felt rather dangerous) and confident expression. Before that she had dared to express herself only on paper. I have found that to be true of many writers and artists; no matter how bold they may be in print or in their art, speaking directly in their own voices is a very different challenge.

Babies and primitive societies use a much freer and more expansive range of speaking and singing than most adults. Many people are vocally inhibited, even though they consider themselves otherwise free.

Practice in voicing your most outrageous thoughts *aloud* (in your head doesn't count!) has surprisingly liberating effects for everybody. Not only does it help your voice, but it stimulates the flow of energy and ideas and produces a carefree spontaneity that might have seemed impossible a short time before.

That moves me . . .
Get a move on . . .
Movers and shakers . . .

To move (vibrate) is to live. "That turns me on" gives us a vivid image of some powerful inner motor being turned on. "I really like the vibrations here" is not just a figure of speech. We can *feel* other people's sonic fields. They're as individual as fingerprints, and they're made of sound vibrations or soundless ones.

A leftover from the eighteenth-century rise of rationalism, our unspoken instinctive attitude is that what we can't see, hear, or touch is somehow not real. But how can we maintain our literal-mindedness when we sit and watch images on a TV or hear the shifting kaleidoscope of sounds on tapes and CDs fill the air as if by magic?

She has "a voice that shatters glass," sang Professor Higgins in *My Fair Lady*. Sounds can have amazing effects on matter. Eighteenth-century German physicist Ernst Chladni scattered sand on steel disks and watched the changing patterns in the sand when he played a violin. He had discovered that inorganic matter (in this case, sand), set in vibration by nothing but sound, creates *new* organic shapes both moving and still.

Every time you raise the pitch of notes on the musical scale, the form changes—a static pattern becomes a moving one. Raise it again, and a new, different static pattern is created. Lawrence Blair in *Rhythms of Vision* observes:

> We see a parallel here with the evolution of civilizations, which consolidate into giant patterns of static form, crumble into phases of movement and creative vitality and get again into periods of conservatism; like the altering Chladni figures, their points of change or "metanoia" are marked by a return to chaos, to a lack of any coherent pattern, before the society begins to respond once more to the new vibratory frequency, or perhaps to the same harmonic, but in a different key.

Not for nothing was the first act of a new Chinese emperor to set—or restructure—the musical scale.

"What has all this to do with my charisma?" you ask.

When you connect with your charisma, you are in harmony with yourself and your world. You feel both your uniqueness and your connectedness. Each of us is a field of resonances, interacting with other oscillating fields contracting at different speeds at different times. When your voice resonates in the head, chest, belly, and throughout the body, you become intensely aware of being alive. In fact, your electromagnetic field expands and affects others powerfully. When your voice is tight, your expressive capacities are limited and you feel less than truly yourself. Your effect on other people is much less than when you are fully resonating. Most people, I find, are not aware of what it means to speak with the body.

"My throat closes when I have to talk in public."

"My voice gets high and shrill."

"People say I can't be heard. I don't know why."

"People don't listen to me."

"My voice feels unreal and far away when I get nervous."

These are common complaints from people who want to learn to speak comfortably in public or private. You can't feel charismatic if your voice is small, tight, or strained. Children have clear and ringing voices—no vocal problems. What happens when we grow up? We have seen the irresistible alternation in nature between static and dynamic that is true in our own development as human beings, too. We learn, we acquire knowledge, concepts, information, and power.

Too often, in the process of learning, however, people are conditioned *not* to express fully. It's impossible to be fully charismatic unless you give yourself permission—especially if it was once withheld by the authority figures in your life—to express your feelings vocally. This means the whole range of human expression from a whimper to a shriek, from crying to singing, from talking to laughing. This is why you need "silly" exercises, the One-Minute Verbal Free-for-All and all the other vocal exercises in this book that may make you balk or wonder, "What has this to do with being charismatic?"

Through your voice you'll be known—and know yourself. You must voice your feelings to really know what they are. As a baby you did it instinctively. Now, of course, it's not always possible or desirable to express them to other people. (Look what happened to the chrysanthemums!) That's why you must liberate your "inner child," energize and express yourself as vocally as you can (at least in private)—without feeling guilty, ashamed, or foolish. It is *not* the same if you never *utter* the sound!

Music has always provided a marvelous neutral outlet for expressing the full range of emotions. Singing or playing a wind or brass instrument deepens the breath and provides a new voice—an intimation of new ways to be alive and expressive, which is deeply satisfying. Something within us longs to know the full range of our possibilities and leaps at the chance to express in new ways. Each human is like a prism with infinite facets. When a new facet develops, the gem glitters more brilliantly, the self expands, and we have more ways to interact with the world—one test of a satisfying life. Most powerful of all is singing—with words.

George Bernard Shaw, that charismatic, indomitable genius, grew up in a household full of music. His mother, a singer, brought a singing teacher named G. J. Lee into their house when Shaw was quite small. Lee not only gave Shaw's mother lessons, he also used their drawing room for rehearsals. Shaw remained grateful ever after to Lee for teaching both him and his mother how to sing effortlessly. Shaw's mother lived to be eighty and kept her voice "without a scrape on it till the end."

When Shaw's adolescent voice broke, he insisted on being taught how to sing properly.

> Following my mother's directions, I left my jaw completely loose and the tongue flat instead of convulsively rolling it up; when I operated my diaphragm so as to breathe instead of "blowing"; when I tried to round up my pharynx and soft palate and found it like

trying to wag my ears, for the first time in my life, I could not produce an audible note. It seemed that I had no voice. . . . But I insisted
on being taught how to use my voice as if I had one: and in the
end the unused and involuntary pharyngeal muscles became active
and voluntary, and I developed an uninteresting baritone voice of
no exceptional range, which I have ever since used for my private
satisfaction and exercise without damaging either it or myself in
the process. . . .

Notice that Shaw admits unashamedly that he had no talent for singing!
Yet he never for a moment questioned his right to sing or play to his heart's
content. All his life he got extraordinary satisfaction from doing both. Certainly this "hands-on," in-depth involvement in music was invaluable for
his career. As a music critic, Shaw was "probably the best that ever lived,"
according to W. H. Auden. But "Corno di Bassetto," as he signed himself,
was doing it to please himself.

I have a strong hunch that his early singing and music making contributed a great deal to his exceptional confidence in his own powers. Certainly he had the courage to be outrageous, sure of his right to express
anything he pleased. After all, he valued his *pleasure* in singing above his
talent! All this played an important role in his extraordinary vitality, pro-
ductivity, and longevity.

> *The root of beauty is audacity.*
> —Boris Pasternak

People who are disappointed in their persona or image or voice usually
sense that they don't command the respect or authority that they would
like. They find it hard to "make themselves heard." It's impossible to be
charismatic with a flat, uninteresting voice. Everyone responds to the magnetism of great voices.

Richard Burton said he developed his voice by shouting Shakespeare at
the sheep in his native Wales. The curious underlying rhythm in Sir
Laurence Olivier's remarkable voice exerted a hypnotic fascination. The richness of the vibration rolls over the hearer like a kind of deep sonic massage. Sean Connery, James Earl Jones, Maya Angelou, Lauren Bacall—how
seductive their voices are!

A voice that thrills us commands respect, fascination, belief, interest—
essential for charisma. Since there are more overtones in a low voice, a high,
thin sound can't have much range or expressiveness. Usually when people
get nervous, their voices get pinched or high or flat or all three. If you stick
your chin out, you cut yourself off at the throat, and it's impossible to connect with the breath and strength of the rest of your body. This is how we
get "uptight" when we're tense. The center of gravity shifts upward, everything "upstairs" gets tense and tight, your throat closes, and you lose your
sense of being in control—both of yourself and the audience.

We all make instant assessments of people based on their voices. We're subliminally responsive to vocal changes in people close to us. When you call home and your husband, wife, boyfriend, or mother answers, you immediately know just from their "hello" if something is wrong. How do we make these split-second inferences?

Our computer-like brains put together vibratory information with our instinctive and learned knowledge that certain sounds indicate certain emotional states, picking up awareness in a flash. For instance, you decide to go on a trip with the children and not stop at your mother's house.

"That's all right, don't worry about me," she says, but her voice, trembling slightly, says very clearly, "I'm hurt, very hurt!"

So often we hear someone say something that she or he clearly doesn't mean; the tone and inflection provide the dead giveaway.

You Mean It, You Don't

Try this exercise for yourself. Say both versions aloud:

You Mean It	You Don't
I'm really glad to be here!	I'm really glad to be here. (Use a downward discouraged inflection—somebody dragged you to the party!)
She's a nice person.	She's a nice person. (Use a dead voice—you don't think so.)
I'd love to go!	I'd love to go. (Resigned, with a sigh)
I'm sorry.	I'm sorry . . . (Sarcastic or with a smile or flippant shrug)
We must get together.	We must get together. (Light, indifferent, voice and eyes roving)
I believe you.	I believe you. (Sarcastic)
You did OK. (With warm approval)	You did OK. (Grudgingly)
I feel fine.	I feel fine. (Apologetic smile—you don't want to complain; or angry, denying; or confused, desperate, faint)
Don't do that.	Don't do that. (Inviting, seductive, or unsure)
It was nice meeting you.	It was nice meeting you. (Unsmiling—actually it was a big strain! Or indifferent; with an unspoken addition of "And I hope I never see you again!" with a curl of the lip)
You look lovely.	You look lovely . . . (. . . considering . . .) ("Forget it, you couldn't.")
That was wonderful.	That was wonderful. ("I really didn't like it much.")

(continued)

I don't mind, really.	I don't mind, really. ("What's the use?—I'm helpless.") ("You're always taking advantage.")
I'm not upset.	I'm not upset. ("I'm mad! I'm not going to let you know I am!" said through clenched teeth)

Sometimes we say things we don't mean—out of politeness, annoyance, fear, indifference, or a dozen other motives. But sometimes, people misunderstand what we say because *our voice does not express* what we are really feeling. If you've been conditioned not to show your feelings, you probably never sound as enthusiastic as you may actually feel.

Do you feel silly when you have to repeat an enthusiastic remark? Practice it—as though each time were the first and most spontaneous. If you have a good deal of free-floating hostility or anger, your voice may sound sharp and sarcastic even when you don't intend it to.

"That's me," Harriet R. sighed. "I can't understand why people think I'm sharp-tongued. I'm always trying *not* to hurt people's feelings." Denying that you have the right to negative feelings has the paradoxical effect of creating "anger leakages"—when the anger you never express for fear of hurting feelings "leaks out" without your knowing it. Other people do! There's no hiding hostility, as we saw in chapter 7.

Oddly enough, I have found that people who lament that they talk too much are those who are secretly afraid to assert their real feelings. When we do the One-Minute Verbal Free-for-All, those people (along with the shy, quiet ones) find it impossible to keep talking. Having been given permission to "talk too much," they suddenly feel shy! Their talking too much is a way of getting back at people who would shut them up, without taking responsibility for rebelling.

"I can't help myself," Wilma L. complained. "Even though my husband tells me all the time I'm talking too much, I can't seem to stop—I say the same things twice, I go off on tangents. I keep repeating—oh, there I go again!" She stopped and laughed ruefully.

Wilma had completely "bought" her husband's judgment and was not aware of resenting his continual put-downs, since she humbly thought he was right. He even belittled her to their seven-year-old son, who started to put her down too.

The turning point came one day when a woman at a cocktail party "cornered me and in this loud, overwhelming voice started complimenting me until I just wanted to crawl away and get out of there. Now what can you do about somebody like that?" (She was still "blaming" someone else.)

"Could you tell her that all the compliments make you uncomfortable?" I asked her.

"Oh, no, that would hurt her feelings!" she answered, horrified.

"It's always legitimate to tell someone what you *feel*," I told her, "without saying, 'You're impossible or you did this and this wrong.' In fact, it's much kinder, because then people know where they stand with you. You were so shaken by this incident because you felt you had no control—you felt bullied. Isn't it so?"

She nodded. "Absolutely."

"It's important not to let anyone bully you, because then you feel like a helpless victim," I said. "The 'I have no control over what's happening' feeling is the most stress-producing feeling of all. Since it's hard for you to speak up when somebody is running you down or riding roughshod over your feelings, let's role-play that. You interrupt her and tell her very firmly, 'All this flattery makes me uncomfortable; that's how I feel about it.' Nobody can argue with your feelings, especially if you preface it with 'I know it's silly but . . .' "

"Pat," Wilma said to another woman in the workshop, "you know Joyce. You play her."

At first it was hard for Wilma to speak up and assert her rights. She laughed and discounted her feelings. But after a few tries she was able to say it firmly. Her voice was clear and her manner friendly but firm—and she stopped "Joyce" cold. We all applauded. "But *why* does she do that to me?" complained Wilma.

"Ask instead what is she feeling when she tries to manipulate people? Do you think her self-esteem is high?"

"No, I guess not. I never thought of that before, but actually she has a pretty empty life—I guess she's afraid we'll all stop inviting her if she doesn't butter us up."

"What shall I do when I feel I'm starting to talk too much?" Wilma asked later. This is the exercise I gave her to "ground" herself and quiet down. It's powerfully effective.

The "No Bars" Hold

This exercise works well for people who feel they talk too much.

1. Press your toes firmly into the ground. Hold. Increase the pressure.

2. At the same time, breathe in slowly (mouth closed), continuously expanding your lower abdomen and back to a count of seven.

3. Hold one count.

4. Release your toes and exhale for seven slow counts. Make sure your shoulders don't go up.

5. Hold for one count.

6. Start again, slowly inhaling to a count of seven.

7. Keep it up.

Practice tensing your toes and *nothing else.* At first, tensing your toes and *not* tensing your stomach and hands may feel like the old game of rubbing your stomach and patting your head at the same time. You'll soon be able to coordinate it with your breath. Breathe very smoothly and noiselessly.

This has all the advantages of the Basic Buddha Belly (p. 254) plus one more: pressing into the ground with your toes will literally ground you and prevent you from "flying high" when you don't want to. It'll also help you slow down and say only what you really want to say. All the other advantages—such as being able to listen better, being perceived as a calm, excellent listener (and actually functioning that way), and getting over nervousness—are amplified and reinforced by the toe press.

You'll be reminded that you're literally being supported by the ground. Sir Laurence Olivier, perhaps the greatest actor of the twentieth century, said this awareness was *the* most important part of his preparation when he went onstage. Once when he played Richard III, he made his entrance appearing in a doorway and stood with his *back* to the audience for fully a minute before he whirled around and savagely began the famous opening speech, "Now is the winter of my discontent. . . ."

When I asked why he made the unusual choice for the opening moment, he said thoughtfully, "Well, you see Richard is a hunchback. It's crucial to get my balance established so I can feel the ground supporting me when I begin. Since Richard is off balance because of his deformity, I needed time to establish the feeling of centeredness in myself before speaking or my voice wouldn't feel or sound right. The shock value of starting with my back to the audience gave me time—as long as I needed to establish the groundedness that's so important—then the rest of the act was no problem." I was fascinated that Olivier felt his being supported by the ground was important enough to actually dictate his choice of how to stage the crucial first entrance.

Since I'd always admired Olivier as the greatest English-speaking actor in the world, when I was singing at the Hotel Pierre in New York, I was thrilled to be asked to entertain at a private party given for him at the Waldorf. Afterward, to my great delight, he asked if he could see me home. He had just appeared in New York in *The Entertainer*, playing a seedy English music-hall performer. We had an absorbing discussion about theater. I told him how much I admired him for being able—after playing all the greatest Shakespearean heroes—to play a third-rater so magnificently. "Oh, no," he replied merrily. "I'm really very much like that, you know!"

Olivier also described how he found the right sound for the shattering scream in his classic performance as Oedipus. "To make the pain real, I had to think of animals," he said. "I thought of foxes screaming, with their paws caught in a trap. Then I heard how they catch ermine in the Arctic. Trappers put down salt, and the ermine comes to lick. And his tongue freezes to the ice. That's what I thought about as I screamed." The perfect vowel sound for screaming "wasn't an *ah* or an *ugh*—more an *err*." It was the terrible living image that gave him the sound he wanted.

Everything is connected. As infants and children, we use our entire animal vocal range and breath freely to express feelings. In order to develop vocal and emotional richness when speaking—so necessary for your charisma—it's important to expand the limited sound spectrum you've been operating with for so long. Loosen up! Limber up! Let fly!

Think about your own voice for a moment. What instrument is it like? What color? Colors? How heavy? How light? Is it thick or thin? Do you enjoy it? Does it hide your feelings? What fabric or substance is it like (wood, stone, velvet, sandpaper, metal)? If it were a fragrance or smell, what would it be? Where is it mostly located? In your face? Head? Nose? Jaw? Chest? Eyes? Throat? Is it a true representation of you? Is it weak? Strong? Monotonous? Varied? What animal is it like? What kind of landscape does it most resemble? Desert? Mountaintop? Lake? Forest? Has it changed much? Since you were a child? An adolescent? In the last five years? In the last ten years? Do you like it? Is breathing easy or an effort? In chapter 9, using some of these questions, you'll be able to chart your own vocal portrait. The spontaneous images you choose (and there are no *wrong* ones) will give you access to unsuspected resources for instant expansion and deepening of your vocal charisma.

II. The Sounds of Your Feelings

The most beautiful words in the English language
are cellar door.
—J. B. Priestly

We all have certain half-conscious associations with words and their sounds. For we each feel certain sounds are more pleasurable than others. Since we know that the sound of what we say is often more important than the meaning of the words, it's valuable to discover the inner palette of sound that pleases you most. When you enjoy the sounds of words, you're more expressive, persuasive, and charismatic.

Sometimes I ask Charismedia students to say a word like *soft.* When they do, with no preparation, it might just as well be *hard* or *June* or *stone.* The word has no particular distinguishing associations, and we certainly can't tell the meaning from the sound.

Then I ask for some associations with the word *soft*—we go around the room: "Feathers." "Fur." "Clouds." "Velvet." "Skin." "Pillows."

"Now," I ask the group, "let's hear the word *soft* again, keeping some of those images in mind."

Now when each person says "soft," it really *sounds* soft. If you have a mental image, it changes the way a word sounds even though your hearer has no idea of what picture you have in mind.

Subliminal Onomatopoeia

On the charisma questionnaire, 75 percent of the answers cited "persuasiveness" as a powerful ingredient of charisma.

You can trigger instant acceptance of your words by making them so juicy with association that people automatically feel attracted by what you're saying. This works even with controversial concepts.

A high government official came to me because people criticized her for talking too fast. She is an excellent speaker, but some of her words got lost when she slurred over them. I asked her to improvise a talk on some topic that she might be speaking on during her week. Without hesitation, she began to speak very fluently about something called—I had to strain to catch it—an urban development action grant.

"Hold it!" I called out. "Is that something your audience knows all about? You dropped your voice and said it in a rush, as though you yourself were rather bored with it."

"No! Oh, did I?" she asked. "On the contrary, this would be the first time they've heard about it. Even the legislators don't know about it yet."

"Oh, then it's important to break it down and make each word interesting and attractive. First, *urban*. Can you think of a positive association for *urban*?"

"Well, it suggests the complexity of the city . . . the planning, variety, and wealth of resources and people," she shot back.

"Now, keeping all those good associations in mind, say the word again." I told her.

"Urban," she said, smiling a little. Now it was more deliberate. It sounded tempting already.

"Now for *development*. That gives us an impression of growth, as though good things were in the offing, a change for the better, auspicious planning. Say it that way!"

"*Development*," she said, taking time, this time, to emphasize the second syllable thoughtfully and promisingly, as though she were visualizing growth.

"Good! Now the next word, *action*, is certainly a positive concept, especially with so much *inaction* and red tape in government. So say *action* very powerfully!"

"*Action*," she grinned, pronouncing it with a crisp glottal attack that sounded like the starting gun in a race.

"Now for the final coup, *grant*. That's a very positive word. It suggests generosity, a large gift; in fact, a magnificent present everybody would like."

"Grant," she said firmly. The *r* was juicy and the final *t* crisp and decisive. The subliminal association with granite added an underground feeling of solidity and reliability.

"Good. Now let's put them all together," I said. "But here's the challenge: make each word *live* with its own association and rich, suggestive background, instead of running them all together as though they're all the same or running downhill in declining importance, so that by the end of the sentence the audience can't even hear what you're saying. A common failing in speakers is dropping their voices completely at the end of a sentence even though they're not at the end of their talk. Remember: dropping your voice is like lowering the curtain. It signifies the end. Keep your inflection at midrange at the end of a sentence so your listeners instinctively know you're going on. Otherwise the audience may either mentally tune out, miss your point altogether, or figure you're ashamed of it!"

The melody of her inflection at the beginning had been like:

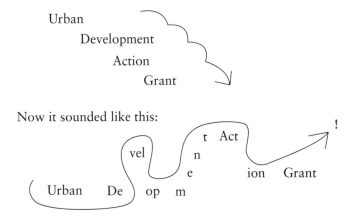

It was clearer, more alive, more varied, and definitely more persuasive. There is another benefit. Applying concentrated attention to each word increases the amount of energy projected in the phrase. That automatically makes it sound more enthusiastic, positive, and interesting. And you increase your charisma!

Sometimes the speaker's negative assumption about how people will respond robs his or her words of energy. Suppose you know there's a lot of resistance to a certain plan among the audience. Anticipating opposition may lead you to sound defensive, negative, or uncertain. Since this happens largely unconsciously, it's important whenever you feel there may be hostility, resistance, or lack of comprehension to put *more* easy energy into your words (to make up for the drainage of confidence). Be careful not to fall into a "justifying" or complaining tone. Nothing is less convincing.

Some people are so unsure of being believed that almost everything they say sounds petulant or aggrieved. People, as you've seen, respond to the *tone* of what you're saying even more than the content. Do you tend to sound complaining? Remember that this comes across as ill-tempered and lacking in authority.

Give yourself this little tone test. Which sentences feel most familiar to you? Tape your answers to hear what you really sound like in these situations. How would *you* react to that tone? Then, try the no-fault alternative, and see how it feels and sounds.

1. The cabdriver ignored your instructions and took a different, longer route. Now you're stuck in traffic and late for an appointment.

    "I *told* you not to go that way!" (Your forehead wrinkles, head juts forward, voice is angry.)

    Better: "Ah, what a shame you didn't go the way I asked you to!"

2. Your friend ignored your advice and bought the wrong color paint for your apartment. Now it's clear that the bright yellow you wanted would have looked better.

    "I *told* you this wasn't a good color!"

    Better: "How disappointing! That really isn't the best color here."

3. You scold a child for breaking her toy after you'd warned her not to throw it on the floor.

    "I *told* you not to throw it on the floor!"

    Better: "What a shame you forgot that toy would break if you threw it on the floor!"

4. An employee ignored your instructions and sent out the wrong letter to an important client.

    "I *told* you to be careful about that letter!" (Glaring, you idiot!)

    Better: "Gosh, now we've got a problem. It was really important that the client should get the right letter."

5. Your friend or relative, who tends to be late, arrived fifteen minutes after the movie was scheduled to begin, and there are no tickets. She had insisted it would work out.

    "You're *never* on time!" (Boy, are you angry! And she'll get defensive.)

    Better: "Oh well, next time we'll get here earlier." (Can you bear it? If you can let go of your fury, maybe the evening won't be ruined.)

6. Against your better judgment, you went to a party—and had a terrible time. Now there's a parking ticket on your car.

    "I didn't want to go in the first place!"

Better: (lightly) "Ah, the end of a perfect evening!" (not tight-lipped, though!)

7. A new hairdresser (or barber) persuades you to cut your hair much shorter than you wanted it. You're not pleased.

"Why didn't you do it the way I asked you to?"

Better: "Gee, I'm really not happy with this."

8. Your boss throws another assignment at you before you finished the first two you're trying to complete.

"I'm only one person! I can't do all of this at once!"

Better: "Please, (laughing) there are only two of me here!"

9. You're annoyed with a friend who doesn't call you as often as you call her.

"Why do I always have to call you?"

Better: (joking) "You don't write, you don't call . . . !"

10. Your teenage son has left a mess in his room.

"How can you live in such a pigsty!"

Better: Close his door.

11. You call up the super, who never seems to be around when you need him.

"We haven't had any heat for three days! Why don't you answer my phone calls?"

Better: "Oh, I'm so glad I reached you. We haven't had heat for three days—please do something, would you?"

12. Your parents don't like your new boyfriend/girlfriend.

"Why do you always criticize? You never like anybody that I do!"

Better: "It hurts me when you criticize my friends. So please don't tell me, OK? I'd really appreciate that."

Then there are the self-pitying complaints. How would *you* fill them in for the column on the left? Do you usually hear yourself phrasing them in the somewhat better-sounding versions, as in the right-hand column?

YOU SAY	BETTER
"You always expect . . ."	"I feel you usually expect . . ."
"You never let me . . ."	"I wish you'd let me . . ."
"You always wait until . . ."	"You tend to wait until . . ."

                                          or "Please don't wait next time
                                          until . . ."
"Why don't you ever . . . ?"   "I'd really like you to . . ."
"Why must I always . . . ?"   "I wish I didn't have to be the
                                          one to . . ."

Notice which of these statements sound complaining or whining. Try saying the same things in a tone of *detached interest*. Cut out "You always" and "You never" phrases; try instead "sometimes," "usually," or "seldom," which are not only more accurate but less apt to make other people defensive.

You'll find that you have much more credibility, and the chances are you'll get a more satisfying response. Most people get defensive or angry when they're complained at. There's something about the sound of someone feeling sorry for him- or herself that is weak and powerless as well as irritating.

This vocal checkup can be a useful guide to unacknowledged feelings. If you find that you tend to have a complaining inflection rather often (notice I didn't say always!), this is a clue that there is a good deal of hidden anger poisoning your system. Are you an injustice collector?

Sentences that begin "I told you . . ." or "Why did you . . . ?" (or "Why didn't you . . . ?") are also likely to act as communication stoppers *if* the tone is complaining.

Here are some other communication stoppers:

"Don't be ridiculous" (or any put-downs, which are sure to produce either ice or fire).

"That's the way I am" (and don't intend to change).

"It won't work" (no hope, no possibility, no compromise!).

"What are you trying to do—make waves?"

Accusations and reproaches, even if delivered in your normal tone, will probably produce a counterattack, almost by reflex.

Shoulds and Coulds—Wistful Wasteland of the Subjunctive

"You should have . . . ," "I would have . . . ," "You could have . . . ," and "If only . . ." all belong in the country of regrets, disappointments, and lost opportunities. They torture us. If somebody is always "right," the other person is terribly "wrong"—a painful place to be. If any emotion is involved, abandon the heady temptation to prove yourself right, because if you win, the other person loses. That's not a rewarding resolution of the conflict. It triggers resentment. Grievance collectors are forever "proving" they're right and everybody else is wrong. By their tone you shall know them! But do they get what they want? Not usually!

If you find yourself complaining a lot, examine your life to see if there are any positive steps you can take to change your passivity. The passive role is basically unsatisfactory and turns other people off as well. First, acknowledge that you're experiencing a lot of anger and frustration and are possibly "dumping" on innocent bystanders. Next, if the amount of anger is out of proportion to the offense, that's a clue that you have to take responsibility (*not* blame!) for dealing with your feelings, rather than blame them on other people. Meantime, the *sounds* of your feelings are getting through loud and clear.

Often in conversation we hear someone express feelings she or he is unaware of, or that don't match the situation. It's impossible to know what the mental buildup was. I'm reminded of a man who found himself out on a dark country road late at night when his car broke down. He decided to knock on the nearest door and ask to use the telephone. But it was so late that he began to imagine that the people who lived in the house would get angry at the disturbance. In his mind he saw them getting furious and saying that not only could he not use the telephone but he had a nerve waking them up at that hour—and to get out before they called the police. By the time he rang the bell, he was thoroughly worked up. When a woman answered the door, before she had a chance to say anything, he yelled at her, "You can keep your lousy telephone if you're gonna be so rotten about it!"

Ella M., a retired schoolteacher, constantly complained in class, "Nobody cares about human misery or politics. I'm always giving people newspaper articles, and do you think they ever act on them? No! I'm very disappointed in people. I seem to be the only person that cares."

The rest of the class grew impatient with Ella's complaining voice and constant criticism of other people. "She is always telling us what to do. It's annoying," one woman observed. "Also she hogs attention all the time." Ella was terribly hurt when someone criticized her!

Ella's need to be "right" and her chronic disappointment in people who didn't "behave right" left her angry, lonely, and bewildered, and the combination of her demands for attention and her self-righteousness produced a good deal of resentment against her. She couldn't grasp that nothing annoys people more than being told what they *should* do and how deficient or negligent they are for not doing it. A large part of it was her tone.

"You *should* write letters to your congressman; otherwise you are a bad citizen!" That was Ella's style, and everybody bristled. Meditation and the anger exercises helped her relinquish the great unexpressed load of old anger she carried around with her. Gradually, she stopped trying to control other people. All of us who need to persuade—and that means everybody at some time or another—must be able to suggest a course of action in a tone that's nonjudgmental and nonmanipulative.

If you're asked for advice, a neutral, nondirective statement of information leaves the other person more freedom to consider it without feeling pushed. For instance, your friend asks you what to do about a problem involving her family. If you take her side, she may resent them more or take some action she'll regret later and then blame you. If you take theirs, she'll get angry and accuse you of not appreciating her feelings. This would apply to a boss-employee relationship, a student-teacher conflict, or any interpersonal problem where someone brings you a problem with a third person.

Fanning resentment is unproductive. So is defending the other side. What can you do?

Be a Verbal "Mirror"

First, mirror the other person's thoughts by restating what she or he has said. "You feel he deliberately kept you waiting for spite?" Invariably, the other person will then explore his or her own feelings more fully. You can then restate what you hear as the other's emotions: "You felt really abused when he didn't show up twice in a row."

Describe Their Feelings Neutrally

Describing someone else's feelings is a nondirective way of helping them ventilate their feelings so that they can move on to others. ("Well, I was mad, but he did have a really good excuse—his boss kept him late both times. I guess I really want to forgive him.") Most important, you're not *telling* anybody what's right and wrong. That would be irrelevant and, worse, not helpful. It simply escalates the other person's sense of grievance. When your friend can share angry or hurt feelings with you, your willingness to listen productively without judging is a tremendous boon. You can always respond with, "Say more about that!" When you listen without judging or commenting, you help the other person process his or her own anger by turning it over on all sides, so that it gets completely explored. Then your friend, having felt heard, understood, and respected, can let it go.

If someone constantly asks for advice, you only foster their dependence by feeding it. "It's better to give a person a fishing rod than a fish," the adage goes. Your being interested but neutral, plus lending your implicit trust that your friend (or relative or colleague) can handle the situation well, is more effective and satisfying than giving direct help. With children, you can call attention to how well they handled an earlier situation and say, "I'll be so interested to see how you take care of this!" *Trust makes people strong.*

Molly went to her friend Evelyn, the former chairperson of her organization, and asked her for help organizing a benefit. Molly felt unable to handle it now that she had been elected president. Evelyn took over, only too happy to have her old power back. Molly, who felt resentful and pushed aside, came to the Charismedia class and asked how she could reestablish her authority at board meetings. Evelyn, running things her own way, now treated Molly as though she were unimportant and had no ideas worth considering. Molly had brought the situation on herself by panicking and running for help. Evelyn, convinced that she was indispensable, was happy to take over—not what Molly wanted.

"How do I get my authority back?" she groaned, very distressed. We role-played a meeting at which she would acknowledge and thank Evelyn for her past contributions and then ask her to now let some of the others in the organization share in the planning; "Please save your comments until they've spoken; we need to have everybody's input." Molly had to practice saying it calmly and authoritatively. This worked out well. Evelyn subsided when she realized Molly was going to be firm. She was satisfied by the acknowledgment of her past contribution, and now respected Molly's new authority. Molly realized she *could* run the meetings herself and was happy that she was able to control the situation without creating an open break with her demanding predecessor. Others on the committee came to her privately and thanked her for handling Evelyn so well; everybody had been feeling overrun!

Let It Be OK if People Accept Your Suggestions—or Not!

If you're asked for information or help, give it neutrally, without a stake in whether or not the help is used. Don't let your self-esteem depend on whether your advice is taken! We all have only a part of the picture anyway. Your considered opinion about the best thing for the other person may not turn out to be the best when all the information is in. This doesn't lessen the value of your insights; it just means we're all like blind people touching a part of the elephant and mistaking our sensations for the totality.

Everyone has a right and a need to get as much information as possible about a problem situation. Only on the basis of maximum information (outside facts and inner feelings) can we make the most productive decisions. A respect for the innate good sense of other people also removes the horrendous need to be right all the time—which clearly nobody ever is. The ultimate responsibility for our actions must rest with ourselves.

With the triple beacons of respect

a.   for the unknown depths of others,

b.   for their right to make their own decisions, and

c.   for the assumption that they, too, are trying to do their best,

your effectiveness and persuasive power will rise sharply.

Ella dropped her aggressive, hectoring tone ("You *should* write letters to your congressman") and said, "If you write to your congressman, we have a good chance of getting this legislation passed. We must make some noise about what we believe in so the legislators know what their constituents want. It's up to *us* to do that."

I congratulated her. By saying "us" instead of "you," you include yourself and detoxify the pointing finger of "Do this!" or "Do that!" which everybody hates. You want to stimulate and inspire people to act, not bully them into it. They must believe that whatever you want to persuade them of is in *their* best interest.

In general, by expecting the best of people and taking for granted that they're acting out of valid motives (though you may not think so), you'll get better results.

A woman complained to her friend that the druggist in their neighborhood gave her terrible service, and she was very annoyed with him. The friend promised to speak to him. A few weeks later they met again, and the first woman said, "What did you say to him? He's been wonderful. You really must have given him a good bawling out!" The friend smiled. "No, as a matter of fact, I told him you had remarked how extremely helpful and cooperative he always was!"

I experienced a somewhat similar situation one day, dealing with a belligerent maintenance man at a school where I was teaching. We were having a TV session in the auditorium, and I decided, on impulse, that I'd like the piano opened so I could accompany one of the students in a song. Ordinarily it was kept closed. (Of course, I should have made arrangements ahead of time!) When I found the maintenance man, he was in no hurry. I'd have to wait, he said, until he finished his coffee. It was clear he would be happy to throw as many roadblocks in the way of opening the piano as he could think of.

"You should have filled out a written request," he glared at me. "Yes, you're right—I really should have. I'm sorry about that," I answered. Not much mollified, he finally—at a snail's pace—grudgingly got the keys for the piano. When we reentered the auditorium I called the class's attention to his "kindness in opening the piano for us." He threw me a suspicious glance, suspecting sarcasm, but I *was* grateful at that point and determined to acknowledge him for it. (After all, it had been hard for him to accommodate me when he was so full of resentment and annoyance at being asked anything out of his ordinary routine!) When he saw I meant it, his attitude changed. Suddenly, he *did* become cooperative. When I asked if we could have the use of the piano for the next hour, he said expansively, "Sure, as long as you like—don't worry about it!" He departed happily to a wave of appreciative applause from the class. Had we gotten embroiled in who was "right" and who was "wrong," I have no doubt he wouldn't have opened the piano at all.

It's a small incident, but a telling one. It is necessary to *let go* of your own resentment and anger if you use this approach. You have to be innocent; otherwise you sound and feel false, and it won't work. The biggest difficulty is that your usual impulse is to get defensive when someone is critical or hostile, to prove you're right. In dealing with antagonism, here's a better strategy:

1. Avoid getting defensive. Recognize when you feel threatened and repeat to yourself, "I am not less valuable or worthwhile even when I make a mistake or someone challenges my ideas or criticizes me." Breathe deeply as you say this!

2. Recognize whatever you can agree with—and express it. If there is *one* small element you can accept in someone else's tirade, do it. It takes you off the barricades and enables your antagonist to start listening to you and stop attacking. This is useful with children as well as grown-ups.

"You're always interrupting me!" shouts your child.

Our impulse is to say, "Well, you never let me get a word in!" or "I am not!" and the battle is joined. A better way (it requires some *hors de combat* rehearsal so that it "takes" viscerally and you can remember to do it in crises) is "Yeah, that's a terrible habit. I'm sorry. Be sure and let me know when I do that. It *is* annoying to be interrupted all the time." Or simply say, "I'm sorry." The explosion will instantly subside. You also have established a principle: it's not good to interrupt people. Next time *you're* interrupted, you'll get a fair response if you ask for equal time. You've provided a model for improved interaction. You're also showing *you're strong enough to admit you're wrong*.

If you can't agree with one single thing the other person says, you can always say, "I see this really bothers you a lot," or "You really feel very deeply about this." (Be careful to use an interested, sympathetic tone, *not* a reproachful one.) This brings up the third way for dealing with antagonism:

3. When the other person is very angry, never deal with the issues! That's not where the action is. *Acknowledge the feelings* and encourage the other person to express them fully. This ventilation always lowers the temperature of the argument, removes the need for defense or attack, and brings you both to a third place. **Well-managed friction leads to a higher level of consensus.**

When you ask, "Why do you feel so strongly about this?" in a sympathetic, nonchallenging tone, you'll be amazed at the results.

The first time I tested this principle, I wasn't at all sure it would work, but the effect was so dramatic I was astounded. I was a guest on a radio talk show. The topic was pornography and obscenity in the theater. The other guests were two producers and a psychologist. One producer (whom I will call Edmund) had a long-running, charming musical fairy tale on Broadway. He was ranting about the evils of pornography. His style was that of a fulminating nineteenth-century preacher. Nobody could get a word in edgewise.

"Obscenity is ruining our youth, corrupting our society's morals, and cheapening our theater," he declaimed. He had a point or two, but they were lost in the torrent of invective and denunciation he unleashed at us. I was beginning to wonder why I had come. The host of the show had actually left the studio! Nobody else was able to get in a word. I thought to myself, "What am I doing here? I might as well go home! OK, I've got to do something. I don't know if this will work, but here goes."

I said to Edmund, "Mr. ———, why do you feel so deeply about this?" To tell the truth, I didn't expect much, or even that he'd stop and respond. To my surprise, he stopped dead. Then he said, in a quiet voice, very different from the thundering tone he'd been bombarding us with, "Well, you see, when I was a kid growing up in New York, my father—he was an Italian immigrant and he didn't know much English—used to use a lot of dirty street talk. I'd beg him, 'Pop, please don't use that gutter talk; it's not nice, you're embarrassing me,' but he didn't listen. He kept right on doing it."

We all sat silent, stunned and moved. All our antagonism at him for monopolizing the panel dissolved. We felt tremendous empathy for the child who had suffered because of his father's "dirty talk." No wonder he hated obscenity! Then the other producer, a man of about thirty who had a nude musical running, remarked, "You know, Edmund, I understand just how you feel. All my life, I've heard four-letter words and they didn't mean a thing. Now that I've got this show, I hear them so much that I wouldn't care if I never heard another one in my life!"

It was an astonishing turnaround. He had agreed with Edmund and demolished his point at the same time! Clearly *he* had *not* been corrupted by obscenities and bad language, as the older man had insisted was bound to happen. There was a warm feeling among the group. We went on to a much more productive general discussion. Edmund dropped his lecturing tone and was able to share the floor with the rest of us.

This was my first dramatic demonstration of the principle: *well-managed friction can create a higher level of consensus*. If pressed to a statement, you can say something like "I see the problem a little differently," or "I can understand your feelings about this." If someone stands up in a meeting and makes totally negative remarks, which you don't want to get into, you can simply say, "Thank you for sharing that with us." Nobody can argue with that! If you *want* to argue the point, do not attack the person or his ideas or "judge" them. These are among the no-nos: "That's ridiculous!" "What a stupid remark!" "You don't know what you're talking about!"

Some adults deliberately go for the jugular when they get angry. They say cruel, hurtful things with an uncanny instinct for your weak spots, your own secret fears and insecurities. Using the power to hurt is *not* a sign of strength. Truly strong people are loving as well. When someone's caustic tongue intimidates you or hurts your feelings, remember to ask yourself, "Why does that remark [or action] lower my self-esteem?" It probably confirms some secret fears or insecurities you have. So you have "bought" the put-down. Often people accuse others of failings that they dislike in their own nature. Or they dislike people who remind them of their own weaknesses. Is that you? Then say to yourself, "I can *choose* my reaction. I *choose* not to be hurt." Change channels; tune it out! Use a visual image of a wall that no one can get over.

If you're on the receiving end, think carefully before you indulge in a sharp put-down. Beware of making a lifelong enemy. Put-downs may be a great short-term satisfaction, but they work best with people you'll never see again. The more elaborate the put-down, the better. Benjamin Disraeli was once attacked by another peer in Parliament who shouted at him, "Sir, you will either die on the gallows or of a pox!" Lord Beaconsfield replied quietly, "That depends, sir, on whether I embrace your politics or your mistress!"

Another put-down answer, just as effective, is to treat the slap as a compliment: "Please, no flattery!" Americans are not very accomplished at slurs. Probably no group exceeds the virtuosity and range of the Hungarians (famous for blasphemy) or the Irish. The Yiddish language is also rich in expressive put-downs ("May you have a palace with one thousand rooms and be unhappy in every one of them").

Few of us could think as fast as Mark Twain did when a Frenchman remarked to him, "When an American has nothing else to do, he can always spend a few years trying to find out who his grandfather was."

"That's so," drawled Twain, "and when all other interests pall for a Frenchman, he can always try to find out who his father was."

Many of us think only too late of what we would *like* to have said when someone takes us unawares with a question or a rude remark. A friend told me what she *wished* she'd said, when a casual acquaintance had surprised her with "Why did your husband leave you?" at a party just after her divorce. "I see," she wished she had remarked, eyeing his rather plump middle, "the only exercise you get is jumping to conclusions!"

If someone catches you off guard, maliciously or not, the first thing to do is *breathe deeply and say nothing*. That'll keep you from stammering or stumbling while you try to collect your thoughts. Sometimes your silence is enough to abash your questioner. A slight smile gives you an all-knowing air.

Wait at least ten seconds before saying anything (breathing quietly and deeply all the time, gazing calmly at your questioner). It's amazing how often, faced with this kind of composed, smiling silence, people will retreat, mumble apologies, and take you off the hook. If you feel an answer is required after that, you can murmur (smiling sexily, of course), "I never give personal information between 3:00 and 6:00 on alternate Fridays" (or whatever time it happens to be). Don't forget to look your questioner straight in the eye with a seductive, teasing expression.

It's a good idea to write down in advance (as I ask participants in the Charismedia workshop to do) ten questions or remarks that make you uncomfortable and *prepare* your response. Remember, it doesn't necessarily have to answer the question. You're not obliged to answer whatever is thrown at you. It's worth studying diplomats' and politicians' answers and nonanswers to questions. You, too, can give people exactly the kind and amount of information that pleases you.

What Kind of Question Bothers You Most?

When I work with top executives of large corporations, I ask them to prepare a list of questions that they would find difficult to answer about their business. This is exactly the kind of question a shrewd interviewer or newscaster will seize on. Then we rehearse not only the answers, but the way the executives look and sound. *The way you behave when you're answering is crucial.* Remember, if there's a conflict between verbal and nonverbal language, it's the nonverbal that's believed! Rehearsal is the key to handling uncomfortable moments well. Richard Nixon looked wonderfully sincere in his "Checkers" speech because he'd rehearsed it thoroughly. Canadians who heard the Nixon-Kennedy debates on radio thought Nixon had won because they didn't *see* him with his giveaway nervousness and shifty-eyed facial expressions. If you don't rehearse, your underlying discomfort at a question will come through and probably be misinterpreted. Negative messages are almost always, as we have seen, read wrong.

Sometimes a question may seem innocuous to an outsider, but for some reason it bothers you. One young lawyer in my group hated to be asked at a party, "What are you doing?" He had taken a couple of years off after law school to look around, see how he felt about himself and law, survey his options, and get his priorities in order. He sounded apologetic when he told us this. We rehearsed his saying, "I'm very fortunate—I've been doing some private research on projects I'm interested in," until he felt comfortable with that. It was true. He only needed to choose *what* and *how* he wanted to disclose; that took the discomfort out of the question.

In a large meeting it's a good idea to repeat the question and address the answer to *other* members of the audience so you don't get trapped in an extended dialogue with one person. From CEOs to the president, a secure executive unhesitatingly says, "I don't know the answer, but I'll have someone on my staff find out, and we'll get back to you."

Another good way of responding is to say, "That's a good [or a very interesting] question," and then go on to make a statement that may or may *not* answer the question.

If the question or comment is not appropriate, tell the questioner, "Can we put that aside for now, sir? I'll be happy to discuss that after we've dealt with the agenda before us. Please see me at the end."

A client who had been a political candidate decided not to run and asked me how to handle his press conference. The truth was he was fed up with the drubbing he'd gotten from the press during the year on some intrastate matters he'd been involved in. He planned to read a formal statement that sounded totally impersonal. Yet because he was uncomfortable, he gave the impression that he was hiding something!

I asked him to choose a positive statement he could say with conviction—because it was the truth, though not the whole truth: "I have decided not to run now. It seems more important to me to support the candidacy of X——, who has been a superb governor, and devote my energies to the international problems I have been interested in." He felt good about this statement and said it with conviction and authority. It also opened the door to an ambassadorial appointment that he preferred. He avoided having to air his rancor against the press, which would have been disastrous. And he maintained his image of a dynamic public figure who knew his worth and could be trusted to take steps in the public interest as well as his own.

If you do decide you want (or should) answer a question you're being asked, there are many ways to do it. Choose an answer you're comfortable with and practice saying it with pleasant authority. A flip answer has to be unusually good to keep the questioner at bay. If it's a question about your age (and most women don't like to answer that after thirty), you can (a) lie or (b) say "old enough"

1. to have accomplished such and such (or to have a grown daughter and son)

2. to know I am still growing.

You might quote Oscar Wilde: "A woman who will tell her age will tell anything!" Barbara Marx Hubbard said, "The older I get, the newer I feel." I sometimes say, "Younger than I was ten years ago." Which is true! You can say, with a smile, "What an indelicate question!" and *say no more*. You can do a really elaborate variant on "I only answer questions like that on alternate Shrove Tuesdays in Leap Year!"

The very feisty mother of a client deliberately shaved ten years off her age (which was ninety-three) when she went into the hospital, because, she said, "They treat you better if they think you're younger."

Lies are, of course, invariably risky, but reconceptualizing information is often not only legitimate but necessary. One executive said that when he only had a shipping clerk's experience, he had told interviewers that he had "been in charge of production supplies" for his company. Look for the positive components of your work (they may not have been included in your title) and add those to your statement. This will also give you a more positive feeling about your qualifications.

Most women whose main life experience has been running a household don't realize that they have had most of the experience necessary to run a government, having handled budgets, supplies, personnel, inventory, etc. Many women, returning to work after having raised a family, feel apologetic about their "lack of qualifications."

> Practice in answering "difficult" questions will help you meet the world with confidence and present the image you want.

Write down the questions you find most difficult or unpleasant to answer. Now *choose* your responses by asking yourself some questions:

1. How much do I want to disclose?

2. Do I want to answer the question or just appear to?

3. Can I state what I want to tell people in a positive, confident way, feeling good about it?

4. How can I phrase the facts I want to disclose in a positive, confident way, telling something but not too much? (Now practice aloud.)

5. Does it sound convincing when I rehearse it out loud? (This is very important! Rehearse until it does. Try it with a friend or supportive relative.)

6. Does this question require any answer at all?

7. If not, what responses (including a silent, knowing smile!) can I prepare that will cover all contingencies?

Ginny R. hated to go home to Ohio because her mother and father were not interested in her career. They kept asking, "When are you getting married? Your cousins are all married!" Exploring how she felt, using the above list of questions, she decided she didn't want to explain or defend her life or why she had no intention of getting married in the near future. I suggested that she address herself to their well-meaning concern for her, while sidestepping the question. You don't have to join other people's games if you don't like the game!

She practiced saying, "Dad, Mom, I appreciate your concern. I know you want me to be happy. Right now, things are going very well. I'll certainly let you know when I plan to make any changes. You must trust me to make the right decisions about my life."

It might not be necessary or desirable to say *all* this at once. The first sentence or two might be enough. But Ginny's attitude had changed. As in an antagonistic situation, it's not the issues you address; it's the attitudes. If you can appreciate and acknowledge someone's concern, your own response is apt to be nondefensive and hence more satisfying. Nobody likes to justify him- or herself—and you don't *have* to. Instead of accepting terms that are not your own, you can bring people onto your turf. They may find it unfamiliar and bewildering, but you'll be a lot happier and avoid unnecessary conflict.

When Ginny went back to Ohio after rehearsing the confrontation with her parents, she had the best visit in years. As in all truly productive conflict solutions, *everybody* was happier. They didn't get an answer to their question (which was rhetorical anyway), but they felt that she appreciated their concern—and she didn't blow up as she usually did. The whole visit was a great success. They even promised to visit her in New York and expressed interest in her career for the first time.

What if a question is less benign? Often we think a question is meant as a put-down merely because we feel uncomfortable about it. A small part of you may feel guilty when faced with the accusing question "Why aren't you married?" or "Have you had enough experience for this job?" or "Why haven't you called me?" Suppose you're worried about your weight. A friend says, "I love your dress! You really have to have a good figure to wear a dress like that." That may sound like a put-down to you, even if none was intended.

If it *was* intended, don't inhale! All chronic "put-downers" suffer from low self-esteem, though their arrogance often fools people. Negativism is a communicable "dis-ease," and a common way of shoring up group and individual insecurities is to indulge in cruel banter, racial jokes, and mean gibes. Allowing such remarks to pass is tacit encouragement. "Say, that's pretty unkind," or "That sounds rather bigoted!" will call other people's attention to the slur, and it often elicits a hasty denial or even an apology. People may derive satisfaction from acting nasty or prejudiced, but they don't want to be perceived that way. Low-key social pressure can fight prejudice and put-downs by saying clearly that they are *not* all right. Avoid denunciation of the critic; your objection is to the behavior, not the critic—a person always has the potential to learn.

If a remark wounded you, observe to yourself that you're hurt, even if it's only a slight, stabbing pain. Repeat your "comfort sentence" to yourself immediately: "I am a worthwhile person; nothing anyone says can diminish my true value." Next, ask yourself if the put-downer feels threatened by or envious of you. You can also respond with a laughing exaggeration: "Gosh, you really know how to hurt a guy . . ."—but make sure you can laugh as you say it!

Marlin P., a young artist, complained that his boss often made remarks like "You could never make it freelance" or "Why can't you get along with anybody?" even though Marlin's talent was generally admired and he got along well with people. I asked Marlin, "Does your boss feel threatened by you?" After thinking about it, Marlin answered, "Yes, I guess maybe he does. He knows he's not as talented as I am, or as young, and he thinks I want his job." Knowing why others feel threatened by you helps take the sting out of their put-downs. You may have to shore up their self-esteem or have some good responses ready—or both.

Verbal Martial Arts

In a Charismedia group I asked people to practice attacking fellow students so that the "victims" could sharpen their responses. One man said to a pretty young student, "Why do you wear dark glasses all the time? To hide your sexuality?" At first she was terribly flustered by his question. I suggested that she practice turning the question back on the questioner. With a wide-eyed, innocent look, she turned to him, smiled sweetly, and said, "Oh, really? What makes you think that?" The attacker stammered, suddenly put on the spot by his own question. Now *he* sounded suspect. This technique of repeating the question can gain time and catch the questioner off guard. When you seriously call the question itself into question (without appearing resentful), the spotlight is turned on the person who asked it, and you may never have to answer the question at all! Again, the principle is: you don't have to play other people's games if you don't want to!

You can also answer with a wild exaggeration. If someone were to ask (unforgivably) how much money you make, a flippant response is in order: "Well, I've decided not to buy the Koh-i-noor diamond this year!" Or you might prefer to give a sober but evasive answer: "Well, I can't complain, but these days money just isn't worth what it was." You have to decide exactly what shade of impression you want to convey.

Seeming to answer while giving little real information is an art familiar to every political figure. Watch *Meet the Press* or *Face the Nation* on television, and observe political statements in the news with an appreciative eye for old and new effective ploys. Different levels of disclosure are appropriate for each situation. You don't have to "tell all" to an interviewer or casual acquaintance.

The head of a leading executive search firm told me that women reentering the job market tend to tell too much in a job interview, as though talking to a personal friend. If you share your feelings fully with someone close or with your private journal, then you can decide how much or how little to tell a stranger, and exactly how you want to do it.

Are You Long-Winded?

One of the secrets of good communication is judging how much the person you're talking to needs to hear and can take in. Lynn S. needed a ride home because her car broke down. When she met a fellow teacher in the hall, with only five minutes between classes, she went into a long whining story about her day's misfortunes before asking her question. All she had needed to say was, "Could you give me a lift home? My car broke down."

Powerful Put-Downs

If a put-down is powerful, it often outlives the relationship that triggered it. One of the oldest is attributed to Heraclitus. When a nobleman sneered at him for his low birth, Heraclitus gently replied, "The difference between us is that your family ends with you and mine begins with me." In the same vein, when renowned artist James McNeill Whistler was asked by a snob in a London drawing room how he had come to be born in such a nondescript town as Lowell, Massachusetts, he answered simply, "I wanted to be close to my mother."

Adlai Stevenson, who enjoyed needling other politicians, was once annoyed by a man from California. Stevenson said, "He is the only man I know who could chop down a giant sequoia, then stand on the stump and deliver a speech on conservation." (The beauty of that denunciation is its extravagantly fantasized scenario.)

Make your own Commonplace Book where you collect the uncommon, quotable sayings, aphorisms, or observations of the great, near-great, or unknown. Collect the most entertaining and effective put-downs you come across. You may never use them, but it gives you a pleasant glow of security to know you can if you choose. They will also help you use *humor*, which takes the sting out of most put-downs and keeps you from sounding angry and losing face.

Every barb should be accompanied by a smile. The Chinese assert that the first person to become angry has run out of arguments and has lost face. When you remain calm and unruffled, you're much less vulnerable to attack.

Dr. Reinhold Aman, editor of *Maledicta, the International Journal of Verbal Aggression*, claims the art of cursing is socially important: it releases pent-up emotions without violence! He says, "Insults should be aimed at behavior, something a person can change." "When I see you," he told his department chairman, "my feet fall asleep." (He had already been fired, so he had nothing to lose!)

The art of hyperbole is useful, but practice flexing it on yourself rather than jumping to put down others. Nine times out of ten there's a better way. Making other people look foolish is a dangerous game. Most people can never forget a really telling slur—nor forgive the perpetrator—especially if it holds the victim up to ridicule. Are you a tease? Ask yourself or the "tease-ees" if you're causing pain. Ask yourself how you would like being on the receiving end.

Knowing your feelings, acknowledging them, and taking appropriate action to express them in ways that you want to are essential to your charisma. If you never insult anybody, practice inventing the most imaginative insults you can, simply to flex your creative imagination. But better not unleash them on the people who bother you!

Using images always gives a powerful boost to your persuasive power. Practice finding images for describing qualities that annoy you, trouble you, or delight you. Successful communicators do this almost automatically. Warning me about a talk show host who flitted from topic to topic in a maddening way, a writer told me, "He has the attention span of a spastic dragonfly!"

> Keep notes on particularly effective images that you hear or read.

Sometimes putting *yourself* down, ruefully and without gravity, can be disarming. "I'm the only person I know who can eat ice cream in bed and make crumbs!"

But what happens if you're deluged with compliments?

Don't Duck the Flowers

"I'm always uncomfortable when people say nice things to me." "I usually mistrust people who pay me compliments . . ." When I ask in Charismedia workshops, "How many people find it hard to accept compliments?" most people raise their hands. Nearly everybody sometimes enjoys admiration, but if you were brought up to be "modest" and self-deprecating, naturally you were also supposed to pretend you were unworthy of compliments or, worse, to actually feel that way. All this makes it difficult to now accept compliments gracefully.

Does it matter? Yes! If you don't accept a compliment with pleasure, the complimenter feels pretty foolish or even put down, as though you had refused a gift or questioned his or her judgment or taste. And in a way you have!

How many times have you heard someone say in response to a compliment about appearance or dress, "Oh, this old thing!?" or "It only cost $2.98." or "It's dirty!" or "Really? *I* think I look terrible!" Or the other person hastily compliments you back. In many cultures, a half-buried superstitious fear of attracting the "evil eye" dictates a modest disclaimer. Most Europeans and Asians would consider the response, "I like it, too," immodest and possibly arrogant. (It's also dangerous to admire something too effusively in a Chinese home—hospitality would demand that your host give you the admired object.) Many people fear envy and jealousy implied in flattery. The Greek idea of *hubris*, or overweening pride or arrogance, suggests that a disastrous fall awaits those who are too pleased with themselves.

Gift giving is often a power play that leaves the recipient at a disadvantage—in the giver's debt. Someone says to you, "Gee, you look great!" You notice he or she is not looking so well; nevertheless, you hasten to respond, "You're looking wonderful, too!" feeling like a shabby hypocrite.

Resist the impulse to give back the compliment as though it were a bomb that might go off if you held onto it. "I appreciate that" or a simple, smiling "Thank you" or "You're very kind" or "That's nice to hear" are better. And there is "What a nice thing to say!"

> Don't worry about deserving the compliment.

There is a rough justice in human affairs. You'll probably find that things you deserved recognition for are sometimes overlooked, so you can afford to accept an undeserved compliment once in a while!

Sometimes people will value an action or remark that you take completely for granted. "It was so wonderful of you not to call attention to the fact that I was fifteen minutes early for my first appointment," a client remarked to me once. I was surprised that she found this "wonderful," but for some reason of her own, it was important to her. I resisted the impulse to say, "Oh, I don't see anything wonderful about that!"

Some compliments may be so effusive that they surprise you ("It was wonderful of you to come—you made the party!"). Although you don't need to agree with equal effusion, accept such compliments simply and gracefully. Although they may be part of a social ritual, they are not necessarily insincere, just a verbal hug!

If you *need* constant praise to keep going, your basic self-esteem may be dangerously low. Ideally, it's better to take both praise and blame lightly. In practice, most people need a fair amount of encouragement. *Too much* can boomerang. Tell a child he's "wonderful," and he'll promptly pull his little sister's hair or do some other mischief to prevent your having such unrealistic notions. (Serves you right for putting an unfair burden of expectation on him!)

The Art of Giving Compliments

I can live on a really good compliment for months!
—Mark Twain

Compliment giving, like other gentle arts, has suffered a considerable decline since Twain's time. Maybe that's why, in this anxious age, people need more of them to achieve the same sustaining effect. A really good compliment shows a subtle appreciation of the person you admire. When you can praise a quality or action that the person values, too, you have enhanced creativity and self-image.

> Acknowledge—Appreciate—Absorb, not only your own but others' good qualities.

This is the nurturing ground of further growth and development. In an era of increasing choices, there is simply too much going on to keep track of without help. Critics offer a consumers' guide in the commercial jungle, but the critical attitude itself creates divisions and rifts. If "ugh" and "wow!" are your usual responses, you're missing a whole range of reactions in between.

What five things would you like people to think or say of you? Which five compliments do you dislike the most?

Consider your motives for choosing each one.

It used to be said that a beautiful woman wants to be admired for her brains and a brainy one for her beauty. (This was before we realized that brains and beauty are not mutually exclusive!)

Sometimes a bouquet can masquerade as a barb. Paul Tabori, the Hungarian-English author and humorist, was a great humanitarian, always quietly helping the steady stream of exiled writers and artists who fled to London and New York to escape tyranny of one kind or another. So the word went out, "Don't go to see Paul—he'll get you a job!"

Don't compliment someone on the obvious. It's almost insulting to gush, "You have a lovely voice!" to Pavarotti or "You're so talented!" to any recognized artist. The more detailed and specific you make your points of admiration, the more valid and appreciated they will be.

"I love the way you phrased that final section in the Mozart!"

"You have redefined that piece for me!"

"Your handling of irony is masterful, especially in the 'bird-dog' story!"

"I've never been so moved by a performance of _____."

"You handled that situation with a great deal of tact."

"I liked your perceptive insight in that paper."

Informed appreciation is rare and treasurable. I once called a researcher who did the fact checking for an article about my work in a major magazine to thank her for the accuracy of her reporting. She said, "Oh, I can't tell you how much I appreciate this! Nobody ever notices what I do since I don't have a byline. This is the first time anybody's called to thank me."

When you praise a child, be just as specific: "I like the way that line curves down the page; you used interesting colors." "I admire your backhand; you get a good swing to the racket."

Is Your Voice Warm?

A good compliment gives insight and warmth and is, therefore, a real gift. In our Charismedia workshops, I ask each person to hear compliments in turn from everyone else in the group. Everybody is asked to offer each person something valid and positive. Even though people have to come up with something different from the comments of others who preceded them, it's remarkable that everybody is able to find *something*, given a few guidelines. "Don't waste time on trivia, like items of clothing," I caution them when somebody says something like "I like your tie!" "Stick to appreciation that is meaningful, even if it's slight or elusive." Forced to make distinctions, people come up with more subtle and valuable messages that they otherwise might not have hunted for: "I really appreciate your warmth in sharing with the group; you always have an insightful comment," or "I learned a lot from listening to you," or "I enjoy the little half-smile with which you tell us something new." Often warmth and helpful feedback might otherwise never have been expressed.

> The habit of defining what you appreciate sharpens your pleasure and stimulates the very qualities you admire.

Everybody learns from feedback, and what we nourish then develops, positive or negative. Expand your vocabulary; learn a new word every other day. The richer your appreciation of language, the more eloquent and articulate you can be. Those are important aspects of charisma.

In general, our culture encourages us to express negatives more freely than positives. "I wish I had told him I loved him!" Rosalind L. sobbed about her father who had died suddenly. "I never did. And now I'll never be able to." Many people find it hard to express their true feelings of love and appreciation to those they love most.

If you want to correct or improve a student, employee, friend, or colleague's performance, give positive feedback *first*, before criticizing. And don't add "*but!*": "You did a good job—*but* it could have been more thorough." It's better to say, "Your points were excellent—on the rewrite it would be good to add more detail to points 6, 9, and 12."

One of the most frequent complaints in business and academia is "I don't know what my boss wants! He never tells me when I'm doing well!"

Expressing positive feelings is related to giving honest and constructive compliments. Both can be deeply satisfying and enhance your relationships and the quality of your life. Earlier you saw how important it is to give positive feedback to yourself. Giving it to others and being able to accept it ungrudgingly *from them* are two sides of the same coin!

The increased flow of information and warmth provides the foundation and stimulus for improved communication. New and unexpected things begin to happen. You raise the energy level, and your own charisma quotient shoots up when you exercise your capability to voice positive and interesting perceptions about other people and to accept theirs about you. That's a gift!

III. The Feelings of Your Sounds

For there is music wherever there is a harmony, order, or
proportion: and thus far we may maintain the music
of the spheres.
—Thomas Brown

Sound, which creates worlds, can draw people to you and enlarge your personal charisma. Its effect can be compelling and dramatic, as if when you vibrate to a certain wavelength, you irresistibly attract people.

"Yes, but aren't you born with whatever voice you have?" you ask. Yes and no! Most people do not really use the full power and range of their speaking voices. Strangely, this is even true for opera singers, whose singing voices are often so much richer and more interesting than their speaking voices that it's hard to guess it's the same person.

In my course for young singers at the Manhattan School of Music in New York (which I half whimsically entitled, "How to Act Although Singing"), it amazed me that more often than not young singers would use a small, rather boring voice to speak, no matter how rich and splendid their singing voices were. This was especially true of the women, possibly because their early conditioning as females was more powerful than their training as singers. It was almost as though they were in hiding from their full gifts.

Many people have told me that when they were children, they were warned not to talk loudly, not to raise their voices, and, if they were girls, to be "ladylike." Just as a poet may be daring in print but terrified of expressing feelings aloud, many women singers have an instinctive sense that it is socially acceptable to be powerful in singing but inappropriate or threatening to use their full voices in everyday life.

Not only women are programmed to be quiet and modest; children are warned not to "show off." Once you begin to guard the expression of your feelings, your voice, too, goes underground. The natural spontaneity of children is dampened, sometimes permanently. Their voices become careful, dull, with very little range or color.

What sounds "normal" to you is largely just what you're used to hearing. That's why so many people are shocked when they first hear themselves on tape. "But I *can't* have such a terrible accent as that!"

Unless you've had speech or voice training, your speech probably reflects pretty accurately the speech patterns of the place where you grew up and the people you grew up with, your family and peers. It's not just the way you pronounce words but the much more subtle business of inflections, ranges, speed, and emphasis. Most Americans have been exposed to standard "mid-Atlantic" speech on radio and TV. Yet their speech still reflects their childhood homes, their educational backgrounds, and the speech of the people they spent the most time with.

Often people ask me to help them get rid of a regional or foreign accent. Most foreigners, however, don't realize that Americans in general are charmed by a foreign accent—as long as it's clear enough for them to understand.

Among foreign accents there is a certain subliminal hierarchy of preference. British, French, and Swedish accents are usually regarded as more glamorous than Spanish, Italian, or German. As George Orwell wrote in *Animal Farm*, everybody's equal—only some are more equal than others. Southerners used to feel that Northerners considered them not quite bright if they used their habitual speech rate. A person with a heavy Brooklyn or New Jersey accent may seem provincial, "dumb," or vulgar. A Mexican accent in California, a Puerto Rican one in New York, an African-American accent—alas, anywhere—may trigger prejudice. Sometimes fashions shift. Since the Carter and Clinton presidencies, a Southern accent is much more accepted. You may even hear a commentator or newsperson with a slight Southern lilt, which adds a nice variety to our increasingly homogenized society. It would be a shame if all regional differences were expunged.

Actors doing commercials are aware that sponsors love a Midwestern accent. Their feeling is that most of the customers are out there in the heartland, and commercials should flatter them by sounding the way they do. Oh, there are a few characters in commercials from other parts of the country, but in general, the Midwestern accent remains the most desirable in commercials, especially for touting the virtues of soap and household cleaners.

When I went to Bennington College, I was exposed for the first time to the nasal semi-Britishism of the eastern seaboard upper-class accent. My classmates with that amazing (to me) nasal drawl had all gone to the small coterie of exclusive private schools, and they addressed each other as "Stokie" or "Smithie." Although everybody dressed in jeans, the subtle segregation by speech patterns was semiautomatic and inevitable.

In England, class distinctions based on speech still exist. Working-class youngsters who attend "public schools" on scholarship are keenly aware that speech is one of the dividers between the "ins" and the "outs." To some extent that has broken down since Monty Python and the Beatles. The rich infusion of talent from the non–U of British society has made Liverpudlian, Birmingham, and Manchester accents more familiar to everyone—and respectable. Even Cockney speech is more accepted. Still, it's not likely that Liverpudlians would be very welcome, even now, in the boardroom of a major corporation—unless they owned the corporation!

In this country some circles consider clear, mid-Atlantic speech "affected." Nevertheless, a number of my students, determined to move up in the world by way of "improving their speech," successfully transformed their speaking style and are very happy at the entrée it has given them into circles that had previously been closed to them.

Changing your accent requires high motivation, lots of perseverance, and a good ear. It's hardest if you're surrounded by people who speak the way you want *not* to. If they think your desire to change is a criticism of them, subtly or not, they may discourage you. Still, some hardy souls succeed in pulling it off.

Diane L., a lovely young airline flight attendant, was in the habit of riding a motorcycle with her boyfriend on her days off. One day, dressed in her usual motorcycle gear of very brief shorts and a sweatshirt, she decided it would be fun to have dinner at a posh restaurant in the suburbs they had just passed.

"We walked in," she reported to me delightedly, "and I could see them getting ready to say, 'I'm sorry, we can't serve you.' But I just acted as if I belonged there. Using my new voice and speech, I told them we'd like to have dinner. They seated us and acted very respectful the rest of the evening. It was just great! I guess they figured if I wasn't somebody important, I wouldn't have the nerve to come in dressed like that!"

Chalk up one more demonstration that:

People do walk through the door of your expectations.

According to the responses to the charisma questionnaire, 90 percent felt that voice was an important element in charisma; 89 percent added that eloquence was probably a prime ingredient, too. Most people in the United States, consciously or not, consider an English accent more elegant and eloquent. The famous drama teacher and actress Stella Adler was shopping in a fashionable Fifth Avenue store when someone asked her, "Pardon me, are you English?" To which the great lady replied disdainfully, "No, dahling, just affected!"

At the offices of the top executives in New York and California, it's a status symbol to have an English secretary. A British paper-industry consultant tells me he's keenly aware of what an advantage speech gives him in negotiations with his American colleagues.

Since the subtle messages of speech are such an integral part of your overall image, they contribute to or detract from your charisma. Much depends on how people in your environment perceive your speech. That does *not* mean you should fake an English accent! It *does* mean that speaking clearly with an interesting, musical, and expressively varied voice is a tremendous asset. It also feels good!

My English consultant friend claims that, by and large, American businessmen tend to have extraordinarily flat, uninteresting voices. Some people, even when they're talking about something they care about, sound as though they're issuing instructions ("Get me a dozen boxes of No. 10 A1").

In addition to obeying messages not to show off, many businesspeople try too hard to seem businesslike or "professional." The professional societies—engineers, lawyers, urban planners, doctors, and architects, all very left-brain-oriented professions—are full of people who speak with virtually no inflection. Their voices are so uninteresting that they put an audience to sleep. Across the length and breadth of the land, charitable, fraternal, and academic organizations are afflicted with speakers who are terrified of speaking and have never learned to do it well.

According to a study of more than three thousand people across the United States, 41 percent were more afraid of public speaking than any other single thing. In a British study by the London *Sunday Times* the women polled were far more fearful than the men. Fear of death rated only seventh on their list, just ahead of flying and loneliness—and after heights, insects and bugs, financial problems, deep water, and sickness.

Do you dread speaking in public? If the answer is yes, check your reasons:

1. I might make a fool of myself.

2. I'll forget what I wanted to say.

3. People won't listen to me.

4. My voice will crack.

5. People will find out I'm not as bright as they think.

6. I won't be able to express myself clearly (related to 1).

7. Other.

Instant Persuasion Power

All of us sound wonderful when we're enthusiastic. So now list ten things you *like* to say. If you're not sure, close your eyes, breathe deeply, and let yourself remember the last time you enjoyed yourself. What did you say? You might list statements such as

1. I had a wonderful time.

2. I love you.

3. That's great.

4. You're wrong!

5. I've finished the job.

6. That's good.

7. I believe *I'm* next.

8. Will you go to hell!

9. Kiss me.

10. You idiot!

11. I can do it.

12. I sold it!

13. I love this restaurant.

Fill in your own list.

Say the sentences aloud with enthusiasm. (The examples, by the way, are all actual sentences various students gave during workshops.)

Now list ten things you *hate* to say! For instance, are any of these on your list?

1. I won't do it.

2. I love you.

3. Stop bugging me.

4. You're wrong.

5. I'm wrong.

6. I'm sorry. (It's amazing how many people just *can't* apologize.)

7. Kiss me.

8. You idiot!

9. Will you please help me?

10. I don't want to see you anymore.

11. I'm going to have to level with you.

12. You don't understand what I'm trying to say.

13. I don't get it.

14. I had a wonderful time.

You'll have noticed that several of the example sentences are on both lists! Some people love to say what others find difficult. This is a highly personal and profoundly important list for you. You may be surprised at some of the sentences you put on it!

The Pleasure Priority Sentence

Now pick the one in the first list that you can say with the most pleasure and enthusiasm. Say it over and over with mounting feeling. Notice the point where you begin to feel silly or the feeling is forced. Then go back to the point just before, and recapture the full expressiveness of that one.

If you find you're losing the original feeling and sound of pleasure, stop. Close your eyes and revisualize yourself in the situation, time, and place when you first said it. Plunge on. Do you find it harder to say positive than negative things? Then practice the Great Wow! Do you find it hard to say negative things? You need courage from the Charisma-cises. Of all the pleasurable sentences, which do you like to say best?

Now that you've identified the Pleasure Priority (PP) Sentence, repeat it and notice how it sounds and feels as you say it. Escalate the pleasure; see how much you can increase it without losing the genuine feeling. What's your face doing? Your eyes? Your voice? Hang on to the image of your happy experience when you first said the sentence. See yourself then. Be able to reproduce the tone of your voice, the twinkle in your eye, and the enthusiasm you felt.

"But that would feel like acting," you say.

It's not acting. It's *reacting* or *reenacting*.

Practice several days. Also take time to spot new pleasure sentences in the course of your day. Write them down, enjoy them, and enlarge them. Whatever becomes *conscious* is then a *usable tool* for greater expressiveness.

> You're increasing your charisma quotient when you increase the amount of pleasure you feel and express.

Experiment with different ways of expressing the pleasure. Vary the tone, the pitch, the inflection, and the speed. Try these on a tape recorder. Watch other people expressing pleasure: your child, your friends, strangers, people on TV. See if you can feel your way into their faces. How would it feel to use your face that way? You'll begin to explore new expressions that you haven't used before.

Mix and Match!

Now take one of your "disliked" sentences and say it in exactly the same tone and with the same expression you used for your Pleasure Priority Sentences.

Suppose you love to say, "That's good!" Take one you hate to say, like "I'm sorry." Ordinarily, you probably mumble it while feeling apologetic or defensive and thoroughly uncomfortable. Now say, "That's good!" noticing how your voice and inflection sound. Immediately follow that with "I'm sorry!"—this time *using the same pleasantness and energy you used when you said "That's good!"*

It's much easier for someone to hear "I'm sorry" when it sounds pleasant and looks friendly, not sullen and grudging. This technique will detoxify a lot of your "hate to say" sentences and take them off other people's "hate to hear" list! Not every PP Sentence will work, but you'll be able to find at least one that will. You can then choose the right sound you want, from a range of positive inflections. This suddenly opens up brand-new possibilities and effective options.

For instance, if "I love this restaurant." was one of your PP Sentences and "I don't get it." was one of your "hates," you'll sound very open and able to smile at yourself if you apply the inflection of the first to the second. If "I've finished the job." was one of your PP Sentences, it might go very well with "I don't want to see you anymore." or "I won't do it!"

Instead of sounding defeated, apologetic, or resentful, you will come across as unthreatened and able to admit a mistake cheerfully. If it's regret you're expressing, you'll sound—instead of indignant, reproachful, or defensive—adult and thoughtful. These are much better for *your* self-esteem, and face-saving for your listener.

On the other hand, if "You idiot!" was a PP Sentence, it might not sound good on "Kiss me." (unless you want to be lightly exasperated or gaily commanding). If you had a little wine and the lights were low and you met the person of your dreams and then you said, "I had a wonderful time." rather dreamily, *that* would apply marvelously to "Kiss me." Or "I believe I'm next." as a PP Sentence would apply perfectly to "That's great." (if that's a negative one for you) or to "Will you please help me?" (pleasant but not abject), "I'm sorry," or "I'm wrong." But it probably wouldn't work quite as well on "You don't understand what I'm trying to say." Try it; it's possible you *will* like it.

Now that you have the principle, you can really begin to be very effective when saying the things that are hardest for you—things that could otherwise cause a lot of misunderstanding and unnecessary suffering. One of my clients, a department manager in a large corporation, called a man he admired to tell him the unpleasant news that the corporation wouldn't be buying from him in the following year. The department manager, Jeff, felt very bad about this, particularly because he had been trying to avert the negative decision. The men were close enough for Jim, the supplier, to say to him, "Say, are you personally disappointed in me? You sound so cold, as though you're angry about something." Jeff was shocked. "Oh, my gosh, no, Jim! I just hated to have to tell you this!" In the Charismedia workshop, Jeff role-played, telling Jim the bad news with warmth in his voice so that the disappointing news wouldn't be twice as bad because he sounded unfriendly.

Homemade Opera

Sing Jeff's sentence in ten different ways. "Oh, but I can't sing!" you protest. Never mind. That doesn't matter in the slightest. Besides, I don't believe it! *Everybody* is capable of singing. Never mind that countless teachers and relatives may have told you you're a "listener" or "just stand there and move your mouth, but don't sing!" or "You have no voice!" Samuel Taylor Coleridge, an early "putter-downer" of bad singing, wrote caustically:

> *Swans sing before they die—*
> *'twere no bad thing*
> *Did certain persons die*
> *before they sing!*
> —"Epigram on a Volunteer Singer"

Never mind! If you can sustain sounds, you can sing. The rest is training your ear.

We all have an innate need to sing. It's part of the human capacity to express feelings. When a child is told, "You can't sing!" a real violation of the spirit takes place, a secret, burning wound. Everyone experiences a deep yearning to utter lyric cries of emotion, pain or joy, in musical form. There are psychophysical reasons for this. Since sustained sound uses much more breath than everyday speech, it offers emotional release, discharge of the psychophysical buildup of stress, and aesthetic satisfaction. Manfred Clynes suggested in his remarkable book, *Sentic Cycles*, that there is a model in the brain for all musical-emotional expression. That's why, when we hear a great artist expressing an emotion with precision and fullness, we *recognize* and are moved and cleansed by it.

We also tend to feel love for the artist. When teenage girls swoon over Leonardo DiCaprio, or opera fans go wild over Luciano Pavarotti, they express a deep inner yearning of human nature.

Expression seems to be just as much a deep human need as eating and sleeping—sometimes even more important. You don't have to be great to sing or dance. Just expressing feelings—especially in some kind of shaped form—not only eases emotional pain but also enhances feelings of innate self-worth. There is a profound satisfaction in shaping something beautiful or expressive from raw emotion. We feel it was somehow of value to have suffered, and the joy of communicating and connecting with other people's deepest emotions is incalculably great. Emotion "remembered in tranquillity" through art becomes a way of managing the world, of connecting with the meaning of existence.

The first Western nation to apply the awareness of music's importance on a nationwide scale was post–World War II Hungary. The Communist government offered Zoltán Kodály, their greatest living composer, the opportunity to revolutionize Hungary's musical education in any way he liked.

Kodály knew that singing is profoundly valuable for children's mental health, concentration, self-esteem, and ability to get along well with people. He started them off before kindergarten. Children between three and six years old sang every day, learned to improvise in song, and sang together. The especially talented ones were sent to special schools, as they are everywhere in the world, but the extraordinary achievement in Hungary was a level of musical skill, expressiveness, and involvement for all children that has literally transformed the musical consciousness of the country.

When I visited Hungary, I asked if I could observe an "ordinary" class of fourteen-year-olds. Having heard about this amazing training, I was curious to hear what these young people could do. When I entered the music room, I was a little surprised to notice there was no piano or other instrument. The teacher began by asking one student to sing four bars in "the style of Bach." Tall and gawky, the boy stood up and unhesitatingly improvised a very graceful and rather elaborate melody of four bars in the style of Bach. Not only was his intonation excellent, but he also was evidently enjoying himself and had no trouble doing the assignment.

Then the teacher pointed to another child and said, "Mari, will you please sing a counterpoint to the subject." To my amazement, Mari, a tall, buxom girl with pigtails, got up and sang an ingenious counterpoint, on the spot, just as the teacher had asked her to do. Next came improvisations in the style of Mozart, then of Beethoven. I was struck by the delight with which the students sang, and how perfectly in tune they were regardless of how involved the melodies became. I doubt if graduates of Juilliard or any other American conservatory could have done better or even as well. It was an astonishing hour.

By starting everybody off so young, no child is unable to sing. Even assuming an exceptionally high proportion of musically talented children in Hungary, it can't be statistically possible that there are no "listeners"— as the ironic euphemism goes—in the whole country! It's simply assumed that everybody can learn to sing—and so everybody does.

"Speech IS Music"

The great Russian director Konstantin Stanislavsky said, "Speech *is* music," and trained his company to sing so that they would speak with a musical line, color, and feeling. Rhythm, tone, and movement added incomparable richness and expressive subtlety. The values of silence suddenly become more meaningful. Ralph Richardson, the great English actor, went so far as to say that "pauses are the most important part of speech." They help "impregnate the words with fresh inner content." A contemporary Japanese composer, Toru Takemitsu, wrote that he wanted to achieve with his music "the eloquence of silence."

Stanislavsky understood that deep feelings are released through the qualities of sounds themselves. In *Building a Character*, he wrote: "Do you realize that an inner feeling is released through the clear sound of the *A* (ah)? That sound is bound up with certain deep inner experiences which seek release and easily float out from the recesses of one's bosom. But there is another *A* sound. It is dull, muffled, does not float out easily but remains inside to rumble ominously—as if in some cavern or vault. There is also the insidious *AAA*, which whirls out to drill its way into the person who hears it. The joyous *A* sound rises from one like a rocket, in contrast to the ponderous *A* which, like an iron weight, sinks in to the bottom of one's wellsprings."

Try these for yourself:

- The euphoric *Ahhh*—when you meet a dear friend you haven't seen for years—"Ahhhhhhh! I'm so happy to see you!"

- The dull depressed groan of "Ahhh, don't bother me! Agh, what's the use?" (More like an *uhh*, preceded by a heavy sigh.)

How perceptive Stanislavsky was when he said, "Do you not sense that particles of you are carried out on these vocal waves? These are not empty vowels; they have a spiritual content."

As the Italians (who gave the world the art of *bel canto*) know, singing is largely the art of sustaining vowels. People who haven't been used to singing usually alter the pitch or shape of the sounds and close them off quickly.

Floating on the sustained sound is itself a form of trust. Vocally, it's like being on a swing—it puts you in touch with a feeling of soaring mastery and power. If the sound is placed right, an interesting thing happens—the note begins to float itself. It seems to grow out of the top of one's head, and you are surrounded by a sea of sound. The singer has become the sound. This is an indescribably exhilarating sensation. But how do you "place it right"?

The Tonal Trapeze

To get in touch with that arcing loop of which you're only a small part, open your mouth just wide enough to say a smiling, easy *ahh*. Allow your jaw to relax; your tongue lies quietly at the bottom of your mouth. The back hinge of the jaw is wide enough for one finger to support the top jaw. Breathe with your mouth open in this position a few times, as softly and gently as you can. Gradually increase the amount of breath, then say *huh-huh-huh-huh-huh* as though you're laughing gently. Then begin singing *haaahh*—with as imperceptible an attack as you can manage. Let the *h* begin the sound. This way you keep the throat open, instead of starting with a glottal catch.

When the sound begins, nothing in the mouth or throat or tongue changes. Feel the sound filling your mouth and then penetrating the upper hard and soft palate and shooting up through the top of the head into the surrounding atmosphere. See where else you feel the vibration; you may find your shoulders, legs, or chest buzzing.

Keep the sound going until you've run out of air. Then, leaving your mouth and jaw in the same position, let the sound end, just fading away, melting into silence. Still not moving anything, allow the back of the throat to be an open door for your breath rising from the stomach. Don't shut it off or start the sound with the twitchy little glottis.

There's nothing intrinsically wrong with the glottal catch. But to produce a free, open vowel sound and gain access to the currents of breath from your lower abdomen, it's valuable to know how to begin a sound *without* a glottal catch (which always starts the sound in the throat). Save that for tremulous emotional moments—when it's very effective. You may find it hard at first to make a vowel sound *without* a glottal catch, but it will pay off in vocal freedom. Here are some sentences to practice on. Have fun with them!

Glottal Nonstop Sentences

1. Esther idled away hours at antiques auctions.

2. Aunt Alice always inquired after all our affairs.

3. Almost everyone enjoys an evening of elegance.

4. Oscar outshines all other outstanding oboists (athletes, engineers, egotists).

5. Edward evidences every attribute of evasiveness.

6. Asters are arranged all over in extravagant abundance.

7. Archaeologists anticipate an enormous array of eye-opening artifacts.

8. Isabella always assured employers of unfailing ingenuity.

9. Each and every assignment energized eager actors.

10. I'd appreciate an uncluttered, uncomplicated existence once in a while.

Note—If you have difficulty doing any of these ten sentences, try the following:

1. Put an *h* before every vowel.

2. Try saying them without any consonants at all. It helps to put the thumb on the hard palate to do this—just hang the head on the thumb. Link all the sounds together.

3. Sometimes it helps to use arm movements.

4. A nice breathless sound to begin each vowel will help you get the hang of this.

5. Be as extravagant as possible in your inflections!

How to Sing Even Though You Can't

Let the back of your tongue press down as you breathe again and start a new sound with the breath *haaaaaah*. Starting softly, gradually increase the sound, filling the cavities of the head and the spaces around your head with the sustained sound of your *hahhhhhhhh*. Keep the mouth, tongue, and jaw in the same open position while you sing the sound.

Begin with a note that's comfortable for you in the middle of your range. Sing that note five times, holding it each time as long as you can. Then start a new note, this time going as low as you can. Feel the sound spreading as you hold it, to your neck, shoulders, and chest and then upward around your head. Feel the back of your head buzzing.

After you've tried that four or five times, keep the image of the sound permeating your head, ears, and the crown of your head, in addition to the neck, chest, and shoulders. Then, still feeling the vibrations in the entire upper body, spread them gradually through your waist and stomach. Feel your ribs and the sides of your spine opening, buzzing, and vibrating with the note you're singing. Really take time to visualize these vibrations opening and spreading your sound energy. Feel the ribs opening as though the air were pushing them apart.

If you aren't sure whether you actually feel the vibrations, just *imagine* you do. Pretty soon you will be able to make every cell tingle with the dense intensity of your sound. Your body will feel both more porous and more intensely awake; it will be tuning in to its own sounds. You'll notice that the sound feels different in different sections—it may tickle in some places, buzz in others, warm you at other points. All this is floated on the breath.

Your main task is not to interfere with the flowing diffusion of sound through your whole system. Let it flow!

The Sonic Embrace

After doing the low *haah* ten times, close your eyes and feel your whole body tingling with the sounds; you'll feel wrapped in a kind of sonic embrace, very warm and cozy. Be sure to make the beginning and end of sounds as gentle as possible. Now hear the sounds continuing after you have stopped. Feel the space around your head and body and under your feet as being completely filled in with vibrations, so that you're swimming in a thick sea of pulsing sound. Sit for two to ten minutes with eyes closed and enjoy the sensations of tingling and warmth and being massaged. Pay particular attention to your back (as though you were being stroked, a soft fur laid around you, or thousands of light fingertips gently caressing you). When you've stopped, release your stomach and breathe in very slowly through your lower belly with your mouth closed.

Sonic Acupressure Massage

Every day in the shower, where the sound is glamorously amplified and everybody is a star, start with an easy hum and check out how your body feels from the inside. Is there a pain, an ache? A slightly sore place somewhere? Send the hum there, a sonic messenger to massage and warm you where you need it most. When you find the right pitch, it will connect with the spot that hurts, almost as though locking into it. Visualize the hum dissolving the edges of the pain and spreading warmth all through your body.

Next, try it with an open *ah* sound. Look for the pitch that connects most deeply with your own vibratory rate. When it "hooks in," you can listen to it as though someone were giving you a giant sonic massage and all you have to do is allow yourself to enjoy it.

Now experiment with different pitches. Make them sound a little higher, a little louder. Stay with that new *haah*. Lower the back of your tongue *without* tensing the sides or the front. A neat trick! (If you can't do it at first, *imagine* it—pretty soon the muscles will wake up and respond.) Now see your body extending to each side as far as the walls, made of pure sound. Then imagine that it's extending up through the upper palate, up, up, out the top of your head. Hang on to the initial image. When you can keep those three directions vibrantly moving outward, then extend downward through the earth. If you're on the fifth floor of the building, make the sound go down below the basement!

Deepen the sound by flaring your nostrils, lifting your rib cage, and opening the "back nostrils" (inside the mouth). Hold it as long as you can. Afterward, sit and feel the sensations in your body. You may find parts waking up that you haven't been aware of before. You may feel excited. You may notice your heart beating faster. You may have a rush of unexpected emotion. When you bathe the body in sound, it triggers reservoirs of feeling. Let whatever wants to happen happen. You will probably feel distinct pleasure and tingling. Each day you try this, notice how the sensations change. Keep checking that your jaw is relaxed, the tip of your tongue relaxed, your breath as steady and even as you can make it, with the edges fading away and beginning again as imperceptibly as the sea fades into the horizon.

Tone Twins

If there's another person around, try matching sounds. First he or she sings, then you match the sound as closely as you can. With your eyes closed, start the *ahhh* very softly, get louder, and then fade away and let your partner begin the sound exactly where you leave off. Then you pick up where she or he stops. Keep this seamless ribbon of sound going until you feel you're a helix of melody twining in and out between you and you can't tell where one leaves off and the other begins.

The Endless Sound

Now put your palms against your partner's palms and start *ahhh-m* and feel the vibrations transfer between you, three to five minutes.

Then, putting your foreheads together gently, choose another pitch both of you are comfortable with. You'll find this very relaxing. Again continue for three to five minutes.

Turn around and stand with your backs leaning against each other, your heads touching. In this position you may have to work a little harder to feel the vibrations as one body. Let the resonance of your backs enlarge the sounds you're feeling and making.

Now you both close your eyes and hear the sounds as though they were coming from some other source; you're simply the receiver or container. Again, don't change anything in your mouth, jaw, and tongue once you've set the shape of the *ahhhhh*. Let go of all judgments about whether your voice sounds "pretty" or not. Just concentrate on making the sounds as even as possible. If you make them louder, make the crescendo as gradual as you can. Notice what it takes *not* to clutch at the end of a sound. (Try to imagine your throat just as open at the back arch as your mouth is at the front.) Let it end without changing anything in the position of your throat, tongue, mouth, or lips. If you notice an involuntary twitch or clutch somewhere, observe exactly where and what is happening, and the next time focus on eliminating it entirely. Even small changes in the position of your mouth, lips, tongue, or back of the throat can alter the sound. The idea is to sustain the sound *without any change* as long as possible—until it "hooks" in and floats itself.

You may find your head buzzing or even that you get a little dizzy—don't worry if that happens briefly. It merely means you're getting more oxygen than you're used to. If you get dizzy, breathe deeply (with closed mouth), pinch the flesh between your eyebrows sharply, and the dizziness will disappear.

Begin to hum and spread the hum throughout your backs. Then alternate with the *ahhhhhh*, spreading the buzzy vibration through every surface that touches your partner's back, and let it continue into the arms and hands. Keep your eyes closed so that you can experience the sounds without being distracted. Feel every millimeter of the skin surface intensely alive with vibration.

The Endless Wave

In Charismedia workshops, groups of people experiment with a continuous sound; they stand in two rows, their hands clasped, foreheads touching, eyes closed. They begin to hum. An immense wave of sound begins to permeate everyone's body; after five or ten minutes you feel as though you have one huge body that is bigger than all the individuals there and you're vibrating with all that power and energy. It's very powerful and pleasant, and afterward everybody's voice is clearer and more resonant, and everyone senses that the group energy has made them feel more alive, more comfortable in their own bodies, and more relaxed with other people, somehow part of them at the same time.

Keep the sound going, either alone or with a partner or group, sustaining sounds as long as possible, moving in and out of existence as imperceptibly as possible—in a very real sense you begin to experience the flow of your own existence as pleasurable beyond words.

The benefits? Your breath control will increase greatly, your energy level will rise, you will feel more centered, and your overall concentration will improve dramatically if you practice this every day. These experiences will also help you to speak in public with greater ease and courage. The risk of making sounds in public will seem a lot less dangerous. You are laying the groundwork for actually enjoying yourself while speaking up!

Pain-to-Pleasure Transformation

It is helpful not to say "I have a pain" but rather "There is a pain." Focus on the neutral energy. By centering on the feeling *without identifying it as pain* you intensify the energy and free it to be spread and diffused through every cell, until it harmlessly drifts into the air surrounding your body. Visualize it as a warm, viscous liquid like warm Jell-O, lapping at and supporting your body. If you think of pain as a form of energy, the power of the feeling will begin to change into heat, which then feels pleasurable.

Remember, the pleasure and pain centers in the brain are very close, so these three steps help:

1. Focusing on the sensations, intensifying them

2. Spreading them throughout the body as energy, starting exhalation, and then—

3. Exhaling fully, passing out the diluted, diffused intensity like heat through cheesecloth, visualizing every cell as a fine, transparent network.

This sequence can change the experience of pain into something quite different. You may be aware of warmth or excitement or pleasure, even triumph!

Be Your Own Sun

The next step is to feel that your inside and your outside are one with only a thin membrane of skin between. The hum is the vehicle of your merging. Feel your hum dissolving your boundaries. Put the center in

a. the soles of your feet,

b. your calves,

c. your thighs,

d. your genitals and buttocks (as you move up, keep the vibration in the lower areas and simply add and spread the hum), and

e. your belly.

Be your own sun. Put the center in

f. your navel point: think of the hum as extending in a sunburst from your navel—in front, to the sides, and out to the back, as far as the horizon. Gradually make the rays longer and larger, until your navel point is the hot center of the radiant sun and you can feel the embracing rays of your own heat extending out toward infinity in every direction. You may feel prickly and tingly. Expand the prickle and tingle out to infinity.

Alternate *mmmmmm* with *ahhhhhh*. See which sound makes the sun more vivid. (The *ahhhhh* and the *mmmmmmm* are now continuous.) Then put the center in

g. your solar plexus—feel the power of the center there radiating like thunderbolts in every direction;

h. your heart—feel your heart grow bigger as though it were now enclosing your entire body, and your body is like a tiny figure inside the enormous gold heart, glowing and translucent. Now add the sun-center radiance from within the "little castle of the heart" and expand it through every individual pore in millions of tiny rays and beyond the "heart-body" enclosing your body. Fill up every space outside your own—above, to the back, the front, the sides, and below. Do this two ways: standing against someone else's back and also standing up alone.

Now put the center in

i. the throat or expressive center—open the pathway to the gut and to the head simultaneously. See the great caverns of the mouth and head and throat extending up into the head and down into the body. Scoop out the whole inside of the mouth and throat with a yawn that reaches in a great curving embrace backward to the horizon as though the back of your neck were totally open. Keep that openness when the yawn is finished. Press down the lower jaw toward the back of your neck. Let the *ahhhh* trigger new yawns each time—make each one bigger (and ruder!) than the last. Let your eyes water. Let the sounds fill the spaces outside the body, still alternating between *ahhhh* and *mmmmm*. (When you close your lips for the hum, make sure you leave them full and relaxed, the tongue low in the mouth, throat even more open if possible.)

Cover every tiny pore on the back of your neck with vibrations shooting out like fireworks. The yawn makes your neck a wider and wider hollow column where the air passes from the lower part to the throat and head.

Let your arms float upward if they want to, so there's maximum stretch while your body is lapped around with the soft embracing airwaves. What color are they? (Some people find they change.) See how you can make the sound without tensing any part of your head, throat, neck, or tongue. Keep your ribs lifted; that'll lengthen the amount of breath you have.

Be Your Own Cathedral

A wonderful way to experience your sound and body fully while you find your ideal spinal alignment is to press your back against the wall, lower your weight, knees bent, feet apart about the same width as your shoulders. The spine, from the midback to the coccyx, makes contact with the wall, every vertebra pressing against it, arms relaxed. The head is a little away from the flat surface, growing organically out of the spine, eyes directly ahead. The shoulders do not touch the wall. In that position, the trunk is relaxed though pressed against the wall.

Sing *ahhhhhhhhhhhh . . . hmmmmmmmmmm* with an open throat (no glottal attack!), holding each note as long as you can, observing the sound vibrate on the roof of the mouth, hook in, and rise straight through the top of the head.

Do this twenty-six times, and you'll find you are in an altered state of consciousness. Your sense of using your whole body to *sound* your vibrations becomes a totally different experience of your own voice. You are your own cathedral. The limitless, echoing expanses of the sounds of your own breath and voice within your head and body and floating out around you energizing your environment will give you an expanded sense of lightness and power. *Notice the moment when the sound seems to be singing itself.* Allow it to float out and mingle with the sound of the room you're in. Soon the room will seem to be singing, not you. If you're singing with someone else, let the sounds mingle and match until you can't tell who is singing; the sound will fill the space between and around you.

After you've completed the twenty-six *ahhhh-mmmmmm*s, listen to the vibration-rich silence. Feel your ears and body tingle, and notice every sensation that you experience. You'll feel expanded and abuzz. The air almost roars with the accumulation of sound.

Silence can never feel empty again after you've experienced this. You'll begin to notice that every silence has its own sound spectrum: the floor or a bone aching or creaking, the dry staccato twitch of a leaf or curtain, the velvet hum of a distant motor or current, the mordant squeal of a faraway dog, the hiss and moan and thump of internal tides, the polyphonic phrases of constant change expressed in faint cues and motifs, as elusive and varied as an atonal kaleidoscope, heard through water.

Now place your elbows on the wall on either side of your body and very gently—not changing your head or torso alignment at all—push off from the wall. Press hard away from the wall with your elbows, so the body remains aligned exactly the way it was when it was against the wall. Your pelvis is cupped like a palm or an ear, the lower back spread and wide, the stomach pressed in against the spine, the head rising from the torso like a flower at the end of its stem.

When you feel your balance is just as solid as it was when you were leaning against the wall, very, very slowly straighten your knees until they're almost—but not quite—straight. Slowly lower your arms to the sides and relax them. Now observe how your body feels, scanning it from the inside. You'll get a new sense of your optimum body alignment. Close your eyes and feel how comfortable it is to stand, both legs and feet supported by the ground, the head so centered that if you were to drop it on a straight line down the center of the body it would fall neatly between your feet after passing straight through your solar plexus, navel point, and pubic bone.

Breathe in the sound-filled silence and exhale it through every pore to join the widening, concentric circles of sound, traveling outward farther and farther with each breath. Each time you exhale, allow the breath to travel still farther outward, and begin the next inhalation by scooping in the energy from that expanded circle.

Each time you exhale, let more and more tension go from your body—not only today's, but all of the past's. Release old angers, fears, irritations, and annoyances, dissolving them into the widening circles. As you enlarge the circles, change into a helix or spiral in a dense complexity of movement that finally weaves in and out in all the directions. See it rimmed in fire, edged with light, dancing, changing, constantly carrying your breath farther out to the edges of the universe. Always widen it in all directions at once . . .

Next, exhale and widen the circle to include first

> *the room you're in*
> *then the building*
> *the block or open space*
> *the city or town*
> *the state*
> *the country*
> *the continent*
> *the oceans around the continent*
> *the other continents*
> *the world*
> *the galaxies.*

Rest in the simultaneous "being" in all this effortless flow, as though your body boundaries now include entire galaxies. It's the universe breathing in and out, and your margins blur into a much larger consciousness.

Through breathing you make the universe aware of itself. Feel space pouring through your bodilessness. You are now part of the largest universe imaginable.

Be Your Own Lullaby

Sit or lie down for this. As you rest in this expanded pulsing sea, you may pick up the sounds of this process or experience sounds as colors. Observe closely but don't force or direct anything. You may suddenly become aware, after some moments of not noticing your body, of a prickling of the hairs on the back of your neck or your foot falling asleep or some other reminder that you're back in your small form. Just notice it and release that sensation, whatever it is, with the next exhalation. Freeing it from your body, send the feeling out, and you may see it, in its shadow form, dancing outside the body. Then dissolve it in the seething energy sea—extra added power, density, and richness in the surrounding texture.

Sonic Tranquilizer

Variation I. Surrounded by the energy sea, with no effort in the throat, make the smallest, most continuous humming sound you can—as though the sound were coming from outside you. Keep experiencing the sound as if it were being generated *outside*, as if you were listening to a strange but deeply comforting steady sound coming from very far away, like a foghorn heard in childhood while you were half asleep, signaling that someone was keeping watch and all was well. We might paraphrase the medieval mystic Meister Eckehart's famous "The eye with which I look at God is the same eye with which God looks at me" as "The sound with which I sing to God (or Nature) is the same as that which God sings to me."

The detachment from one's own sound has a wonderfully calming effect. To hear the sound of one's own voice as though it were coming from outside has the effect of equalizing the energy outside and in. To sustain the feeling of this sound, make the beginning and end as imperceptible as possible. If the sound was always there and you didn't start or end it, you can merge with it. It was always there, waiting to be uttered. One can only invent ("sound") what already exists. Acknowledging, giving it voice, makes it sing.

Variation II. Imagine you're going to focus in on *the* sound of the universe. When you match the pitch, it will sing itself; you'll know by the way the inside and outside become the same. Listen to the silence and let your throat open to prepare itself. (Your mouth is open just a little.) When the pitch rises irresistibly from the silence, allow it to sound without planning or controlling it. Important—let it happen as though it had always existed (which indeed it has) and you've just permitted your body to resonate with it. *Complete relaxation of the throat, lips, tongue, and shoulders is essential.* Sometimes the sound may surprise you by being very high or then very low. The less you do, the better. Just allow it to continue as long as possible. Feel how it originates outside you and comes *into you* from all sides. It's not issuing from you. The pitch will probably be different on different days. Wait patiently for it to happen.

After this, sit very quietly and close off one nostril with your thumb and listen to the pitch of your breath. At first you may find it hard to tell what it is. But your breath, softly coming in and out of your nostrils, actually does have a pitch. Try the other one. The pitch will be middle C. Your breath sings! You have to be *very* quiet to hear it. The subtler the sounds you're attuned to, the more relaxed you are, the more power and sense of ease you can generate in your electromagnetic field. The more subtle your breath, the greater is your power.

Results? Greatly magnified charisma.

Variation III—love sounds. Think of someone you love. Avoid thinking in words. See that person with as much sensory detail as possible: light, color, smell, sound, and kinesthetic movement. Allow yourself to focus on all these impressions for a few moments, knowing that at a certain point a song will rise out of those impressions and shape itself without your doing anything but allowing it to flow out of you. All you have to do is to keep your awareness focused on the soft, warm feelings in your chest and wherever else they appear and simultaneously concentrate on the thought forms of the person you love.

As soon as you feel your concentration slipping, or you become mesmerized or distracted by the act of singing or by the song, *stop!* Refocus on the love you feel and the person who draws that love. You'll find that you're able to sustain the concentration more and more, so that the song of your love sings itself with ever less interference. Use *lalala*. Using this syllable strengthens your electromagnetic field and compensates for any negative experience or feelings by stimulating the thymus and restoring the equilibrium of the left and right hemispheres. If you can't sing aloud or you're with other people, all you have to do is *think* the *lalala* and lightly tap your tongue over and over against the ridge just behind your front teeth as you do when you sing *lalala*, and the same revitalizing effect is produced.

As you focus on the image of a person you love, let the sound emerge from that image so that the song is coming into you and you hear it as it strikes off the image, not as though you had produced it at all. Start it quite softly so you don't have to worry about *making* the sound and so the "edges" are imperceptible. This helps sustain the illusion that you're receiving the song fully formed, rather than doing it yourself. Your heart expands with warmth, light, color, and sound. Spread the sound through your body. The love sounds sustain and float around you.

Sound plus visual imagination equals the experience. Now you know what it means when they say, "When you're in love, your heart sings!"

You can in fact produce the same feelings of euphoria; it's almost like *being* in love!

9

Your Persona–Projecting the Charisma Within

Charisma is to image as electricity is to the wire that carries it. Conscious or not, everyone has a self-image and projects a persona that may or may not match the internal one. Are you projecting your real charisma or the static that interferes with it? A lot is at stake. "Nobody," remarked Garry Shandling, "gives prizes for lack of confidence."

You've seen how judgmentalism and lack of self-confidence interfere with your creativity, your health, your confidence, *and* your charisma. Ninety-five percent of respondents to the charisma questionnaire cited confidence as a key factor in charisma. The color, shape, size, and nature of your charisma are unique because you're unique. So blanket instructions on what to do won't touch the central issue: defining (and realizing in action) who you really are.

We all have a complex, subtle "feeling sense" of what we are like inside. This is hard to put into words, yet it dramatically affects how we project our "image" to other people.

A lot of factors are obviously involved: how and where we grew up; the communication styles of our culture, families, and associates; our basic sense of enjoying life; our most hidden assumptions.

You can define yourself according to your roles: "I am a businessperson," "I am a professional," "I am a student," "I am a parent," "I am an artist," etc. Or you can define yourself according to your qualities: "I am a loving person," "I am a responsible adult," "I am a hard worker," "I am intuitive" (or, less favorably, "I am oversensitive," ". . . unstable," ". . . stubborn," etc.). Astrological charts—"Are you a Gemini? I usually get along well with Gemini people" or "He's a Leo, that's why he's so domineering" or "I'm a home-loving Cancer person"—set up constellations of expectations that may reflect or influence your inner sense of yourself.

We now know, according to the principle of the hologram, that each part suggests the whole. A person's DNA contains the instructions for the *whole* organism. That's why one can "read" a person by analyzing his astrological chart, by observing body language and voice, by (if you're trained to understand the information) checking the iris of a person's eye. *Everything* is potentially a source of information about the whole person. According to our left-brain habits of thinking, we name four or five qualities or talents or predilections and come to a conclusion of some sort about ourselves or other people. The reality is much more complex, however, and harder to pin down.

When you have put yourself in touch with specific qualities that please you and that you connect with (you recognize and "own" them), it's possible to reprogram your inner image, that subtle-beyond-words computer. Through visualizing yourself in a different (perhaps only slightly different) way, you'll begin to project a different image.

An image is powerful; it can encapsulate an incredible amount of information in a microsecond. So when you imagine something deeply enough, in a relaxed state, with no forcing, you really *see* it as though it were happening right now. The mind-body programs this as a reality. That's how people with powerful dreams realize their ambitions. They "see" everything not as wishes but as *reality*. The mind and body only carry out the detailed subconscious instructions of the mental imagery. This is how healing can be programmed through imagery, and it also is why TV and films affect us so profoundly.

The beautiful part is that everybody has the capacity to imagine. We do it all the time, sometimes without realizing it.

"Is that why I sometimes get my best ideas just as I'm dropping off to sleep?" asked a young corporate executive at one seminar.

"Yes, exactly!"

If you *try* to stop thinking altogether for a moment, you'll notice it's no use; thoughts and images flash into your brain anyhow. "Oh, I must take my coat to the cleaner's" is overlapped by a picture of your neighbor's dog racing past you that morning, a fight you had with the kids, and a dim awareness of six or seven other half-formed thoughts and elusive pictures that slip out past your consciousness, some of them bearing no relation at all to the others or to your daily life. Out of this welter of information overload, we can begin to solicit a useful randomness. This is not exactly free association, but it's more right-brain than linear thinking, and it gives us access to intuitive knowledge we didn't know we had.

When people in my Charismedia workshops fill in the upcoming Vocal Self-Portrait, there's always a subtle but real and *immediate* change in their voices and speaking styles. The process consists of two parts: first you write down the answers to the questionnaire; the second part is answered aloud.

The act of describing aloud your minute reactions to your thoughts and sensations enhances learning ability. It works like this: the feeling state is a right-hemisphere activity; *describing* these feelings aloud involves left-hemisphere processes. Any activity that uses *both* hemispheres improves the coordination and working efficiency of both. That's why when children learn to sight-sing and play an instrument at the same time, their general intelligence improves. Remember, the left cerebral cortex does the work with words, analytical thinking, logic, and analysis; the right deals with perspective, music, intuition, pattern recognition, insight, and the aesthetic sense. Most of our culture is left-brain-oriented. The counterculture tried to shut down the left brain through drugs to reach a right-brain experience. But this is just as big a mistake. You need the two working together to produce a high level of creative ability and intelligence.

Homemade Opera (see chapter 8, part III) is another method of stimulating your dual brain. Dr. Denis Gorges in Cleveland developed a brain synchronizer that allows the brain to synchronize its electric rhythms for both sides, as well as front and back, through sight and sound and magnetic field induction all working together. This improves communications within the brain and probably affects emotional balance and physiological well-being. One of the most fascinating training experiences I've had was with Dr. Jean Houston, president of the Foundation for Mind Research, who, with Dr. Robert Masters, has done comprehensive work integrating the whole person through the body-mind connection. Their invaluable books detail dozens of exercises to increase the subtlety, complexity, and creativity of body-mind functioning.

Dr. Win Wenger, in his book *Beyond* OK, writes that he was amazed at the dramatic heightening of a wide spectrum of abilities as a result of describing spontaneous, visual image flow aloud. He writes, "Spontaneous visual imagery is a right-brain function; verbal description of such imagery is a left-brain function. Integrating functions from both sides . . . builds connectedness between the two hemispheres. . . . This *permanently* heightens general ability, regardless of the particular activities and problems to which describe-as-you-observe mental-imaging is directed."

In Western culture, only poets, writers, and artists are accustomed to describing internal impressions and the *feel* for experiences. Yet this intuitive cross-sensing and pattern recognition is the ground from which all creativity, problem solving, and insights arise, as well as the sense of right-wrong or true-false. If you have always wanted to play the piano like Art Tatum, then go to the piano with all the memories alive in your consciousness that you've ever had of hearing, seeing, and reading about his wonderful piano playing. All that information is stored somewhere deep inside, and if you go through it with all your senses and then apply that to actual playing, you'll learn about one hundred times faster than the conventional way. The idea is to go back and forth from your "inner virtuoso" memory to your learning.

This is why hero worship (or having a role model or guru) helps immeasurably in learning to become what one wants to. Not just information (left brain) but also the *complex feeling state* of what it means to be or do as that person is or does is being transmitted.

In Bali, where everybody is an artist and nobody stops to ask if you are "talented," children are taught to dance between ages six and eight. The teacher simply molds their bodies, instead of giving a verbal explanation.

At that age, the flexibility and plasticity of the mind and body are so great that the learning capacity is almost unlimited.

A simple way to practice visualization is to observe your "image-flow." Just breathe slowly and deeply, relaxing more and more with each exhalation. When an image flashes by, describe it aloud, whatever it is: some colors, a landscape, part of a face, some geometric shapes, whatever. If you keep describing it aloud, you will gain some interesting insights and a deep respect for the awesome richness of your inner images. If you see only some color, breathe in that color slowly and deeply a few times until the picture clears.

This is a good experience to share with a friend. Ask her or him to relax and to breathe slowly and deeply with closed eyes. When you see a slight shift under the eyelids, that eye movement is the signal that your friend is experiencing a visual image of some kind, although he or she may not be aware of it. Sometimes you'll see changes in body position, breathing, or facial expression.

After you see any of these signs, ask quietly, "What was in your awareness then? What was your impression just now?" Encourage your partner to describe the visual impressions she or he is receiving as soon as the individual becomes aware of them, even if you don't ask. At first, your friend may protest, "I don't see anything." Quite soon, though, images will start to come.

After a dozen experiences or so, pick one interesting image and ask for a more and more sensory-detailed picture. Special insights will surface when enough details are filled in. Suddenly, the "meaning" becomes clear.

Now have your partner do the same for you.

It was after experimenting with "image-flow" that I hit on the notion of using our capacity for image sensing to reprogram our voice sense. *This is one of the fastest and most effective ways to enhance your own vocal charisma.* It invariably produces rapid and subtle changes that are exactly what people have wanted for themselves.

Your Vocal Self-Portrait

Write in your answers.

What would my voice be if it were
1. a material (i.e., wood, leather, stone, silk, rubber, corduroy, etc.)?

2. a texture?

3. an animal?

4. a color?

5. a landscape?

6. a shape?

7. a flower?

8. a tree?

9. a vehicle?

10. a dance?

11. a fragrance or smell?

12. a tempo?

Is your voice

13. a musical instrument?

14. warm or cold? thick or thin?

    Does your voice

15. match your body?

16. match your face?

17. match your feelings?

18. fully represent you?

19. Is it an effort?

20. Where does it come from? (throat, chest, head, etc.)

21. Is it big or small?

22. Is it strong or weak?

23. Is breathing easy or difficult?

Accept whatever images come to you—don't reject any, even if you think they're uninteresting!

In a Charismedia workshop, I asked everybody to describe their answers. Janet, a quiet, neat administrator, was first: "I saw my voice as nubby wool. Then I had an image of a fox, but I also had a fleeting image of a horse or a wolf." She hesitated. "I guess I like the fox running over cultivated terrain, but the strength and solidity and rhythmic gait of a horse—and the wildness of a wolf. Is that OK?"

"That's fine. It's your fantasy, so you can make it anything you please," I told her.

"I saw the color as deep blue, and it was pancake shaped, thick, and cold. The flower is an organ pipe cactus. The fragrance was rich earth."

"Did you pick the cactus because of the stickers?" someone asked.

"Well, more because of its rich solid base. But I guess," she admitted with a smile, "also because of the stickers. I like sounding a little prickly!"

She couldn't feel an instrument. Her vehicle was a compact sports car going merrily over a hill.

Ellie, an extremely inhibited, shy, tall young woman of twenty, said her voice was corduroy, and the animal was a tiger, the shape an octagon, that it was thin and cold, and her throat was the center. Her dance was free-form, and her flower was a tulip. The fragrance she thought of was a men's cologne. Her instruments were the drums and guitar, and her vehicle a Volkswagen. The smell was burning leaves.

Mel, a sixty-year-old amateur ornithologist and retired engineer who had at first looked skeptical and baffled, said, "I got fog; the color—blue; the animal—a bear; and it was thick and warm." He grinned with enjoyment. "I feel it in my whole head and throat, and it does match my face and body. The dance it most resembles is the rumba, and the vehicle is a boat."

"What kind of boat?" I pressed.

"Oh," he said, considering, "not a little boat—a yacht!"

"The tree is an oak, the smell is leather, and the rhythm is slow and even."

Having protested at first that he "couldn't think that way!" Mel found he could visualize quite easily and thoroughly enjoyed coming up with all these unexpected associations.

Natalie, an affable and very large fourth-grade teacher who had a decided dramatic flair and a strangely monotonous voice ("I feel really sorry for my kids, who have to listen to me all day!" she remarked), had the following list: "Velvet, or cotton corduroy; the color is yellow, the shape is a rectangle, the animal is either an elephant or a cat, the sound is thin and warm; it does *not* fully represent my feelings, I feel it most in my forehead. It does match my appearance." (This surprised me—since her voice was much more babyish than her large solidity would suggest.) "The smell is soap, pure castile. The flower is pussy willow, and the tree is weeping willow. The rhythm is a slow, maddening, oscillating ceiling fan, and the dance is a fox-trot."

Jenny was next—a young chemist, sensitive, brilliant, and dedicated. Her voice was so thin and small she could barely be heard more than a few feet away. "I got an image of glassy ice, with cracks in it. A bird—a seagull. The color was pale yellow—with splashes of violet. The shape—a narrow cylinder (like an attenuated wire). It is thin, cool. It doesn't fully represent my feelings or match my face or body. It's too monotone. Sometimes it matches," she corrected herself. "I feel it in my throat and upper chest. Sometimes it's pleasurable to me, but I often find breathing an effort. I think of the waltz and a plane."

"What kind?" I interrupted. "It's important to be as detailed as possible. A 747?"

"Oh, no," she laughed, "a Piper Cub. The smell is of pine needles, the tree is a pine tree, the flower is a petunia, and the tempo is staccato."

The whole class looked amazed. The images "fit" Jenny more perfectly than any description we could have come up with.

When asked to chart her Vocal Self-Portrait, soft-voiced Amy, who had a gentle, self-effacing manner, remarked, "I can see easily what image I'd like to have, but an image for my voice the way it is now seems more difficult."

"You know," I told her, "there are no wrong or right choices. If you tried making new choices six months from now, your images *might* be entirely different. That's fine too!"

With some encouragement and prodding, she was able to come up with the following list: for texture, balsa wood; and for shape she selected round. The flower she chose was a daisy and the color was yellow; the landscape, Central Park. Then she decided on some changes. The flower she preferred for her vocal image was the pussy willow and she chose ice blue instead of yellow. These two alterations seemed to mean the most to her. "Oh, and I'd like Newport instead of Central Park—I like the sense of adventure and the beauty of the sailboats, the cleaner whiteness, open sky, and the beautiful music. Oh, and I'd rather be a cello than a piccolo."

Suddenly Amy realized to her surprise that it had been quite easy.

"You're speaking in your new voice," I pointed out.

She laughed and protested, "I feel self-conscious!" Still, she went on talking.

"Do you hear the difference?" I asked, turning to the group.

"Yes. Her voice is deeper, more definite somehow."

"So is her whole personality!"

"More clarity. Crisper!"

"She sounds and looks more assertive now."

Amy looked pleased. "Thank you, everybody," she said with a delighted smile. "I'm going to try to keep this new voice going all the time. It's the *me* I want to be."

Someone commented, "These are all such extraordinary self-portraits; we really get a rich, complex impression from all these associations." It was true. Their accuracy and subtlety were generally astonishing. Then I asked everybody to consider the following questions. Do this now at home.

Look over your list of written images. Then, again close your eyes and breathe deeply. Get an overall feeling about all the associations you decided on before.

1. What would you like more of in your voice?

2. What—if anything—do you want to give up to get that?

3. Can you feel or sense any other changes you'd like to make to have your ideal, charismatic voice?

4. Say them aloud and write them down. Be as detailed as possible, including your reasons.

5. Now hear your *new*, improved sound, visualizing yourself using it, with all the qualities you want enhanced or transformed as you just formulated them. Spend a few minutes, hearing and seeing and sensing yourself—in your mind's ear—expressing yourself in this new, more fully *you* way.

6. Now open your eyes and begin to speak *in this new voice*. Share with us what changes you made.

7. Which of these images will you use to produce this new sound—and how?

Janet said, "I stayed with the fox, adding the freedom of the wolf and solidity of the horse, but I changed the color from blue to a much richer brown. Instead of the pancake, I prefer streamers. I like the thickness, but I changed the cold to warm and from the center of the sound in my chest, I expanded it to include my whole body, particularly the hands and feet, which almost never seem to get any circulation. They're always cold, and I can hardly feel them!"

"Good! Now when you want to quickly put yourself into this newly enlarged charismatic state, what will you do?"

"I'll use the streamers to spread the energy all over my body. Especially to my hands and feet."

"Right!" I was delighted that she had instantly seen the creative process she herself could use to transform her own functioning with an image that had meaning for her.

"Do you notice how different your voice sounds?" I asked her.

She smiled happily. "Yes, it feels richer and more expressive."

Ellie was next, and she surprised everybody: "First of all, I'd like to change the corduroy to velvet. I want to keep the tiger, but make the octagon a circle. From thin I want to change it to thick, from cold to warm. I'll keep the free-form dance, but I'd rather have a daisy than a tulip."

"Do you get a sense of why?" I asked.

"Yes." She hesitated a little. "It feels to me like a tulip is too closed— I want to be open and friendly. I'll keep the drums and guitar, but I'm going to change the Volkswagen to a Rolls-Royce."

"Hooray," cheered the class, " 'atta girl!"

Ellie grinned shyly. "Yeah, I like the quiet purring of a Rolls-Royce. It's steady, reliable, and luxurious, not uneven like I tend to be."

The whole group could see the flowering of her personality just through this exercise.

Mel said, "Boy, I'd like to see you in six months, Ellie, if this is what you could accomplish in ten minutes!"

She blushed and looked pleased. "Yes," she admitted, "it feels really good!"

Natalie, the massive but pretty-faced teacher, said, "I want to get more *cat* in my voice. I don't need more elephant, and I'd like to change the thinness. I'd like it to represent my feelings more, and to move the sound of it from my forehead to my legs and feet. I'd like less pussy willow and more weeping willow, with its long slender swaying branches and graceful trunk. Most of all," she paused mischievously, "I'd like to change the fox-trot to a tango! I want a slow, even tempo with a lot of depth."

"How are you going to put that into practice?" I asked her.

"Oh, I'm going to talk a lot lower," she said, "and with a lot more rhythmic variation to match the ebb and flow of my thoughts. I forgot to tell you the smell—it was of rich wood and the instrument is a cello!"

As she had been speaking, she had taken on much more authority than usual. She suddenly seemed not just large, but important—not childish at all, but a person to reckon with.

The group spontaneously applauded, and Natalie bowed with her usual sense of theater, this time without self-irony. She was assured and graceful.

Jenny said then, "I'd like mine to be silk instead of ice, with a liquid shimmer (no cracks!). I'm going to give my seagull more room. I love the feeling of freedom and flight and the endless open sky all around for me to play and swoop in. Instead of a narrow cylinder, I transformed into a kaleidoscope, with rapid changes of color and pattern, constantly transforming without ever losing character or definition. I felt more crackle and crunch, and I wanted to give up the coolness and thinness and get more depth, more richness. The petunia changed to a peony, very full, womanly, and generous."

"When you felt yourself using this voice, how did you use this new knowledge?" I asked her.

"I was able to open up and express my thoughts and feelings with power and spontaneity. It felt marvelous!" Jenny's eyes were shining and her voice was noticeably stronger, firmer, and deeper than we had ever heard it.

This questionnaire has an amazing power to trigger a complex, rich awareness of inner gifts, which itself produces heightened confidence. The more specific the image, the more pleasure it gives. For instance, if your first definition of the vehicle is a train, ask, "What kind? How big? What era?" Jim, a brilliant wit and a highly successful literary agent, at first said only, "A train—long-distance." When I asked him to be more specific, he added more details: "A long, highly sophisticated train with an air of mystery and glamour—in fact, the Orient Express would be perfect!" Interestingly, Jim didn't have a particularly sensuous voice quality, but he was very pleased with his own sound. As he had been highly persuasive all his adult life, his images were rich and powerful: "velvet, lion, red, the flower a rose, the tree an oak." His inner self-perception actually communicated itself to his hearers, exactly as if he really had a beautiful voice. When I asked him if there was anything he wanted to change, he said no. The only thing he wanted to alter was a tendency to tire if he did long, sustained speaking. But since he never had to do this kind of speaking, he didn't feel he had a problem.

Even people who were satisfied with their voices began to speak with more depth and variety. Jason, a business writer and executive who was also an artist and photographer, grinned with embarrassment when he began. "This is so revealing!" he remarked. But he, too, grew fascinated by his choices, and his voice began to take on more color, life, and richness from the multilayered images that flooded his consciousness.

Universally, it seems to be a pleasurable, life-affirming procedure. For people who want to contact their charisma, it is an astonishingly effective and powerful tool. For those who are already sure of theirs, it's a surprising, many-textured confirmation of their richness.

Everybody who does the Vocal Self-Portrait experiences an increase in tonal variety, subtlety, and color (even those with monotonous voices), as well as more expressive and appealing rhythms and intensity. All this suggests that we're really meant to be expressive and interesting—and are, by nature!

During a newspaper interview a few years ago, I remarked, "Nobody is boring!" The interviewer was skeptical.

"How can you say that?" she protested. "I know so many boring people!"

"Well, of course, we've all met 'boring people,'" I agreed. "But inside nobody's boring! Everybody is a maze of such incalculable richness and complexity that it's positively awesome!"

The Vocal Self-Portrait confirms my early feelings. The voice, as the most faithful, subtle index of inner intuition, is only the outward evidence of the limitless treasures of each individual's charisma.

Maggie H., a dynamic feminist, perceived her voice as coming "from the outside—at fingertip, outstretched, arm's length—from the electromagnetic field around me."

No two portraits were alike, although certain images appeared frequently. Some people chose one color, some several. Maggie asked for rich purple, deep brown, and silver. Some people smelled deep earth, burning leaves, fresh-baked bread, or cologne. Vehicles ranged from transatlantic liners to Model T's and kayaks or sleighs. Sometimes people would cross-sense; when asked what shape his voice was, Martin S., a banker and specialist in Japanese culture, saw a *gyotan*, a Japanese fruit with a particular ovoid shape. The literary agent chose for his tempo a "moderate, steady one— Big Ben." Others ranged from "boring ceiling fan oscillation" to "machine-gun fire." Like the Vocal Self-Portrait, the next exercises use your own synergistic imagery to reach a new state of heightened awareness. At that level, not only is nobody boring, but everybody is a poet!

How to Find Your True Voice

Most people only use a fraction of their real voices. Do you know how yours really sounds?

The key to projection is relaxation and release of vibration. With your new interior image in mind, you're now going to connect to your inner sounding board and experience how your body and head feel when they are really resonating fully.

Is your voice harsh? Nasal? Too high? Too monotone? Breathy? Too thin? Too throaty? Uninteresting? Uneven?

To start off, let's get in touch with the sound as if it came from your gut. This will immediately double your power!

The Ape

Bend over from the waist and let your arms dangle. Let them fall as loosely as possible. Let your head drop too. Now, with a deep sound that comes from the lowest part of your abdomen, say: "*Huhh*! *Huhh*!! *Huhh*!!" The only thing that moves is your stomach; it moves sharply *in* as you release the sound. The jaw is totally limp. Jump with both feet at the same time you say the *huhh*! Now jump around the room, slowly (on both feet simultaneously), heavily, like an ape. Always sound the *huhh*s exactly as you come down on both feet. Keep your head and arms totally relaxed and dangling the whole time. (If they get stiff when you jump with both feet, practice relaxing them while standing upright.) Repeat ten times. Feel the sound go right through the floor. Feel it in your back as well.

The Santa Claus Laugh

Once the Ape is easy for you, do a big *ho ho ho*, still keeping your jaw very limp for the *ho*s, standing upright this time. With each *ho*, your stomach moves in sharply, as though somebody kicked you and it recoiled. Keep the sound very big and deep, next door to a yawn. If it isn't deep enough, *yawn*. Your throat probably isn't really open *enough*.

The Inner Yawn

Can you make yourself yawn yet? Remember, if you draw your lips up off your teeth and stretch real wide, you should be able to start an involuntary yawn. If you can't, keep opening wider, until it begins to happen. When you yawn, notice how open the back of your throat gets. Now see if you can yawn with your mouth closed, just as you've done lots of times in a boring meeting! Put your fingers on the cords at the back of your neck (sides). You should feel them being pushed outward if the yawn is really wide enough. If at first you can't feel this opening, keep directing your attention to it and ask it to open—it will start to wake up and respond. This is very important for throat relaxation.

Whenever you're going to make a talk or presentation, practice pressing down your tongue and opening the back of your throat. That way, you'll prevent yourself from getting "strangled" by nervousness. By doing that before you get up to speak, you'll prevent trouble.

"When I get up to introduce speakers at the PTA, I feel my throat closing up," moaned Sally S.

"The same thing happened to me," Don B., a journalist, added. "I thought I would die on camera. Then I did the Inner Yawn and it opened up again. Boy, that was scary until I got that under control!" He is now a regular on TV as a talk-show host. Sally, who at first couldn't feel the back of her neck expanding with the Inner Yawn, gradually was able to locate those muscles; she never had that trouble again.

The Helmet of Hum

First hum, loose-lipped, thinking of something pleasurable that turns you on. Then press lightly with your fingertips at the sides of your face, feeling the vibrations there. Then touch another spot. Then another: forehead, chin, nose, temples, top of the head, sides of the head, back of the head, back of the neck. In each area, if you don't feel as much vibration as you did in the first one, consciously *send* more to your fingers through that spot. Imagine that every pore on your face and scalp and neck is exuding electric vibrations *equally*.

Jack and Jill

Put your thumbs in your ears while your pinky fingers close off your nostrils. Gently! Now, keeping your mouth *closed* (yes, closed) but your jaws parted, say this familiar verse:

> *Jack and Jill went up the hill*
> *to fetch a pail of water.*
> *Jack fell down and broke his crown,*
> *and Jill came tumbling after!*

Say it as loudly and with as much vocal variation as you can. Naturally, you'll have to push hard to get your sounds through since all the openings are closed off.

1. Now take away your left thumb, keep everything else closed, and repeat the whole rhyme.

2. Put back the left thumb, take away the right, and repeat the nursery rhyme. Notice whether there is a difference between how you hear on one side and the other.

3. Put back both thumbs, and remove the left pinky from your left nostril; now only the right one is closed off. Repeat the verse.

4. With thumbs still closing off the ears, remove the right pinky from the right nostril and repeat the verse. Note any difference.

5. Now repeat with pinkies closing off both nostrils but both ears open.

6. The same, but with only the *left* nostril blocked off.

7. The same, but with only the *right* nostril blocked off.

8. Now, still with the mouth closed, but with ears and nostrils open, repeat, making it as articulate as you can without opening your mouth.

9. Open your mouth, but keep your teeth clenched and repeat the verse.

10. Now, finally, say it normally.

You'll be astonished at how loud your sound is after going through this sequence. Having forced the vibrations through the inside of your skull, you feel your head as a resonating cage of bones. Now you'll be able to *experience* the full resonance of your voice as it should sound.

Practice this sequence every day for three weeks, and it'll have an astonishing effect. Your voice will be large and resonant without effort!

The Helmet of Hum (continued)

1. Start humming again, the jaw very relaxed and tongue lying low in your mouth. Feel the hum at the top of the inside of your skull, at the back of your head, and around the sides.

2. Now hold up your palms two inches in front of your face and keep humming. Feel the entire surface of your hands massaged by the hum.

3. Move your palms away from your face a little farther—perhaps four inches. Keep humming. Keep sending the vibrations to bathe your hands. At any point, if you can't feel the buzzing in your hands, move them closer again until you can.

4. Move the hands a little farther away, then farther until they're at arm's length. Make sure you can really feel the vibrations bathing the entire surface of your palms.

5. Slowly move the arms apart a little. *Stop* so the left palm (still facing you) is out about twelve inches from the left side of your head and the right palm on the opposite side is the same distance from the right side.

6. If that's still buzzing nicely, move the palms out to the sides at ear level, still looking straight ahead, and make the palms buzz out there.

7. Move them sideways around to the back and intensify your humming.

8. Move them above your head, first close, then as high as you can reach. Extend arms upward. Intensify the humming.

9. Close your eyes and visualize the entire field around your head as a dense helmet of buzzing hum, at arm's length, in every direction: sides, top, and back. Make sure you can really feel your palms buzz before you move them to the next position a little farther away. Anytime you're not sure you can feel them buzzing, move them closer until you can feel the buzzing vibration easily. You will generate a lot of tingling energy in your hands as well as around your head.

10. Now speak, sending the sound out *from the back of your head*, visualizing the sound radiating out from the back.

Your voice will feel and sound at least twice as strong and vibrant as usual. Practice this every day for a month, and your normal way of speaking will be dramatically improved. After that, you can probably maintain it without difficulty by doing it only once in a while to remind yourself of the way your expanded voice feels.

Now that you've relaxed your body with the Ape, felt the sound coming from your lower stomach, and activated the Helmet of Hum around your head, you're ready to combine the two for your newly expanded voice.

The Whole-Body Sound

Sit or stand straight.

1. Put your left hand flat on your upper back and your right hand on your diaphragm, fingers spread so they are splayed across your stomach.

2. Now, say, as slowly and as sustained as possible, without any interruption of sound and so you can feel both hands vibrating: "AAAHHHH-HHHHHHH-EEE WANNNNNNNHHHHHHHHHHHHHHHHHNT (breathe) Tooooo FEEEEEEEEEEEEEEEEEEEEEEEL (breathe) thuhh-hhh SAHHHHHHHHHHHHHHHHHOOND (breathe) of mahhhhhhhh-hheee VAWWWWWWWWWWWWWWWWWWWWWWEECE (breathe) Lahhhhhhhh-eeeke A WIHHHHHHHHHHHHHHHHHH-HHHND (breathe) aaaaaaaaaaaaand uhhhhhhhhhh WAAAAAAAAAA-AAAYYYYYYYYYYYYYVE (breathe) THROOOOOOOOOOOOOUGH MAHHHHHHHHHHHHH-EEE (breathe) WHOOOOOOOOOOOO-OOOOOOLE BOHHHHHHHHHHHHH-DEEE!" You're saying, "I want to feel the sound of my voice like a wind and a wave through my whole body"—and you should experience your whole body sounding as though you are your own cathedral. Feeling your hands vibrate with your own sound is a very pleasurable sensation, and it will make you aware of the *back* of your body as a sounding board, too. (Most of us feel as though the voice comes out of a narrow hole in the face!)

The Enchanted Stream

In *bel canto* singing (literally, "beautiful song"), the Italians, the masters of this sustained and pure tonal style, taught the world that long, pure vowels are the secret of a beautiful, continuous, and melodious sound. Most people who have not had voice training never really sustain *any* sounds long enough. The result tends to be choppy, disconnected, and unmusical.

To feel and produce the sustained sounds of the vowels flowing smoothly one into the next, sing the same sentence you did for the Whole-Body Sound: "I want to feel the sound of my voice like a wind and a wave through my whole body." Only this time *leave out all consonants*! Like this:

AHHHHHHHHHHHHHHHHHHHHHHHHEEEEEEEE AHHHHH-HHHHHHHH (breathe) OOOOOOOO eeeeeeeeeeeeeeeeeeee (breathe) uhhhhhhhhhhh ahhhhhhhhhhh uhhh ahhhhhhhhhhhh awwwwwwwwwwwwweeeeeeeeeee (breathe) AHHHHHHHHHHH-HHHHEEEEE UHHHHHHHHHHHHHH IHHHHHHHHHHHHH* (breathe) ahhhhhhhhhhhhhhhh uhhhhhhhhhhhhhhh ayyyyyyyyyyy-yyyyyyyyyyyeeeee (breathe) ooooooooooooooooo ahhhhhhhhhh-hhe (breathe) uhhhhhhhhhhhhhhhhhhhoooooooooo ahhhhhhhhhhh-hhhhhhhhhheeeeeeeee!

If you do this right, you'll be able to feel the sound shooting right up through the top of your skull and also emanating from the sides and back of your head. It's exciting to feel this suddenly "take over" and become larger than you are!

When I studied opera on a Fulbright grant in Italy, my teacher had me practice all the early Italian art songs this way, with no consonants! At first it drove me crazy, but it was a marvelous way to learn how to connect the vowels in a pearly, unbroken line. Try doing this with the Glottal Nonstop Sentences (page 180). Try it with *any* sentence. It's not easy! It requires considerable mental alertness. For instance, the sentence "It drove me crazy!" would read: "Ihhhhhhhhhhhhhhhhhhh ooooooooooooooooooooo [uhhh-hhhooooo] eeeeeeeeeee ayyyyyyyyyyyyyyyeeeeeeeee!" The idea is to connect all the vowels on one breath, without interruption. Keep the jaws relaxed, separated, and unmoving!

Once you've practiced this sustained sounding, you'll enjoy speaking a lot more because of the secret melody underneath. And other people will find you infinitely more interesting to listen to—without realizing why.

Remember, it's the sound—much more than the words—that seduces! When you talk without these "underground melody streams," your speech is not only less musical but less interesting and sometimes even hard to

---

*Pronounce like the *i* in *pig*.

understand. You never give the sound a chance to hook into the vibratory stream, which, being closer to singing, is more expressive and pleasurable to feel and hear.

Part of the difficulty arises from the desire to enunciate clearly. If your tongue is agile, you can make clear sounds and yet not lose this all-important connecting stream. The exercises presented above will help you maintain the personality expansion you experienced when you drew your Vocal Self-Portrait. Practicing these will make your new way of speaking feel comfortable, natural, and eventually automatic. If you exercise these new muscles and sensations of coordinated sound and body relaxation, your whole level of functioning will become more and more like your ideal vocal image. Otherwise, old habits can creep back and take over. As you build your new technique, the exercises will give you practical, multisensory image reinforcement.

The Vocal Self-Portrait invariably enhances self-esteem by giving you a richer sense of your own nature. People are often surprised by the beautiful, satisfying memories this exercise evokes, which are a source of refreshment, renewal, and growth. These self-chosen images are a sort of conscious cellular coding—a set of built-in, attainable instructions—portable, powerful, and private—to access your true charisma.

10
Overcoming Performance Anxiety

"If I have a presentation to give, for days ahead I'm tense and nervous. No matter how much I prepare, it doesn't help. Sometimes the nervousness doesn't go away during the whole time I'm on."

"I'm always terrified before I go onstage."

"I can't even bring myself to ask a question in class—or make a comment."

"I have such terrible stage fright I turned down a job I wanted because I'd have to speak in public."

"When I get up to speak in court, I feel I'm going to black out."

"My little girl said she didn't want to be a concert artist if she had to throw up like me every night before a concert."

"Before a job interview my head throbs, my heart beats terribly fast, my mouth is dry, and my knees shake."

"All I had to do was introduce the speaker, and I was paralyzed. My stomach hurts. I can't catch my breath. My voice gets tight and high, my palms are wet . . ."

"I forget what I was going to say."

"I can't remember the notes."

"After years of starring roles, I suddenly felt like a novice and couldn't remember my lines."

All of us suffer from performance anxiety, or stage fright, at some time in our lives. I can't think of anybody who claims *never* to have gone through it. I know several famous musicians who have given up playing live concerts altogether because of their terror. Careers have tottered and even failed because of it. On the other hand, many stars claim it's essential for a good performance.

What *is* stage fright? The dictionary says, "The nervousness felt by a performer or speaker before an audience." Yet people who have never stepped on stage have felt it too—perhaps before meeting an important client, before their first date, before their wedding, or before a battle or an athletic contest—even before sex. The fight-or-flight syndrome steps up the adrenaline and the release of hormones; all of your body and mind are gripped by a stress reaction. How you deal with it can affect your life, career, health, and well-being.

Nobody really understands the mechanics or causes of stage fright very well. Oddly enough, there's little research on the subject, although interest has grown as more and more people find they must communicate with different groups and be able to talk on TV, at a PTA meeting, or in a business setting. People who never thought of themselves as performers now appear in public, and the communications explosion is just beginning. So performance anxiety is a real concern to growing numbers of people.

The main causes seem to be these:

1. Fear of not doing as well as you want to

2. Insufficient or inadequate preparation

3. Fear of what people (the audience) will think

4. Earlier negative experiences

5. Inadequate enjoyment of what you're doing (probably due to 1, 2, 3, or 4)

Many people in my workshops confess at the beginning of the course that they have to take tranquilizers or other medication before speaking in public.

"You'll never have to take one again!" I tell them. And after they learn how to calm themselves with breathing exercises and other de-stressing techniques they don't. Taking tranquilizers dulls your perceptions. It is far better to transform the energy of your nervousness into available adrenaline to energize your performance. (There was much talk during the 1980s of a drug called Inderal to reduce nervousness; some psychopharmacologists claim it's effective and without side effects. But since nobody knows exactly how a drug may affect different people, it's much safer to use control techniques that are nonpharmacological.) Changing your conceptualization, meditating, de-stressing your body, and controlling your breathing are simple, safe, and effective; they require no equipment and cost nothing but time.

A safe, gentle, harm-free resource is the remarkable set of Bach Flower Remedies, which work on subtle energy levels and are so effective that they have been called "Nature's Prozac." I muscle-test them for clients, so their bodies indicate exactly which are the best for them. For performance anxiety, Rescue Remedy and Larch (to eliminate terror and boost confidence, respectively) are marvelously effective. You can get them in health food stores and take a few drops in liquid or under the tongue; they help enormously.

People who have had good experiences speaking or performing sometimes find it hard to understand why their less fortunate friends or colleagues are so terrified. An editor of *Fortune* who interviewed me and some of my students hinted in his article that people who were afraid of public speaking really only needed to "get hold of themselves." Himself a good speaker, he was unable to understand the problem or believe there really is one—despite the fact that 41 percent of the U.S. population admit they are more frightened of public speaking than any other single thing!

Some people begin to suffer days or weeks before their performance ordeal, some only moments before going on. Others are calm until they start but then are suddenly gripped by panic. Some feel it until they step onstage; then everything is all right (this pattern is most common with experienced performers). Many professionals recognize that the stress buildup can be a valuable source of heightened energy and performance readiness.

Reactions are highly individual, and variable even for the same person. Some lucky people claim they can't wait to get out onstage and only feel insecure when they haven't rehearsed enough and "done the homework." One woman in my class said she enjoys public speaking of any kind and will gladly address any group of any size, but she suffers "horrible" stage fright when she has to take exams. A certain conductor found himself yawning and getting sleepy before performances—a kind of withdrawal.

Then there is the curious phenomenon of situation-specific stage fright; it only attacks in a particular environment. This type usually stems from one special, unpleasant early experience.

James F., a distinguished patent lawyer who took up a successful acting career late in life, confessed that although he loved singing, dancing, and acting, addressing a small group of his peers made him so nervous that he had turned down the presidency of a nationwide bar association. He even felt uncomfortable at meetings of his own firm. When I asked him if he could remember some early negative experience speaking in public, he said, "Yes, I remember now—I was in high school and I did something I shouldn't have—can't remember what. The principal called me into his office and ordered me to get up in the assembly on Monday morning and, *as punishment*, deliver some sort of speech. I have no idea now what it was about. All I know is that I was terrified; I slunk in, got through it, and crept out, feeling horribly humiliated and whipped. I never realized the connection before, but I see now that must have been a real injury. Later in college, when my fraternity had weekly meetings, I always managed to sneak out every time without getting up and talking. Yet at the same time I was appearing in shows up and down the vaudeville circuit and loving it! All my life I've ducked speaking situations if I could. It's a wonder people didn't realize! But it actually hampered my career." Here was a very cause-specific performance anxiety, which only affected him in situations vaguely similar to his traumatic early experience.

Then there's reentry stage fright. No matter how experienced you are, if you've been away for a while, you may experience some of the nervousness and stage fright you felt when you first began. Performing isn't exactly like riding a bicycle! *But the heebie-jeebies won't take as long to disappear as the first time.* The experience and maturity you acquired in other areas of your life help to ease the transition.

Performers, if they talk about stage fright at all, tend to divide into two camps. Each side feels (somewhat snobbishly) superior to the other. Most stage fright sufferers regard their agonies as somehow necessary and valuable and tend to disdain anybody who *doesn't* get nervous as insensitive or lacking in fineness of perception. The fearless ones are apt (like the *Fortune* editor) to be unsympathetic and can't understand why the others make such a fuss.

On evidence, whether or not you have stage fright does not seem to correlate with your artistic sensitivity, although it does reflect the state of your nervous system. Opera singer Richard Tucker was reputed to be "iron-nerved." He never lost his cool before or during a performance. Pianist Vladimir Horowitz suffered so badly from stage fright that for years he didn't play at all. (He returned to the concert stage when he suddenly began to enjoy sharing his music with a new generation of appreciative music lovers—his pleasure overrode his old fears.) Actress Stockard Channing told me matter-of-factly, "Stage fright is just part of your inner preparation and creativity."

Usually (though not always) nervousness diminishes with increased experience. Sometimes a performer will be totally at home in one medium and suffer anxiety in another. Actors who have to appear on talk shows have come to me for help because they feel so uncomfortable and uncertain without a script. Peter Falk remarked about talk shows, "It's very difficult! I don't even know which camera to look at or if I should look at the camera at all." An instrumentalist who turns to conducting may feel completely at ease on the podium, although subject to terror in solo recitals. I used to get nervous before singing, but not before acting (which seemed easy by comparison!). Whenever you don't feel your self-esteem is on the line, you tend to be much less vulnerable.

The brilliant English actor-director Helen Burns told the actors she was directing in *The Cherry Orchard*

> When we suffer from stage fright it's as though we feel we'll be attacked by wild animals. We all have wild animals in our minds and hearts—but they're just going down to the pool to drink, and when they drink they don't attack anybody. They're just there. . . . So we need to remember that they won't hurt us, and just let them be.

People who suffer from chronic performance anxiety usually have a scarcely heard "tape" going round in their heads. "They won't like me." "I'll make a fool of myself." "They'll think I'm boring." "I'm not good enough." Sometimes such a message is so ancient that you're not even aware of it, just of the physiological reactions it causes.

If you're to give a talk, you can install positive "tapes" instead. Say very consciously, loudly, and clearly, "I have something interesting and valuable to say, and people really want to hear it!" Then put it on a cassette and play it to yourself over and over until you believe it! Repeat it silently, but with lots of conviction, just before you get up to speak.

Richard M., an amateur ornithologist, said, "I was afraid my bird slides were not good enough for my group. Then I remembered to tell myself, 'I have something really interesting to show them, and they're very interested.' It was true. I can't tell you how that helped me! After that, everything was fine. It turned out they really did enjoy them."

Unfortunately, not all stage fright is that easily dispelled. Being thoroughly prepared is crucially important. For many people, preparation means overpreparation: learning their speech (or part) by rote and doggedly repeating it over and over until all the pleasure has gone out of it. Instead, if you can thoroughly *immerse* yourself in what you're doing, your pleasure in the talk (music, play, or whatever) will protect you from many of the discomforts of nervousness. It's important to want to share your talk or performance with others. Remember these words from famed Russian director and innovator of method acting Constantin Stanislavsky, "Love the art in yourself, rather than yourself in the art."

Composer-pianist-conductor Lukas Foss said, "Stage fright is very narcissistic. The more committed and dedicated, the more *serious* you are about music, the less you suffer. Of course, nothing is as awful as worrying whether or not you're going to be humiliated in front of an audience. One is much more likely to worry playing solo than when conducting. If I worry whether my fingers are going to hit all the notes, I become unserious. When I conduct, I'm worrying about other people—whether the horn will manage to hit the high note, whether the timpani will come in on the right beat, and so on. That's much more real because I'm thinking about the *music*. The more dedicated you are, the less you think about yourself. No, I don't get stage fright onstage now. I love a captive audience in the concert hall or in the classroom. But I get nervous at home where I have to introduce people to each other at a party. I can never remember people's names!"

"Did you ever have stage fright when you were starting?" I asked him.

"When I was a little boy, my father told me, 'Look at the audience and imagine they're all naked!' " He laughed. "Somehow that made them much less frightening!"

The critical competitiveness that is the normal working atmosphere of many businesses, schools, and conservatories makes it hard to retain your joy in what you're doing. Luckily, the physiological changes that accompany stress can be eased or reversed through slow, deep breathing and preperformance exercises. When you discharge built-up tension through the Depressurizer, the Karate Chop, the Steam Engine, the Elbow Propeller, the I-Don't-Care Swing, the Horse Laugh, and the Wibble Wobble, you make the *energy* of your nervousness available to you again. You send oxygen to your brain, discharge lactic acid from your muscles, and stimulate your own energy level and desire to perform.

All creativity is born of excitement. Everybody who ever lived was conceived because some man got excited! The dopamine system of the brain is aroused by aggressive exercise. It's like a built-in "speed" drug. Serotonin released by "moving meditation" or even tennis (if you play with a certain detachment) behaves like mind-changing mescaline. You really can manipulate your brain systems with exercise—without drugs. Very competitive exercise has an "angry-upper" effect, which is then followed by depression, a "downer." But with a calm attitude, you can get high and stay high. The elevated mood can last for days, even weeks.

Utilizing our new knowledge of how the brain functions, we can discharge the fright in stage fright through powerful preperformance exercises. The next step is to calm your entire organism and normalize it, even bring it to a heightened state of optimum functioning through deep, even breathing. Add to this a meditation period and then a chant that reestablishes equilibrium of both hemispheres of the brain, and you're then able to enjoy the fruits of all your preparation. You'll be at your best—even when you don't feel like it!

Now that you've learned good breathing habits, you can concentrate on that process. The habit of shifting concentration from your fears to the business of breathing is comforting and supportive. Knowing you can control at least *that* element gives you much-needed confidence.

It's impossible to be relaxed and anxious at the same time! If you can relax your muscles at will, you can mentally rehearse the feared situation and experience yourself going through it with complete success, visualizing every detail with pleasure and confidence. The moment you have a problem "seeing" or feel some nervous symptom overtake you (the familiar clutching at your throat or a sinking feeling in the stomach), abandon the visualization and coax your body back to physical relaxation. Sure enough, you'll notice a slight clenching somewhere, a tiny grabbing at one set of muscles or another. By slowing your breathing and deliberately letting go of that tension spot or spots, you can again prepare yourself to "rehearse" *only* when you are deeply relaxed.

The more you do it, the easier it gets! When you're able to go through a whole performance mentally and with pleasure, just as though you were really experiencing it, you will have taken a tremendous step. The body-mind doesn't know the difference—at that level—between the real and the imagined. It's just as though you had already *had* a good performance and experienced your own success. In a deep sense you have. When it comes time for the actual performance, it seems like *the second time*.

The more positive experiences you have, the less frightening your momentary inner leap of excitement will feel. *Your stage fright will be transformed to stage readiness*, that deliciously exhilarating feeling of being challenged and ready to do your best. Some people, like gamblers or racing car drivers, are "hooked" on this excitement.

A few summers ago, I found myself alone on a ski lift in Aspen, feeling rather frightened in the open car. There was no way I could get off. Close to panic, I forced myself to breathe very slowly and deeply. Suddenly an inspiration hit me. I'd pretend, like any nine-year-old, that I was a queen surveying her subjects ranged on the mountainside to greet me. It worked! As soon as I "saw" the massed throngs of my adoring people and felt their love and admiration supporting me, I straightened up and enjoyed the ride, though I was still aware of an undercurrent of acute danger. Dimly I recognized as distinctly familiar the transformation from paralyzing fear to a sense of being alive in a larger way than before, of being poised midway between peril and flying mastery. It was very much like stage fright and the transition to a good performance—on opening night!

Arrange Your Own Success—It's a Gift!

If fears of not doing as well as you can or of what people will think are your main stage fright problems, the chances are they stem from earlier negative experience. You need long-range confidence building. In addition to meditation, chanting, breathing, and the stress-relief exercises, you have to program successes in miniature test situations. For instance, if you have a talk coming up in your work, offer to teach the children at a neighboring school something you know well, just to have the experience of presenting information publicly. Or start practicing telling stories to your friends and relatives when you're sure of getting appreciative responses. Let them know how you want them to respond.

Be creative in finding opportunities to volunteer your knowledge or skills in a less demanding situation than the one you face at work or socially. The practice can help boost your confidence, especially when you give people something they need and wouldn't have if you hadn't volunteered. You can always offer to read to patients in hospitals or spend a few hours a week telling stories to children at the library or nearest neighborhood center. Somebody somewhere needs and will appreciate a gift of your time, concern, and skills.

"When I finish my hour helping underprivileged schoolkids with their math problems," remarked Stuart S., a market analyst who regularly helped out at an inner-city school, "*I* feel good! It does as much for me as for them."

Ruby R., a retired widow who had owned a cosmetics company, offered to teach teenage orphans in her community all about makeup. They were so happy to have her come and share her beauty secrets that her social confidence (which had plummeted after the death of her husband) rose sharply. Feeling useful and seeing how much her experience was appreciated, she no longer felt the stage fright and shyness she had been suffering on meeting new people in social situations since her husband's death. Connecting with others in a generous, giving way that uses some of your personal skills helps overcome the "narcissistic" fears of stage fright by increasing your own sense of real self-worth.

Every performance is a form of sharing with others. When you feel you're truly giving service and are a channel to transmit something of value, you're part of your own audience. That bio-rapport that's such an essential element of charisma rests on being able to overcome the "small self" stage fright because you're focused on something larger that you want to communicate to people. Getting your "small self" out of the way is the problem.

That old automatic fright response is left over from a time when your self-esteem was injured by a negative experience. "Every time I step on a platform, my heart jumps into my throat exactly as if my life were being threatened; it reminds me of the first public speaking experience I had when I was about nine—I stuttered and couldn't get the words out and everybody laughed at me," said Roland M., a management executive. By gritting his teeth and forcing himself, he managed to get through speaking engagements in his work without collapsing. But the internal cost was heavy: "I feel I'm going to die—it's ridiculous! Everybody thinks I'm calm, but I go through agonies. I've got to get over that! It really poisons my life every time I have to get up and talk before a group." Doing the Personal Success Factor Workshop (see below) changed all that.

We all need a safe place to fail, where we won't be laughed at, fired, humiliated, thrown out, or "killed" if we make mistakes. Nasa, the space agency, worked out some of the most complex and difficult explorations ever attempted. Mistakes are inevitable with so many unknown factors. Interestingly, they never use the word *failure* or even *mistake*. Their term is "negative successes." Can you see how this would alter attitudes toward a plan that hadn't succeeded? One can learn from it and go on without wasting energy on breast beating, guilt, or shame. This creates a highly productive atmosphere in which risk taking is valued, not punished.

Your Personal Success Factor Workshop

If you have an early negative memory still triggering unwanted automatic responses like paralyzing stage fright, you can reprogram yourself through this process. As with all deconditioning processes, you start by relaxing totally.

Relaxing

1. Sit in a comfortable position, feet on the floor, hands relaxed on your lap. Starting with your feet and working your way up your body, deliberately release every muscle group in turn. (If you can't feel it, tense it first and then let go.)

2. Breathe very slowly and deeply, and mentally begin to count. On one inhalation count to yourself 1,000; 2,000; 3,000; 4,000; 5,000; 6,000. Hold for one beat, then exhale slowly, counting down: 6,000; 5,000; 4,000; 3,000; 2,000; 1,000. Repeat both sequences seven or eight times or until you are thoroughly relaxed. At first it helps to hear another voice giving you gentle, complete directions on a relaxation tape. After a while, your body will get the idea and be able to do it by itself, having learned the specific steps from the tape. When you begin, it'll probably take about twenty-five minutes; later, you'll achieve total relaxation in about three minutes.

3. Now decide your objective: for instance, "I'd like to perform or speak in public without being paralyzed by stage fright." Let your little finger lift when you've decided on your objective.

First Steps—Consensus Within

The part of you that always gets frightened was acting *to protect* you—a valid instinct of survival engendered by your first negative experience. What was that part trying to protect you from? Call that part of you "Little ——— (your own first name)," and answer the question. The answer might be "Little Tom wanted to save me from being criticized and mocked. I understand now that the fear was a protective measure so I wouldn't undergo such pain again." Let your finger rise when you see this.

Ask Little ——— if she or he would be willing to *give up* this old way of "saving" you from destruction if Big ——— (you) could come up with a new form of protection that would be more appropriate and effective in your life now. Raise your finger when you have an agreement from Little ———.

Important—if the part of you that is "Little ———" *won't* agree, ask her or him this question: "Would you be willing to *try* a new way and decide later if you think it's all right to give up the stage fright?" Usually, Little ——— will give this conditional agreement. Let your little finger rise if it's all right to proceed.

Visualization

Now, think back to the last time you felt completely comfortable and happy performing or talking to people. Let your little finger rise when you've done this.

See yourself going through that experience in great detail. Hear it. See all the people who were there, see the appreciative expressions on their faces. Remember how everything tasted, smelled, and felt; where you were; what time of day or night it was—the entire scene. Take a few minutes to experience it as completely as you can. Enjoy it fully. Let your little finger rise when you've done this.

Finding Your Resources

Now, ask yourself: What were three qualities or personal resources that helped you in that situation and made it so successful and rewarding for you?

For instance, Neil S., a textile designer who wanted to be more spontaneous and comfortable talking to people, picked a time when he was made class captain at the age of fifteen. He decided that the three qualities he possessed then were resourcefulness, intelligence, and a genuine interest in people. He realized that he was using his intelligence and resourcefulness but, somehow, had lost contact with his interest in people.

Having grown up on a Caribbean island, the son of a distinguished Anglo-Indian family, he was very conscious of social hierarchies, and when he came to this country, he was afraid to reveal himself to anyone lest people find him either superior or inferior! He was afraid that he might, in a new and unfamiliar society, make himself too vulnerable if he was spontaneous and open with people. "I thought people wouldn't be interested in my experience—I see now that that was when I began to lose interest in *them*. I became cold, shy, and mistrustful."

Now, ask yourself: *How can I use these three qualities* I've named as my best resources to learn a new way of handling the old challenge . . . for example, feel confidence instead of stage fright? How will these resources protect me against the "danger" of humiliation and satisfy the "Little" me?

Neil's answer was: "I can prepare intelligently, use my resourcefulness to notice new points of interest I have in common with people, and trust my interest in people to arouse their interest in me."

A singer's answer to this question was: "I have a beautiful tone, a great love of music, and good judgment. The first and second are what I can count on to offer people in performance; the third will protect me from going out unprepared or from giving a bad concert. I got in touch with other resources I have, too. I'm creative and a damned good musician, and I've worked hard so I deserve to succeed. I have an excellent stage presence, and I am grateful for the privilege of performing—after all, I waited on tables and did accounting and other things that aren't any fun for me so that I could do this singing, which is what I love. I really want to do this! It helps a lot to realize that I'm *choosing* to sing because singing gives me more pleasure than anything else."

A construction company executive said, "I have a keen knowledge of people, a thorough background in my business, and a likable personality. I realize I have a lot to contribute. I used to worry that my formal education wasn't good enough, and I was afraid to get up and speak. Now I see that I actually have experience of a wide range of people and have been very successful in my business, and people really want to hear what I can tell them. And I do love to play the expert! So, I'm going to enjoy the opportunity next time."

If you perceive more than three resources within, that's fine. Acknowledge them all and absorb them. If you have trouble finding three, use the one or two you are able to come up with. More will emerge later.

Practicing with Your Inner Resources

Now, keeping these three resources very much in mind, visualize a situation coming up where you respond *in a new way*, using all your resources and enjoying it very much. See the situation in great detail: taste, smell, touch, colors, people, sounds, faces. Go through it just as you want it to happen, feeling just as comfortable and good about it as you did in the happy experience you remembered. Take a few minutes to do that. Enjoy it thoroughly; elaborate on it. Notice how much in command, how at ease, you are. Relive it. Let your little finger rise when you've done this. If it's a performance or a talk or a presentation or a meeting, *see* it happening with this new feeling of success that is you at your best—remembered from your success memory.

Visualize another situation and go through it in the same way, utilizing your internal awareness of your success resources. Again, *see, smell, touch, taste, hear—be there*. Take five minutes to enjoy this.

Repeat the process, this time making your fantasy as satisfying as the best experience you ever had.

Locking in the Positive Responses

Now, notice how you are sitting. Don't move. Observe closely. This position is your Body Trigger, with which you'll always be able to activate your Success Factors. Your head may be to one side, your fist on your chin. You may notice your arms are folded across your chest and your legs crossed. Just take careful note, and whenever you want to get back into that state of feeling unscared and in touch with your own charisma and personal power, assume this position and visualize your upcoming challenging situation. *The physiological reinforcement of your happy memories serves to lock in the new positive responses.*

Close your eyes and take a moment to get in touch with Little ———. Thank him or her for trying so hard in the past to protect you against humiliation and failure, and ask if it's safe now to let go of the old Little ——— because you've found a better way. Assure Little ——— that you will always be there for protection and support, and that she or he has nothing to worry about anymore. This internal conversation can take place just with feelings—a wordless exchange that is nevertheless real. Some people even feel their "Little Self" placing a small hand in theirs and expressing trust. It's amazing that one can feel so comforted and confident, having nurtured the small frightened person that, for most of us, still exists inside in some situations. Having taken care of your "child," the "child" knows it's safe and will stop getting in the way of your grown-up self.

If you had a skeptical, resistant Little Self, ask now, "Do you feel OK about changing the way you're going to protect me now?" If the "child" is still not sure, ask him or her to help you try out the new way anyway. Get a positive response. Thank your "child."

Periodically, when you have a performance or situation coming up that evokes some of the old stage fright, run through this process again to reinforce your success resources and rout the old shadow responses.

All successful performers eventually find ways to master their stage fright, even if some never manage to lose it completely. Everyone evolves his or her own "system." Know your own tension spots, use the exercises in this section, and experiment to see how they affect you. Then you can select and use those that work best and fastest for you.

Finding Your Own Methods

Meditation is another important tool that demonstrably reduces stress for millions of people. It can give you just enough detachment to make all your preparation pay off. Meditation lowers blood pressure, slows the heartbeat, and gives you a deeper rest than normal sleep. Because there is usually a great deal of spontaneous, borderline imagery during meditation, the period of REM (rapid eye movement) imagery in sleep is unnecessary. You may well find, therefore, that you need far less sleep. I used to need eight hours' sleep. After a number of years of practicing meditation, I am perfectly happy with five. For a quick rest, I find that a ten-minute shoulder stand is as good as two hours' sleep.

The Alternate Breathing, the Emergency Energy Lift, and the Breath of Fire are all fast energizers (see chapter 12).

When you prepare for a performance or an especially important presentation, interview, or meeting with people who make you nervous, don't forget the importance of eating and drinking wisely.

The most common cause of high stress in the United States is malnutrition, according to Dr. Warren M. Levin, an orthomolecular physician. Poor eating habits aggravate the effects of all other stressors on the system. Avoid "empty" calories (sodas and snack foods) as well as bleached flour, sugar, and refined foods. It's even more critical to eat wisely when you're under stress. Rushing and gulping food guarantees inadequate food absorption. Thorough chewing is necessary for good digestion. An enzyme in our saliva called ptyalin stimulates the production of hydrochloric acid in the stomach. It's only released by adequate chewing. (Try twenty times for each bite—it's a wonderful way to keep your weight down, too. It's difficult to overeat when you chew long and well.) We can't be well nourished without good digestion.

It's important to have fresh foods—preferably organic—without additives and chemicals as the mainstay of your diet. Many stars drink freshly made vegetable juices, high in minerals and vitamins. Tennis pros claim that a carrot-celery cocktail gives them a great lift between matches. Many people are turning to vegetarianism. Meat, which takes days to digest, is frequently contaminated with hormones and chemicals, which then pass into our systems. We need less red meat and sugar and greater emphasis on whole grains and vegetables.

While we're constantly reminded that smoking is a deadly hazard to our health, many people don't know that it destroys the vitamin C in our bodies. Even nonsmokers lose vitamin C when exposed to other people's smoking.

Never eat when you're nervous! If you're scheduled to speak after dinner, beware of overloading yourself with food. Eat very little and chew very thoroughly. ("Chew your drink and drink your food!" Grandma used to caution.) Avoid iced drinks; ice chills your stomach and increases your discomfort. Skip liquor altogether. Heavy coffee drinking increases stress and nervousness and robs your system of B vitamins. Coffee is a drug that can make you a lot more jittery than you would otherwise be. If you're aware of being nervous, keep up the slow, even breathing; it'll do wonders. Peppermint tea, too, is soothing to the stomach. I always carry little bags of peppermint and green tea with me when I travel; it's easy to get hot water and make tea yourself in hotels and coffee shops. Chamomile tea is soothing, too, but may make you sleepy. Try it at night for insomnia.

It's better to have frequent, small, light meals rather than one heavy one. A few nuts and raisins, carrot sticks, alfalfa or broccoli sprouts, an apple—these will give you quick energy when you're under stress without making you logy. When your stomach is busy digesting food, your mind can't be as alert as you'd like.

Somebody once estimated that the effect of a performance on an actor's nervous system is roughly equal to the shock of a minor car accident. This is true, to some degree, of all performances. You must treat your system with attention and intelligent care. A regular exercise routine (yoga, jogging, dance, or outdoor walking) is helpful for cutting down preperformance nervousness, too, because it improves the state of your entire nervous system. Above all, do the deep, slow breathing; that's the *master control.*

Experiment with the stage fright exercises and suggestions given here to find the best combination and timing for you. Preparation is absolutely essential for your best performance. Everyone develops certain preferred rituals and is meticulous about observing them.

Luciano Pavarotti loves to kid around in rehearsals, but prepares entirely alone and with great seriousness for an hour before every performance. Aretha Franklin prays and meditates. Many stars do yoga and vocal warmups.

Give yourself all possible support in terms of adequate rehearsal, destressing exercises, nutritional backup, chanting, meditation, or prayer.

When you want something more than you fear it, you can act freely.

Peter Serkin, the concert pianist son of the late distinguished pianist Rudolf Serkin and grandson of another great musician, Adolf Busch, rebelled and dropped out of music for a year. He went to live in a little Mexican village where there was only the native music. One day, on a classical radio station, he heard a Bach Brandenburg Concerto and thought to himself, "Wow! How wonderful that I can make music like that!" He returned to his career, feeling now that he was choosing it himself. Music became his joy, and stage fright took a back seat.

If you get nervous even practicing your presentation or performance, do your stage fright warmups before rehearsal. As a matter of fact, it's a good idea to do them even if you're not nervous. You'll find you're able to work more efficiently and with a lot more pleasure. It seems so simple and natural when everything is going well that it's hard to realize what an extraordinary boost the de-stressing exercises will give you. We *are* under a lot of stress most of the time, and to recover the childlike spontaneity and pleasure in what we do and join that to the knowledge and skills of our adult achievements is tremendously satisfying.

Every moment is an experience in itself, as well as preparation for the future. When you see the connections between your past successes and what you want to do, you can trust yourself more to bring the preparation you've already had to your new tasks.

Linda L., vice-president of a paper-manufacturing company, moaned, "When I have a presentation to prepare, I write everything out and memorize it, but it sounds dead and I feel miserable about it."

In Linda's Personal Success Factor Workshop, she remembered (as her three greatest resources) her sense of humor, her enjoyment of new experiences, and her pleasure in communicating with people. Then I asked her to talk on something she was passionate about. To her own surprise, she talked fluently with expressive body language and no notes on mountain climbing, her hobby.

"You see," I pointed out, "you just learned what your real style is—from your own spontaneous moments. That's the style you want to catch in your business talks. It's a lot easier and more natural than what you were trying to do. Don't write out the whole speech. Outline the points you want to make, know your first sentence and last, have notes only for statistics you want to refer to, rehearse six to eight times, and you're ready—not to lecture, but to *talk* to people! Every talk is a dialogue between you and the audience. Only you have to use your imagination to fill in what they would like to know and ask you."

Eye contact! Enthusiasm! Energy!

Linda became an accomplished speaker for her company and, with her new ease and enjoyment of public speaking, was elected president of a major professional association.

Make Stage Fright a Tingle Instead of a Torture

Grab opportunities to talk to people on subjects other than the one you're required to do. Experience makes everything easier if it's good experience. The ease of speaking *when it doesn't matter* takes the pressure off. Having spoken comfortably where it wasn't required and given a lot of pleasure to people who responded with appreciation, you will find that your confidence will soar. Any success, even minor and unrelated, is wonderful preparation for more difficult challenges.

Do three *nice things for someone else* every day, for no reason, expecting nothing in return. (Try for a face-to-face exchange so you can enjoy the pleasure and warmth this will generate, first in yourself and then in others.) This too is confidence building. You will have *acted*, instead of passively suffering fear and apprehension; this makes you feel more yourself, more powerful, generous, and charismatic. *You will have done something because you chose to, regardless of what other people expected.*

Sharing a *laugh* with people every day is profoundly helpful in reducing anxiety. Seize every opportunity to enjoy a light moment, even with people you only see briefly: taxi driver, mailperson, doorman, another passenger waiting at a bus stop. Establishing connections makes you feel you're supported, not alone. Brief, friendly encounters with strangers make audiences seem less strange and alien. Your private self has expanded a little in a warm outreach. The world itself seems suddenly more friendly. Then it's easier to share what you're doing with others and concentrate on shaping your "gift" to them, whatever the performance happens to be.

All this sharing and everyday communication will help you move your "small self" out of the fright and into the light, enjoying the warmth, connecting with your "larger self," the one that is confident, in command, and in touch with the audience, enjoying the shared warmth of your time together.

That's where your charisma can really shine, shedding light as well as warmth all around you!

Performance Anxiety Exercises

The Butterflies Chaser

This is great for last-minute (or earlier) preperformance nerves.

1. Stand with your feet apart, knees bent a little, back straight, and arms relaxed and hanging loosely at your sides.

2. Without taking any additional breath, do twenty-six short bounces, saying "Vuh!" on each. Do this as energetically as possible, making the *vuh* a short, sharp, forceful sound (coming from the gut). If you're unable to manage twenty-six bounces at first, do as many as you can and gradually work up to the full amount. Punch downward on each *vuh* with both fists.

3. Relax and (with the mouth closed) inhale slowly and very deeply.

4. Exhale in a steady stream (*sh-h-h-h-h*) with mouth slightly open, letting the body sink into the knees.

Repeat three times; follow with long, slow breathing. Follow immediately with the Sa-ta-na-ma Chant.

Sa-ta-na-ma Chant

This chant balances the two sides of your brain and provides a cooling, reassuring sense of smoothness and flow. It's particularly good when you're waiting to go onstage. It can be kept up under your breath and will keep you calm and steady in performance.

Ra means sun; *ma* means moon; SA TA NA MA is *sat nam* (truth, essence) broken into component parts for the cycle of Birth, Life, Death, Rebirth. Hear the steady hum underneath the words, and keep that going. The sounds should be continuous, and each double syllable should take only the same time as each single one: "Rama" and "Mama" are said twice as quickly as "Ra" and "Ma" so that all syllables take only about one-half second.

Ra	Ra	Ra	Ra
Ma	Ma	Ma	Ma
Rama	Rama	Rama	Rama
Mama	Mama	Mama	Mama
SA	TA	NA	MA

Repeat for at least five minutes.

Energy Expander

This exercise is helpful when you are weary, sleepy, or need energy.

1. Contract your middle as though it had been kicked by a horse, and at the same time, let out a short, sharp *huh* sound. Do as many as you can without breathing, gradually working up to at least ten.

2. Relax and inhale, expanding your abdomen and diaphragm.

   Repeat ten times.

The Depressurizer

Skip this exercise if you have high blood pressure.

1. Stand in a doorway and press your palms against the door frame on both sides. Hold your breath and keep increasing the pressure—you'll feel warmth rushing to your face, head, and neck. Hold as long as you can.

2. Release totally, with a rush. Drop your hands as you exhale.

3. Inhale deeply.

   Repeat three times.

Karate Chop

1. Stand with the legs shoulder-width apart, bend your knees, and clench the fists at your sides next to your knees.

2. Pretend you're lifting a heavy bucket filled with sand, giving three short, sharp bursts of inhalation (mouth closed) so that by the third you're stretched upward, arms overhead as high as they will go, fists still clenched.

3. CRASH! Bring both fists down together in a tremendous karate chop, at the same time yelling, HEHHHHHHHH! or HAHHHHHHHH!

Repeat five times.

Steam Engine

1. Stand with the legs shoulder-width apart, knees bent, head erect, and mouth closed. Make fists with both hands.

2. Pull your right arm straight back and, at the same time, punch the left arm forward (without leaning into it) as powerfully as possible, exhaling forcefully.

3. Draw the left arm back, inhale as your fists pass each other, and as the right arm punches forward, exhale forcefully. Maintain a steady, even rhythm, and keep the mouth closed.

Repeat as powerfully and steadily as you can for three to five minutes. This produces tremendous energy release through the chest, shoulders, arms, hands, and neck. It enhances your courage and releases tension instantly.

The I-Don't-Care Swing

The ability to let go of our effortfulness is essential. Any tension that is sustained without release will lead to reduced efficiency in functioning and eventually stress the body-mind enough to produce an illness or breakdown. If we're too stressed, we don't absorb information well, listen productively, think creatively, or interact effectively with others. We need to achieve a childlike release of tension—often! Becoming aware of and sensitive to your own biofeedback instrument—your body-mind—and what it is registering is the first step to discharging stress and renewing energy. As children, we have natural anti-stressing techniques, which we forget as we grow up. Getting in touch with the playful spirit and rebelliousness of a child is enormously rewarding and an effective device for quick, easy tension release.

1. Stand with the feet shoulder-width apart. Fling the whole torso-neck-head as *one* piece to one side, then the other, moving the whole upper portion of your body as a unit. Do this a few times, freely and rhythmically.

2. Let your arms swing freely from side to side at shoulder level, until they loosely wrap around your body as *you* swing from side to side, the whole trunk and head turning.

3. As your torso swings first to the left, then all the way to the right, freely shout "*I don't care!*" or "*No, I won't!*" or "*You can't make me!*" Enjoy yourself! Do this at least twenty times. Make sure that your head goes all the way around with the torso.

This exercise is great for a mid-morning office break. If you allow your eyes to unfocus as you swing, this becomes an effective eye-relaxing exercise as well.

A Courage Exercise—The Elbow Propeller

For stimulation of the chest and heart, relaxation of shoulder and neck tension, and your increasing ability to *take risks* and feel energized, this exercise is tops.

1. Stand with the feet apart, knees slightly bent, elbows at the sides, forearms raised, and hands hanging limply from the wrists.

2. Begin to rotate the arms, leading with the elbows in the largest vertical circle possible, close to the body, ten times forward, then ten times backward—as rapidly and energetically as possible, with the mouth closed.

3. Finish with three long complete breaths (in and out) and relax.

This will give you instant alertness when you're tired, logy, or diffident, stepping up your vitality.

Preperformance Exercises

These exercises, several of them described in chapter 12, are especially helpful before performances.

1. The Pointillist Necklace (Drunken Head Roll; see p. 260); three times in each direction.

2. The Helium Ball Yawn (see p. 285)

3. Head Alignment

    a. Drop your head on your chest.

b. Slowly, slowly unroll neck from the back, one vertebra at a time (eyes open), keeping chin in, with the slowest possible continuous movement.

c. When head is exactly at the end of the spine, like a flower at the end of its stem, *stop*! Note the position. Is it higher or lower than usual?

d. Feel that you are looking straight ahead with your entire body—your head very much part of the whole trunk.

e. Maintain your open throat, straight back, proud head, and direct gaze. Notice the feeling of power and integration this gives you.

4. Preperformance Look

   a. Smile broadly.

   b. Drop the smile from your mouth, but leave it in your eyes and cheekbones. The eyes sparkle; cheekbones are lifted and round.

   c. Inhale and feel the resultant look: "Something good is about to happen!" "I have a wonderful secret!" Great when you're being introduced on a dais, on TV, or at a party.

5. The Horse Laugh (see p. 285)

6. Wibble Wobble (see p. 285)

7. Hand Heartener (see p. 289)

8. Basic Buddha Belly (see p. 254)

11

The World Inside Your Heart

Within the city of Brahman, which is the body, there is the heart, and within it, there is a little castle which has the shape of a lotus . . . within it dwells that which is to be sought after, inquired about and realized.

. . . Even so large as the universe outside is the universe within the lotus of the heart. Within it are heaven and the earth, the sun, the moon, the lightning and all the stars. Whatever is in the macrocosm is in this microcosm also.

. . . Though old age comes to the body, the lotus of the heart does not grow old. . . . Untouched by any deed, ageless, deathless, free from grief, from hunger and thirst, its desires are right desires and its desires are fulfilled.
—Chandogya Upanishad

When we really connect with people, when our charisma is clear and shining, we "touch" the hearts of others. Everyone secretly longs to communicate in this "heartfelt" way. Yet many people are so enclosed in heavy emotional armor that they seem hidden to others. It is always to guard against being hurt that we hide our naked hearts.

Johann B., a handsome, stoically reserved half-German, half–South African venture capitalist, came to me to learn to be "more expressive." Since he barely spoke, people found him boring. He had spent his early childhood years fleeing across Europe from the Nazis. Forced to be very quiet for fear of discovery and arrest, his early childhood messages were "Be proper," "Don't show feelings," and "Don't get angry." This was not only the message of his family, but also of the upper class he grew up in.

He found it impossible to lift his voice above a quiet, cultivated monotone. The only release he enjoyed was lovemaking. He was extremely, almost painfully, "correct" and apologized frequently.

He had taken the injunction against speaking so literally that he had never told anyone, not even his wife, the story of his terrifying childhood flights across Europe. "I don't want to burden people," he said. "They wouldn't be interested."

What Are You Passionate About?

If there is a large part of your life that you've never shared with anyone, chances are you feel cut off from expressing deep feelings. This has a subtle dulling effect on your ability to communicate directly and warmly to people. It's as though your inner self, deprived of the right to speak, loses confidence (literally "loses heart") and retreats into an impersonal, safe grayness that neither offends nor calls attention to itself.

To be charismatic you must have heartfelt connections with what you're saying. This means giving yourself permission not only to know what you really feel about your life experiences but also to express your inner thoughts openly. Ellis M. was dismayed at his discovery: "I haven't felt passionate about anything in years—I don't know where it went." He needed to recapture the childlike enthusiasm and eager excitement he once felt. A surprising number of people are like Ellis. A key for them is being able to talk about something personal without the fear of being disapproved of or criticized. Only then can the intensity they once felt instead light up everything they talk about, public or private.

We all have leaky margins. Freeing yourself in one area automatically frees up others. *If you can talk openly about something personal, then you can talk about something open personally.* Think about it.

Johann practiced the One-Minute Verbal Free-for-All, the "I Have a Right" (page 230), the I-Don't-Care Swing, the Golden Sunflower, and the anger exercises, and he kept an Anti-Judgmental Notebook for several weeks. He could then begin to still the internal censor that constantly chipped away at his spontaneity. He found himself laughing and enjoying his life more. When he shared some of the secrets of his childhood, he began to talk louder, his voice took on more color; his personality seemed less formal, warmer, and more appealing.

The One-Minute Verbal Free-for-All is an indispensable tool for freeing the capacity to connect with your individual heart's essence. Through this tool you can discover that we are all inextricably (and heartwarmingly) connected with each other. **If you consider yourself shy, or you'd like to improve your verbal fluency and rid yourself of a fear of speaking in public, try it!** It's astonishingly effective.

The One-Minute Verbal Free-for-All

When I speak to a large group, several hundred or a thousand people, I usually ask for a show of hands: "How many people here know how to hide?" Every hand goes up! It's not surprising. We all learn very early how to lie low and stay out of the way of adults who may not be friendly or approving. Then I ask people to face each other in pairs and for one minute, nonstop, to shout at each other (without listening to the other). "Take a mental Polaroid of how your body feels before, during, and after this exercise," I suggest. Stopwatch in hand, I tell them, "OK, now yell as loudly as possible. It doesn't matter what you say or even if you're making any sense; just keep going until the minute is up. Go!"

As was discussed in chapter 2, people who find it difficult to "hold the floor" are amazed at how hard it is for them to do this exercise. They report feeling silly or embarrassed or think they have "nothing to say." But once they get into the knock-down, drag-out spirit of it, they find it a tremendous amount of fun, and everybody feels alive, warm, and energized. In fact, it's one of the fastest ways to bring up energy in a group of any size. The mock battle leaves everyone breathless and laughing, and it has the power to make a roomful of strangers suddenly feel at home with each other!

The One-Minute Verbal Free-for-All is both a superb diagnostic and an incredibly effective transformative exercise. It tests something very basic: *how willing are you to take attention?*

Since your body has been faithfully recording all your experiences all your life, if you ever had a negative experience speaking, it will show up in this exercise—as a reluctance to take attention (because long ago it wasn't safe!). However, the good news is that through this psychophysical exercise, the body can relearn in a surprisingly short time *a newly enjoyable way* of experiencing public speaking. The first time you do the exercise, you will get an accurate reading of where you stand. If you feel more relaxed when you finish (most people do), your body is ready to learn to enjoy speaking. If you feel more tense than when you began, it just means that it feels like a dangerous situation to you. But every time you practice the exercise and speaking, it gets easier. You are building in new, positive experiences for the body-mind, which override the old messages and replace them with a pleasurable, spirited fluency. This is what I mean when I tell clients, "Spontaneity takes great preparation!"

Carter S., a distinguished but shy scientist, came to me before a scheduled appearance to testify in Congress. He felt paralyzed with fear at the prospect. When we first did the One-Minute Verbal Free-for-All, he hated it—he was barely able to say anything at all! Nonetheless he went home and practiced it grimly for several days.

"At first," he reported the following week, "it was very difficult, but I kept trying to do it, and at a certain point something funny happened. It was as though I suddenly realized, 'Hey! I did this taboo thing and nothing bad happened!' I didn't lose my prestige, my dignity, my family—nothing! I felt as though I was putting something over on people. From that point on, it got easier and easier every time I did it. I even began to enjoy it and to be surprised and interested at the things that were coming out of my mouth. When I went down to Washington less than a week later, to my amazement I felt just as comfortable testifying in Congress and talking to senators as I do in my own research institute or with my closest family and friends. I could hardly believe it. Normally I would have been petrified! I owe it all to that remarkable exercise."

This no-holds-barred, no-agenda One-Minute Verbal Free-for-All is the first stage of the exercise. When you get comfortable enough with it to be able to do it anywhere, anytime, without hesitation, you're ready for Stage II. In Stage II you pick a subject and "riff" on it for one minute. (By the way, this is a marvelous way of planning a speech or presentation—do the One-Minute Verbal Free-for-All about seven times on the opening paragraph. At the end of that time, you'll know exactly what you want to say, and you'll know it cold! Then you do the same process to find out how you want to finish your talk.)

Why does this work? The secret is that when you're not nervous, you exchange thoughts and ideas with people easily, all the time: your unconscious continuously feeds you responses. But when you are gripped by anxiety, the door to your unconscious clangs shut, and you've lost the connection with your own rich inner resources.

You may remember in Jonathan Swift's *Gulliver's Travels* that Gulliver is shipwrecked and wakes to find himself a prisoner. He's lying flat, he can't move, and hundreds of little men are swarming all over him. Suddenly he realizes that the reason he can't move is that he's tied down with hundreds of incredibly fine, invisible ropes! This is a perfect metaphor for inhibitions: when we're inhibited by old negative experiences, we're literally tied up and shut down!

The One-Minute Verbal Free-for-All is an indispensable life-changing resource to give you back what is yours—your spontaneous thoughts, moment-to-moment observations, feelings, and memories—and with them, your confidence! When you can comfortably do Stage I and Stage II of the One-Minute Verbal Free-for-All, you're ready for the next step, "I Have a Right."

"I Have a Right"

1. Standing up straight, say in a loud, firm voice: **"I have a right to feel what I feel!"** You may realize you don't believe it—notice how your voice sounds. Is it timid, or perhaps defiant (as though arguing with somebody in your past who didn't think you *were* entitled to your feelings)?

   Say it ten times, and *mean it!* By the tenth time it should feel and sound as though you own it!

2. **"I have a right to say what I feel!"** Again, do it ten times. If you're not sure you do have that right, tell yourself that you have the right, but you can choose whether or not you *will* say it. If you honor your inner hesitations by noticing them, then you can negotiate with them.

3. **"I have a right to know what I know."** Say it ten times!

4. **"I have a right to enjoy saying what I feel!"** Say it ten times, with feeling! A quiet young Chinese artist asked in one of the Charismedia workshops, "Does this work just as well if you say it to yourself?" "Let's muscle-test it!" I suggested. We were all amazed when muscle testing showed that saying a positive phrase internally did not strengthen the body; only saying it aloud had that effect!

The Golden Sunflower

1. Imagine a huge, golden sunflower shining in your chest at the heart's center. See all the petals in great detail. Close your eyes and imagine the sunflower in the heart center of someone you love. Send your radiance to their flower, and feel theirs connecting with yours.

2. Next, imagine the golden sunflower in the heart center of someone neutral (a stranger on the street, for instance). See his or her sunflower just as intensely, and connect it with yours as you did before.

3. Now think of someone you dislike or fear. See the golden sunflower radiant in the center of that person's chest. If you have trouble imagining this, go back to the sunflower of the person you love and then transfer it! Send your heart warmth to the person you dislike. (One United Nations diplomat told us this process got him through boring official parties.) Everybody responds at the heart's level, so then it doesn't even matter what you say: there's a warmth between you that is palpable.

4. Always imagine the golden sunflower in your own, and others', hearts before you meet new people or address a group. Everybody responds with warmth and friendliness because you are connecting from your heart centers. This is a great way to avoid being affected by others' negativity.

How You Can Actually Improve Your Heart's Health

Recent research at the California-based Institute of HeartMath (IHM) has demonstrated striking connections between positive emotional states and the heart's electrical patterns. Doc Childre, founder of the nonprofit institute, and Rollin McCraty, IHM research director, discovered that through emotional self-management people can generate consistent positive changes in the output of their electrocardiograms (ECGs).

"When people entered loving states, ECG spectrum patterns, which are typically scattered and chaotic, became much more coherent and orderly." People who practiced heart-centered consciousness produced coherent patterns 30 to 50 percent of the time. Untrained control subjects reported higher daily levels of mental and emotional stress and produced less consistent ECG coherence. In fact, subjects' patterns became disordered when they were asked to experience negative states like anger or frustration.

ECG coherence was linked to increased levels of S-IgA (secretory immunoglobulin gamma-A), a key factor in the body's immune system. These results confirm a well-known Harvard University study by David McClelland showing an increase in S-IgA among all the students who watched a compassion-inducing videotape of Mother Teresa (even the ones who didn't believe in her).

The *heart's electrical amplitude* is about fifty times as strong as that produced by the brain. In fact, in order to get an accurate electroencephalogram (EEG), the signal from the heart must be filtered out. The heart's electrical system and its corresponding electrical fields permeate *every cell in the body*!

Crystal-like structures in the heart act as transducers, converting the positive "heart intelligence"—such as positive mental and emotional states (e.g., sending love with the Golden Sunflower)—into electrical frequency data, which are reflected in the ECG. Through human DNA, this "information" then communicates directly with all cells in the body. So it is easy to see a direct impact on our health.

Clearly, the heart's intuitive information-processing field forms a sort of "superconscious" that directs the conscious mind. The mind then communicates with the brain, which executes physical commands.

"Both heart and mind ultimately exist in a nonlocal quantum domain," observed Glen Rein, a former Stanford University researcher. "We believe the quantum field of the heart embraces the mind, consistent with the Buddhist conception of the mind residing in the heart."

Back in the 1950s researchers John and Beatrice Lacey suggested that one's heart rate "tunes" the senses and alters the brain. But for a long time nobody thought to pay much attention to the cardiac impact of positive emotional states. Medicine was about sickness, not human potential.

Now rigorous scientific research in a new field—cardioneuroimmunology—is providing validation of ancient spiritual truths, like the power of love to heal. As a result, scientists seriously exploring the *physiological* benefits of love, compassion, and other positive emotions no longer regard the body as a somewhat faulty machine. Psychology, too, has been shifting from an emphasis on pathology to greater interest in what makes us most human and even divine. A sense of reverence has crept into the discourse.

The internal coherence created by caring, loving thoughts (emotional focusing as in the Golden Sunflower) can actually be measured electrophysiologically. This coherence is characterized by improved sympathovagal balance and increased secretory immunoglobulin-A levels. At the same time, salivary cortisol, a stress factor, is considerably reduced. *Now we know that a therapist's positive cardiac field is registered by the patient and amplified.* New studies by Linda Russek and Gary Schwartz, done from 1995 to 1997, find that people who are more accustomed to receiving love and care are better receivers of others' positive signals.

The IHM's groundbreaking research has demonstrated not only that a loving intention produces very desirable coherence in the electromagnetic field of a person's heart, but also that the EEG field affects brainwave activity in a second individual. Our emotions affect others at a basic physiological level. For the first time we have a scientific basis for understanding the actual physiological individual and interpersonal effects of charisma! The amazing positive impact of Mother Teresa's loving presence, *even communicated through a film*, on the immune systems of the students who watched it shows that these love-generated electromagnetic fields are real and powerful positive forces not only for individuals but also for groups—people who aren't even in the same place or time!

Physicists call the mechanism by which a person's positive emotional intention creates the physiologically powerful and highly desirable effect of increasing internal cardiac coherence *nonlinear stochastic resonance*. The original Greek for *stochastic* meant to "aim at a mark" or "guess." In current usage it means "randomly determined, so its behavior may be analyzed statistically but not predicted precisely." This is a nice description of something everybody has witnessed but nobody has been able to pinpoint and define—the operation of charisma.

Having a positive, caring intention and wanting to share your passion with others, it now becomes abundantly clear, is not simply good for your health but also for your charisma!

The Passion Ploy: Voicing Your Feelings

The first talk people in my workshops give is three to five minutes long on something they feel passionate about. Once you share your true feelings with a group of strangers, it's much easier to talk about business, politics, philosophy, or anything else that interests you.

A lot of people have a hard time with this assignment.

"Nobody will be interested!" said a student.

Stuart M., a corporate executive, gave a talk on his hobby, biophysics. As he spoke, he kept rubbing his nose with his hand, an unconscious signal that he didn't think the audience would understand or appreciate what he was saying. When I asked him if that was what he felt, an embarrassed smile spread over his face. "I'm afraid that's just what I was thinking!" he answered.

Do you secretly fear your audience may not understand or be interested? If you notice you're feeling doubts, you can go ahead without being undermined. Otherwise your energy level will swiftly and mysteriously drop, and you'll telegraph uncertainty and a lack of confidence to your audience.

Stanford L., a distinguished professor and author of eight books, took the class because he was terrified of speaking. Comfortable enough seated on a panel, he didn't dare accept solo speaking engagements. He gave his first talk for us on the U.S. Federal Communications Commission (FCC). Although, he'd written a prizewinning book on the subject and was deeply interested in it, nobody would have guessed it from his platform behavior. His face was expressionless, his large, burly frame slouched miserably, and his voice was toneless and uninteresting.

"Please, Mr. L., talk about something personal!" I begged him.

The following week he got up and gave one of the most memorable talks of the semester about three risks he had taken. The first was riding the whitewater rapids in Colorado with his daughter. Braving the rough waters and feeling he had held his own turned out to be an enormously exhilarating boost to his self-esteem. The world looked a little different to him after that adventure. The second risk was taking the Charismedia workshop. The third was that "for the first time in twenty-five years I talked back to my father-in-law." The change in Stanford was remarkable. His face was animated, his voice colorful. He even stood up straighter. We were all fascinated. For the first time we all had a sense of who he was because he had shared important experiences and perceptions with us and had allowed us to know his vulnerabilities. He was, suddenly, very human and appealing. (I later found out that his father-in-law was a world-famous songwriter who was a notorious curmudgeon!)

The Charm of Being Vulnerable

If you admit you're not perfect and share that with the audience, that's engaging and warms everybody; we can all relate to imperfection. Perfection is not only unlikely and unreal, it's boring! Programmed as most of us are to revere success and equate it with perfection (the impossible dream), it's a great relief to hear about someone's bumbling efforts to master a personal problem. Lewis Thomas, the wise physician, wrote in *The Medusa and the Snail* that "the capacity to leap across mountains of information to land lightly on the wrong side represents the highest of human endowments. It may be that this is a uniquely human gift." He claims if we were not "provided with the knack of being wrong, we could never get anything useful done."

What a relief it is if we plunge ahead and not only admit but are amused at our mistakes! It enhances rapport. People feel they know and like you.

Of course, you want to be "right" in an important report for your company or a research paper, but it's marvelous practice to speak openly of personal feelings, without having to be right, when you want to connect warmly with people.

Can You Name Three Passions?

What's your "passion quotient"? Could you give three talks on subjects you're passionate about? Remember, anything you care deeply about you're probably an expert on. You don't need weeks or even days of research to prepare a talk about something you're very involved with.

Name your passions:

1.

2.

3.

The first two should be about feelings and experiences, not public issues: perhaps "the most important decision of my life" or "my passion for driftwood." Don't write out the whole talk. If you do, you'll feel you have to read it, which will kill all spontaneity. Audiences need eye contact with you—when you read a speech, you lose connection and sound stuffy, impersonal, or dull. Randomly brainstorm your ideas for a day or so and then jot them down, not necessarily in order.

Then, on your feet, do the One-Minute Verbal Free-for-All, six to eight times, on the opening part of your talk. Tape this—but you don't have to listen to it! When you've finished, you'll know exactly how you want to start. **Important!**—know your opening sentences cold. Rehearse out loud. Doing it in your head is not the same!

Now give yourself permission to say the same thing twenty times, each time with as much expression as the first time.

"But that feels phony!" you protest.

For your audience, it *will* be the first time. Remember, spontaneity is the result of great preparation. Preparation can be a lot of rehearsal or a lot of experience. The aliveness and enthusiasm of spontaneity is an important element of charisma. Eighty-nine percent of respondents to my questionnaire listed eloquence among the essential ingredients of charisma, and eloquence is not just *what* you say but *how you say it*. Don't kid yourself—this does take practice!

Who Is Your Ideal Listener?

To find the tone of greatest interest and connection with your audience, close your eyes and visualize your ideal hearer. It may be your mother, sister, husband, colleague, a childhood teacher, your dog, or even your goldfish.

Alison R. remarked, "You know, that's really hard for me. I keep seeing my family interrupting me, which makes me so tense that I want to bludgeon through before they stop me."

Other people have the opposite reaction—when they're interrupted, they feel uninteresting and shrink back, sometimes without saying anything at all. Margo R. protested, "I could never get a word in edgewise in my house. But I just flashed on an old lady I met in the country last summer who loved to hear me talk about photography, my hobby. When I talked to her, I felt everything I said was interesting and important. I'll concentrate on her!"

Trial lawyer Edward M. laughed and remarked, "The first thing that came into my mind was the look on the face of a girl I was madly in love with when I was eighteen. We talked about everything—she was the first person who really listened to me. It was because of her that I applied for and got into law school. Now most of the time I see adversaries when I'm talking, but it certainly changes things to visualize my first girl." Next time he tried it, he won his case!

Janine L. said, "Believe it or not, my best listener is my ten-year-old son. Everything interests him! I love to tell him what I'm thinking, and he really listens."

If you signal mistrust of your hearer or show doubt of a listener's willingness (or ability) to get your message, you automatically lose your audience. Worse, you may come across as unfriendly, weak, discouraged, or snobbish. Keep in mind that whenever there is a conflict between verbal and nonverbal signals, the nonverbal ones are believed!

Regardless of what your old family experiences were, here's a key to taking and holding people's attention: what makes you interesting is *your own interest in what you're saying*. It doesn't matter whether you are passionate about orthodontics, semiotics, Glagolithic script, stamp collecting, or rock 'n' roll. *Assume* your listeners are just as fascinated as you are; then they will be. That's the "entrainment process" of charisma. Plunge right in. Never begin with "I am going to talk about . . ." or "Today I want to tell you about . . ."

Start with a provocative sentence: "September 8, 1974, may have been the most extraordinary day of my life."

Or lead off with a question: "Who would have guessed a few short years ago that the Australian dugong would become the world's most desirable mammal?"

Or cite a quotation: "Alexander Woollcott once said, 'When I feel like exercising, I lie down until the impulse goes away.' Well, I used to feel that way, too!"

If you're inexperienced, just throw away your first sentence (the one that begins "I'd like to tell you about . . .") and start instead with the one where you really get into the topic. Go through your main points, noting a couple of "key words" for each of them on three-by-five-inch cards to help you remember the order. Keep your notes brief, make drawings if they help, and resist the temptation to write everything out. Don't get bogged down in trivia or apology. Feelings are important, and the audience can identify with yours, but don't tell them you're nervous, tired, or feeling unprepared. Why burden them?

Decide ahead on your last sentence or last two. Do another few One-Minute Verbal Free-for-Alls to loosen up. Wrap up the main points of your talk. End with a quotation, a call to action, or a powerful sentence to leave the audience thinking. Avoid "In conclusion, . . ." or "I'd like to close by saying . . ." Let your audience know that it's the end by the weight and importance you give your closing words and your silence and eye contact after you've finished.

Practice talking about something personal—nothing is more interesting to an audience than what you bring of yourself—your "baggage" of knowledge, experience, feelings, and reactions. That special combination is a unique package. If it's heartfelt, it's charismatic. And remember the old acronym KISS (Keep it simple, stupid!).

The Power of Sound Bites

A short pithy phrase—often an image—can accomplish more than hundreds of words. The term "population bomb" undoubtedly contributed to the tremendous drop in the birthrate in the United States and Europe over the past few decades.

When Rachel Carson wrote a book on ecology, her publisher asked for a catchy title. A few days later, Ms. Carson received a letter from an old friend, who wrote, "I found two more robins dead on the lawn today; I guess it's going to be a *silent spring*."

"That's it!" said the publisher. The book became a classic, and the title summed up its cautionary message.

Finding the right simple words is far from easy. Fall in love with language—it's always changing. The larger your vocabulary, the more things you have to say, as well as ways of saying them! You'll see more subtleties and more nuances. Beware of cliché generalities: "Oh, it was just wonderful." "It was really terrific, marvelous." "It really pisses me off."

If you want your hearers to share your experience, fill in sensory details: sight, sound, taste, feeling, hearing. Allow meaningful pauses. Describe problems you overcame: it's more dramatic to hear about some setbacks than an unbroken string of successes. Every passion is a tale of adventure.

Marjorie L., a writer in my workshop, told us she became intrigued with a prehistoric boat found in England and decided to write a book about it. She told us she'd written to all the people and organizations she could track down that might have something to add. Then she described her frustration when she got a flat turndown from the owner of the property where the relic was found, and how the little old curator of the local library invited her to tea and later cajoled the owner into admitting her onto the estate.

Her car broke down, her money ran out, her husband came to the rescue—one clue led to another. Finally she showed us the completed book, just published. We had all listened entranced as the story unfolded, because she shared with us all the disappointments, dead-end leads, and her sense of growing excitement. She took us into her life.

This is what you do when you talk about a passion. You take your hearers into a whole world. Shape your talk to a strong ending and decide which details will enrich and clarify and which are irrelevant or repetitious. You can create whatever impression you want to. If *you* were listening to this talk, what would *you* really want to know? Imagine your ideal listener with eager eyes asking you questions:

"What happened then?"

"What made you pick that particular road (or bowl, day, city, whatever)?"

"What did it (he, she, they) look (feel, sound, talk, act) like?"

Every solo talk is a dialogue, even if the audience is silent. Avoid practicing in front of a mirror or you'll feel lost without it when you face an audience. Use a mirror only to check on a particular expression, phrase, or gesture, but don't get hypnotized by your own image!

Practice louder than you normally speak (even if it feels silly at first). You raise your energy level and increase your vocal and expressive range when you speak louder. Say very loudly "*I enjoy being outrageous!*" flinging your arms in the air. You might feel your heart beating rapidly, as though you were doing something dangerous, but the more you practice, the more quickly that will subside. (To get your energy level up fast, try jogging as you're talking—this is also helpful when you're doing the One-Minute Verbal Free-for-All—it's impossible to be boring while jogging!)

If you do have an ideal listener in the house, ask him or her to check you—but only for volume. At this stage, politely but firmly explain you're just practicing and don't want their reactions—yet (unless it's genuine, unqualified enthusiasm!).

The Importance of Following Your Instinct

Ashley G., a serious, extremely intellectual young writer with an important new book, was a guest on a late-night talk show one evening; his publisher had asked me to watch. To my horror, I witnessed a small massacre. The host and another guest had decided to attack Ashley: "Your style stinks!" they chortled gaily. Ashley, unprepared for such rudeness, didn't know what to say. Nonplussed, he began to defend himself, at excruciating length. It was painful.

When he came to see me, I asked him, "When they lit into you, what did you *feel* like saying?" He looked surprised. "Oh," he answered slowly, "I felt like saying, 'For this I turned down the Letterman show?!'"

Right! That would have been a great response. The audience would have laughed and applauded, and he'd have had no further trouble with his host (who just wanted to create controversy and an interesting show). By taking a deep breath and tuning in to his intuition, he'd have uttered the most natural, heartfelt response—usually the best riposte.

More on Sound Bites

A TV show isn't a normal social situation—it's a simulated one, and ordinary rules of courtesy often don't apply. You must *take* attention, not wait for others to give it to you. There's very little time to make your point. Sound bites use images, metaphors, quotes, and colorful stories to get ideas across as fast and memorably as possible.

A New England senatorial candidate begged me to help him: "I get hopelessly long-winded at press conferences when reporters ask me to comment on, for example, the economy. I just can't seem to give a short answer," he complained.

"Who's the youngest person you enjoy explaining things to?" I asked him. His face broke out in a smile. "My nine-year-old daughter, Christina."

"OK," I said, "How would you explain the economy to Christina?"

"Well," he said promptly, "you see, the economy is like a three-legged stool. One leg is farming, one is tourism, and one is industry."

"Perfect!" I told him. "That's clear, interesting, and vivid. Any time you need to explain something to a lay audience, think of Christina. We're all nine-year-olds on matters we know nothing about. As Will Rogers remarked, 'Everybody is ignorant, only on different subjects.'"

Life is so complex that we're almost all what Miguel Unamuno called "vertical savages." That is, most people would be hard put to explain the basic inventions of our age. I know if I were whisked back to the eighteenth or nineteenth century, I'd have a tough time explaining airplanes or nuclear fission, let alone computers! Nobody can possibly know everything—we're all ignorant in lots of fields. By respecting the "dumb" questions an intelligent but uninformed listener might raise, you'll know how to put the information in user-friendly chunks, so *people will feel you respect them and are taking care of them.* This is just as important in business, in politics, and on TV as at home. Since TV has altered our nervous systems, everybody has shorter attention spans, is used to rapid multisensory stimulation, and is less willing to tolerate boredom. So we all need to learn more pithy and situationally effective communication skills.

Here's Looking at You!

When your eyes express concentrated pleasure and interest in what you're talking about, people are drawn to you as if by magic. Visualize in your mind's eye what you're talking about, and people will "see" something in your eyes, although they may make a different internal picture from yours. The human face is capable of about twenty thousand expressions, but the eyes are still the "windows of the soul."

Facial expression is an international language. Intense emotions like joy, sadness, fright, and contempt are instantly comprehensible to people from all cultures. Paul Ekman of the University of California at San Francisco took photos of six different emotional states and compared the interpretations of them by people of five different cultures. A high percentage of the associations were the same. Even blind or deaf children who can't imitate facial expressions they haven't seen express their feelings the same way (according to Irenäus Eibl-Eibesfeldt's studies). To be human transcends all national and physical barriers.

If you're talking to a group, large or small, make sure that at some point in your talk you include everyone in your gaze. Find a friendly face and address a sentence or two to that person, then transfer your attention to someone else. Really connect with each person you look at for at least two or three remarks. A nervous, darting eye scan doesn't satisfy anyone! Include people at the sides and back of the room (and try to avoid having anyone behind you, if possible). You may find you instinctively look more toward one side than the other. One client realized he always ignored people on his right. Once he was aware of it, he got new glasses.

Look up or beyond the audience when you're reflecting, remembering, or visualizing. If the audience can *see* you thinking, they'll be interested. Looking down is like garlic—a little goes a long way. It not only cuts people off, it also may give the impression you're shy, nervous, or ashamed. There's no need to give these messages!

When your heart center is open, people feel and respond to that.

"But how can I protect myself from people who might take advantage?" you ask. Being open doesn't mean you're a sucker. On the contrary, when your instincts are keen, you'll be able to protect yourself effortlessly. There is a story of a Zen master whose "one-pointed" control was legendary. Although he seemed completely relaxed, sitting quietly in a doorway, when a bandit tried to attack him from behind, the master cut him down with his sword so swiftly that *nobody saw it*!

This is very different from the fearful self-protectiveness that makes some people walk around half-expecting an attack, worrying about cancer, the bomb, or being robbed or mugged. Aileen, for example, depended on "magic" to get her through the day, and she lived in fear of the "evil eye." Yet she was an extremely bright young woman; she simply felt she had little control over her life. Her charisma was buried under her "armor."

Do You Have Too Much Armor to Enjoy Your Life?

If you're constantly expecting disaster or are always wary of being ill-treated, you live in a state of fear and tension. Your personality may seem guarded, constricted, or hostile. It's hard for people to feel your warmth through your fearful armor.

Through breathing and visualization we can let go of "stuckness," fear, limitations, and pain. When we transform our sense of being alive, *the moment is enough*—being in the quiet inner world of the heart is so satisfying that nothing else matters.

Let's explore how finding your center and going inward for peace and strength can enhance your joy in life—and help your charisma emerge clearly.

When Aileen complained that she wished she could enjoy her life, I suggested, "Close your eyes and breathe slowly and deeply." As she relaxed in her chair, hands in her lap, her breathing grew quiet. Her stomach rose and fell. Then I continued, with pauses to allow Aileen to follow:

> *Feel a great space between your ears . . . be aware of the space between your shoulders . . . between your ribs . . . between your sides . . . between your hips. . . . Now feel the space within the body. . . . Visualize yourself floating in the spaces and just be there . . . be aware of any emotions, thoughts, or pain that is in your body and dissolve them in the space flowing through. . . . Watch the colors as they change, flowing through and around the space. . . . Let all the spaces around your body, under the chair, over your head, flow through the body and melt with the space flowing out through the walls, up into the sky, down below the earth, into the sea, and past the endless horizon, all is swirling lightness . . . feel that you are all space . . . it is dissolved in you and you in space . . . no boundaries anywhere . . . just a flowing of lightness . . . space and radiance. . . . Allow yourself to let go of your body completely . . . imagine yourself letting go . . . dissolving easily . . . you are diffused through the universe . . . exhale . . . and let go . . . (after a long pause) . . . . Now choose to be born again . . . as a tiny baby anywhere and in any way you wish . . . you choose your new life . . . When you open your eyes you will see everything as though for the first time . . . you are reborn . . . with each breath, you die . . . as you exhale and let go completely, and with each inhalation, you are born again . . . rested . . . fresh . . . new. . . .*

Aileen opened her eyes, smiled, and sat silently for a few minutes. Then she said, "Oh, that was wonderful! I have never been able to relax like that. At one point I had the most wonderful image: I was an angel, flying over me with outspread wings. That was the first time in my life I ever felt *my own angel* watch over me. It was peaceful and exhilarating. Until now I was only aware of my devil. I just feel this is one of the most important things that's ever happened to me."

She sat quietly, a smile on her face. "You know," she said, "I'm breathing really deeply but very gently—it feels so easy—the way babies breathe; it's no effort at all. And my whole body feels soft and light. The strange thing is that it's as though I knew this all along—it's like coming home."

The World Heart Embrace

I asked her to stand up and stretch. Then we continued:

> Inhale and hold both arms out as though you are embracing the universe. Really feel you're *stretching to embrace the whole world*. This is the most life-affirming gesture, the *primal loving welcome of the eternal mother*. Merely seeing this gesture strengthens your life force! (Muscle-testing shows this.) When you embrace the world, your heart center opens and expands your electromagnetic field; your charisma is moving out to strengthen others. Now hold that stretch, and visualize that you really are including the whole world in your arms: hold your breath . . .
>
> When you've held your breath as long as you can, slowly, lovingly, bring your arms together until your hands fold over each other and rest on your breast. Feel that you have brought the love of the whole world to your own heart; feel the warmth of that flowing into you through your fingers. Now again stretch and embrace the universe, and then allow all this concentrated love to sink in and nourish every cell of your body; spread it to your fingertips and your toes, to the topmost cell of your brain, to every single muscle, ligament, and neuron. Feel all of you warmed and bathed in the warmth and radiance of that love . . . spread it with your soft full breath through your body and beyond the boundaries until the world and you are one—there is no distinction. All warmth and energy is flowing to you, through you, and you feel with every cell, love pervading and penetrating everything.

Do the World Heart Embrace three to nine times.

The Anger Transformer

If you feel anger toward somebody or something in your life, add these exercises even before the World Heart Embrace:

1. Anger Discharger

Standing with the feet apart and elbows bent, bring both hands up in front of your face, palms facing outward (as though somebody said "Stick 'em up!"). Make three or four small circles, with both hands (palms still facing outward) moving together toward the *right*. Your head follows, eyes soft-focused, looking just above the hands. When you get all the way to the right, suddenly push hard, straightening both hands as you shove away something you want to get rid of. Shove it as far as possible; let a sound *ugh!* come out of you at the moment of the violent push.

Then, immediately move both hands gently, making four or five small circles to the center and to the far *left*. Then do exactly the same thing: *shove as hard and as suddenly as you can*, flinging away the person or problem you have negative feelings about. As you say "*Ugh!*" the air is forced out of your lungs, and your flung arms straighten. Then immediately do the very small, soft circles to the far *right*. Again fling away the person or problem you hate as suddenly and violently as possible, the *ugh* escaping from you as you do it.

Do this cycle five times, alternating to the right and left.

2. *The Transformer*

Then inhale, expand and open your arms wide, and embrace the whole world. Stretch upward and outward as fully as you can, as though your heart center were the world being stretched and opened and you had become larger than life. Hold the posture (and your breath) for at least thirty seconds. Then bring the whole world into your embrace, gather that love, exhale, and lay your hands on your chest. Hold . . . do this three times. On the fourth time, transform the negative image you pushed away, by zapping it with love, and lay it on your breast, transformed from hate or dislike into love. Hold. Feel the love penetrate every cell.

This is an amazing exercise. It really works and has a healing effect on your life. If you find it hard to transform the negative image, then practice the World Heart Embrace alone. Really internalize the good feelings this produces. At another time, do the Anger Discharger, remembering to start softly and gently and then, with all your might, fling away (*ugh!*) the person or problem you hate.

I have watched this exercise revitalize and refresh all kinds of groups. In a business workshop, it eases the tensions that build up in the room because of business problems. The warmth and currents of ease that flow through the group as they finish are always visible on people's faces and in their bodies: smiles, a relaxed look, laughter. It's a marvelous, safe, nontoxic way to discharge the buildup of anger and tension that produces constraint and discomfort in so many groups. This exercise works for everybody, regardless of the causes of the friction. There is nothing competitive about it. Everyone can do it—it requires no athletic ability. People who usually resist "exercises" don't resist this one.

Alternating very gentle, easy-moving, small motions and the sudden violent discharge of feelings is like the hidden movements of emotions themselves. We think we're calm ("That doesn't bother me!"), and suddenly there's a terrific flash of anger or rage. It's disarming to start off so softly and gently and then experience a satisfying surge of power when you suddenly fling away, *without warning*, everything that may have been secretly bothering you. The most mild-mannered people throw themselves into this exercise with great abandon. The violent motion happens so suddenly that one can lie low and play "meek" right up to the moment of explosion. Like the flow of your feelings, you allow yourself to go from a gentle state to a fierce and total discharge. It's safe, yet swift as an adder's tongue. Busy with what you're doing, you don't watch anyone else, and the violent part is brief enough, followed again by the soothing massage of slow, gentle, small hand circles, so that you get both a release of sharp violent feeling and a sense of instantly renewed control.

This sequence is characteristic of Tibetan Kum Nye relaxation exercises, a wonderful system of detailed psychophysical stretches and releases that tune the mind-body and balance the emotions. I recognized the origin of this style of release when Walt Anderson did this exercise at a Washington, D.C., conference for the top one hundred government policy makers and the leaders of the human potential movement, who had come together to brainstorm and "soulstorm the possible society." People had come from very different mind-sets, and there were some tense confrontations. It was amazing to see how the atmosphere in the room changed after we did this exercise. Defensiveness melted; barriers eased. People who had been arguing before left the room arm-in-arm, smiling, and talking together.

When communication breaks down because of anger and dissension, *nobody's* charisma can prevail. Perhaps there is such a thing as group charisma—when the bio-rapport is so powerful that *everybody* feels enhanced, richly effective, and turned on. A person who gives a marvelous speech makes everyone listening feel he or she has spoken for them all. When you can directly express what's in your heart, other people who might not have had the courage to speak up (or be completely aware of what they felt) feel understood, validated, and supported.

We seem to be like radio transmitters. If there is a lot of static (i.e., stress), we get a great deal of noise and disturbance and only limited programming, mostly heavy-metal rock music, shrieks, reports of murder, and more static. When we fine-tune, the choices will be much wider: more interesting music, poetry, and information of all kinds.

Meditation is a practical method for this fine-tuning, or stress release. When we can drop our fears, hates, and old scars, we have access to more of ourselves and our intuitive understanding of reality.

It's always easier to see the connection between events from the top. Patterns become clear. A beetle doesn't see the tiny blade of grass he laboriously crawled over a minute before; that's already in the past. But for the falcon, the hill he flew straight up over fifteen minutes ago is still there. He has a larger view of the present. That is what enables mediums, mystics, and physicists to accomplish their remarkable feats. They report that at their creative best, time is unified: past, present, and future are one.

Ordinary people suddenly find they have access to extraordinary capacities. Sometimes we experience a powerful answer to that essential question: what matters most in my life? (Ask yourself that now.)

"What Matters Most in My Life?"

I once spent an Easter weekend in the mountains with Swami Muktananda and several hundred other people. Stories floated about—what "Baba" had done for this one, that one. A skeptical rationalist, I had been meditating for a number of years, but still I had the typical Western reluctance to "surrender" to any guru, whatever that meant. In the early morning chill hundreds of people filed silently into the carpeted meditation hall. Fragrant incense vapors curled lazily toward the ceiling, as devotees softly clanged cymbals and we chanted sacred Sanskrit songs for an hour.

Then we sat silent, the room darkened, and Muktananda, a great scepter of peacock feathers at his side, stepped up to a kind of throne. While we closed our eyes and meditated, Muktananda moved quietly among us, softly touching people with the peacock plumes. All around me people were making strange sounds: crying, gasping, laughing, growling, even something that sounded like wings flapping. Some of the noises were spine-chilling. At first I thought, "Oh come on! Some people will take any opportunity to yell their heads off." I noticed with surprise that tears were running down my face, although I was not feeling sad. I had come with some idea of what I wanted to ask, but suddenly all that fell away and I knew only that this was a Christlike human being who communicated love through his presence. If it was possible for a living human, all I wanted was to be like that. I felt I had never wanted anything so much in my life. To be able to live in perfect love seemed both miraculous yet completely real and attainable.

When the meditation ended, people spoke up and shared their very different experiences. Some people were Christian, some Jewish, others agnostic, but they all felt something very deep that would change their lives. The form it took depended on their history and background. The man who had growled said, "I want to tell everybody that was not an unhappy sound; I was experiencing a great joy and thinking, 'I am the only son of the only father!' I know it sounded scary, but that's what I was actually experiencing. All my life I've suffered from being rejected by my father at a very early age, and in that moment during meditation after I had received the *shakti* (energy) from Baba, all that was wiped out. I felt I had been restored to my true place."

When I got home the next day, Ellen, a writer-client, begged me to go with her to the Muktananda Center to meditate, as she was anxiously waiting to hear if her publisher was going to buy her latest manuscript. Without expectations, I went with her; we meditated for an hour and then left. As we parted, I gave her a small pot of African violets to sweeten the long hours of waiting. I knew, somehow, that she wouldn't hear anything till after the weekend, and Monday I knew the publisher would buy her book. It all turned out exactly as I had foreseen. *I was astonished. How did this happen?*

Then I realized that the meditation had fine-tuned my intuition so I could receive the information. Ellen's great anxiety, on the other hand, was a stress "static" that prevented her from getting it.

That Easter weekend I had felt mistrustful of all the adulation of Baba. What was all that stuff about "surrender" to the guru? Wasn't that giving up your free will? Abandoning your precious right to choose? "God is within you—love the God within" read signs all over the ashram. Then why surrender? I wasn't sure what was meant by "God," and I felt wary of groups that talk about God. Ever since the Crusades, religious wars caused more suffering in the West than did any plagues or natural disasters. What exactly are you surrendering to when you surrender to the "divine" in Baba?

A few days later, I found that I had lost my menstrual period, and I had severe pains in my ovaries, something that had never happened before. "OK," I thought rather angrily, "let's see what happens if I turn this pain over to Baba! They said he would take away the pain." Feeling a little ridiculous and totally skeptical, I thought, "OK, Baba, I'm giving this to you. Take away the pain!" To my amazement, the pain actually went away! And I didn't "believe" in him.

Suddenly I understood what "surrender" meant. When we're suffering or stressed, we function from a limited spectrum of sensorimotor frequencies—our "radio transmitter" is out of tune, limping along. Fear and pain shrink our electromagnetic field. We clutch and tighten, fearful as a baby. When we "surrender" the problem, however, turning it over to a higher power ("It's out of my hands"), we allow ourselves to relax and connect with the infinite powers of the universe. "Letting go" permits the natural homeostatic powers of body and mind to heal and make us whole. One of the hardest things to do when you're sick or frightened is to *let go of fear, to detach and trust, to visualize health as the present reality, seeing oneself as safe and well.* Turning the problem over to a higher will creates that deep relaxation of the small, terrified self, which can open the door to healing. People who pray are tuning in to their higher selves, that synchronicity of the individual self with the universal mind. Sometimes when people pray, they're really only bargaining: "Please make me well (or rich, or send me a mate), and I'll be good, give you money," or whatever promises desperate people make.

But experiencing that return to a unitary consciousness where all things are present and possible in the "secret world of the heart" may be the most profound prayer of all. "The eye with which I look at God," wrote Meister Eckehart, "is the same eye with which God looks at me."

In our anxiety to control our lives, at a time when we feel less certainty and more fear than ever before, probably our deepest need is to release our stranglehold on the limited reality of our usual functioning. It just isn't good enough. It's as though we're in a desperate race to get somewhere and stay alive—with ten thousand bandits in pursuit. We have to stop time, to get off the track. When you tune in to your own creative consciousness, you are part of the collective consciousness of everything that exists: "Not only is the drop of water contained in the ocean, but the ocean is contained in a drop of water" (the Upanishads).

Like someone who hasn't ridden a bicycle and can't believe it could possibly stay upright, you can't imagine this unless you've tried it. Yet everybody has *experienced* it. The unself-consciousness of a child is a state we instinctively long to recapture, because it allows us to "flow" and be one with the world. In that unstressed state, our senses function with great subtlety. The human eye can discern more than 10 million colors; we also have elaborate neurological awarenesses for touching. We can sense temperature through touch or a heavy and medium and light touch. Smell and taste, equally mysterious, reverberate to memory.

Chinese Taoist literature harps on "no-mind," which is not unconsciousness, but un*self*-consciousness. In this state of spontaneous flow, the mind functions easily, naturally, and effectively, without the Inner Critic standing over it criticizing and making matters difficult. In a more restful, free state, right action is possible, and the necessary decisions will come without the chatter and racket of the judging mind. That critical self only gets in the way, making us feel "not good enough" and preventing us from realizing our potential and connecting with others.

When we communicate effectively with people, when our charisma is clear and shining, we do connect directly to others' hearts—if we allow ourselves to. Of course, everybody knows people who are extremely bright, or even intellectually brilliant, but who are quite insensitive to others. (Motivational speaker Lisa Curtis refers to them as the "smart stupids.") They lack what Bruno Bettelheim called "the wisdom of the heart." Arthur Koestler has another splendid name for such people—*mimophants*. A mimophant is someone who is as sensitive as a mimosa when it comes to his or her own feelings but as insensitive as an elephant when it comes to the feelings of others!

Nevertheless, we dare not give up on anyone. The human heart is a mystery, and no one knows what may suddenly open another person's heart. It could even be something as hidden and subtle, but powerful, as the Golden Sunflower . . .

As the thirteenth-century Persian poet Rumi wrote:

A True Human Being is never what he or she
Appears to be. Rub your eyes,
And look again.

By de-stressing, you expand your senses and open up your hereditary capacities for learning and evolving. By opening your heart center, you expand the power of your brain, that still vastly underused palace of potentiality.

The instruments of your development that enable your charismatic gifts to unfold are *awareness* and *intention*. You see the possibilities like a wonderful garden that lies just beyond the wall. You despise nothing trivial that may lead, like a golden thread, to the essential mystery and answer.

The deeper you go into your inner world, the more you can let go of old fears, hatreds, and emotional wounds. Every time you can forgive yourself and others (and most of us have to do it over and over), you will feel more compassionate and patient. You will travel more lightly, take more pleasure and delight in other people's quirky humanness. The Tibetan Buddhist prayer "May I find good explanations for all living beings!" and the daily vow to dedicate oneself to the happiness of all sentient beings help lift the heavy burdens of self: both are somehow immensely freeing. It becomes more satisfying to relate to other people, and this activates both your charisma and theirs.

The experience of feeling your *own* heart center as open, loving, and radiant will expand to others. Then they too are "touched" with the light of the extraordinary brain and the limitless powers of the heart.

12

Your Charisma-cises
(Care and Maintenance of
Your Charisma)

Charisma-cise Contents—What Exercises to Do for Specific Problems and Situations

1. **Stress—before**—when you are feeling nervous or apprehensive.

2. **Stress—during**—when you are feeling uptight.

3. **Stress—after**—when you are feeling immobilized or exhausted.

4. **Anger**—when you are feeling rage, indignation, or humiliation.

5. **Quick energy**—when you are feeling listless, dispirited, or tired.

6. **Relaxation**—when you are feeling tension or exhaustion.

7. **Vocal ease**—when you want to release and develop your true voice.

8. **Courage**—when you want to be assertive, hold your own, or take risks.

9. **Performance anxiety**—when you are feeling panic, alarm, or anxiety.

10. **More control of your life**—when you want to expand your powers.

11. **Mood change**—when you are feeling negative, sad, or depressed.

12. **Good relations with others**—when you want to be tuned-in to others.

13. **Pain**—when you are feeling physical distress or discomfort.

14. **Body alignment**—when you want to center and balance yourself.

15. **Waking up**—when you are feeling sleepy, tired, or lethargic.

16. **Inducing sleep**—when you are feeling restless, fretful, or worried.

17. **Better sex life**—when you are feeling inhibited, bored, or distracted.

Exercise Finder

Exercise	Section/Page
Alternate Breathing	Waking up (p. 308)
Anger Transformer	Anger (p. 269)
Ape, The	Anger (p. 270)
Back Rock	Relaxation (p. 279)
Basic Buddha Belly	Stress—before (p. 254)
Basic Yawns	Vocal ease (p. 284)
Beat Out Anger Release	Stress—after (p. 265)
Belly Dancer's Bump	Body alignment (p. 306)
Be Your Own Cathedral	More control of your life, chapter 8, p. 185
Be Your Own Sun	More control of your life, chapter 8, p. 184
Brain Cleaner	More control of your life (p. 294)
Breath of Fire	Waking up (p. 308)
Butterflies Chaser	Performance anxiety (p. 291)
Calming Energizer	Mood change (p. 298)
Cannonball Headroll	Stress—after (p. 265)
Cat Crawl	Waking up (p. 309)
Caveman Whump, The	Stress—before (p. 256)
Centering with Sound	Mood change (p. 299)
Crazy Scale	Vocal ease (p. 287)
Depressurizer, The	Performance anxiety (p. 291)
Dream Machine	More control of your life (p. 295)
Drugless Painkiller	Pain (p. 304)
Elbow Propeller, The	Stress—before (p. 256)
Electric Eye	More control of your life (p. 295)
Emergency Energy Lift (or Right-Nostril Breathing)	Quick energy (p. 276)
Emotion Cooler, The (or Left-Nostril Breathing)	Stress—during (p. 261)
Energy Expander	Performance anxiety, chapter 10, p. 222
Environmental Control	More control of your life (p. 295)

continued on next page

continued

Exercise	Section/Page
Straight Standoff—The Spine Lineup	Body alignment (p. 307)
Sunrise—Superenergizer	Waking up (p. 310)
Swinger, The	Stress—after (p. 268)
TongLen	Good relations with others, chapter 6, p. 115–17
Toothache—"Eeeeeeeeee"	Pain (p. 305)
To Sleep	Inducing sleep (p. 311)
Tranquilizing Triangle	Anger (p. 273)
Wibble Wobble	Vocal ease (p. 285)
Woodchopper	Anger (p. 273)
World Heart Embrace, The	Anger (p. 274)
"You Bastard!"	Anger (p. 275)
Zaps	Quick energy (p. 277)
Zicker (Bumblebee)	Quick energy (p. 278)

Section 1/Stress—Before

When you are feeling nervous or apprehensive

What Exercises to Do:

Basic Buddha Belly

Breath Balloon

The Caveman Whump

The Elbow Propeller

Golden Cocoon

The I-Don't-Care Swing

Meditation on R-aah-mm

Meditation on Sat Nam

Meditation on So Ham

The Pointillist Necklace

Basic Buddha Belly

How to Do It

Preparation: Sit on the edge of a chair, with your back straight and your feet on the floor. Interlace your fingers loosely around your lower abdomen (the back of your hands rest on the upper thighs).

1. Exhale fully with a big, audible sigh; deflate the stomach all the way down to your groin, and stay empty a few seconds. Release any tightness you feel in your face, neck, jaw, shoulders, head, back, and chest.

2. Begin to inhale very slowly, with your mouth closed, feeling your lower abdomen swelling in your hands. Visualize the entire area from your groin to the rib cage as a balloon. (The air enters as though from between your legs.) Make the balloon a beautiful, favorite color, and watch it inflate slowly and evenly all around, filling up from the bottom. Expand it totally.

   - Keep your shoulders relaxed. Don't let them hike up!

   - As you inhale, consciously draw in pure, fresh energy; feel it massage every cell, filling your body with vital force.

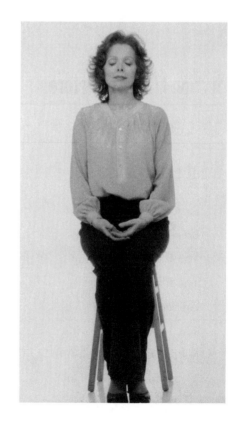

3. Hold for one slow count.

4. Exhale slowly, watching the balloon deflate, until your abdomen is completely flat.

5. Start by practicing with ten slow breaths, but work up to continuing indefinitely.

If you experience a little lightheadedness or dizziness when you first begin to breathe deeply in the Basic Buddha Belly, don't worry.

You are simply taking in more oxygen than you are used to; with a little practice the sensation will disappear. Meanwhile, if you do feel dizzy, simply pinch the bridge of your nose between thumb and forefinger, breathe slowly, and the dizziness will subside.

How It Helps

If it's done right, the Basic Buddha Belly will rid you of stress and recharge your entire system with energy. When you're sitting at a desk, it should be invisible. Breathing changes the chemistry of your consciousness. Most people breathe between twelve and eighteen times per minute. If you reduce your breaths per minute to seven or fewer, you greatly increase your composure, stamina, intuition, and personal authority.

- You will feel less worn down by daily wear and tear.

- You will be a better listener, take in more information; others will feel you are really understanding and responding to them.

- You prevent the escalation of stress.

- You'll be able to act on your intuition.

- You can keep up the breathing throughout conversations (except when actually speaking).

Note on Breathing Exercises

These must be practiced *before* you need them and frequently enough so they become automatic. Since the patterns are the *reverse* of the kind of breathing most people have been accustomed to all their lives, it takes a lot of practice to make this organic and vital breathing perfectly automatic. It's worth the effort.

Breath Balloon

How to Do It

Preparation: Lie on the floor. Put a little cushion under your head for comfort. The important thing is to have your back flat. Raise your knees if you need to so you can feel your whole spine touching the floor.

1. Inhale slowly and continuously for eight counts. Visualize a rubber barrel filling with air all around or a balloon. Pick a lovely color! Feel your breath start sharply and evenly from the lowest point of the belly, just above the groin. If you can't expand as long as eight counts, you just need to start smaller because you're probably inhaling too fast. Make the beginning as subtle and imperceptible as you can.

2. Hold your breath for a count of four. Check to see if your shoulders are relaxed; drop them if they're tense.

3. Exhale, with a steady hiss, for sixteen counts. Make the breath as steady as a laser beam. Empty totally. If you find you haven't enough breath left, you need to start more slowly. You're probably exhaling too fast. Husband your breath so it's very even.

    At the end of the count, your middle back or ribs will expand or lift; your chest and shoulders should remain quiet. If you find you're starting the breath in your chest or solar plexus, *stop*. Start again.

Note: After you've experienced the breath pressing against the floor in back and learned how to isolate your lower belly so your shoulders don't get into the act and you can really feel the breath expanding through your whole body, then you can do this exercise sitting in a chair, standing, or walking.

How It Helps

Changing your breathing pattern, combined with visualization, gives you access to instantaneous de-stressing. It removes the buildup of lactic acid from your taut muscles, calms and oxygenates your whole system within seconds, and lowers the heart and pulse rates and cholesterol.

The entire system benefits from increased circulation of oxygen in the body. Learning to inhale and exhale fully will improve your health, stamina, creativity, and capacity to handle stress efficiently.

The Caveman Whump

Beat your chest, shoulders, and back with your fists. This breaks up tight feelings, stimulates circulation, and opens your heart center.

The Elbow Propeller

How to Do It

1. Stand with your feet apart, knees slightly bent, elbows bent, and forearms raised, hands hanging limp from your wrists.

2. Begin to make vertical circles with your elbows, making the biggest circles possible, keeping elbows close to the body. Do the circles backward ten times, then forward ten times, as rapidly and energetically as possible. Keep your mouth closed.

3. Stand still and take three long, slow, complete breaths (in and out), slow your heartbeat—and relax.

How It Helps

You'll feel energized immediately and will act freely—without being afraid!
Great for your chutzpah (courage) level! This exercise stimulates circulation in the chest and heart; increases air intake, which releases tension and
raises your energy level; and relaxes shoulder and head tension.

Golden Cocoon

How to Do It

1. Take a deep breath, exhale, and relax.

2. Visualize yourself surrounded by a radiant cocoon of deep golden relax-
    ation. Feel it all around yourself; feel it particularly thick and golden
    wherever there is tension in your body. You're completely surrounded
    by this cocoon. It relaxes you completely. This is particularly good for
    dealing with irritable people—your cocoon protects and insulates you
    from them.

3. Now inhale and exhale again and visualize all poisons, toxins, aggra-
    vation, anxiety, and tensions draining out of your body. After each exha-
    lation, stay relaxed and empty for several seconds. Relax the shoulders,
    feet, hands, and back.

4. Your mouth should be closed when inhaling, but it may be slightly open
    for exhaling.

5. Do ten to twenty-six complete breaths anytime during the day for a
    quick de-stressing and recharging of your entire system with energy.
    (While sitting at a desk, if you do it right, this breathing is entirely invis-
    ible.)

6. After you've mastered this breath, you can add a heartbeat or pulse
    count to it.

    • On the inhale, count very slowly 1-2-3-4-5-6-7 pulse beats; hold one
      count.

    • Exhale very slowly in the same rhythm, 1-2-3-4-5-6-7 (make sure you
      are empty); hold one count.

How It Helps

This breath needs to be practiced and mastered so you can truly breathe
slowly and fully during all tense situations, which will keep you calm,
authoritative, and in control. Use this whenever you're not speaking and
you need composure and alertness.

The I-Don't-Care Swing

HOW TO DO IT

1. Stand with the feet about shoulder-width apart. Swing your torso, neck, and head as one unit first to the left, then to the right.

2. Let your arms begin to swing freely as your body turns from side to side, until they wrap loosely around you at shoulder level.

3. As your body swings from left to right and back again, shout, "I DON'T CARE!" as loudly as possible.

4. Enjoy yourself. Keep repeating. Switch to "No, I won't!" or "You can't make me!" if the impulse seizes you. Repeat twenty times or more.

- Make sure your head follows your torso all the way around when you swing to each side.

- Keep it as loose and free as you can.

HOW IT HELPS

Children have natural de-stressing techniques, which we forget as we grow up. Getting in touch with the playful spirit and rebelliousness of a child is enormously rewarding, as well as an effective device for a quick, efficient release of tension.

Meditation on R-aah-mm

HOW TO DO IT

1. Breathe slowly and deeply ten times, eyes closed.

2. Sitting with a straight back, the eyes closed, begin to repeat mentally, "Rr-ah-M," "R-ah-M," "Rrahm" (a mantra).

3. When thoughts come into your mind, just notice, "Oh, that's a thought," and return to the mantra.

4. At the end of twenty minutes (keep a watch on your lap, close the door, and turn off the telephone), rub your hands together, stroke your face gently upward, and, when ready, open your eyes. Don't rush.

5. Set aside regular times—before eating, in the morning, and early evening or before bedtime—to meditate.

6. Let go of expectations. Your nervous system will take exactly what it needs from each meditation.

   • Allow yourself to stay as still as possible.

   • Boredom is a form of restlessness and indicates you really need the meditation just when you have the least patience for it. If you're very restless, jump rope, jog, or do strenuous exercise for ten or fifteen minutes before meditation.

How It Helps

By lowering your respiratory rate, blood pressure, and heartbeat rate, meditation provides a deep rest for your mind-body. You then have more of an emotional margin and are less affected by stress. It's easier to take ups and downs calmly. In an emergency, meditate just before the important situation; in the long run, daily meditations will bring peace of mind and greater mental clarity.

Meditation on Sat Nam

How to Do It

Note: When you choose a mantra, stick with it, and don't discuss it. It should be part of a completely private experience.

1. As you inhale, think *sat* (sät); as you exhale, think *nam* (näm)—*sat* meaning "truth" and *nam* meaning "essence."

2. Repeat with the rising and falling of your breath over and over for ten, fifteen, or twenty minutes.

(The other directions are identical to Meditation on R-aah-mm.)

Meditation on So Ham

How to Do It

1. Use the mantra *so ham* (so häm), or "that I am."

2. The rest of the procedure is the same as for the Meditations above.

Stay with your mantra at least forty days to see results.

The Pointillist Necklace

How to Do It

1. Drop your head from the first vertebra until your chin practically rests on your chest. Imagine that there is a necklace gracing your clavicles and at each point on it someone will press gently and *that* will move your head. It'll start moving of its own weight without your help. Keep asking, Is my head as heavy as a cannonball? Is my neck as long as a giraffe's?

2. Now let your head start moving around in the circle. Feel each point. Your head should move as slowly as possible without stopping. Don't turn it; let it *be* moved!

3. Circle three times clockwise, three times counterclockwise.

   - Breathe deeply, especially if your neck hurts. Open your mouth slightly, but breathe mainly from your nose.

   - If your neck "cracks," go back and "iron out" the cracks.

How It Helps

The Pointillist Necklace benefits you in many ways:

- Irons out all neck tension
- Relaxes the shoulders
- Normalizes the thyroid
- Calms and balances the mind
- Helps you sleep
- Opens the throat

Section 2/Stress—During

When you are feeling uptight

What Exercises to Do:

Basic Buddha Belly

The Emotion Cooler (or Left-Nostril Breathing)

Heart Relaxer

The Magic Breath

Rushing Relaxation

Basic Buddha Belly

See section 1, Stress—before (p. 254), for this exercise.

The Emotion Cooler (or Left-Nostril Breathing)

How to Do It

1. To calm your nerves, get over an emotional moment, or give you strength for a difficult confrontation, place your thumb on the right nostril, lightly blocking it off.

2. Start by exhaling slowly, soundlessly, and completely through the left nostril. "See" all toxins, poisons, stresses, and negatives draining out of your body.

3. Inhale slowly and fully. "See" pure radiant energy filling your body.

4. Do twenty-six times.

HOW IT HELPS

By sending oxygen rapidly to the right hemisphere of the brain (the "emotional" side), this exercise quickly balances your nervous system and gives you emotional control.

Heart Relaxer

HOW TO DO IT

1. Suddenly drop your jaw.

2. At the same time, rotate your shoulders slowly in full, smooth, luxurious circles. Keep breathing smoothly! Keep your jaw dropped.

3. Do six backward and six forward circles. Do this exercise *every half hour* during a hectic or stressful day.

HOW IT HELPS

When your mind works intently, your jaw and shoulder muscles tense. You may also notice you clench your teeth and the backs of your shoulders feel tight and tense. The heart is ready to speed up and rush more blood to the fighting muscles. This "crouched for action" tension whips the heart into a spasm-ready state. The Heart Relaxer relaxes the muscles in the backs of your shoulders (trapezius muscles), alters the brain wave into a normally functioning pattern, and relaxes your heart.

HOW YOU BENEFIT

You protect your heart, de-escalate your tension buildup, and at the same time increase efficiency and energy. Everything looks light and brighter. You can enjoy life again!

The Magic Breath

A note to purists—this exercise tells you what happens in your body when you breathe fully and completely.

HOW TO DO IT

1. Sit or stand erect with spine straight, keeping your shoulders and arms relaxed.

2. Inhale steadily through the nostrils, expanding the lower belly. This fills the lower part of the lungs. The diaphragm drops and presses on the

abdominal organs, pushing the stomach outward. Don't let your shoulders rise!

3. Continue to inhale slowly, filling the middle part of the lungs, pushing out the lower ribs, breastbone, and chest. Imagine that you're blowing up a balloon from the bottom.

4. Continue to inhale slowly, now filling the upper portion of the lungs, lifting the chest (but not the shoulders!). The upper six or eight pairs of ribs will move outward. In this final movement, the lower part of the abdomen will be slightly drawn in, which gives the lungs support and also helps to fill the highest part of the lungs.

    Important: This is a continuous inhalation. Keep it very steady, smooth, flowing, and even—no jerks! Feel that you are drawing air in from the whole universe, up through the feet and legs, through your body and around your head—more and more energy is at your disposal each time you inhale this way.

5. Exhale slowly and evenly. Keep your chest high. Draw in the abdomen slowly as the air leaves your lungs (imagine a balloon deflating). When the air is completely exhaled, relax chest and abdomen, but don't collapse!

6. Stay empty briefly; then begin again.

How It Helps

This breath exercises every part of the lungs, including the most remote air cells. Your lung capacity is greatly increased, your energy level vastly enhanced. It's like an air laxative, cleaning and purifying the system! Holding the breath a few seconds purifies the air still in the lungs from former inhalations, discharges as much accumulated stress and toxins as possible, fully oxygenates the blood, and leaves you more room to take in energy and strength on the next breath.

Rushing Relaxation

When you are in a rush, have to get a thousand things done by yesterday, or are late for an appointment, try this.

How to Do It

1. Walk quickly but breathe as *slowly as possible*, expanding the abdomen as in the Basic Buddha Belly, imagining a colored balloon inflating and deflating. Your shoulders must not ride up. Start by counting four steps as you inhale. Then exhale evenly on eight steps. Work up to ten—inhale, twenty—exhale.

2. *The faster you go, the slower you breathe.* Continue indefinitely.

3. *You must practice before you need it* so you will be able to use this relaxation exercise with ease and without thinking about it.

HOW IT HELPS

The brain uses three-quarters of your oxygen supply, so when you breathe shallowly under stress, the brain doesn't function well and memory and concentration suffer. The Rushing Relaxation assures you of an astonishing expansion of time, smooth functioning, steadiness, and calm. The increased oxygen intake steps up your mental efficiency.

- You will be able to listen accurately, take in more information, and respond with intuitive rightness.

- You will give the impression of being composed, calm, and authoritative, even in difficult situations—and you will be!

Section 3/Stress—After

When you are feeling immobilized or exhausted

What Exercises to Do:

Beat Out Anger Release

Cannonball Headroll

The Elbow Propeller

Heart Relaxer

The I-Don't-Care Swing

Instant Vacation

The Magic Breath

Neck and Shoulder Relaxers

Pressure Breaker

Rag Doll Shakeout

Shoulder and Midback De-Tenser

The Swinger

Beat Out Anger Release

How to Do It

1. Hit your bed or sofa with a tennis racket or some rolled-up newspapers, a mailing tube, or a towel while shouting, "NO!" or "I won't!" from the gut with an open throat.

2. Do this at least ten times.

3. Follow with slow, deep, even breathing.

You might also use the Karate Chop and the Steam Engine (see section 4, Anger).

Cannonball Headroll

How to Do It

1. Stand or sit straight. Drop your head on your chest. Feel the neck muscles stretch out. Keep breathing!

2. Roll the head very, very slowly around, feeling the base of motion as all the way down at the clavicle. Imagine a ball bearing inside your head. As the weight shifts, your head rolls. At each point on the circle ask,

   - Is my head as heavy as a cannonball?
   - Is my neck as long as possible?

The Elbow Propeller

See section 1, Stress—before (p. 256), for this exercise.

Heart Relaxer

See section 2, Stress—during (p. 262), for this exercise.

The I-Don't-Care Swing

See section 1, Stress—before (p. 258), for this exercise, which gives you instant alertness when you're tired or tense and steps up your vitality. It is an effective eye-relaxing exercise, too. Do it before going to bed. (For best results, do it one hundred times.)

Instant Vacation

How to Do It

1. Sit comfortably, close your eyes, breathe deeply, uncross your legs, relax every part of your body.

2. Go to your favorite natural place (e.g., a beautiful garden, seashore, mountaintop).

Be there completely. Feel the sun on your face or body, the breeze, the smell of flowers or pine. Hear the rustling of leaves or water or tide, whatever natural sounds belong in your vacation.

The Magic Breath

See section 2, Stress—during (p. 262), for this exercise.

Neck and Shoulder Relaxers

How to Do Them

1. Place your head on your right shoulder (keep the shoulders relaxed, the neck long). Move head slowly in a forward half-circle to the left shoulder. Do this over eight counts, making a complete circle with the head. Reverse, starting on your left shoulder. The head slowly moves to the right, then to the back and the left shoulder by eight.

2. Roll your shoulders forward, shrug up, and then roll back in one continuous movement. Inhale forward; exhale back. Then reverse: start with the shoulders back, shrug up, and then roll the shoulders forward. Keep the hands relaxed.

3. With feet apart, clasp your hands behind you and extend the arms straight back. Inhale and swing left. Exhale, and swing right as far as possible eight times.

4. In the same position, the arms out in front of you, clasp your hands and swing left (inhaling) and right (exhaling) eight times.

5. Use the same position—clasp your hands and stretch the arms in back. Lean forward until your nose almost touches the ground (or as close

as you can get), stretching upward with your arms. Inhale going down; exhale coming up. Repeat four times.

6. In the same position; raise the right hand over your head as high as you can and, inhaling, swing it down to the outside of your left foot (knees straight!). Look back at your raised arm. Exhale.

    Inhale and reverse, bringing the left hand up over your head to the right foot. Try to touch the ground outside each foot. Repeat sixteen times.

How These Help

They unkink tensions through shoulders, neck, and back; release energy flow; and relieve accumulated strain. They're good for an office break or anytime you need flexing and stretching.

Pressure Breaker

How to Do It

Lean forward onto a desk or table, arms extended and head down. Inhale; hold breath. Jog in place twenty times as hard as possible, as though racing. Exhale all the way with a sigh. Then inhale, hold, and jog thirty times; exhale; inhale and jog three to five times; exhale.

The harder you run and the harder you hold, the more release from tension you will get when you do the exhale. Tighten everything—face, hands, and body—when you're running in place.

Skip this if you have high blood pressure!

Follow with slow, deep, even breathing.

How It Helps

This exercise increases the tension of anger but then releases it; provides a satisfying physical outlet for angry feelings; and is even great for the complexion!

Rag Doll Shakeout

How to Do It

1. First shake out one hand, then the other. Then shake your head like a rag doll (let your mouth hang loose). Then shake out each leg (just add each limb; keep shaking out the rest).

2. Then hop, shaking the feet. Then jump and wiggle your pelvis and throw your arms and elbows and hands all around every which way and make noises! Shake out for three to five minutes.

How It Helps

Every muscle and nerve in your body gets a workout. Your circulation increases. You breathe more deeply, sending oxygen to every part of your body. You discharge all tensions completely.

How You Benefit

Your body no longer feels frozen, tight, tense, or tired. Your body and brain hum and buzz from the stimulating activity, and you loosen up. You're less withdrawn, you're not afraid, and it's easier to speak up and be spontaneous. You get instant energy!

Shoulder and Midback De-Tenser

How to Do It

1. Lean back on a desk or table, fingers facing forward, head down, knees slightly bent, body slumped (as though you were ashamed).

2. Inhale. Arch your body back, like a bow; drop your head back. Stretch. Straighten your legs. Press the toes against the floor.

3. Hold for a count of four and feel the stretch in your back muscles. To get the stretch higher or lower in your back, simply move your hands farther apart or closer together. S-T-R-E-T-C-H!

4. Now exhale, bend your knees, and come back to starting position.

5. Repeat the sequence six to eight times.

The Swinger

How to Do It

1. Clasp your hands behind your back, and swing your whole torso and head to the left, breathing in. Then swing to the right as you exhale.

2. Do this twenty times. Imagine there's a point in the middle of your chest and you are suspended from the ceiling by a string attached there. Imagine the "wings" of your back touching as you swing.

Section 4/Anger

When you are feeling rage, indignation, or humiliation

What Exercises to Do:

Anger Transformer

The Ape

The Groan

Karate Chop

Steam Engine

Tranquilizing Triangle

Woodchopper

The World Heart Embrace

"You Bastard!"

Anger Transformer

If you are feeling anger or there is somebody in your life who is the focus of negative feelings for you, before doing the World Heart Embrace, practice this exercise.

How to Do It

1. Stand or sit. Bend your arms at the elbows and put your hands up, about a foot in front of your face, with the palms facing *away* from you (as if somebody had said "stick 'em up!").

2. Make little clockwise circles in the air with your hands (like polishing a window), gradually (with bent elbows) moving your hands all the way toward the right. Your head follows, your eyes softly focused.

3. When you get all the way to the right, make a sudden violent pushing movement with both hands, straighten both arms and push hard as though throwing away something you want to get rid of. Push away your anger or negativity or the person you're mad at. Throw it as far as possible, and make a sound like *ugh*! or *uhh*!

4. Immediately afterward, put your hands to the center again and then, making counterclockwise circles, "polish the mirror" to the far left. Then shove as hard and as suddenly as you can to the left, pushing away your "enemy."

5. Repeat five times in each direction.

6. Immediately after this, do the World Heart Embrace.

How It Helps

- Gets you back to "normal" mode fast and safely
- Discharges hormonal stress
- Lowers your blood pressure
- Satisfies the need to "explode" with anger—safely

The Ape

How to Do It

1. Bend over from the waist, your arms and head dangling loosely like an ape's, the knees slightly bent.

2. Slowly jump heavily—landing on both feet—around the room, arms and head still dangling loosely. Stay relaxed, almost limp from the waist up.

3. With each jump, make a deep, open-throated grunt that you can feel way down in your stomach, your legs, even your feet: "Ugh, ugh, ugh." Make sure the grunt coincides exactly with your landing each time you jump.

Stamping on the floor provides a safe and satisfying "grounding" of anger, hostility, and frustration. This seems to be a universal expression, ranging all the way from a child's tantrums to jogging and to the elaborate and precise rhythms that drumming and rhythmic dancing use to express emotions and influence events (a war dance, a rain dance, a fertility rite to ensure a good crop).

Pope John Paul II, in a visit to the United States, surprised observers by uttering deep, rhythmic grunts in response to audience adulation. This centered and protected him from the engulfing waves of sound bombarding him.

How It Helps

- Releases a deep body sound
- Loosens upper body rigidities

- Grounds and centers your energies
- Provides rapid, deep release of muscular tension
- Reestablishes hormonal balance
- Gives your body a feeling of power and ease
- Disinhibits old constraints
- Releases anger through the feet
- Stomping on the floor is a satisfying expression of strong emotion
- Balances overintellectualizing; counteracts worry

The Groan

HOW TO DO IT

Sit down comfortably in a chair or stand with your feet slightly apart (knees bent). Place one hand on your stomach, one hand on your forehead. Close your eyes and start to groan. Groan softly. Enjoy it.

HOW IT HELPS

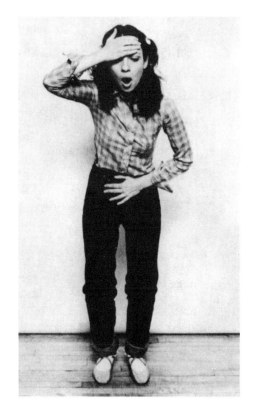

When you groan with maximum vigor, your voice gets connected to your entire body, and you feel the sound coming from your entire body, not just your head. These vibrations add the rich, deep, quality to your voice that is so exciting. Once you become experienced, you will also know when these vibrations are missing. You can eventually learn to control these vibrations and let them "color" your speaking. When you have learned to maximize the innate qualities of your voice, you'll be able to communicate more effectively through the variety you'll find in your vocal intonations.

Express your feelings and experience release of all that pent-up tension. When you're back in "neutral" you can deal with the situation more effectively.

Karate Chop

HOW TO DO IT

1. Stand with your legs shoulder-width apart, knees bent. Hands are at your sides—clench the fists. With your mouth closed, draw your arms up in three short, powerful inhalations (as though pulling up heavy weight in a bucket) until you are stretched upward with fists overhead as high as they will go.

2. Then: *crash!* Bring both arms (and powerful fists) down together in a tremendous karate chop, and say as loudly as possible, with your throat open, "*Hahhhhhhhhhh!*" Bend your knees.

3. Repeat five times as powerfully as you can.

HOW IT HELPS

- Beats stage fright

- Instantly discharges anger, hostility, or fear

- Gives you immediate energy

- Gives you immediate courage

Steam Engine

HOW TO DO IT

1. Stand with the legs approximately shoulder-width apart, knees bent, head erect, and mouth closed. Inhale and then pull your right arm straight back, and, at the same time, punch the left arm forward (without leaning into it) as powerfully as possible. Exhale powerfully.

2. Reverse, drawing back the left arm; inhale as your fists pass each other, and exhale again as the right arm punches forward. You will be exhaling with each punch. Your rhythm is steady and even.

3. Start slowly. Continue as rapidly, powerfully, and steadily as you can for three to five minutes, *mouth closed*!

How It Helps

This releases blocked energy in your chest, shoulders, neck, and arms; steps up your oxygen intake; and increases your ability to take risks.

Tranquilizing Triangle

How to Do It

Stand with your legs apart and put your hands on the floor. Keep the legs straight, so you feel a stretch in back of the thighs. Let your head dangle. Breathe slowly and deeply for two to six breaths.

How It Helps

- Restores calm
- Sends blood to the brain
- Increases mental alertness and memory

Woodchopper

How to Do It

1. Stand with your feet fifteen to eighteen inches apart, the toes pointing a little outward and the knees almost straight but relaxed, and clasp your hands.

2. Inhale and swing your clasped hands as high over your head as they will go.

3. Immediately swing your clasped hands down between your legs as far as they will go, bending forward and exhaling. At the bottom of the swing, shout "*Hah!*" as loud as you can. Your knees are bent.

4. Inhale and swing the hands up again overhead.

5. Repeat this sequence without stopping, ten or twenty times.

It is important to keep your mouth closed as you inhale until you bring the arms down for the "Hah!" More oxygen reaches the brain with the mouth closed, and the exercise is much more powerful.

How It Helps

- Regulates your biorhythms
- Stimulates the adrenal glands in the lower back, which control the rhythms of hormonal secretion

- Safely releases lactic acid from the muscles

- Lets off steam, dissolves anger, keeps you from being prey to your emotions, and fills your brain with fresh, new blood

The World Heart Embrace

This exercise should be preceded by the Anger Transformer (p. 269).

How to Do It

1. Inhale, feel yourself expanding, open your arms, embrace the whole world, stretching out and up as though your heart center is the world being stretched and opened. You become larger than life.

2. Hold at least sixty seconds. Bring the world into your embrace, gather that love, and lay it on your breast, your hands on your chest, pressed gently one over the other.

3. Do this whole cycle four times, transforming the negative image you have pushed away while doing the Anger Transformer. Love it, bring it in, lay it on your heart, transformed from hate to love.

Note: if you can't "let go" of the anger yet, repeat the Anger Transformer, do the Beat Out Anger Release exercise, or try some jogging or other exercise.

Keep testing to see if you're ready to transform anger into love.

How It Helps

- Converts the energy of anger to positive love power

- Increases self-esteem

- Expands the electromagnetic field

"You Bastard!" (or "Dastard," Whichever You Prefer)

How to Do It

Stand with the feet firmly planted, about shoulder-width apart, knees a trifle bent (to give your feet a good grip on the floor). Relax your hands at your sides, and begin to swing your arms up to the left (like a golf swing), as high and free as you can. Breathe *in* on the first swing to the left (mouth closed). Exhale on the second swing to the right; inhale (with mouth open) on the third swing to the left. Then (after the three-swing preparation) on the fourth swing (to the right) shout as loudly and as long as possible:

YOU-U-U-U-U-U B[D]-AAA-A-A-A-A-S-TARD!

Swing right for the shout and then swing left.

Begin the whole sequence again with the three-swing preparation (inhale-exhale-inhale). Then again shout:

YOU-U-U-U-U-U B[D]-AAA-A-A-A-A-S-TARD!

It's important to make sure your breath, movement (swings), and voice are perfectly coordinated. If you find that the words are not in synch with the motions, if they are coming before or after the gesture, you've probably been programmed as a child not to release anger as easily and freely. You may find that your throat tightens.

It's important to open your throat and release the sound freely at exactly the same time as the breath and the swing. Repeat the sequence at least ten times.

How You Benefit

A tremendous increase in spontaneity and freedom result from this exercise. (One man said that after doing this exercise he was able to dance in public for the first time in his life!) It transforms anger.

Section 5/Quick Energy

When you are feeling listless, dispirited, or tired

What Exercises to Do:

Emergency Energy Lift (or Right-Nostril Breathing)

Fast Energizer

The Great Wow!

The I-Don't-Care Swing

Karate Chop

The Magic Tongue-Tap

Zaps

Zicker (Bumblebee)

Emergency Energy Lift (or Right-Nostril Breathing)

How to Do It

1. Place the left thumb on your left nostril, lightly blocking it off. Exhale slowly through the right nostril, imagining any tiredness and strain leaving your body.

2. Inhale slowly through the right nostril. Imagine new strength and energy coming into your body.

3. Repeat this cycle twenty-six times. You'll feel new energy!

Fast Energizer

How to Do It

1. Inhale and tighten all the muscles in your face, neck, shoulders, hands, abdomen, buttocks, genitals, arms, legs, and feet—all the muscles you can.

2. Hold as tightly as you can. Hold your breath for as long as you can.

3. Then—whoosh!—exhale with a big sigh and let go of all tensions.

The Great Wow!

How to Do It

Crouch. Take a deep breath. Now straighten up slowly, softly saying, "Wow!" Repeat eight times, getting louder and louder, more and more animated each time, until on the final "Wow!" you're leaping, jumping, and flinging your arms toward the ceiling.

The I-Don't-Care Swing

See section 1, Stress—before (p. 258), for this exercise.

Karate Chop

See section 4, Anger (p. 272), for this exercise.

The Magic Tongue-Tap

How to Do It

For quick energy and to restore confidence, tap the tip of your tongue against the ridge behind your top front teeth, as though you were silently saying, "la-la-la-la-la-la-la-la" very rapidly.

How It Helps

The tapping stimulates the thymus gland and restores the balance between the two hemispheres of the brain. This produces a feeling of well-being.

Zaps

How to Do It

Repeat over and over "Zap! Zap! Zap!" getting louder with each one. As you say each "Zap!" fling your arms in front of you, above, to the sides, everywhere—consciously zapping all obstacles with as much power and force as you can.

Zicker (Bumblebee)

How to Do It

Seated on the edge of a chair with your back straight, open your mouth and, with teeth closed, say "*zzzzzzzzzzzzzzzzzzzz*," vibrating with the buzz as you get louder and louder. Feel the vibrations all through your head.

Now walk around the room buzzing.

Continue for three minutes.

How It Helps

It stimulates and wakes up energy all over your body, increases circulation, and unblocks energy channels.

Section 6/Relaxation

When you are feeling tension or exhaustion

What Exercises to Do:

Back Rock

Basic Buddha Belly

I Am at the Beach

Infinite Shrug

Laughing

Piecemeal Poop-Out

Prayer Pose

The Secret Smile

Shoulder Rolls, Shrugs

Specific Tension Points

Back Rock

How to Do It

1. Lie on your back, bend the knees, and bring them up to your chest. Clasp your hands around your knees.

2. Rock back and forth along the length of your spine. Feel each vertebra being massaged as you rock. Press your stomach in. Don't forget to breathe deeply.

How It Helps

You massage all the sore points, stimulate the nerve endings all along the spine, and erase tension from your back and shoulders.

Basic Buddha Belly

See section 1, Stress—before (p. 254), for this exercise.

I Am at the Beach

How to Do It

Imagine you're at a beautiful sandy beach all by yourself. It's completely private, yours alone. Imagine trees around you, decide what kind, and visualize them. See flowers and the fish in the water. It's your favorite time of day. Imagine as clearly as possible everything you want to make this your perfect beach.

To get to your beach you have only to close your eyes, breathe deeply, and say, "I am at the beach," and there you are. Now, with your eyes closed, imagine yourself lying on the sand at your beach. Feel the warmth of the sun, hear the waves in the ocean, smell the salt water, feel the slight breeze on your body. Feel yourself relax totally in the sun.

Stay at the beach as long as you like. When you feel refreshed, open your eyes.

How It Helps

You'll feel as if you are having a short, wonderful vacation.

Infinite Shrug

How to Do It

1. Sit with a straight back, your eyes closed.

2. Breathing very slowly and deeply, begin to raise your shoulders as slowly as possible. *It should take anywhere from five to fifteen minutes!* Keep your arms, hands, and the rest of your body relaxed (especially the stomach).

3. When your shoulders are touching your ears, hold them in this position for one minute.

4. Begin to lower your shoulders as slowly and continuously as you raised them, breathing deeply and evenly. (This should take as much time as raising them did—from five to fifteen minutes.)

How It Helps

This expands your sense of time, stimulates the circulation, and releases deeply held tensions. It also sharpens concentration. Each person has a different—and fascinating—experience.

Laughing

How to Do It

Laugh for three minutes. Start by just saying "ha, ha, ha" until you're genuinely laughing. Laughing continuously takes a lot of energy; it also *produces* a lot of energy by relaxing many involuntary muscles and stepping up oxygen consumption and circulation.

How It Helps

- Provides a "soul bath"
- Relieves tension
- Steps up energy
- Dissolves anger

Piecemeal Poop-Out

How to Do It

1. Lie on your back, arms at your sides and the palms facing up. You might like to have some quiet, soothing music playing.

2. Take a few deep breaths from as low down in your body as you can.

3. Now say to yourself, "My feet are relaxed; they're feeling very heavy," and feel that happen. Breathe very slowly and deeply.

4. Now say to yourself, "Now my ankles are very relaxed. They feel very heavy." Feel your ankles relax and all tensions leave them. Continue through the whole exercise to breathe very slowly and deeply.

5. Continue in this way, saying "My ———— are relaxed," and then relaxing that part, proceeding in this order: lower legs, knees, upper legs, buttocks, genitals, lower back, upper back, belly, chest, hands, forearms, elbows, upper arms, shoulders, front of neck, scalp, forehead, eyes, cheeks, lips, chin, jaw.

6. Now concentrate on your lower belly: feel it move out with the inhale and in with the exhale. Imagine that you are lying on an ocean and that the waves are moving your belly up and down, up and down. You are a small, light wave, bubbling buoyantly in the ocean—which supports you.

7. Take ten to fifteen minutes to do this deep relaxation. Then, open your eyes and sit up slowly.

How It Helps

As you slow down your breathing and put your attention in various parts of your body, you relax all tension.

How You Benefit

Better than a nap, this exercise makes you feel totally refreshed and relaxed, clear of the worries of the day.

Prayer Pose

How to Do It

Sit on your knees, bend over, put your forehead on the ground, extend your arms and hands past your head, with the palms together. Relax your stomach. Breathe slowly and deeply, until you feel relaxed—and then a little longer.

The Secret Smile

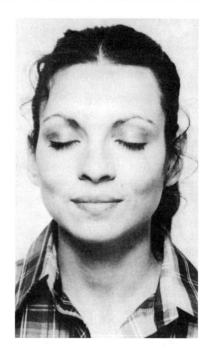

How to Do It

1. Close your eyes. Now imagine a huge ball of helium in your open throat.

2. With your lips loosely closed, start humming, increasing the intensity as you begin to feel the vibrations all over your face and head. Touch your face, your cheeks, your forehead, your chin, and your head to intensify the vibration. Continue as you hum to imagine the helium ball in your throat.

3. Think of something you really enjoy. Maybe it's lying in a meadow or being with someone you enjoy or making love or eating your favorite dish. Whatever it is, recall that particular pleasure and feel it. Spread it with the hum all through your face and head. Tingle with pleasure.

How It Helps

When you're tense or afraid, your breath shortens. When something pleasant happens to you, you automatically breathe deeply. By deliberately recalling some pleasurable experience, while humming, you can re-create all the relaxed body sensations that went with it the first time.

Shoulder Rolls, Shrugs

How to Do It

1. Make six big backward circles with your shoulders, the arms hanging loose, inhaling with the mouth closed with each circle. Now make six circles forward, exhaling through your mouth with each circle.

2. Now shrug one shoulder up as you inhale strongly (your mouth again closed); then let it drop as you exhale sharply through your mouth.

3. Reverse.

4. Repeat ten times for each shoulder.

5. Now shrug both shoulders as high as you can—as you inhale strongly—and let them drop as you exhale sharply through your mouth. Repeat this three times.

Specific Tension Points

HOW TO DO IT

Wherever you feel tension, massage it! Your own hands are your magic healing and tension-relieving tools. First rub your hands together thirty-six times to generate chi (energy). Breathe slowly and deeply as you massage yourself. Imagine, as you inhale, that the breath is flowing directly to and relaxing the tense places, and that you diffuse and exhale out of the entire body all fatigue, soreness, discomfort, and tension, bringing in light, warmth, and well-being.

Section 7/Vocal Ease

When you want to release and develop your true voice

What Exercises to Do:

This is a good sequence for throat, face, and jaw relaxation:

Jaw Releaser

Basic Yawns

The Helium Ball Yawn

The Horse Laugh

Idiot Fingers

Wibble Wobble

Here's an excellent sequence for tonal color and variety:

The Secret Smile

"You Bastard!"

The Helmet of Hum

Jack and Jill

Glottal Nonstop Sentences

And here are some others:

  Jogging Before Speaking

  Crazy Scale

  Instant Opera

  The Pointillist Necklace

Jaw Releaser

How to Do It

1. Open your mouth wide; stick your tongue out and down.

2. At the same time, open your eyes wide. Hold the tongue out for three breaths.

3. Now, pressing the jaw into your neck, wag your tongue from side to side and then up and down—without moving your jaw.

4. Now circle your tongue as slowly and smoothly as possible outside the mouth, imagining the tongue touching your nose, cheeks, chin. Now circle the other way. Keep the jaw still!

How It Helps

This jaw release relieves throat tension, enabling you to speak more clearly and loudly. It frees the tongue and jaw and increases circulation in the throat (which is a good antidote for sore throats).

Basic Yawns

How to Do It

If you have trouble starting the yawn, lift the lips away from your teeth as though you were snarling, inhale deeply, and open your throat wide; crinkle your nose and eyes, and then open your mouth as widely as you can so that the muscles in your neck stand out and you hear a roaring in your ears. Only by exaggerating the yawn can you really get into the feeling that will take over and thoroughly relax your whole face, neck, and throat.

Now do it with your mouth closed. Feel the muscular reactions. Your tongue is as low as possible at the back of the throat, lying on the bottom of the mouth; the tip is flat and the sides are in contact with all the gums. Press the middle of the tongue down hard.

The Helium Ball Yawn

How to Do It

Now imagine there's a huge ball of helium in your mouth pressing the roof up, the back out against the back of the neck, and the sides and bottom down. Yawn as slowly and smoothly as possible.

How They Help

- These yawnings release facial tension, preventing a "freeze."

- They relax the face, tongue, lips, and throat; they also increase spontaneity.

The Horse Laugh

How to Do It

Start with your lips lightly together as though you were going to say "*p*." Blow outward so your lips ripple continuously like a little motor.

Idiot Fingers

How to Do It

Move your index finger up and down rapidly across your absolutely lax lips, saying "*Brrrrrrrrrrrrr.*"

Wibble Wobble

How to Do It

Keeping your lips absolutely limp, shake your head from side to side. The lower part of your face will wobble. If you're really relaxed you may even drool! It should be easy and smooth.

The Secret Smile

See section 6, Relaxation (p. 282), for this exercise.

"You Bastard!"

See section 4, Anger (p. 275), for this exercise.

The Helmet of Hum

How to Do It

1. With lips and jaws relaxed, start humming loudly.

2. Put your hands on your cheek-bones; feel the hum vibrating there. Now move your hands up and feel the vibrations of your forehead: on the top of your head, the sides, and the back of your head.

3. Continue humming, cup your hands in front of your face, and feel the humming vibration fill them. Now move them farther and farther away in front of your face, still feeling the vibration filling them. If you lose the vibration, bring your hands closer to your face until you feel it again.

4. Send the vibration to your hands at arm's length. Then move your hands apart and to the sides, then above your head, then behind your head, making a huge "helmet of hum" all around your head. Feel that your head becomes a resonating cage of bones.

How It Helps

When you fill your head with humming vibrations, they bounce off the different parts of your face and head. They relax your throat, face, and head and also provide pleasurable, confident, and powerful feelings. This exercise is stimulating and generates energy.

Jack and Jill

See chapter 9, page 202, for this exercise.

Glottal Nonstop Sentences

See chapter 8, part III, page 180, for this exercise. The voice is the first thing to shrink when you feel diffident or shy. These sentences help give your voice underlying melody and color.

Jogging Before Speaking

How to Do It

Jogging shakes up the accumulated rigidities and tensions, and it lightens your approach to speaking. If you run *in place* before rehearsing, as part of your warm-up, you will become more in touch with your whole body, your voice will be louder and freer, and your gestures will become larger, more relaxed, and spontaneous. Practice singing and speaking while jogging in place. Follow with long, slow breathing.

Crazy Scale

How to Do It

Practice talking with the wildest extremes of pitch, going "crazily" up and down the scale. This gives you access to unsuspected tonal ranges of your own voice, and will add some new colors to the sound.

Instant Opera

How to Do It

When practicing your speech, sing your lines as if they belonged to an opera. Use large arm movements. Having done that, you will find that your rhythmic variety and tonal possibilities expand without further effort. Once you have been wildly extravagant vocally, your "normal" will be more interesting and varied than it was before the exercise.

The Pointillist Necklace

See section 1, Stress—before (p. 260), for this exercise. Since vocal freedom is impossible without relaxation in the throat, jaw, and neck, the Pointillist Necklace is very valuable here.

Section 8/Courage

When you want to be assertive, hold your own, or take risks

What Exercises to Do:

There are two types of exercises for courage: those to be done just before
a difficult encounter or a situation when you need courage, and those to
be practiced daily to build up your general courage level.

For Emergency Courage

> The Elbow Propeller
>
> The I-Don't-Care Swing
>
> Karate Chop
>
> Steam Engine
>
> "You Bastard!"

For Building Courage Daily

> Basic Buddha Belly
>
> Hand Heartener
>
> Meditations
>
> Prespeech Visualization
>
> Rhythmic Poetry—Speak Aloud Every Day
>
> Sing

The Elbow Propeller

See section 1, Stress—before (p. 256), for this exercise.

The I-Don't-Care Swing

See section 1, Stress—before (p. 258), for this exercise.

Karate Chop

See section 4, Anger (p. 272), for this exercise.

Steam Engine

See section 4, Anger (p. 272), for this exercise.

"You Bastard!"

See section 4, Anger (p. 275), for this exercise.

Basic Buddha Belly

See section 1, Stress—before (p. 254), for this exercise.

Hand Heartener

How to Do It

Rub your hands together—hard. When they're quite warm, keep rubbing and imagine the warmth spreading all over your body.

Now reach up your hands as high as you can: imagine you are embracing the sun. Draw down that energy and place it on your heart and chest. Feel it warm you and glow, penetrating your back, spreading throughout your body.

This is also a good thing to do before speaking if you don't know what to do with your hands. They'll have so much warmth in them that they'll feel relaxed and natural!

Meditations

See section 1, Stress—before (p. 258–60), for these exercises.

Prespeech Visualization

How to Do It

Visualize the place where you'll be giving a speech. See it as a warm, cozy place. Imagine that the people who are there are all interested in hearing what you have to say; they have only good wishes for your success and love in their hearts for you. This will enable you to let go of your fears and negative thoughts.

If you're confident and think other people think well of you, they'll step through the doors of *your* expectations.

Rhythmic Poetry—Speak Aloud Every Day

How It Helps

Speaking poetry has a calming effect. It produces equilibrium in both sides of the brain. Therefore you feel less anxiety and tension. Find some poetry you enjoy, memorize it, and recite it aloud every day.

Sing

HOW IT HELPS

Singing is also excellent for calming the mind and establishing equilibrium in both sides of the brain. It also opens up the throat, improves breath control, and gives more color to your speaking voice.

Section 9/Performance Anxiety

When you are feeling panic, alarm, or anxiety

What Exercises to Do:

There are exercises you can do right before you perform and exercises to do every day to make you feel more confident in general.

For Preperformance

This is an excellent sequence:

Butterflies Chaser

The Depressurizer

The I-Don't-Care Swing

Woodchopper

Karate Chop

Steam Engine

The World Heart Embrace

Here is another good sequence:

The Horse Laugh

Idiot Fingers

Wibble Wobble

The Elbow Propeller

Basic Yawns and Helium Ball Yawn

Butterflies Chaser

Preperformance Look

Sa-ta-na-ma Chant

For General Confidence

Rhythmic Poetry—Speak Aloud Every Day

Sing

Meditations

Relaxation Rehearsal

Energy Expander

Butterflies Chaser

HOW TO DO IT

1. Stand with your feet apart, knees a little bent, back straight, and the arms relaxed and hanging loosely at your sides.

2. Without taking any additional breath, do twenty-six short gentle bounces, saying "*Vuh!*" on each. Make the *vuh* a short, sharp, forceful sound (coming from the gut). If you are unable to manage twenty-six bounces at first, do as many as you can and gradually work up to the full count.

3. Relax and, with your mouth closed, inhale slowly and very deeply.

4. Exhale in a steady stream ("*sh-h-h-h-h*") with your mouth slightly open, letting the body sink into the knees.

Repeat three times; follow with long, slow breathing. This exercise and the next one are great for last-minute preperformance nerves.

The Depressurizer

HOW TO DO IT

1. Stand in a doorway and press your palms against the door frame on both sides. Hold your breath and keep increasing the pressure—you will feel warmth rushing to your face, head, and neck. Hold as long as you can.

2. Release totally, with a rush.

3. Inhale deeply, smoothly, and slowly.

Repeat three times.

The I-Don't-Care Swing

See section 1, Stress—before (p. 258), for this exercise.

Woodchopper

See section 4, Anger (p. 273), for this exercise.

Karate Chop

See section 4, Anger (p. 272), for this exercise.

Steam Engine

See section 4, Anger (p. 272), for this exercise.

The World Heart Embrace

See section 4 Anger (p. 274), for this exercise.

The Horse Laugh

See section 7, Vocal ease (p. 285), for this exercise.

Idiot Fingers

See section 7, Vocal ease (p. 285), for this exercise.

Wibble Wobble

See section 7, Vocal ease (p. 285), for this exercise.

The Elbow Propeller

See section 1, Stress—before (p. 256), for this exercise.

Basic Yawns and the Helium Ball Yawn

See section 7, Vocal ease (p. 284, 285), for these exercises.

Preperformance Look

HOW TO DO IT

1. Imagine something pleasant; smile.
2. Now drop the smile from your mouth, leaving it on the eyes and cheekbones (gives you a dynamic, charismatic look). Everyone is drawn to an expression that says, "Something good is about to happen."

Sa-ta-na-ma Chant

See chapter 10, p. 222, for this exercise.

Rhythmic Poetry—Speak Aloud Every Day

See section 8, Courage (p. 289), for this exercise.

Sing

See section 8, Courage (p. 290), for this exercise.

Meditations

See section 1, Stress—before (p. 258–60), for these exercises.

Relaxation Rehearsal

How to Do It

Tense and relax your entire body, starting with the toes and working upward. You can use relaxation tapes, including mine, available from Charismedia Services, 610 West End Avenue, New York, NY 10024-1605; tel. no. 212-362-6808; fax no. 212-362-6809; E-mail: charismedia@earthlink.net.

When you are deeply relaxed, visualize the scene or talk you want to rehearse. See yourself going through it exactly as you'd like it to go; visualize every detail as if you were there. If you feel any nervousness or can't visualize it, relax further or begin again. When you can easily go through the entire scene, you're ready. The actual event will be easy—like the second time!

Energy Expander

See chapter 10, page 222, for this exercise.

Section 10/More Control of Your Life

When you want to expand your powers

What Exercises to Do:

Be Your Own Cathedral

Be Your Own Sun

Brain Cleaner

Dream Machine

Electric Eye

Environmental Control

Golden Cocoon

The Golden Sunflower

Infinite Shrug

Kinesthetic Body

Onion Flower

Party Promoter

Programming for Success

Relaxation Rehearsal

Be Your Own Cathedral

See chapter 8, part III, page 185, for this exercise.

Be Your Own Sun

See chapter 8, part III, page 184, for this exercise.

Brain Cleaner

HOW TO DO IT

Close your eyes. Imagine a broom sweeping out sense after sense, sweeping out all the doors of your perceptions—your sight, your hearing, your sense of smell, your sense of taste, your kinesthetic feelings. This cleans out your senses, makes them fresh. Take three to five minutes for each sense. Breathe deeply. Open your eyes.

Dream Machine

HOW TO DO IT

At night, before you go to sleep, say, "I'm going to remember my dream." Put paper and pen by your bed (or a tape recorder), and when you wake, immediately write down or tape what you remember of your dream. Then think of what this dream reminds you of and what associations you make. The dream doesn't have to be logical; it belongs to dream time, to the dream world.

HOW IT HELPS

Remembering your dreams puts you in touch with parts of your life that are often hidden, enriching your fantasy life and giving you cues to intuition.

Electric Eye

HOW TO DO IT

Imagine that your eyes expand to the sides of your head. Now inhale through these enlarged eyes, taking in everything. This makes your face and eye muscles relax. You feel more open and expanded.

Now imagine a central eye in the middle of your forehead, like a big blue pearl. Connect this with the expanded large eyes. Feel that the light that comes in is an extraordinary, radiant light.

Next imagine that you have eyes in the back of your head and can see everything behind you. Feel that this makes your head feel light and spacious.

Environmental Control

HOW TO DO IT

Listen to sounds, take them in, then breathe them out completely. Don't resist them. For instance, in the subway where it's very noisy, breathe in these noises and let them go out. Don't tense up against them. Feel the noise as energy and transform it into power by filtering it outward and equalizing the sound.

Golden Cocoon

See section 1, Stress—before (p. 257), for this exercise.

The Golden Sunflower

How to Do It

Imagine a huge, very golden sunflower shining in your chest. See all the petals in great detail. When you meet someone (particularly if you are having trouble dealing with him or her), "see" a big golden sunflower shining in his or her chest, too. Ignore negative messages from the top level (the mouth). Respond to their sunflower. Others will respond with more warmth and friendliness because you are connecting from your heart center—a great way to prevent yourself from getting "sucked in" by other people's negativity.

Infinite Shrug

See section 6, Relaxation (p. 280), for this exercise.

Kinesthetic Body

How to Do It

1. When you have some physical task to do (for instance, skating, dancing, walking across a stage), breathe deeply; imagine in your mind how the movement goes, and visualize yourself doing this movement as it should be done.

2. Next actually do the movement, as you have imagined and "programmed" yourself to do it. (This will erase previous "tapes" or memories of being awkward, clumsy, or not able to do it.)

3. Repeat the visualization, which will deepen your sense of how it "feels" to do it marvelously. Use a mental picture of an expert or virtuoso doing it. If it's skiing, for instance, see Jean-Claude Killy skiing. If tennis, pick your favorite tennis stars—Bjorn Borg, Andre Agassi, or whoever. Imagine you're inside *their* bodies—moving with perfect flowing grace and effectiveness.

4. Then go back to physically *doing* it!

5. Keep alternating—kinesthetic rehearsal and real practice.

Onion Flower

How to Do It

Deeply relax. Now imagine your favorite flower (maybe a smooth yellow tulip, a fluffy white chrysanthemum?). Now *be* that flower; use this flower for your image of yourself, focus on it, and meditate on it.

How It Helps

When you're under stress you will be able to remember the image of your favorite flower and how it feels to be this flower. This will have an instant de-stressing and calming effect on you.

Party Promoter

How to Do It

Before you go to a party, imagine that the whole event is a show put on *for your benefit*. Therefore, *whatever happens* at this party is happening for *you*.

How It Helps

You will find that instead of being worried, shy, or afraid, you will be interested in everything going on and enjoy the whole spectacle. You let go of all expectations (future) and fears.

Programming for Success

How to Do It

1. Relax deeply.

2. Imagine a situation in the future, perhaps giving a presentation at work or meeting someone. Now imagine yourself giving this presentation (or whatever) with perfect calm and authority, and imagine the other people hearing it with interest. Put into your scenario whatever elements you want, and imagine yourself in the best possible light, doing the best job you can possibly do. The trick is to imagine specifically, to visualize clearly that you are as you would like to be.

3. Remember a situation that has already happened that you were dissatisfied with. Go back over this situation in your mind, visualize it as you wish it had happened, imagining what you wish you had done or said and what you wish others had done or said. In this new scenario, be as you wish you could have been.

4. Both of these steps are rehearsals for the way you would like to be and can really be. They will help you program yourself for success, instead of failure, by having success in your mind instead of the fear and subsequent image of failure. They help you to act differently than you would have otherwise.

Relaxation Rehearsal

See section 9, Performance anxiety (p. 293), for this exercise.

Section 11/Mood Change

When you are feeling negative, sad, or depressed

What Exercises to Do:

Anger Transformer

Calming Energizer

Centering with Sound

The Elbow Propeller

The Emotion Cooler (or Left-Nostril Breathing)

Golden Light

Lazy Lemon

Letter from Your Higher Self

The World Heart Embrace

Anger Transformer

See section 4, Anger (p. 269), for this exercise.

Calming Energizer

This can be done anywhere you can close your eyes for fifteen minutes. It is guaranteed to calm and refresh you.

How to Do It

1. Visualize a warm, glowing pink light around your heart center. Hold it there for a slow mental count of nine.

2. Move the glowing pink light to just over the top of your head, and hold it for a slow mental count of fifteen.

3. Surround your entire body with a field of glowing pink light; sit in the middle of it for a slow count of twelve.

4. Visualize a radiant blue light at your throat level, and hold it there for a slow count of nine.

5. Move the radiant blue light to just over your head and hold it there for a slow count of fifteen.

6. Surround your body with a field of radiant blue light; sit in the middle of it for a slow count of twelve.

7. Visualize a glowing white light at your forehead level; hold it there for a slow mental count of nine.

8. Hold the glowing white light just above your head for a slow count of fifteen.

9. Surround your body with a field of white light; sit in the middle of it for a slow count of twelve.

10. Observe how you feel and enjoy it before opening your eyes.

Centering with Sound

How to Do It

1. Close your eyes and sit with your back and neck straight.

2. Inhale and exhale slowly and deeply, three times.

3. Inhale and make a very low, deep *om* sound. Feel the vibration cover the whole area from the base of your spine to your solar plexus (including the abdomen). Repeat twice more. Notice your feelings.

4. Inhale again and make a midrange *om* sound. Let it vibrate through the heart center and chest. Repeat twice more. Feel the effects.

5. Inhale and make a very high, loud *om* sound. Make it vibrate through your whole head. Repeat twice more. Observe your sensations. Open your eyes. You will feel strong, grounded, and confident.

How It Helps

This exercise is very effective when you're feeling scattered and want to center yourself.

The Elbow Propeller

See section 1, Stress—before (p. 256), for this exercise.

The Emotion Cooler (or Left-Nostril Breathing)

See section 2, Stress—during (p. 261), for this exercise.

Golden Light

How to Do It

1. Close your eyes. Sit with a straight back.

2. Imagine that you are sitting on a soft white cloud, which gradually lifts off the ground and soars up, up into the sky.

3. A great golden waterfall of warm light is high above you, cascading down. Your cloud approaches the base of the waterfall, and the warm golden light pours down over your head.

4. You feel your skull, face, neck, shoulders, chest being bathed by the warm golden light. It pours down until it reaches the center (*dan t'ien*) two inches below your navel. It rests there a moment.

5. Now the light rises to your waist and divides in two—one part starts down your left side; the other starts down your right, down past the hips, thighs, knees, calves, and ankles until the soles are bathed in the warm golden light. Pause.

6. Now the light rises up the inside of each leg until it reaches the crotch and meets again in the *dan t'ien*.

7. Then the light goes to the base of the spine and slowly moves up the spine, toward the middle of the back, the shoulders, and the base of the skull, rising, rising until it reaches the crown of your head. There it rests, bathing the entire head with its golden shower of warmth and light.

8. Do this journey three times. You will feel peaceful and energized. If you practice it nine times successively, you will move easily into deep meditation and find your creativity and intuition are greatly enhanced.

How It Helps

This is a wonderful preparation for meditation or a meditation in itself.

Lazy Lemon

When you experience complete enjoyment through any of your senses, your breathing becomes deeper, your oxygen supply increases, and tensions drain away.

How to Do It

1. Cut a fresh lemon or orange in half, or open a bottle of your favorite perfume.

2. Sit down in a comfortable position, close your eyes, relax your body, take deep breaths, and enjoy the fragrance.

HOW IT HELPS

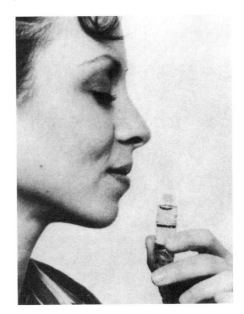

- This exercise helps you build up a satisfying field of pleasure, to be drawn on at will. It's an instant vacation—which breaks up and prevents stress.

- It restores perspective and your capacity to enjoy life.

Letter from Your Higher Self

HOW TO DO IT

Write yourself a letter of encouragement, as though your most developed self is addressing you. Acknowledge your fears and your good qualities (*all* of them), and express faith and confidence in your abilities, efforts, and accomplishments. Be as genuine, compassionate, and specifically supportive as you can. Write yourself what you would like most to hear, what you feel you need from the most supportive person you would like to have in your life. Keep this letter where you can reread it when you need to hear encouraging words.

Variation—record the letter on a cassette and play it whenever needed.

The World Heart Embrace

See section 4, Anger (p. 274), for this exercise.

Section 12/Good Relations with Others

When you want to be tuned-in to others

What Exercises to Do:

Anger Transformer

Fireworks Fling

The Golden Sunflower

Mirror-Matching

Party Promoter

Preperformance Look

Programming for Success

TongLen

"You Bastard!"

Anger Transformer

See section 4, Anger (p. 269), for this exercise.

Fireworks Fling

HOW TO DO IT

1. Lightly curl your fists and fling your arms up into the air as you say, "Ah!" Imagine a shower of fireworks issuing from your outspread fingertips as you fling them up in the air (at ninety degrees on either side of your head). Hold. Visualize the sparks cascading down all around you.

2. Inhale (mouth closed) and bend your elbows, drawing in your arms close to the body again.

3. Repeat the "fling" on an "Ah!"

4. Do ten of these. Make each one bigger and more spectacular than the last.

The Golden Sunflower

See section 10, More control of your life (p. 296), for this exercise.

Mirror-Matching

See chapter 5, page 86, for this exercise.

Party Promoter

See section 10, More control of your life (p. 297), for this exercise.

Preperformance Look

See section 9, Performance anxiety (p. 292), for this exercise.

Programming for Success

See section 10, More control of your life (p. 297), for this exercise.

TongLen

See chapter 6, pages 115–17, for this exercise.

"You Bastard!"

See section 4, Anger (p. 275), for this exercise.

Section 13/Pain

When you are feeling physical distress or discomfort

What Exercises to Do:

Drugless Painkiller

Headache Remedy

Pain-to-Pleasure Transformer

People Purr

Piecemeal Poop-Out

Sonic Acupressure Massage

Sore Throat Soother

Toothache—"Eeeeeeeeee"

Drugless Painkiller

How to Do It

Sit or lie down. Breathe deeply and slowly; relax. Now direct your brain to send endorphins, the body's own painkillers, to the spot that hurts. Visualize these endorphins as sparkling white lights going directly to the pain, absorbing the pain, dissolving the pain, and leaving sparkling white light in its place. Exhale the atomized pain.

Headache Remedy

How to Do It

Visualize your pain: its exact dimensions, how big it is, where it's placed, what shape it is, what color it is. (Is it round, square, rectangular? Is it two inches or six inches? Is it yellow, green?) Now breathe slowly and deeply into the pain; imagine it getting smaller and smaller. Watch it disappear.

Pain-to-Pleasure Transformer

How to Do It

Ask what message is this pain or illness trying to give me? What can I learn from it?

Focus on the energy of the feeling, without identifying with it as "your" pain. Intensify the energy and visualize it becoming a warm, viscous liquid (like Jell-O), lapping and supporting your body.

The pleasure and pain centers in the brain are located very close to each other. Concentrate on

1. focusing on the sensations, intensifying them;

2. spreading them throughout the body as neutral energy;

3. exhaling completely and passing the diluted, diffused intensity of that energy like heat through cheesecloth, visualizing every cell as a fine, transparent network; and

4. transforming the energy into white light, bathing the whole body in healing light.

You may change the experience of pain into warmth, excitement—even something actually akin to pleasure.

People Purr

How to Do It

Try the People Purr as a walking meditation. You purr as you walk along—very, very lightly. This keeps the expenditure of air very, very economical and even.

Piecemeal Poop-Out

See section 6, Relaxation (p. 280), for this exercise.

Sonic Acupressure Massage

How to Do It

Get in a nice warm shower. Begin to hum (with relaxed, slightly parted jaws and loose lips). Feel the hum massaging the sides, back, and top of your head with soft, stimulating sonic "fingers" from the inside. (See p. 181 for a fuller explanation.)

How It Helps

- The healing streams of water intensify the warm vibrations.
- It relieves pain and makes you feel pleasantly light, clear, and alert.
- It stimulates energy and well-being.

Sore Throat Soother

How to Do It

Put a rubber band around the second knuckle of your thumb for nine minutes. Gargle with one tablespoon apple cider vinegar in a glass of water—then swallow it, every hour, until you have finished the glass.

Avoid meat, starches, sugar, citrus fruit, and dairy products. Eat steamed greens (so the body becomes more alkaline, not acidic).

Toothache—"Eeeeeeeeee"

How to Do It

For tooth pain, say "Eeeeeeeeee" in a high tone. Direct vibrations to the painful area, and visualize the sound breaking up and dissolving the pain. Match the intensity of your sound to the pain—neutralizing it.

Section 14/Body Alignment

When you want to center and balance yourself

What Exercises to Do:

Belly Dancer's Bump

Massage

Pelvic Clock Rock

Plumb Line

Straight Standoff—The Spine Lineup

Belly Dancer's Bump

HOW TO DO IT

Stick your fanny out like a duck. (Don't tip forward with your torso!) Bring your pelvis sharply forward with a "bump." Don't move the top half of your body. This tucks your pelvis under and aligns your body, with the knees slightly bent, thighs under your shoulders.

Massage

And don't forget massage for your body! You can massage yourself; your magic hands do know what to do. Even better, massage a friend and exchange massages. (Use only oils you could eat on your skin—almond, coconut, avocado, peanut—*not* mineral oil!)

Pelvic Clock Rock

HOW TO DO IT

Feet slightly apart, imagine you are the center of a clock: 12:00 is in front of you, 3:00 at your side, 6:00 at back, 9:00 at the other side. Now move your pelvis around the clock, back the other way, very, very smoothly. Now try moving it from 12:00 to 3:00, from 9:00 to 12:00, from 9:00 to 6:00, etc., as though it were an oiled ball bearing. Try going from all hours to all others—smoothly and evenly.

HOW IT HELPS

- Promotes sexual responsiveness

- Increases range of feeling and enjoyment
- Releases abdominal tension
- Promotes good digestion
- Improves coordination
- Helps you enjoy dancing without self-consciousness

Plumb Line

See chapter 5, pages 85–86, for this exercise.

Straight Standoff—The Spine Lineup

How to Do It

1. Stand against a wall. Bend your knees. Press the spine and small of your back against the wall. Breathe for a minute; pay attention to how this straight back feels.

2. In this position, sing *Ahhhhhhh* as deeply and evenly as possible; then *Mmmmmmmmmm* two to six times.

3. Then push off with your elbows away from the wall, keeping the same alignment. Your pelvis is cupped like a palm, the lower back feels spread and wide, the stomach is pressed in against the spine, and the head rises from the torso like a flower at the end of its stem.

4. When you feel your balance is just as solid as when you were pressed against the wall, slowly straighten the knees until they're *almost* straight. Relax your arms. Scan your body from the inside. See how it feels.

Section 15/Waking Up

When you are feeling sleepy, tired, or lethargic

What Exercises to Do:

Alternate Breathing

Breath of Fire

Cat Crawl

Sunrise—Superenergizer

Alternate Breathing

How to Do It

1. Close off the right nostril lightly with the right thumb. Exhale slowly and evenly through the left nostril. Inhale slowly through the same nostril.

2. With the little finger of your right hand (same hand), close off the left nostril and exhale through the right nostril. Inhale.

3. Again, thumb on the right nostril, close it, exhale through the left nostril, then inhale through the same nostril. Then close the left nostril as before and continue—five minutes (or until nose is clear).

   - As you exhale, visualize poisons, phlegm, and negativity leaving your entire body. On inhale, visualize air being drawn into your nasal passage, then up into the head, clearing it and bringing oxygen and energy (*prana*) to the brain. Then spread it through your entire body.

   - Move smoothly from thumb to pinky, only letting go of one nostril when you close off the other.

How It Helps

- Clears your head and nasal passages
- Balances your energies
- Oxygenates your brain
- Makes you feel alert and optimistic, calmer
- Makes you happy to start a new day

Breath of Fire

How to Do It

Important—Mouth is kept closed.

1. Exhale powerfully (with a short, sharp, unvoiced "HMH!") by pulling in the navel point and abdomen toward the spine (as though someone had kicked you in the solar plexus); immediately relax the abdomen and allow the breath to come in naturally and easily by itself (as part of the relaxation).

2. Then exhale again powerfully, and relax to inhale—this should be a continuous rhythm, fairly rapid, with no pause between inhale and exhale. Focus energy at the navel point—you should feel the pull of

the muscles in that area. A steady, even rhythm is more important than speed.

3. Do this for one to three minutes.

How It Helps

Long-range, this exercise helps build endurance, stabilizes shaky nerves, and generates mental and physical constancy. It can help you if you cannot keep a promise, intention, or train of thought without constant distraction. It's great anytime you're tired, bored, or sleepy. This is a fast energizer, an instant waker-upper that

- cleanses the entire bloodstream in three minutes,
- raises the voltage of the nervous system,
- increases circulation, and
- releases old toxins from the lungs, blood vessels, mucous lining, and cells.

If you are toxic due to drugs, smoking, or poor nutrition, this exercise may stimulate a temporary self-toxification. To aid in cleansing, increase the amount of exercise you normally do daily, and lighten your diet with vegetables, fruits, and nuts for a week or two. This helps your body drop the heavy load of toxins it has carried.

Cat Crawl

How To Do It

On your hands and knees begin to crawl very slowly around the room (so that, for example, your left knee is under chest and right leg is fully extended in back). Look over first one shoulder, then the other, slowly twisting as far as you can. *Streeetch.* Change legs very slowly, being sure the straight leg is totally extended.

Do ten times (each leg) as slowly and luxuriously as possible.

Variation—you can combine this with counting to your pulse or heartbeat. Exhale six beats, hold three; inhale six beats, hold three.

How It Helps

- Gently stretches the spine and body
- Eases the transition from sleep to full alertness
- Gets the kinks out without strain

Sunrise—Superenergizer

How to Do It

Sit with a straight spine, cross-legged or kneeling (fanny on heels) and with your eyes closed. You will feel like the sun yourself, surrounded by your own circle of warmth, energy, and radiance.

1. Extend your arms out to your sides at a forty-five-degree angle—thumbs pointing up, fists closed.

2. Do the Breath of Fire for one minute (80 to 120 breaths). You will feel your face and neck get warm.

3. Inhale deeply, while you bring straight arms up slowly over your head until your thumbs meet. Hold for six counts.

4. Exhale slowly while lowering the arms straight out to the sides—and then all the way down.

How It Helps

- Wakes you up
- Stimulates you
- Centers your magnetic field
- Balances energies in anticipation of the day
- Gives an optimistic energy to your day

Section 16/Inducing Sleep

When you are feeling restless, fretful, or worried

What Exercises to Do:

Presleep Rerun

Sonic Tranquilizer

To Sleep

Presleep Rerun

How to Do It

1. About an hour before you go to sleep, rerun the film of your day.

2. Sit or lie down; take a few deep, relaxing breaths. Begin in the morning, remember everything that happened that day.

3. Take note of the things that pleased you, that you liked. Acknowledge how great they were.

4. Look at the things that you were dissatisfied with, gently and without blame or guilt. Visualize how you would have liked them to be; make the scenario better than it was, making yourself and everyone else act the way you would have preferred.

5. Finish off the rerun with a thought of gratitude for the good things you experienced, for the lessons you received, and for the problems you got to work on and began to solve.

6. This wipes clean your day, finishing up all the loose ends and worries, and allows you to sleep with a clear, relaxed mind. You wake up fresh in the morning, ready for the next day's movie!

Sonic Tranquilizer

See chapter 8, Part III, page 188, for this exercise.

To Sleep

How to Do It

1. Don't eat for two hours before bedtime.

2. Drink chamomile, valerian, or passionflower tea.

3. Drink hot milk, with or without honey.

4. Do the Piecemeal Poop-Out (section 6, Relaxation, p. 280) to relax you.

5. Try 5HTP (hydroxytryptophan) or calms-forté, a homeopathic remedy, a half-hour before bedtime. They are natural sleep inducers.

6. Lie on your left side and softly purr, feeling the vibration driving out all thoughts.

7. *Be your own lullaby* (see chapter 8, p. 187). Lie down, feel the sea of energy all around you, observe sounds, prickling of your hairs, small sensations . . . Dissolve all thoughts with your purr.

8. Avoid stimulation or anxiety-provoking work, reading, or talking just before bedtime. Wind down. Put on soft, soothing music or a relaxation cassette. Let go of all worries—see them tied up in a huge garbage bag and floating up and away out of sight.

Section 17/Better Sex Life

When you are feeling inhibited, bored, or distracted

What Exercises to Do:

Belly Dancer's Bump

Pelvic Clock Rock

Pelvic Flow

Pleasure Checklist

Sensualizer

Belly Dancer's Bump

See section 14, Body alignment (p. 306), for this exercise.

Pelvic Clock Rock

See section 14, Body alignment (p. 306), for this exercise, which

- increases your flexibility,
- increases your subtlety of movement, and
- increases your ability to respond and feel pleasure.

Pelvic Flow

How to Do It

Undulate and weave around the room for ten minutes. Lie on the floor, lift pelvis, release spine. Let pelvis initiate the action. Move arms and legs smoothly and sinuously. Improvise without stopping. Move in ways you haven't done before, and don't worry about how it looks. Feel good! Keep the movements lazy, legato, and sinuous.

Pleasure Checklist

How to Do It

Each day, at the end of the day, check whether you have had at least one pleasant experience of each of your senses:

- Did I see something beautiful and feel pleasure today?

- Did I taste something good and savor it today?

- Did I smell something fragrant and enjoy it today?

- Did I hear something beautiful and enjoy it today?

- Did I touch something pleasurable and enjoy it today?

- Did I feel any warm, loving thoughts and spread them through my body?

Keep a record for a week. If you notice that some of your senses get less pleasure than others, consciously make an effort to use those senses more and to enjoy more with them.

Sensualizer

How to Do It

Run your finger as lightly as you can down your own or a friend's arm and hand. Barely touch the skin. Do it very, very slowly; see if you can touch just the hairs. Let your friend do it to you.

Acknowledgments

"... By the Glittering of our Eyes ..."

My idea of gratitude was permanently affected by a fascinating anthropological conference I once went to in Bali, reevaluating Margaret Mead's famous book on Balinese culture. Mead had written, among other things, that the Balinese are ungrateful people, since they never say "thank you" when they receive gifts. I will never forget the tall, imposingly bearded Balinese priest who rose in place and told us, eyes flashing,

> We believe it trivializes gratitude merely to say "thank you." We teach our children and their children that when someone has done a good deed for us, they must remember it all their lives and do good deeds themselves for the family of that person in honor of that original kindness. The only way we *show* gratitude ourselves is *by the glittering of our eyes!*

So, eyes glittering, I would like to express my deep appreciation for the many people who helped and inspired me in preparing this new expanded and revised edition. To Claire Gerus, my gifted and resourceful agent, who suggested some of the reorganization and encouraged me to add a great deal more; to Christine Allen for her warmhearted and heartwarming generosity; to Joyce Engelson for her unstinting kindness in sharing her vast publishing knowledge; to Elly Stone, Phyllis Grunauer, and Lisa Curtis, whose friendship and warm appreciation buoyed my spirits; to Brian Lang, whose poetic depths and insights often enrich and amaze me; to Pema Chodron and Sogyal Rinpoche for their soul-nourishing teachings; to John Nolan, Matthew Carnicelli, Kristen Eberhard, and Linda Gray at NTC/Contemporary Publishing; to the conscientious and thoughtful copyeditor, Anne Heiles; to my computer guru for "being there"; and to the thousands of clients, colleagues, and friends around the world with whom I have been privileged to work, and who have taught me so much—to each of you, my grateful, heartfelt thanks.

In the words of the lovely Buddhist prayer, may all this virtue gathered together, and whatever merit I have accumulated, become a seed for the enlightenment of all beings.

—Doe Lang

Index

About the Author

Internationally recognized motivational speaker, lecturer, therapist, and speech and performance coach Doe Lang, Ph.D., has helped more than one hundred thousand people of all walks of life to be more comfortable, effective communicators—in business, in personal life, and on TV! She has taught charisma skills and leadership training for such clients as Honeywell, Xerox, government agencies, and stars of entertainment and international politics.

Dr. Lang, a graduate of Bennington College, earned her Ph.D. in psychology and communication from the Union Institute and has taught at Columbia University, Temple University, and the New School. She has been cited for Distinguished Achievement by the International Who's Who in Education and the International Who's Who of Women. An accomplished concert pianist, opera singer, and actress, she was awarded a Fulbright for opera to Italy and has performed on and off Broadway and at Carnegie Hall. On TV she sang with Leonard Bernstein and acted in *As the World Turns*, *Another World*, *Edge of Night*, and innumerable commercials. Her books and audiotapes are popular in twenty-five countries and have been translated into eight languages.

For a catalog of charisma skills training tapes, write to Charismedia, 610 West End Avenue, New York, NY 10024-1605. (Please enclose a self-addressed, stamped envelope with your inquiry.) Telephone: 212-362-6808. Fax: 212-362-6809. E-mail: charismedia@earthlink.net

Dr. Lang will be delighted to receive your comments on your experiences and reactions to *The New Secrets of Charisma*.